CAHIERS DU CINÉMA

Published by Routledge in association with the British Film Institute

Volume Four: 1973–1978: History, Ideology, Cultural Struggle
Edited by David Wilson
Introduction by Bérénice Reynaud

David Wilson is a freelance editor and film script consultant. He is the former Editorial Director of BFI Publishing and André Deutsch and has written extensively on film and television.

Bérénice Reynaud, a regular collaborator on *Cahiers du Cinéma* since 1987, currently teaches film theory and history at the California Institute of the Arts.

Previously published volumes:
Volume One: The 1950s: Neo-Realism, Hollywood, New Wave
Edited by Jim Hillier
Volume Two: 1960–1968: New Wave, New Cinema, Re-evaluating
Hollywood
Edited by Jim Hillier
Volume Three: 1969–1972: The Politics of Representation
Edited by Nick Browne

CAHIERS DU CINÉMA

Volume Four
1973–1978: History, Ideology, Cultural Struggle

An anthology from *Cahiers du Cinéma*
nos 248–292, September 1973–September 1978

Edited by David Wilson
With an introduction by Bérénice Reynaud

Watkins College
of Art & Design

Published in association with
the British Film Institute

London and New York

First published 2000
by Routledge

11 New Fetter Lane, London EC4P 4EE

Simultaneously published in the USA and Canada
by Routledge
29 West 35th Street, New York, NY 10001

Routledge is an imprint of the Taylor & Francis Group

Original French articles © Les Editions de L'Etoile 1973–8
English translations and editorial material © 2000 The British Film
Institute

Typeset in Garamond by
J&L Composition Ltd, Filey, North Yorkshire

Printed and bound in Great Britain by MPG Books Ltd, Bodmin

British Library Cataloguing in Publication Data
A catalogue record for this book is available from the British Library

Library of Congress Cataloging in Publication Data
A catalogue record for this book has been requested

ISBN 0–415–02988–0

CONTENTS

CONTENTS

CONTENTS

CONTENTS

PREFACE

This final volume of selections from *Cahiers du Cinéma* aims to reflect the principles underpinning the series which were outlined by Jim Hillier in his Preface to the first two volumes. In particular, we have tried to ensure that this volume is self-contained, is representative of the period covered and is accessible to the non-specialist reader.

In general, the texts in this volume *are* more 'accessible' than many of those in Volume 3. This is not because of any editorial decision on our part. It simply reflects the editorial shift in *Cahiers* which became increasingly discernible during the later 1970s – a shift echoed by the journal's decision to abandon its austere format (no pictures) of the early 1970s. *Cahiers* continued to occupy, and develop, the political and theoretical positions elaborated in the post-1968 period, in particular questions concerning the place of the spectator (the influence of Lacan's psychoanalytic work is still very evident), and questions about politics and history arising out of the writings of Michel Foucault, Marc Ferro and others. But, as Bérénice Reynaud shows in her Introduction, these positions became gradually less entrenched than they were in the immediate post-1968 years. *Cahiers*, as it were, began to argue with itself.

A continuing overall commitment to understanding the nature and operation of mainstream cinema, through a systematic re-reading of both films and film history, criticism and theory, began to be complemented by an equal commitment to explore alternatives to this cinema, whether in the deconstructed European cinema of Godard, Straub/Huillet and others or in the 'anti-imperialist' cinema in, for example, Algeria, Palestine, Chile. There was also a renewed interest in French cinema, and in the way in which a genuinely 'national' cinema needed to be generated and understood. In this sense, questions about cinema and cultural struggle remained at the top of the *Cahiers* agenda: what could a radical film journal contribute to political struggle on the cultural front?

A note on translations

Translation always poses problems about accurate rendition, especially when the original writing is often difficult. The English language does not take kindly to Gallic abstraction, as witness the none too successful attempts by some Anglo-American film journals to import, unadapted, the neologisms of French critical theory. It would be foolish to pretend that we have not occasionally experienced problems of translation; but we have tried throughout to be sensitive to the original nuance without being slavishly literal. Too many translations from the French have been seduced by *faux amis*: we hope we have avoided them.

The French terms *auteur* and *mise en scène* have long been familiar in critical discussion in English, but *auteur* in particular did not always have some of the meanings which have since been attached to it. We have usually retained *auteur* when 'author' might have been a direct translation and *mise en scène* where 'direction' might have been a suitable rendering, but we have tried to reflect the varying usage of these terms. The same principle has been applied to such theoretical terms as *écriture* for which there is no wholly adequate translation.

Les Cahiers du Cinéma (literally 'Cinema Notebooks') are plural, but we have preferred to refer to *Cahiers* – the usual abbreviated form – as if in the singular.

Notes

All notes are the editor's, except when specifically designated as authors' or translators' notes.

ACKNOWLEDGEMENTS

We are indebted to *Cahiers du Cinéma* for the agreement to produce these volumes of anthology from their material.

I owe thanks to Paul Willemen for inviting me to take on this volume; and to Roma Gibson and Dawn King, whose support in often difficult times was invaluable. My belated thanks also to Andrew Sarris, for enlightening conversations about *Cahiers du Cinéma*, and cinema, in late-night San Sebastián and Berlin.

I am especially grateful to Bérénice Reynaud, both for her illuminating introduction to this volume and for responding to my queries about some of the more recondite references in the French texts.

Translation is an achievement too rarely acknowledged, so I am pleased to acknowledge the work of the translators for this volume: Jill Forbes, Liz Heron, Chris Darke and Annwyl Williams. It was only when I undertook several translations myself that I fully appreciated the difficulties they faced. I hope the other translators will understand if I express my particular thanks to Annwyl Williams, whose conscientious work on three volumes of this anthology has been exemplary. I am happy to acknowledge the work of Phillip Drummond in the original selection of texts for this volume. Sylvie Lyall has tolerated my absences during the years I have worked on this volume, and I am grateful to her.

Routledge and the British Film Institute gratefully acknowledge the help of *Cahiers du Cinéma* in the compilation of these volumes.

INTRODUCTION

Cahiers du Cinéma 1973–1978

Bérénice Reynaud

The story's outline is now plain: the untiring search for a human
soul through the barely perceptible reflections cast by this soul
on others.

Borges, *The Approach to al-Mu'tasim*

In the early 1970s the *concours de l'agrégation* in Paris presented the candidates
for the position of philosophy teacher with an intriguing topic for a paper: 'crisis and criticism'. Candidates were expected to build on the etymology of the
word 'crisis' (from the Greek *krinein*, to distinguish, to separate) in order to
weave a Hegelian dialectical analysis of the relationship between the unfolding
of a crisis and the work of criticism. For the students who were involved in, or
had simply witnessed, the May '68 events and the various militant/political
struggles that followed, the subject was more than simply academic: it was the
very fabric of their lives. Similarly, the history of *Cahiers du Cinéma* between
1973 and 1978 is both fascinating and difficult to write because the generation
of writers that came of age at this time decided, with real intellectual courage,
not only to face the crisis undergone by French society but to make it the subject, the core, the motivation of their theoretical practices as film critics.
Political crisis, inter-generational crisis, crisis of identity, of civilization – but,
first and foremost, crisis of cinema. Those who accused *Cahiers* of forgoing its
'object' (the specificity of cinema) were unaware that maybe there was nothing
now to forgo. The idea of 'cinema' that had given birth to a certain form of film
criticism no longer represented what was happening in the cinemas themselves, in private living rooms where television sets were turned on, or in people's minds. In the years following the May '68 events, alternately losing and
rebuilding their 'object', *Cahiers* critics were to discover that, as Jean-Luc
Godard's *Numéro deux* has it, 'despair is the ultimate form of criticism'.
    So the history of *Cahiers* at that time is fractured, turbulent, sometimes
exhilarating, sometimes bitter, always engaging; it abounds in ruptures,
contradictory positions, fearless enthusiasms, suspicions, disgusts, stringent

self-criticism or amused hindsight. The editorial and visual format of the journal changed more often in these six years than during the rest of its history. From the November 1972 issue (241), for example, it was decided to stop reproducing photographs both on the cover and within the pages of *Cahiers* and to adopt a more 'austere' presentation. Images did not return until the cover of the January 1976 issue (262–3) with a drawing by the political cartoonist Willem denouncing 'advanced liberal censorship': it showed Charlie Chaplin, in a tuxedo jacket but naked from the waist down, exhibiting a long, thin penis which a policeman was preparing to cut off. The journal returned to a conventional magazine format only with the issue of July–August 1976 (268–9), with glossy paper and full illustration. These visual changes reflected changes in the journal's editorial policy.

Recounting the history of *Cahiers* at that time also means, even indirectly, recounting the history of the individuals who made it. For the written texts orchestrated a complex polyphony, echoing, alluding to, quoting or criticizing articles published a few issues before (or in the same issue), pursuing an argument in a discontinuous manner from text to text and issue to issue, and, more often than not, re-evaluating, refining, amending, invalidating statements, theses and positions that a writer (sometimes the same writer) had previously defended. *Cahiers* was a laboratory, a palimpsest, a factory/landscape (see *Numéro deux* again, for if ever there was a text that could function as a metaphor for *Cahiers*'s development at this time, it is Godard's film) where some ideas were worked out to become *material forces* – or to be forgotten by history.

The March–April 1972 issue (236–7) included a collective text 'deconstructing' a popular political talk show on prime-time French television (*A armes égales*) and signed 'Groupe Lou Sin d'intervention idéologique'.[1] The leader of the group was Serge Toubiana, who had been actively involved in Maoist militant groups such as VLR (Vive la Révolution) and who played an important role in *Cahiers* from then on. Another hardcore Maoist, Philippe Pakradouni, became very active at about the same time. In February 1972 Bernard Eisenschitz, who had been involved with *Cahiers* since the 1960s and had collaborated on the special Eisenstein issue in 1971, was expelled after a mock trial because of his membership of the Communist Party. The editorial of the November 1972 – January 1973 issue (242–3) reflected *Cahiers*'s subsequent political and intellectual evolution. It announced that, with their agreement, Jacques Doniol-Valcroze, Pierre Kast and Jacques Rivette, who had not been actively involved with *Cahiers* for some years, were deleted from the masthead. The editorial team was now composed of a non-hierarchical list of writers: Jacques Aumont, Pierre Baudry, Pascal Bonitzer, Jean-Louis Comolli, Serge Daney, Pascal Kané, Jean Narboni, Jean-Pierre Oudart, Philippe Pakradouni, Sylvie Pierre and Serge Toubiana. During the next few years these writers' input was irregular. Comolli eventually stopped writing in order to direct *La Cecilia*. Kané managed to stay away from any direct involvement in the journal's Maoist positions, and eventually directed *Dora et la lanterne mag-*

ique. Sylvie Pierre – the first and only woman to write for *Cahiers* for years – was living in Brazil, from where she expressed her puzzled disagreement with the new Marxist-Leninist line, though she remained on the masthead until the July–August 1973 issue (247). In March 1973, Baudry wrote a letter (published in the following issue) announcing his resignation, frustrated by *Cahiers*'s 'politicism' (the subordination of film criticism to cultural criticism, and of cultural struggle to political struggle). Strangely enough, the arguments used in Baudry's letter[2] were to reappear, in slightly modified form, in the self-critical evaluation published in *Cahiers* 250, May 1974 ('Les *Cahiers* aujourd'hui'), and Baudry resumed writing for the journal in the late 1970s (an article entitled 'Remarques sur la télévision, la radio et le cinéma' marks his 'comeback' in *Cahiers* 274, March 1977). On the other hand, the rupture with Pakradouni, sanctioned by a long letter published in the October–November 1974 issue and attacking *Cahiers*'s new 'revisionist' line, was bitter and complete. (In their spirited reply, the editorial board accused him of dogmatism.) Pakradouni's departure signified that *Cahiers* was turning a new leaf, gradually giving up hard-core Maoist positions and preparing to go back to 'film criticism' *per se*.

Meanwhile Oudart and Bonitzer pursued their own theoretical explorations of the language of cinema – which for Bonitzer were to blossom in a well-received series of books (where his essays for *Cahiers* were collected) before he turned to scriptwriting (for Alain Resnais, André Téchiné and Chantal Akerman). The three leading figures of the journal were now Narboni, Toubiana and Daney. Narboni had come (as a medical student) from Algiers in 1960, where with his friend and colleague Comolli he had been active in the local *ciné-club*. With his brilliant, polemical style he fought on several fronts, defending militant and Third World cinema, attacking the 'revisionists' and other ideological enemies, while finding time to teach at the new, experimental Vincennes University and to get involved in the collective film *The Olive Tree*, about the Israeli–Palestinian conflict. The mid-1970s also witnessed the growing importance of Toubiana, culminating in his becoming editor-in-chief in the 1980s. For a long time, he worked in tandem with Daney: the two men became close friends, respected each other's different capabilities (Toubiana was a first-rate manager with a keen political sense, Daney was the intellectual impulse of *Cahiers*) and together assumed editorial responsibility when, in Daney's words, 'the journal was given away to whoever was willing to pick it up'.[3] The masthead of *Cahiers* 265, May 1976, lists Daney and Toubiana at the 'secrétariat de rédaction', and in June 1977 they became 'chief editors'.

Toubiana's role was to be immense, for he assumed sole editorial responsibility from 1981 (the year Daney left to write for *Libération*) until roughly 1992 (he still has a notable influence on the journal). He designed and implemented the new format of *Cahiers* in 1989. Yet if Toubiana was one of the most brilliant minds writing for *Cahiers* in the 1970s, the intellectual contribution that most marked the decade was Daney's.

Born in 1944, a reader of *Cahiers* since he was fifteen, Daney founded the short-lived *Visages du cinéma* with his friend Louis Skorecki, who was later occasionally to write for *Cahiers*, especially in the late 1970s. Daney published his first text for *Cahiers* in 1964. Unusually for a French film critic, he travelled widely (USA, India, Africa) until the editorial responsibility for the journal happened to fall to him. 'Nobody had asked Serge to play this part,' Toubiana wrote in the special issue devoted to Daney after his death in June 1992:

> He . . . happened to be available. The only thing I could offer him was that I was *there*. He accepted my assistance, more out of friendship than for my abilities. For years we shared the same dark office . . . His contribution was essential: principles, an immense culture, an editorial project based on the desire to echo our most powerful and wildest cinematic experiences.[4]

In January 1973 a group of former leftist militants, under the direction of Serge July, founded the newspaper *Libération*, which was to become a daily a few months later. A number of *Cahiers* writers, including Daney and Toubiana, contributed articles to it. For Daney, the decision to write in a daily reflected a desire to be even more in touch with the present, a desire which for him had become an ethical principle. This explains his decision to leave *Cahiers* in 1981 to assume editorial responsibilities at *Libération*; the late 1970s at *Cahiers* were marked by a continuing dialogue between the daily paper and the monthly journal, between two kinds of *journalism*.

Journalism: the production of a series of texts aimed at influencing the present, not the eternity, as Gertrude Stein noted. Daney bypassed this contradiction, for it was only after leaving for *Libération* that he started publishing collections of his texts.[5] Yet, as revealed by the title of one of them (*Ciné-journal*), these books are in fact intellectual diaries. What they embody is the *singularity* of the author's trajectory. Strangely enough, in spite of the Marxist-Leninist standardization and codification of the arguments in the first part of the decade, the texts produced between 1972 and 1978 reflect a wide array of singular paths, beliefs and relationships to cinema. The difference between these 'non-legendary years' and those preceding them was not the lack of strong individualities but the near impossibility within the tenets of Maoism of saying 'I', of writing a text in the first person. Hence the convenient ploy of writing texts collectively, in order to be able to say 'we'. Yet the overwhelming presence of the first person plural cannot be written off as a simple dialectic-materialistic device. *Cahiers* writers were striving to define their position as intellectuals within the class struggle, but, more existentially, they were also working at expressing their experience as *a generation*. The first person singular came back only with the post-1975 'journalistic' years – which was also the time when militancy in France started to dissolve into insignificance, boredom and renewed individualism.

All this means that *Cahiers* texts of the 1972–8 period are difficult to anthologize. There are no 'obvious' choices, and a selection can reflect only an individual point of view, the echo made by a particular argument in the mind of the reader. So every selection will necessarily be partial (in both senses of the word). For in the rich exchange that marked these often misunderstood years, in the complex dialectic between the militant impulse, the journalistic impulse and the ambiguous role played by theory, every text conceals another, generates another, answers or criticizes another. This introduction – itself the result of a personal trajectory – aims to define some lines of analysis, presenting a picture of the interconnections and reciprocal influences between the texts reproduced here and those that are not, as well as locating them within their historical context and the 'spirit of the time'. For the 1970s was the decade in which the question of the *present* (the present of politics until 1975, the present of history afterwards), of the *real* – missed, constructed or impatient – was posed with the greatest acuity.

Chairman Mao's structuring absences

When the editorial team of *Cahiers*, with the exceptions mentioned above, embraced Maoism in October 1971, the decision, albeit controversial, represented a desire to become an accurate reflection of the ideological struggles of the time. May '68 had generated a crisis in representation in France, opening a gap within discursive practices, and it is within this gap that *Cahiers* was to be positioned for the next few years. Maoism had played a major role since the onset of the May '68 movement, as a practical/theoretical tool to change society. For French intellectuals and activists who, after ten years of Gaullism, had a sense of being divorced from history, Maoism represented a triple advantage. It embodied a successful revolution, one that had taken China from a still feudal age to the 'four modernizations'; its achievements were based on an impressive body of theoretical work, opening up new ways of combining theory and practice and using 'intellectual production' as a tool for social change (little did French Maoists know that, during the Cultural Revolution, intellectuals were sent to re-education camps or to the countryside); and finally it came from the Third World, where a large fraction of French left-wing activists (aptly called *tiersmondistes*), despairing of the possibility of a revolution in industrialized countries, saw the future of socialism. The delay with which Chinese cinema came to be known in France also worked in favour of Maoism. With film production in China practically halted between 1967 and 1973, French *cinéphiles* were discovering with delight the only revolutionary productions allowed during the Cultural Revolution, such as Pan Wenzhan's and Fu Jie's 1971 version of *The Red Detachment of Women* for the China Dance Drama Troupe (which graced the cover of *Cahiers* 236–7 in April 1972), blissfully unaware of the version directed by Xie Jin in 1961.

Cahiers came to Maoism relatively late, at one of the most difficult times of post-'68 despair and social tension. In June 1969 Georges Pompidou was elected as president; shortly after, his Prime Minister, Chaban-Delmas, set out his technocratic programme for a 'new society'. In April 1970, the 'anti-casseurs' law allowed the leaders of political groups to be prosecuted for any incident taking place during a demonstration they organized. Feeling threatened, ultra-leftist political groups – strange bedfellows from anarchists to Trotskyists to Maoists – regrouped under the name of Secours Rouge to organize huge demonstrations in protest against political repression. These demonstrations, all illegal, were ruthlessly attacked by the special police force (CRS) created after May '68; during one of them Richard Deshayes, a leader of the militant group VLR and an editor of its 'counter-cultural' magazine *Tout!* ('All!', as in 'We want it all!'), lost an eye when a tear-gas grenade exploded in his face. In May 1970 the GP (Gauche Prolétarienne or 'Proletarian Left'), founded in October 1968, was dissolved by the government but Jean-Paul Sartre assumed editorial responsibility for their paper, *La Cause du Peuple*, and he, Simone de Beauvoir, François Truffaut, theatre director Patrice Chéreau and other well-known cultural figures started selling it in the streets. Other major intellectuals got involved. In early 1971, as imprisoned Maoist militants were on hunger strike, Michel Foucault announced the creation of the GIP (Groupe d'Information sur les Prisons). In April the same year Maria-Antonietta Macchiochi's *About China* was published, increasing tension between *Tel Quel* and the Communist Party when the book was prohibited for sale at the yearly fair/celebration of *L'Humanité*, the Party's daily newspaper (*Tel Quel* had just taken a firm position against the 'revisionism' of the French CP and in favour of 'Maotsetung thought'). In March 1972 two hundred thousand people followed the funeral procession of Pierre Overney, a Maoist militant killed by a security guard in front of the Renault-Billancourt factory. Responding to the killing, and to the French Communist Party's ambiguous reaction to it, a text in *Cahiers* 236–7, April 1972, identifies 'revisionism' as the main enemy: 'Revisionism is . . . the ally of the bourgeoisie, its agent within the working class, the specific form of its class dictatorship.' A number of French intellectuals left the French CP to join Maoism at this time, and their letters of resignation were published in the same issue of *Cahiers*.[6] At the same time, an article in *Le Monde* noted that 1,035 extreme-left militants had been sentenced to prison terms.

In this climate of social restlessness and thwarted expectations, while Maoism represented the spearhead of the intellectual and political thought of the time, it also, maybe not surprisingly, solidified into a 'terrorist' structure of symbolic power. It was no secret among militants that, in spite of the presence and involvement of women, the movement was male-dominated, heterocentrist and quite puritanical. Feeling under- and misrepresented, women started to organize and created the MLF (Mouvement de Libération des Femmes). Fighting on different fronts, they campaigned for abortion rights (often within the MLAC, the Movement for the Liberation of Abortion and Contraception), strove to redefine sexual power within and without the (heterosexual) couple, sought to rewrite history from the point of view of women and set up a publishing company (Des Femmes). Similarly, homosexual movements such as the FHAR (Front Homosexuel d'Action Révolutionnaire) sprouted, and Guy Hocquenghem published his book *La Révolution des homosexuels*. In October 1970 the magazine *Actuel* was founded, providing an outlet for a different kind of alternative culture, much inspired by the United States: mind-altering drugs, sexual revolution, communal life, psychedelic music, post-beat-generation literature etc. The phrase 'idéologies dominées' ('dominated ideologies') was used quite frequently at the time (it even appeared in *Cahiers*) among intellectuals struggling with the idea of misrepresentation and marginalization. However, Maoism dogmatically failed to conceptualize these different centrifugal tendencies, even though they could legitimately claim to be the by-products of the various May '68 movements, substituting ideological and poetic creativity for their painful political failure. Similarly, these tendencies were hardly represented in *Cahiers* at all. For example, the collective text that spells out the programme of the 'Front culturel révolutionnaire'[7] lists a number of fields in which the Front ought to intervene: 'specific cultural practices' (theatre, music, cinema) through which 'transverse connections' are necessary; the cultures of national minorities (Provençal, Breton, Basque, Corsican) which have been 'reduced to silence by the central power of the bourgeoisie'; and the cultures of the immigrant proletariat, unnamed in their national and ethnic specificity and lumped together as 'class brothers' of the French proletariat. No mention of women as being an under-represented minority or a subculture, nor of feminism as a cultural front in its own right.

Cahiers did, however, devote several articles to the outlawed militant film *Histoires d'A* (1973), which defended women's right to abortion and, moreover, represented a woman being aborted by the new Karman method, at the centre of a long scene in which 'we see her successively speaking and being "spoken", acting and being "acted" ', as Daney writes, adding that *Histoires d'A* is one of the best examples of political cinema: it asserts not only that abortion can be practised but also that it can be *shown*. Its staging represents 'a space that had been reconquered and temporarily snatched away from the enemy'.[8] So *Histoires d'A* (directed by Charles Belmont and Marielle Issartel) was praised more as an example of revolutionary *mise en scène* than for its feminist applications. Between 1974 and 1985, two women, Thérèse Giraud and Danièle Dubroux, wrote regularly for *Cahiers*,[9] but their witty, often acerbic, texts did not generate larger discussions on issues of feminism or sexual politics *per se*. (The notion of 'sexual politics' was quite foreign to French intellectual life at the time. Kate Millett's book, for example, was translated as *La politique du mâle*, i.e. 'Man's Politics', or 'Male Politics'.) Homosexuality was somehow taken for granted as an 'unconscious' underlying element of the male bonding involved in cinephilia. Writers' sexual identity, or their revolt against gender-biased forms of representation, were expressed at an individual level, as part of their personal relationship with the film, the idea or topic discussed, and not structured by a more militant, more globalizing discourse – this being a marked difference from the theoretical texts on cinema produced in Britain at the time.

Later, when writers such as Jean Narboni or Louis Skorecki attempted to discuss issues of sexual politics, they did so within the restricting framework of the discussion of cinephilia, the former to decipher its unconscious yet 'essential' homosexual connotations,[10] the latter to notice that 'cinephilia is *first* a masculine phenomenon that concerns . . . only men. I have to confess that, when a female film-maker, annoyed by the habits and mannerisms of cinephilia, pointed out that it was an exclusively masculine passion, the obviousness of her statement was such that I didn't doubt it for a moment.' And Skorecki adds, somehow closing what could have been a possible discussion on 'the pleasure of the spectatrix' (which was to be foreclosed for many years on both sides of the Channel and the Atlantic), 'I am less interested, *today*, in why women aren't involved in cinephilia than in explaining how men experience it.[11] This resistance to all forms of 'system' or 'militancy' is much more representative of the form of *écriture* generated by *Cahiers* than their intense, though short-lived, involvement with Maoism.

Does this mean that *Cahiers*'s Maoist period should be considered an aberration – or, as the editors later wrote in their 'self-criticism' of 1974 ('Les *Cahiers* aujourd'hui', *Cahiers* 250, May 1974), as naivety? This seems to be the opinion of Antoine de Baecque, currently a member of the editorial team of *Cahiers* and author of the two-volume *Les Cahiers du Cinéma: Histoire d'une revue*. Published in 1991, the book does not avoid a 'teleological' view of history, reading it *a posteriori* from the perspective of the more open-minded, more commercial, less political framework of the late 1980s.[12] While impressed by de Baecque's scholarship and presentation, I would argue that, as far as the 1970s are concerned, he fails to provide a materialistic reading of this quintessentially materialist phase of *Cahiers*'s history.

Indeed, from the point of view of survival, diffusion and even readability, the Maoist period was a disaster. In 1972, six issues were published, in 1973 only four (the journal did not appear again on a monthly basis until 1976), readership decreased (as low as three thousand), debts accumulated. Some of these 'hardships', however, were the result of conscious political or intellectual decisions. The irregular publication of *Cahiers*, for example, might have been disturbing for its readership but it also reflected an editorial policy. 'Toubiana and I,' wrote Daney, 'would gravely wonder if we had enough "personal" material to quickly produce a simple issue, or if we had to wait for another month to produce a "double" issue.'[13] What was at stake, for *Cahiers* writers as for most French intellectuals at the time, was not to build a career, even less to make money, but to articulate the primacy of a certain form of reflection in the face of the desolating events of the period. Jan Palach had sacrificed himself in Prague, Salvador Allende's forced suicide ended the socialist experiment in Chile, Solzhenitsyn published *Cancer Ward*, Palestinian camps in Jordan were eradicated following the Black September massacre, the Baader-Meinhof gang was committing collective 'suicide' in Germany and political militants were imprisoned in France. The sense of urgency expressed in *Cahiers*'s dogmatic positions (defining a 'Front Culturel Révolutionnaire' according to a strict Marxist-Leninist orthodoxy), as well as in their often quixotic attempts at 'cultural animation' (such as the Avignon 'training sessions' from 1970 to 1973), reflected the demise of most of the utopias that had been at the heart of French leftist political thinking since the Liberation (and which functioned as a form of suturing process): Communism in its Soviet version, 'socialism with a human face', the Czechoslovakian and the Chilean 'Springs', the possibility of revolution in industrialized countries, etc. What was left was an immense void, which could be filled only by death (some former militants did commit suicide), universal cretinization (the period marks the real beginning of mass media in France), narcissistic experiments to 'liberate' one's sexuality and/or unconscious (the Californian counter-culture), or, conversely, a pretty stern combination of theory and political activism. That theory itself, at the forefront between 1968 and 1971, should now be dismissed as a symptom of 'petit-bourgeois thinking' is highly revealing of the intellectual crisis faced by *Cahiers*: it had become urgent to *think* the heritage of May '68, but fact after fact had proved the futility of such an endeavour. Theory seemed to be functioning in a void. Chaban-Delmas's 'new society' was consolidating de Gaulle's project to bring France up to the standards of modern, competitive capitalism, and French people had voted en masse against revolutionary change.

What makes it more difficult, from a contemporary standpoint, to evaluate and fully understand *Cahiers*'s intellectual position at the time is that it was mostly built *against* the texts through which the journal became known to English-speaking readers as a main force in film theory – such as the often-quoted text by Oudart on 'Cinema and Suture', or the collective deconstruction of Ford's *Young Mr Lincoln* and Sternberg's *Morocco*.[14] In a first critical assessment of their 'intervention' in Avignon, published in 1972, *Cahiers* writers were reflecting on the journal's past history, especially what they called its 'structuralist period' (1969–70) – now denounced as 'revisionist' – and its 'avant-garde period' (1970–1):

> Our mistake then consisted in thinking of contradiction and ideological struggle in terms of non-relevant oppositions: latent/manifest, visible/non-visible, full/empty . . . This implied an idealistic belief in 'the intrinsic strength of the true idea' . . . As if bourgeois ideology and the artistic products it governs were going to collapse (like a vampire) as soon as they were exposed to daylight. Ideological struggle was thought of in terms of 'criticism' and it was not appreciated that a 'criticism' not sustained by an alternative to bourgeois production, that a deconstruction without construction, was not a real destruction.[15]

In other words, for the 'critic' must be substituted the 'militant' and film criticism itself, rather than being an effort to describe, understand or deconstruct
filmic texts, should acquire a 'prescriptive' quality. The journal's self-
proclaimed goal was 'how to politically use political films'. Again, this attitude
was very much in the spirit of the time (we need only think, as far as Britain is
concerned, of the first texts by Claire Johnston and Laura Mulvey). The down-
side of *Cahiers*'s forceful Maoism was that theory was to be abandoned for a few
years.

However, the tide kept changing, as proved by the long controversy that
began with the release of Jean-Luc Godard and Jean-Pierre Gorin's *Tout va bien*.
An extensive text published by the 'Lou Sin' Group in *Cahiers* 238–9, June
1972, praised it (as a film that knew the position of its makers, actors and spectators in the class struggle) against Marin Karmitz's *Coup pour coup* (denounced
as 'fantasizing' the working class from a petit-bourgeois perspective). Less than
two years later, Bonitzer acknowledged that it had been a mistake to oppose
two films so different in their intentions and modes of production, as if 'a single level of apprehension of film existed and should exist – which would imply,
for example, that the ideal revolutionary movie should occupy the place currently held by *The Adventures of Rabbi Jacob*'.[16] Similarly, Daney went on to criticize 'the famous couple ideology/science' (the basis of many Maoist analyses)
as

> castrating. In *Vent d'est* Godard and Gorin tell us: cinema gives you
> pleasure and yet it is a real war machine erected by the bourgeoisie
> against you. We have to criticize it. But once it's been put through a
> riddle, what about pleasure? ... Ideology gives pleasure ... That
> doesn't mean that getting out of ideology means getting out of plea-
> sure, exchanging one's illusions for the (scientific) gain of an all-
> encompassing gaze or an uneasy conscience (without pleasure).
> Pleasure does not exist only where one is blinded.[17]

Yet at the time the isolation experienced by *Cahiers* during the Front Culturel
Révolutionnaire accurately reflected the avatars of contemporary thought: its
alienation, its split from what was conveniently termed 'reality'. As readers of
Lacan, we have learnt to consider that 'the real' is no more than what is left
unaccounted for by the symbolic and the imaginary. Let's say that, in the early
1970s in France, because of the impasse reached by the imaginary (demise of
the utopias), and the difficulties in symbolizing the recent historical past (the
causes of the failure of the May '68 movements or various socialist and revolutionary experiments), the real became very heavy. The uncanny (and painful)
accuracy of *Cahiers*'s position at that time is to have correctly perceived and
embodied this split between real, imaginary and symbolic as it presented itself.
So *Cahiers*'s history can be read as two parallel lines: what it did, and what it
missed. And the part of the 'reality' it missed was enormous. It stopped paying

attention to the films released in the cinemas.[18] No mention was made of Fassbinder until April 1977 – to the chagrin of the German film-maker.[19] Jean Eustache's *The Mother and the Whore* (arguably the greatest filmic text of the post-'68 generation) was dismissed in a way that completely baffled its author: in *Cahiers* 247, August 1973, a text by Bonitzer describes the film as 'deeply reactionary' and puts it on the same level as two other 'petit-bourgeois' movies, Marco Ferreri's *La Grande Bouffe* and Bertolucci's *Last Tango in Paris*. Having split with Truffaut (who withdrew from the editorial board in 1979, while remaining a stockholder of the publishing company), *Cahiers* ignored *Les Deux Anglaises et le continent*, *Une belle fille comme moi* and *La Nuit américaine* (*Day for Night*). It also bypassed the first films of Pialat and Doillon, and ignored Chabrol's production at the time. American cinema came to be denounced, by Louis Skorecki, as 'the worst in the world',[20] and, apart from John Cassavetes and Robert Kramer, *Cahiers* even lost touch with what they continued to term 'the American underground', which they actually knew very little about. There was no dialogue with British and American critics and theoreticians which could have introduced them to various theoretical practices of alternative film-making on both sides of the Atlantic.

The main criticism that *Cahiers* writers addressed to themselves after the fact was that they had lost their initial object, cinema. Or at least lost touch with it, which may not be entirely the same thing. Again, in this articulation of the loss I see the outline of an important truth that became clear only later: that the love of movies, classical cinephilia, the fetishization of the film-viewing experience, was not essential, or at least not sufficient, to construct a discourse about cinema. The texts of the time of the Front Culturel Révolutionnaire may not have discussed *mise en scène* (the phrase returns with a vengeance in Pascal Bonitzer's review of Marguerite Duras's *India Song* in *Cahiers* 258–9, August 1975, translated in this volume), but they were analysing other parameters that have to do with the way a film is constructed as a cultural and ideological product. One often tends to forget that the early writers of *Cahiers* displayed noted rightist tendencies, and that the aestheticism of some of their filmic analyses can be read as reflecting a desire to foreclose, or dismiss, the notion of class struggle. If the most visible part of 'reality' was missed (what we would call 'current news about cinema'), its *'part maudite'* (to use Georges Bataille's phrase) was eventually recovered through a slow and laborious burrowing. Reflecting about the 1970s in a double special issue, Daney analysed Godard's career at the time in a way that could have applied also to *Cahiers*'s intellectual trajectory: 'Godard, after '68, turns his back on his career to follow his time even in its own impasses (militant cinema and its criticism, television and its criticism).'[21] The 'passion of/for the idea' embodied by *Cahiers*'s intellectual positions at the time may be read as a form of Hegelian alienation. Because reason is 'canny', and advances only through a series of side-steppings, the concept must undergo trial, negativity, misunderstanding: such is the price paid for dialectical progress.

What *Cahiers* missed as well, of course, was a readership. Granted, most of the texts were deemed 'unreadable' even by *Cahiers*'s closest supporters. But so were Lacan's *Ecrits* ('They were not *supposed to be read*', its author superbly said in one of his *séminaires*), and yet they changed our understanding of psychoanalysis. Yet, again, this 'unreadability' suggested a displacement of the problematic of communication, a resistance against the transparency of social signs that Chaban-Delmas's 'new society' sought to impose on France, and which the nascent ideology of mass media was soon going to trumpet through every television set. As Serge Daney was to write years later: 'Culture is a misunderstanding that succeeds. The opposite of culture is the "Roger" of a "successful" communication functioning as a loop.'[22] The opacity of the *écriture* at *Cahiers* was an accurate rendering of the murky political climate, the social impasses, the muted anxiety of the time. As Godard said in *Numéro deux*: 'It is not anxiety that is complicated and things simple but things that are complicated and anxiety simple.' The ideologists of transparency who reproached *Cahiers* for its obscure style wanted in fact a simple, *naturalized* social reality, an unbroken communication pattern, a real flattened and exposed without loss or dark corners.

There was a third thing acutely 'missed' by *Cahiers* around 1971–5, and it was the 'Other'. Not only the audience, although Daney came to ask why it was that two films defended by *Cahiers* such as René Allio's *Rude journée pour la reine* and Godard's *Tout va bien* totally missed their target audience (see note 33):

> *Rude journée pour la reine* is an important film, a film that is 'looking back at us' . . . *Tout va bien* had been another commercial failure, another film we found important, another gap between our point of view (or shall I say our *interests*) as critics and a disappointed audience that balked. And it was no longer possible to attribute this gap to the advanced aesthetics of an avant-garde film-maker as opposed to the backwardness of the audience since . . . Godard yesterday and Allio today were simply trying to reach the *largest possible audience*.

It was mostly in the late 1970s that *Cahiers* tried to reformulate a theory of the spectator, within a political context, especially with a series of texts written by Toubiana in 1977 on 'the place of the spectator within the leftist fiction' – the 'leftist fiction' (*fiction de gauche*) being films with a 'progressive message' presented in the most conventional narrative forms of identification, representation etc. Yet what was at the heart of *Cahiers*'s problematics in the early 1970s was the Other as it was built by the process of representation itself. 'In its generalized critique of representation, the leftism of the 1970s could be described as a certain mystical rage. The *other* had some rights. He had the right of not being spoken for "in his name", and he had the right to be missing in the place [where he was expected]', recalled Daney, who explained that, if *Tout va bien* was once judged superior to *Coup pour coup*, it was because it expressed 'the aristocratism of an eloquent absence (the absence of a people represented by a void)'.[23] For *Cahiers* at that time, as for Godard, the Other is structurally missing, and it is significant that the model for theoretical thought and revolutionary political action should come from faraway mainland China. Yet even the 'close' Other is missing, as Godard masterfully rediscovered with *Ici et ailleurs*, in which his 'unusable' footage of Palestinian camps shot in 1969 shortly before the Black September massacre leads him to an analysis not only of the way the images of their dead bodies are 'consumed' by the news, but also of how we use the bodies of others – the unemployed in France, for example – to construct the signifying chains of our own discourses.

While Maoism isolated *Cahiers* from practically everybody, it allowed a reconciliation with Godard. The latter had broken with the journal in late 1968 to express his disagreement with the commercialism of its editor, Daniel Filipacchi. *Cahiers* ended its association with Filipacchi in 1969, but Godard, already involved in the Marxist-Leninist practice of the Dziga Vertov group with Gorin and Pierre-Henri Roger, would not forgive its writers what he saw as their 'revisionism' and their closeness to the Communist Party. (In fact, Bernard Eisenschitz was the only *Cahiers* critic to be a member of the CP.) Maoism finally constituted a common ground, where *Cahiers* and Godard could meet again. *Vladimir and Rosa* was on the cover of *Cahiers* 232 in October 1971; the same issue reproduced the Poretta Terme statement, through which a Maoist version of Marxism-Leninism was adopted.[24] From the May–June 1972 issue (which featured *Tout va bien* on the cover), *Cahiers* endeavoured to write a systematic history of the Dziga Vertov group, starting with the long text by the Lou Sin Group mentioned above. From then on, texts on Godard appeared regularly, culminating in Pascal Bonitzer's *J.-M. S. and J.-L. G.*, which analyses the films of Straub (in particular *Moses and Aaron*) and Godard (*Numéro deux, Ici et ailleurs*) as generating a *jouissance* in 'the gap in representation, the off-screen space, the black screen, the white screen, the empty screen . . . a white hole that classical cinema has always tried to fill'.[25] Bonitzer then analyses Godard's work in *Ici et ailleurs* as a

> dismantling, dismembering, unchaining/unbridling of . . . the representations that the apparatus of seduction (posters, press, television, cinema) produces and organizes for an *ordered* circulation of desires. The 'whole' offered to desire by these representations (the 'whole' object of *jouissance*, of knowledge, etc.) undergoes fragmentation, the imaginary immensity of the 'elsewhere' (everything that is elsewhere: the object of representation) is swallowed back to the sphere of the 'here'.

As 'the working class' (represented *in full* in Karmitz's *Coup pour coup*) is missing in *Tout va bien*, whose entire movement represents a failed effort to reach it (the strikers lock up the journalists with the boss instead of allowing them to share their space), cinema can reach 'the real' only by acknowledging that the place of the Other is occupied by a void in representation. In other words, that the truth of cinema lies in the off-screen space.

The off-screen space as the field of the other; or, Lacombe versus Rivière

It is in Bonitzer's texts that one finds the most articulate expressions of the notion of 'off-screen space',[26] which may be considered as one of *Cahiers*'s major contributions to film theory. The 1970s witnessed a further refinement of the notion's dialectical implications in the reading of contemporary cinema. When in *Cahiers* 257, May–June 1975, four members of the editorial board – Serge Daney, Pascal Kané, Jean-Pierre Oudart and Serge Toubiana – decide to reassess collectively 'a particular trend in French cinema',[27] the political climate was murky but the question was clear: seven years after May '68, what were the conditions which, in France, generated the process of thinking (or: thinking as a process/*en procès*/in trial)? The classical articulation between off-screen and on-screen, as better expressed by Bresson in either *Pickpocket* (a film referred to by Daney throughout his writing career) or *The Trial of Joan of Arc* (the film about which Oudart wrote his 'Cinema and Suture'), was no longer possible. Daney notes:

> Bresson provided the *ideological and formal* model for the *mise en scène* of these fringes of society. He furnished the ideological model by making the heroes of his films characters . . . who were least susceptible of recuperation . . . And he provided the formal model by filming the gaze which nothing in the world or out of the frame . . . could satisfy or *suture* . . . French cinema around 1975 records something different. Its problem is not that some person or thing has been completely excluded from it but that various groups have been relatively privileged.

What is at stake, in this reformulation of the off-screen space, is a displacement of the subject, putting into crisis the couple spectator–*auteur*, the placement of the Other, the role of *écriture*, of marginalized practices. Having served time in the desert of the Front Culturel Révolutionnaire, the editorial team of *Cahiers*, intent on reclaiming cinema as its lost object, set out to explore its boundaries and limits – intimately aware that enlarging the field (*champ*) of filmic inquiry also meant enlarging its 'off-screen space' (*hors-champ*) and exploring more specifically the various strategies at work in devising reverse angles (*contre-champs*).

The initial project of the journal – *Cahiers du Cinéma* implies *one* cinema – presupposed the existence of a *single* operational concept that in turn divided the world of mediatic experiences between cinematic and non-cinematic objects. It is interesting to note that this notion rarely came to a crisis. In his 1976 text (see note 25) Bonitzer briefly mentioned that 'Straub and Godard

... stand at the two opposite poles of filmic modernity. They each hold one end of what we call "cinema", they make up the two focuses of the ellipse in which the world of cinema has opened up, flattened and decentred itself: so we can no longer talk about "*the* cinema".' Then Bonitzer brilliantly adds that

> Straub, like Godard, takes as his starting point that all cinema is a lie. That everything which is currently done in cinema is false, fascistic, perverted, pornographic. The interest of this radical position – which is nothing but an ethical stand – is that it comes from *within* cinema itself ... Straub and Godard are made of cinema [*sont des êtres de cinéma*] ... This position commits them to struggle with cinema.

Thus the text ends by restricting even more the concept of cinema. The possible opening of the notion, hinted at in the beginning, does not happen.

The notion of *le cinéma* – and with it that of *cinephilia* – came to a crisis much later, as expressed in an article by Louis Skorecki entitled 'Contre la nouvelle cinéphilie' (see note 11), which the editorial board of *Cahiers* hesitated before publishing, finding it, in the words of its author, 'problematic ... not so much because of its discrepancy with the (implicit) line of the journal, but rather because it does not mark its position vis-à-vis *Cahiers*'. Skorecki first establishes that the events of May '68 and the semiological research that followed sounded the knell of a certain form of cinema and marked the death of classical cinephilia, thus sarcastically summarizing a great part of the discussions of the early 1970s:

> If cinema is apt at producing such a powerful alienation at the very moment when a new awareness (disalienation) is taking place, it is because (1) it might somehow be responsible for this general alienation. It is guilty. It must pay for it; (2) there might be a way to use cinema, as the partial cause of this evil, to serve the opposite interests ... to awaken consciousness, to question, to promote another form of politics and a new, wider and more revolutionary struggle.

In other words, the pleasure of the spectator (even though it is not named as such) manifests itself in the category of guilt – and the only way to resolve this guilt is to move cinema in another direction, that of revolutionary action, or, as stated in the texts written around the time of Poretta Terme, to make 'politics the order of the day'.

For an English-speaking reader, this analysis rings a strange bell. If one substitutes for the Catholic or Jewish-accented 'guilt' the more classically puritanical position of English academia, one is not very far from Laura Mulvey's will to 'destroy cinematic pleasure' as being the effect of narrative, patriarchal and post-Oedipal alienation.[28] It is not so surprising, though, that these two texts – *Cahiers* openly repudiating what it had adored and Mulvey heroically renouncing the pleasures of Hollywood – never intersected. The first reason, as I indicated earlier, is that the 'spectator' referred to by Skorecki is, irreducibly, male. The second is that he is a cinephile, while the one posited by Mulvey is more of a consumer (and indeed the most interesting avenues taken recently by feminist film criticism have developed the relationship between the emergence of the female spectator as a social/symbolic force and the transformation of the patterns of consumption within the history of capitalism and/or the history of cinema[29]). Consumers and cinephiles have different patterns of identification with the filmic image. For the consumer it will be with the star (male or female, depending on complex levels of identification and masquerade), or even with 'the point of view of the camera' or 'the development of the narrative' – in other words, with various elements of the diegesis. For the cinephile, identification will create the 'pervert' couple spectator–*auteur* (both of them, in classical cinephilia, being male, hence its 'essentially' homosexual character).

Years later, Daney strikingly described this process: 'For the spectator who, as I did, had forgotten his own body in the theatre, the good mediation was provided not by the actor but by the one about whom I imagined that, behind the camera, he articulated all the angles of vision from a unique point of view, *his* point of view: the *auteur*.'[30] For Daney, this couple create the only *space* open to film criticism – in which the desire of the cinephile/critic can communicate with the desire of the *auteur* – while for Mulvey, if there is a 'desire of the *auteur*', it is essentially, at least in classical Hollywood fiction, a male desire, and its goal is to subjugate the imaginary of the (female) spectator, not to enter into a dialectical relationship with it. 'The critic feeds on what he criticizes', adds Daney. 'Basically, answering another's desire is what legitimates him. Someone has *desired* the film as such, and, incognito, the critic throws the ball back at him.'

What happened in May '68, then, was an immense outburst of desire that could be found everywhere: in the streets, the universities, the factories, under the stones on the beach, but no longer in a personal relationship with the films of Hawks, Renoir or Harold Lloyd. So, writing ten years after May '68, Skorecki could notice only that 'there are no cinephiles any more, and we shouldn't look too far for the reason: there is not . . . one cinema any more. To be more specific, there is no *auteur* cinema any more, there are no cinema *auteurs* any more . . . there are only films, and *that's fine*.' Yet Skorecki's challenging statement, instead of opening the door to new directions, remained marginalized in *Cahiers* (probably because of Skorecki's self-acknowledged 'peripheral' position vis-à-vis the journal at the time). Maybe it came too late. While it would have been relevant in the heyday of Maoism (but who would have been interested in listening to it then?), it was slightly out of place at a time when *Cahiers* was struggling to recover its seemingly 'lost' object (cinema). And it is probably no accident that the member of the editorial team chosen to respond to Skorecki was Pascal Kané, who continued to write about

Hollywood cinema while everybody else was writing about class struggle, the cultural front and Maoist dialectics. (It might also be significant that, in the same issue in which Skorecki's text and Kané's response appeared, *Cahiers* published a 'dossier' on Douglas Sirk, a film-maker who had never been part of the canon, and was moreover much criticized for his political ambiguities by an *auteur* like Straub.) Anyhow, having reclaimed their object in its glorious specificity, *Cahiers* writers weren't ready to scatter and divide it. While exploring the cinema of the 'Others' (Palestinians, Chinese, Chileans), *Cahiers* writers rarely doubted that there was *one* cinema, in its infinite and contradictory manifestations. What they couldn't avoid, though, was the crisis undergone by the couple spectator–*auteur*.

No critical concept has been more misunderstood than that of *auteur*, especially in English-speaking countries. The *politique des auteurs* was mistranslated as the 'auteur theory' by the enthusiastic pen of Andrew Sarris.[31] If such a mistake was made, however, it was because it was tempting: tempting to focus on a romantic, essentialist notion of the *auteur*, and to forget that the term had been coined as a space of resistance, as a polemical argument against the system of commercial production. In other words, you had *auteurs* only because you had spectators – Hawks and Hitchcock, and Renoir or Lang during their Hollywood years, and Rossellini during his Bergman period, were *auteurs* in so far as Godard, Rivette and Rohmer could *read* them as such and from then on find in this reading the energy to impose on the industry and on the world their own 'desire of cinema'. Both *auteurs* and spectators were posited in a situation of resistance against a stifling normalization – claiming the value of Renoir's American period (and consequently praising *Woman on the Beach*) or Hitchcock's *Rear Window* against both *la qualité française* and various forms of 'literary' film criticism. In his text against the 'new cinephilia' Skorecki correctly, though paradoxically, asserts that 'all the *auteurs* of Hollywood cinema are ... its negative. There is no great American film-maker who has not revealed (either as an accomplice or a denouncer) the other side of the system and its structures.' Daney was to resume and synthesize such insight by writing in 1984 that the *auteur* was maybe nothing other than 'the truth of the system from which he extricates himself ... the *vanishing line* through which the system is not closed, can breathe and has a history'.[32]

Daney can be credited for restoring the *'fonction critique'* in *Cahiers*, in a series of articles published between September 1973 and October–November 1974, as a way of 'intervening', establishing how 'for each film *someone is saying something to us*'. In a brilliant conceptualization, he formalized this as the 'relation between two terms: the *statement* (what is said) and the *enunciation* (when it is said and by whom)'.[33] This method – quickly adopted by the other *Cahiers* writers (see in particular the collective discussion on Marker's *Le Fond de l'air est rouge* in *Cahiers* 284, January 1978) – was used by Daney to further two goals. First, to reclaim the specificity of cinema against the 'politism' of the Maoist years (yes, 'the bourgeoisie imposes its vision of the world', but *how* does it do it, for *each film*?). Second, to expand his long-waged battle against the fetishization of 'The Name of the Author'[34] – this itself within the context of the unmasking of a double negation (in the psychoanalytical sense of *Verneinung*[35]). A negation that 'someone is speaking' (in the 'neutral', 'naturalist' discourse of television news, for example); or, in the case of *auteur* cinema, a negation that, beyond the subjectivity of the film-maker, a discourse is articulated.

In his brilliant analysis of Marco Bellocchio's *In the Name of the Father*,[36] a text that precedes, announces and contextualizes the first part of his analysis of 'the critical function', Daney gives a name to this *auteurist* illusion: revisionism, i.e. the political/cultural position of the French Communist Party, against which most Maoist positions were constructed. 'What is the class position that commands the [film-maker's] gaze? Eschewing this question means falling into the trap of revisionism that thinks that "once an artist looks at the world, only good results can come out of it".' Daney demonstrates that if, at the end of the film, Bellocchio presents as unavoidable both the failure of a movement that would unite the revolt of the students in an upper-class religious school with the strike of the lumpenproletariat staff, and the ambiguous, premonitory triumph of the young fascist Angelo, it is because

> from the outset the film distinguishes . . . between the characters . . . who are conscious of the crisis experienced by the school . . . and all the others, swamped in their own fantasies. This opposition of conscious/unconscious . . . capital for Bellocchio . . . prevails over all political contradictions . . . The example of the religious school [as a metaphor for Italy] is not an innocent choice on the part of Bellocchio. [His] class analysis developed in the microcosm of the school brings face to face a degenerate bourgeoisie and a pathological proletariat, two unconscious and irrational masses which a small number of conscious individuals attempt to control.

Yet Daney goes much further than describing Bellocchio's pessimism and nihilism as 'the position of a revolted petit-bourgeois'; much further even than seeing that, in spite of his class position, Bellocchio's strength consists in filming situations that 'are always interpretable in political terms'. He analyses the *text* of the film and tracks down the *negation* hidden in some of its formal devices.

> The last shot of the film has to be taken seriously. We see Angelo . . . driving a car. Next to him is Tino, one of the workers in the school . . . One might point out that at this moment, through a 'subtle' backtracking movement, the shot critically recontextualizes what it shows. We don't believe much any longer, however, in the critical value of such procedures, which are rather like negations.

What Daney, a reader of Freud and Lacan as well as Mao and Marx, called *negation* was also termed 'false consciousness' or 'false class position' in the political jargon of the time. And as such it was, ironically, a good description of the position of *Cahiers* writers in their 'naive' attempt to constitute a 'front culturel révolutionnaire' while 'as we understood it the process of liaison-subordination to the Marxist-Leninist movement was lived out, or else conceived, sometimes formulated, as the *renunciation* of any *anchorage* to a specific site, even the one by which we had been constituted: the cinema' ('Les *Cahiers* aujourd'hui'). In other words the naivety of *Cahiers* writers was a lack of political consciousness leading them to deny their specific position within the class struggle and the process of intellectual production – a naivety mirrored, of course, by that of the *auteurs*, who, trapped in their own narcissism as artists, forgot that their class position and/or the structure of the means of cinematic production spoke through their work.

If there is negation, there must be repression. When, in their collective text of 1975, Daney, Bonitzer, Kané and Toubiana attacked the 'bad faith' of French cinema, they used another term for it: 'naturalism'. By then, in the last of his articles on 'the critical function' (*Cahiers* 253, October–November 1974), Daney had further specified the effect of 'revisionism' on the representation of class struggle and history in France and in particular on the 'retro' fashion of films like Louis Malle's *Lacombe Lucien* and Liliana Cavani's *Night Porter*:

> You cannot with impunity [as 'revisionists', i.e. the French Communists, do] present class confrontation in terms of a peaceful rivalry, you cannot ask the masses to choose, on the evidence presented to them, the *least bad manager* of bourgeois affairs, without making them more aware of the ideological hegemony of the petite-bourgeoisie.

Both films displace the terrain of historical representation, Cavani's by 'offering' the spectator a choice between a 'human' Nazi and an unrepentant one, and Malle's by creating a 'barbaric', 'unconscious' protagonist, incapable of thinking the historical processes (Nazism, collaboration) that *act through him*.

The wave of 'retro' films had been deemed so dangerous by *Cahiers* that they devoted a number of articles and 'interventions' to it. Bonitzer, Daney and Toubiana first interviewed Michel Foucault (*Cahiers* 251–2, July–August 1974), not only because the latter had publicly taken a stance against *Night Porter* but also because he had published in book form a text discovered during his archival research: the first-person account of a horrifying series of murders committed in nineteenth-century France by a young peasant who, having baffled the medico-judicial system, was sentenced to life imprisonment and later committed suicide. The book – *Moi, Pierre Rivière, ayant égorgé ma mère, ma soeur et mon frère . . .* – was later brought to the screen by René Allio, a film-maker whose films, such as *Les Camisards* and *Rude journée pour la reine*, were much admired by *Cahiers* in the mid-1970s, which led to another interview with

Foucault in November 1976 (*Cahiers* 271). While *Lacombe Lucien* takes it for granted that 'the masses' are not aware of their own history, Foucault's research explores the different modes of constitution and survival of popular memory: 'ordinary people, I mean those who don't have the right to writing, the right to make books themselves, to compose their own history, these people nevertheless have a way of registering history, of remembering it, living it and using it,' he explains in the interview.

Popular memory and cinema/television make up a couple of inversely proportional opposites. Since the end of the nineteenth century, during which the memory of popular struggles was carried through various forms of oral tradition, songs, etc., Foucault notices that an increasingly more sophisticated apparatus (pulp literature, compulsory education, then cinema and television) has been set up to recode popular memory: 'the historical knowledge that the working class has about itself is becoming less and less all the time.' What is at stake, then, in movies like *Lacombe Lucien* or, to a lesser degree, Ophuls's *The Sorrow and the Pity* (*Cahiers* writers were more severe on this film than Foucault[37]), is the occultation of the *real struggles* waged by Partisans during the Occupation. *Lacombe Lucien* is the story of an underpaid, marginalized hospital attendant who, politically unaware, ends up working for the Gestapo, denounces Resistants, and has a love affair with a young Jewish girl. The film is entirely marked under the sign of *disavowal*: disavowal of the fact that the working class, slowly 'repoliticized' through the Spanish Civil War, took an active part in anti-Nazi activities and in the Resistance – and that political choices were possible, even for the ignorant, victimized loser such as Lacombe. 'Such is the main artifice of the film, as well as its goal, in which we can identify the bourgeoisie's desire: *making History guilty*, short of being able to stop it', writes Bonitzer in his review of the film:

> The film attempts to strip *any political decision* of meaning, to render it insignificant . . . or at least to combine Nazism, collaboration and Resistance within the idiocy of every historical choice (that History is stupid is a reactionary commonplace). Lucien is not very bright . . . Yet if he is endearing it is because his stupidity is ultimately taken on by History.

Conversely, in one of the texts of the 'dossier' that precedes Foucault's second interview (about the film *Moi, Pierre Rivière . . .*), Toubiana notes the specificity of Rivière's decision to write a report, to have a discourse about what he did: 'Among all the gestures he uses to revisit his act, whether it is writing, speech or memory, there is none whose goal would be to lessen the import of his act, *none is a disavowal*, that particular form of self-criticism so appreciated by the law.'[38]

Lacombe and Rivière represent two different figures of the Other. Lacombe is a sort of anthropological portrait, designed to give the spectator the illusion of *knowledge* over the subject. It is because Lacombe is a 'primitive' and not too

20

bright that his motivations and his actions seem obscure, 'telluric'. In fact the diegesis sets out not only to explain (unhappy childhood, lack of sympathy and understanding on the part of some adults, etc.), but also to partially excuse and, eventually, 'naturalize' them ('this is the way people are'). Lacombe has no 'voice' for himself, but the film displays his psyche with a voyeuristic and arrogant 'pretence to see or to *own* the others' *minds*, whose *knowledge* these others cannot, supposedly, have themselves', to use Trinh T. Minh-ha's description of the anthropologist's reductionist fallacy.[39] To Lacombe's lack of insight, made parallel with and caused by History's own stupidity, the film smugly, contemptuously, opposes its own knowledge and plays the spectator against the protagonist.

Conversely, in Foucault's publishing of Rivière's report, as in Allio's staging of the same text, Rivière is clearly 'the one who knew too much', as acutely described by Toubiana in his critique of the film: 'Pierre [Rivière] is a "case" that teaches the penal system about itself; while it thought it knew everything about the marginals it is used to treat, to judge and to lock up, the system discovers one who prevents the code from functioning, the norm from normalizing, the law to be exercised.' Rivière's 'otherness' retains its opacity, not as an exotic object of study, to be understood or sympathized with, but as an authentic, irreducible site of resistance against the norm. Lacombe was to be taken as a 'natural' element of the French socio-historical landscape. Rivière is a scandal, even to himself. He is a void within the social fabric, a 'failure' of the signifier who yet strives to constitute himself as a set of signifiers (he writes), i.e. *as a subject for another subject*, to borrow Lacan's striking phrase. Rivière's radical otherness escapes any form of 'naturalization'. It is *his* type of discourse (when the Other, who doesn't fit the norm, strives to speak as a subject rather than being the object of inquiry of the dominant discourse) that is actively repressed in the commercial French cinema of the 1970s, which prefers to represent the Other as historically mute (the collaborator Lacombe, who doesn't think through his historical situation and will be shot, presumably without trial and without understanding why, at the Liberation) or as blinded by stupidity, racism and sexual repression (the 'average Frenchmen' in Yves Boisset's fable about racism, *Dupont Lajoie*). While the 'case' Rivière stands in splendid isolation, as an element of disruption of the dominant discourse on family, pathology, criminality, Lacombe and Lajoie are treated as 'natural' objects of that same discourse, as 'types'.

To go back to the series of fragments defining 'a particular trend in French cinema', it is significant that they appear in the same issue as *Cahiers*'s interview with historian-turned-film-maker Marc Ferro, who defines the relationship between cinema history and propaganda in terms of a dialectic between the said and the unsaid:

The historian's primary task is to restore to society the History which the institutional apparatuses have dispossessed it of. To question society, to begin to listen to it – to my mind, this is the primary duty of the historian. Instead of settling simply for using archives, it is equally important to create them . . . to make films about and to ask questions of those who have never had the right to speak and be a witness.

The role of 'naturalism' and 'typecasting' is to repress and negate the fact that the dominant discourse is based on a dialectics of exclusion. What is important is the *work* through which previously excluded categories of population attain the right of being represented. It is the crisis of French society between 1968 and 1975, the restructuring of the means of production under a new bourgeoisie, the state of the class struggle, the various ideological battles, that *produced* the conditions allowing the publication of Pierre Rivière's report as well as the various 'retro' films. Naturalism, as a denial of history, takes for granted the presence of recently under-represented categories of people within the field of representation, which Daney expresses by writing:

> Naturalism is the game of readjustment where those such as young people, immigrants and peasants who were previously forbidden from making films . . . are now suddenly included in fiction films (and in traditional fiction films) as though they had always been part of them . . . But what is glossed over in this process . . . is how and why they *break into* the story.

In other words, 'naturalism' eliminates the dialectic between on-screen and off-screen, and trivializes the processes of *mise en scène* itself, since the latter consists in articulating these two fields *within a certain point of view*.

We'll see the impact this analysis has on a new reading of *la politique des auteurs*. But in this series of fragmented, Barthes-like, polyphonic texts that analyse 'a particular trend in French cinema' *Cahiers* critics were more interested in attacking certain manifestations of French cinema than in promoting the films they liked. Mainstream movies such as Bertrand Blier's *Les Valseuses* (1974), Pascal Thomas's *Les Zozos* (1973), Claude Sautet's *Vincent, François, Paul et les autres* (1974), Claude Berri's *Le Mâle du siècle* (1975), Costa-Gavras's *Section Spéciale* (1975), and, on the other hand, *auteur* films which concealed the process of class struggle to 'function as reserves of individualism and subjectivity' (Oudart), such as Jean Eustache's *Mes petites amoureuses* (1973), Jean-Louis Bertucelli's *On s'est trompé d'histoire d'amour* (1973), Jacques Doillon's *Les Doigts dans la tête* (1974), Yannick Bellon's *La Femme de Jean* (1974) or Claude Goretta's *Pas si méchant que ça*,[40] were analysed as *symptoms* of what was seen as repressed in French cinema. Like the 'revisionism' of 1973, 'naturalism' was analysed as a fantasmatic projection on the part of film-makers and audiences alike, whose result was to conceal what was really happening both in the social arena and at the level of its representation. Again Daney was quick to point out that what was missing in French cinema was not its apprehension of the real, but its 'reserves of imagination' – thus recontextualizing, via a mention of the mirror stage, the question of suture. The suturing process allows the spectator to project him/herself in the diegetic space through a process of identification with the 'Absent One' (see note 14). According to Daney, French cinema of the 1970s was foreclosing this process by 'skirting around' the dialectics of the absence.

On the other side of this specular illusion there is the question of the 'majority', as mentioned by Kané. If the ultimate goal of 'naturalism' is to integrate the Other within a rather shapeless majority, then the majority of spectators can have only an abstract image of themselves. 'The majority refuses to consider itself as a group. It is a group with no image of itself.' It is, in other words, a sort of 'degree zero' of representation, oppressive because it pretends it does not exist. In his 1988 article 'White', Richard Dyer notes that 'white power secures its dominance by seeming not to be anything in particular', and that it is in a sense easier to study images of 'groups defined as oppressed, marginal or subordinate – women, the working class, ethnic and other minorities'. Yet since 'the impulse for such work lies in the sense that how such groups are represented is part of the process of their oppression, marginalization or subordination', there is a danger in constructing such groups *as owing their identity to their very alienation*, as 'departure from the norm'. (And Dyer is fond of stating, quoting Marcuse, that 'power in contemporary society passes itself off as embodied in the normal as opposed to the superior'.) 'Meanwhile the norm has carried on as if it is the *natural*, inevitable way of being human.'[41] Dyer's text sheds a new light on *Cahiers*'s position in the mid-1970s, but it also underlines the different directions taken by British and French theoreticians. *Cahiers* was always more interested in analysing racism (as a form of representation) than race itself (as a cultural construct). With the exception of the Iranian Fereydoun Hoveyda (who wrote for *Cahiers* during the 1960s), the editorial team never included a 'person of colour'.

When Daney denounces the lack of 'reserves of imagination' in the French cinema of the 1970s, he is also alluding to a major difference between French and American cinema: what Marxist philosopher Jacques Rancière, interviewed in 1976, defined as 'the absence of a dominant fiction in France', as opposed to the founding myth of the United States, the 'birth of a nation'. Native Americans were annihilated, while the French bourgeoisie could not wipe out the resistance of the working class: this in turn explains the capacity of the United States to offer its citizens the image of a social consensus with which they are invited to identify. For Rancière this generates two different types of fiction: the American one is an endlessly renewed explanation of the origins ('this is where we are coming from'), while the French one, more modestly, tends to describe 'the way we are':

Power in our country does not offer itself to our love as *law* . . . More discreetly, it tries to be accepted/forgotten . . . as a representation of social diversity in which the policeman, for example, is less the representative of the law than a voyeur going through a collection of social types . . . In the corresponding fiction . . . class struggle is neither represented nor suppressed; it is taxonomized.[42]

So the use and misuse of 'typage' – as denounced in mainstream French cinema of the 1970s – is in opposite relationship to the existence of a socio-political consensus in France. As Daney was to say later:

> France . . . is a country that finds it difficult to reach a consensus, that is not terribly imaginative in this matter. When I suffer from this lack of consensus, I look at postwar Italian cinema, or towards America. The manufacturing of American ideals is not incompatible with great films, those of Capra, McCarey, and especially Ford.[43]

Yet while it is apparently easy for someone versed in cultural criticism to oppose, from a Marxist point of view, two forms of dominant cinema for their inability to talk about class struggle, Rancière goes further, and opposes two film-makers much admired by *Cahiers*, Robert Kramer and Godard, as being, in spite of themselves, the bearer of these opposite forms of fiction generated in the dominant modes of representation:

> Kramer's *Milestones* is able to give voice to the American left, to make it tell its own story because it is a film posited within a culture in which it is natural to represent oneself under the guise of a travelogue. Yet . . . it does not raise any issues of 'representation', and it is a bit disturbing (deceiving) to see these characters who are both given as real, who ask questions of each other in front of the camera and are organized within a fiction of hope. Conversely Godard in *Numéro deux* denies the left the possibility of telling a story. He radically deconstructs all the lies of the figuration of the left, which also means that he bars any possible reflection about militant history by confronting, from the outset, all militant discourse with its own lies, with its collusion with the modes of fiction of power and of capital.

Rancière's interview appeared less than a year after the *Numéro deux* 'dossier' published in *Cahiers* 262–3, January 1976 (from which three texts – by Toubiana, Giraud and Daney – are reproduced in this volume) and about a year and a half after the no less enthusiastic section devoted to *Milestones* in *Cahiers* 258–9, August 1975 (in which the 'presentation' written by Kramer and his co-director, John Douglas, is followed by a round-table discussion of the film by *Cahiers* writers). In contrast with the interview with Foucault about *Moi, Pierre Rivière* and with Deleuze about *Numéro deux*, Rancière's intervention was not designed to contextualize, comment on or expand *Cahiers*'s position on a film, but rather to mark a certain distance from previous positions. So maybe one shouldn't be surprised that, while Kramer remained a *Cahiers auteur* (there is another 'dossier' on him in December 1978), Bonitzer wrote, in his belated review of Monte Hellman's *Two-lane Blacktop*: 'We . . . missed it. We talked about *Milestones* and we didn't talk about *Two-lane Blacktop* . . . Yet one may prefer the latter film because Monte Hellman is less taken in by notions of truth, interpersonal communication, tribal speech and revolutionary messianism.'[44] In the collective discussion of *Milestones* Toubiana admits that he is mostly interested in the 'off-screen space' of the film, i.e. the American political reality, but also in the thoughts generated by the screening in France about 'a certain way of talking about politics . . . a dialogue with oneself and others'. Clearly, *Two-lane Blacktop*, as a variation on the B-movie genre, stands by itself as a film, while *Milestones* is a film still drenched in militancy, a film whose ultimate importance lies in the information and the message it conveys. From this point of view the various positions taken by *Cahiers* about *Milestones* are extremely interesting. August 1975 might be interpreted as the apex or the swan song of the journal's militant period, and Bonitzer's text on Monte Hellman, published only nine months later, leads the way towards a more cinephiliac reappraisal of Hollywood, its *auteurs maudits* and its mavericks. As a B-movie, *Two-lane Blacktop* fits in the tradition of the insider-outsider – exemplified by such films as Ulmer's *Detour* or Jacques Tourneur's *Wichita*[45] – creating a fiction within the national consensus while suggesting values, a life-style, a way of constructing subjectivity, of representing death and sexuality, etc., that are indirectly in contradiction with it. Conversely, *Milestones* denounced the consensus, stating from the start, as Kramer and Douglas explain it in their text, that 'the origins of the United States . . . are blood-stained, deformed by the excess, the violence and the arrogance of Western civilization', i.e. the extermination of the Indians and the enslavement of the blacks. In his interview Rancière suggests that *Milestones* attacks the national consensus only *in its content*, reproducing it structurally in its form, its mode of address, its optimism, etc. Not questioning representation as a process, *Milestones* is doomed to produce signifiers that are as naively 'full', undivided, 'realistic', as those produced by Godard's *Numéro deux* are 'empty' and return any fiction to insignificance. In spite of itself (and maybe mostly because of the way it was received in France), *Milestones* is still of the order of the myth, even if the mythological element is no longer the US cavalry but the American left. I suggest that if *Cahiers* found *Milestones* – and Kramer in general – fascinating, it was partly because *c'était encore l'Amérique*. Another America, indeed, one that was critical of the policy of its own leaders, militant, courageous, marginalized, but infinitely more exciting than the drab reality of the slow death of the post-'68 movements in the mid-1970s in France.

So the enthusiasm generated by *Milestones* among *Cahiers* writers can be interpreted as a strange 'return of the repressed'. The Maoist years had foreclosed any real discussion of American cinema. In the mid-1970s the 'founding question' that is at the root of the *politique des auteurs* came back with a vengeance. Faced with a mainstream American cinema that often conveys questionable ideological values, and with a certain French or European cinema that, while pretending to be 'ideologically better', manages only to be formally inferior, *where* is it possible to find a critical discourse *within the very institution of cinema*? In the authorial obsessions of well-established Hollywood directors or in militant films such as Firestone's *Attica* or Kramer's *Milestones*? In the B-movies? Or, in Europe, with a more 'artistic', intellectual or personal cinema? (We might note, in passing, that *Cahiers* never looked at avant-garde or experimental cinema long enough to consider it as a possible critical alternative to the mainstream – another major difference from British and American critics of the time, such as Peter Wollen or Annette Michelson.) In the heyday of Maoism, Daney and Oudart had proved merciless against the pretensions of 'classical European cinema . . . [that] presents itself as a kind of "uneasy conscience" of Hollywood cinema, a tableau/critique of a society (where Hollywood cinema offers complete ideological accord between the values of cinema and those of society) – as a "critical realist" cinema.'[46]

In *Cahiers* 289, June 1978, Yann Lardeau, a newcomer to the journal, came up with an original answer. His text, *Le Sexe froid*, proposes that the real 'uneasy conscience', the actual 'critical truth' of Hollywood, is nothing else than pornographic cinema: 'It is cinema itself, as a medium, which is pornographic . . . It is not sex that is obscene but, fundamentally and in the literal sense of the word, cinema, the ob-scene crystallized by the close-up.' As analysed at length by *Cahiers* in the texts of the previous decade, Hollywood functions on a strict separation between the dream and the repressed reality. If Lardeau can state that pornographic cinema is a 'critical genre' that summarizes and crystallizes the crisis experienced by cinema, it is precisely because porn has 'naively' crossed the bar separating real and imaginary, and its violence lies in having shown the artificiality of such a limit. In an article about René Allio's *Les Camisards*, Jacques Aumont reminded the reader that, for Barthes, 'in a system the lack of any element is in itself significant'.[47] A number of texts written for *Cahiers* at the time strive to redefine the problematic of the lack, conceived in terms of negativity, negation, return of the repressed. If for Daney and Skorecki the *auteurs* are the 'negative' and the 'vanishing line' of commercial cinema, for Lardeau porn reveals what mainstream cinema (or, for that matter, *auteur* cinema, at least until Jean Eustache's *Une sale histoire*) functions to hide.

Yet porn uses – while subverting them – the same devices that identify *mise en scène* as such: variations in framing, in camera movements, in point of view, dialectic between the visible and the invisible, what is hidden and what is represented. So, far from being atypical, Lardeau's text on porn (which, significantly, ends with a negation of sexual difference rather than with an exploration of it, probably because, once again, the text does not open towards a theory of the *gendered* spectator) should be read in the wake of a series of

26

insights offered by various *Cahiers* writers at different moments of their texts on the pornographic essence of cinema.[48] Not only Narboni defining cinephilia in his critique of Wenders's *The American Friend* (see note 10), or pondering in his text on Chantal Akerman's *Je, tu, il, elle* on 'the existence of some disturbing kinship, of an essential connection between obscenity and the obsession with realism, pornography and the representation of . . . any object',[49] but also Toubiana when he reflects on

> the position of the spectator in the *fiction de gauche*, sliding along the metaphorical meaning of 'position' in which he sees an allusion to porn cinema, and analysing the cinematic apparatus as 'inscribed . . . in this slight shift that causes the spectator to disrobe and take off his imaginary before entering the theatre, and to put on someone else's clothes during the screening'.[50]

Even more to the point, Daney, in 'Le thérrorisé' (on Godard's *Numéro deux*, *Cahiers* 262–3, January 1976), defines obscenity as a by-product of a cinema in crisis: cinema is 'a bad place, a place of crime and magic. Crime: that images and sounds should be *taken* . . . from living beings. Magic: that they should be exhibited on another scene . . . for the pleasure of those who see them . . . That's where the real pornography lies, in this change of scene: it's literally the ob-scene.' In another often-quoted text,[51] in which he distinguishes between the *voice-off* (voice over), the *voice-in* (commentary that comes from within the image), the *voice-through* (the voice that seems to come out of the body, as when a character who speaks is shot from the back) and the *voice-out*, Daney defines the latter as

> plainly, the voice as it comes out of the mouth . . . The *voice-out* partakes of pornography by making it possible to fetishize the *moment* of emission (the lips of the star, Marlene Dietrich applying lipstick in front of the firing squad in Sternberg's *Dishonored*). Similarly, porn cinema is entirely centred on the spectacle of the orgasm as it happens for the male, i.e. *in its most visible aspect* (coitus interruptus, ejaculation).

While Daney's text outlines a geography of the off-screen/in-screen through a dialectic of the different kinds of voices, Lardeau's article, in its obsession with framing, can be read as a distant echo of the fascinating research conducted by Bonitzer on the composition of the filmic image between 1976 and 1978. The title of the most famous of these texts, *Décadrages*, was used also for the collection of Bonitzer's essays published later by *Cahiers* in book form.[52] This text (*Cahiers* 284, January 1978) is important also in respect of *Cahiers*'s theoretical evolution, through the influences it acknowledges. One of them is Panofsky and his work on the Renaissance perspective – even though, during the Maoist years, the interpretation of Panofsky's thesis and its application to the space created by the camera had caused heated discussion between *Cahiers* and *Positif*. The second is Bazin's ever-useful distinction between 'frame' and 'masking', an elegant way to redeem Bazin from the idealistic 'hell' where he had been confined (notably in 'L'écran du fantasme', a 'double' text written in parallel by Bonitzer and Daney[53]). The third is Oudart's text on suture, which, along with a reference to Foucault's deconstruction of Velázquez's *Las meninas* in *The Order of Things* (*Les Mots et les choses*), clearly marks a return to a more classical vision of the relationship between theory and film criticism, a vision that had been harshly criticized in the name of the primacy of politics during the Maoist years. 'The portrait is not', states Bonitzer, 'this manic reduplication of the visible; it is also a conjuring up of the hidden, a game of truth with power and knowledge.' With characteristic elegance, Bonitzer glosses the work of contemporary painters like Cremonini, Bacon, Adami, Goings or Monory,[54] cartoons by Alex Barbier, even a painting by the writer Dino Buzatti, to analyse the specificity of 'deframing' in the films of Bresson (whom he opposes – significantly – to Eisenstein), Straub, Duras and Antonioni, who are 'also painters'. It is useful to compare this text not only to Lardeau's but also to an earlier text by Daney, 'Un tombeau pour l'oeil' (to which both Oudart in 'Diffamations', *Cahiers* 266–7, June 1976, and Toubiana in his text on 'the position of the spectator' allude to), which takes some recent films by Straub as a pretext to discuss reverse-angle shots, porn and the silent work of power in the filmic image.[55]

'Le sexe froid', 'Un tombeau pour l'oeil' and 'Décadrages' are in various degrees 'Lacanian', which means, among other things, that they don't take 'the gaze' for granted, but as a complex process involving a dialectic between the visible and the invisible, power and enunciation, pleasure and *jouissance*. While Lardeau discovers that one of the effects of 'the close-up's fragmentation of sex is the absenting of the body, its exclusion (which, one might say, is systematized in pornography)', Daney pursues his reflection on Jean-Marie Straub and Danièle Huillet's *Moses and Aaron* by writing: 'strangely, Straub's cinema makes us understand that the naked body has such an exchange value, constitutes for the capital (porn cinema) such a precious signifier because it holds nothing of History, it makes History disappear [*il n'accroche rien de l'Histoire, il la fait perdre de vue*].' Along this line, Bonitzer analyses 'deframing' as 'a perversion, one that adds an ironic touch to the function of cinema, painting, even photography, all of them forms of exercising the right to look'. Yet, from this point of view, painting is a more 'sadistic' art form because of its absence of the reverse-angle shot to fulfil or soothe the viewer's expectation about what is lurking off-screen. This is itself an echo of Daney's insightful analysis of two 'images of power': a photograph representing the corpses of Paris Commune militants just after they been shot, and a B52 about to take off to drop bombs on Vietnam:

These images ... also tell us that the camera was American, that the photographer was paid by M. Thiers [who had ordered the repression of the Commune]. The non-neutrality of such images is not only that they present us with something horrible, it is that they show us something for which no reverse angle exists ... (which would be, for example, a photograph taken by the Communards, or the B52 seen from the bombed field – i.e. the impossible).

In its own way, each of these three texts is resolving the theoretical impasse of the early to mid-1970s, Daney providing brilliant insights and theoretical directions on which the others will later elaborate with their particular talents and 'poetics'. After spending so much time dissecting how a filmic text was a reflection of the class struggle, how it articulated either the power of the bourgeoisie or the uneasy conscience of the petite-bourgeoisie, *Cahiers*'s task was then to retrieve 'the pleasure of the text' without, however, losing sight of the way power is expressed through it. The *auteur*, having lost his sacred aura, no longer reigned supreme in the off-screen space. Yet it was no longer possible to claim that space as entirely occupied by socio-political determinations. The real Absent one, which re-emerged in *Cahiers*'s texts, was desire. Paradoxically, Lardeau's text forecloses sexual desire, probably because, in the perverse dialectic woven by porn, nothing is what it seems: sexual difference is resolved in its opposite, eroticism transmuted as a pulsion of death, desiring bodies are shot like dismembered corpses, organs in motion become the mechanical elements of an infernal machine. The device that allows such transformation is framing and deframing which Bonitzer describes as 'tedious and without humour. Photography ... which is the art of framing and deframing par excellence (a slice of life caught hot or cold in a snapshot or a composition), is an art basically bereft of humour.' Yet the difference between photography and painting, on the one hand, and cinema, on the other, in the representation of death is that 'photography does not have film's power, it can only portray death agonies or the corpse itself, but not the imperceptible passage from one to the other', writes Lardeau, quoting (again) Bazin, and emphasizing the 'sort of ontological obscenity' of cinema that is thus revealed.

In addition to this obscenity – depicted in Lardeau's text from a rather moralistic point of view, without asking *why* people take pleasure (horrified or not) in seeing other human beings put to death – in addition to the 'Sadean' impulse of framing and *mise en scène*[56] – since the Sadean impulse eventually results in the death, at least symbolically, of the object of desire (and Pasolini's *Salò* was an extraordinary demonstration of the connection of such an impulse to a certain theory of power and class struggle[57]); in addition to its semi-clinical cutting out of bodies,[58] cinema also has the power to represent *the opposite of death*, which is not life but *work*. This is why Bonitzer's text ends with two film-makers who have particularly emphasized how the notion of work haunts cinema: Godard and Eustache. Godard because, for him, everything is 'work':

sex, love, desire, survival, even death (cf. his famous text on how to represent concentration camps). And of course representation, 'just an image', or how what Bonitzer calls 'anything that upsets the frame' is already *work*, *duration*, *process* on the part of the image itself before being the work of 'reading' demanded from the spectator. And Eustache because of his exemplary film, *Une sale histoire*, which is a fable about the relationship between desire and its retelling, framing, repetition, obsession, the pulsion at work and the work of the filmic text. A man (Jean-Noël Piq) discovers one day a certain public toilet where one can, by lying down on the floor, peep through a crack in the door at women urinating. He becomes, in spite of himself, a Peeping Tom, and comes back again and again to the fatal crack. Years later, having broken the habit, he takes a certain pleasure in retelling the story, especially in front of women. A film-maker (Jean Eustache) hears about it, and one day brings a 16 mm camera and films one of Piq's narrations. Then he transcribes the dialogue thus recorded and asks a famous actor (Michael Lonsdale) to re-enact the situation, in front of a 35 mm camera and with some glamorous women playing the 'audience'. Later he edits the two parts together, and that makes it one of the most disturbing – yet humorous, says Bonitzer – films of the late 1970s in France.

This obscure object of criticism

In the second of his articles on 'the critical function' (*Cahiers* 250, May 1974), Daney redefines criticism by its method, and no longer by its object (as a certain right-wing interpretation of the *politique des auteurs* might have done in the past):

> the struggle must encompass point of view as well as choice of subject ... For film-makers ... a single problem emerges: HOW CAN POLITICAL STATEMENTS BE PRESENTED CINEMATICALLY? HOW CAN THEY BE MADE POSITIVE? ... This cinematic presentation carries another name: enunciation. ... That is why criticizing a film doesn't mean shadowing it with a complicit discourse ... It doesn't even mean unfolding it or opening it out. It means *opening it up* along this imaginary line which passes between statement and enunciation, allowing us to read them side by side, in their problematical, disjointed relationship.

In the same issue, in his text on *Lacombe Lucien*, Bonitzer defines film criticism through different linguistic parameters: the opposition between *connotation* and *denotation*, the former being the real object of criticism, for it 'implies that there is always *a surplus-meaning [un plus de sens]*, or *a left-over meaning [un reste de sens]*, to be accounted for by a secondary language (a metalanguage)'. Hence, 'Criticism consists in adding meaning, in exhibiting a "latent content", in revealing overdeterminations: in enunciating – to bear judgment on it – what the object undergoing criticism eludes, disavows or half-says. So criticism is a matter of truth.' This 'truth' is the result of a process of construction, not of unveiling: it is not something that would always have been there, hidden. Conversely, denotation is on the side of the apparent function of communication of language (as in 'pass me the salt, please') and implies 'an ideology . . . of the true meaning, the full meaning, the self-sufficient meaning. About two decades ago some film critics thought they had discovered such health, such self-insurance and such plenitude in American movies; a cinema without fault or left-over [reste]. What was extolled by the *politique des auteurs* was the rectitude of denotation.' Interestingly, Bonitzer puts classic Hollywood cinema *and* Chinese revolutionary cinema back to back, as trusting denotation too much and somehow foreclosing connotation. The work of film criticism is to find the 'left-over' under the lures of the denoted discourse of the film: the ideological substratum of films implicitly defending a certain social order (Hollywood, China), or something more intangible that will allow *Cahiers* to define a new *politique des auteurs*.

Daney identifies the questionable aspect of the opposition between connotation and denotation in that it remains too much within the problematics of the signified and forecloses the issue of power:

> By seeing in the iconic content of the image only what can be passed – or decanted – from the realm of connotation to the realm of denotation, one leaves aside the fact, but a simple one, that in the present of the film projection something (but what?) functions as an authority that says 'Here it is'. Something, someone, a voice, an apparatus *gives* us something to see.

This silent authority, continues Daney, 'is always on the side of the part of the cinematic apparatus which is the most heavily invested with bourgeois ideology'. So 'the filmic image is as though hollowed by the power that allowed it to be made'. What Daney adds to his political interpretation of *énonciation* as *mise en scène* is the dimension of desire. To Bonitzer's idea that the denotation tends to 'age, fade, change' Daney opposes the distinction between the life and death of an image (for images, like statues, also die):

> As long as an image is alive, as long as it has an impact (ideologically dangerous or useful), as long as it hails an audience and gives pleasure, that means that in this image, around it, behind it, something that partakes of *énonciation* is at work (power + event = 'Here it is') . . . In cinema, *énonciation* might be, hidden somewhere, a little machine wound up to repeat the Lacanian phrase: 'You want to look? Well, look at this.'[59]

This polemic was to be fruitfully pursued throughout the late 1970s, and was actually helpful in redefining the notion of *auteur* during this time. For example, in his long review of Chantal Akerman's *Je, tu, il, elle*, Narboni defines 'the movies that matter to us today' as 'those in which one can perceive the work of the counter-production within production, the co-presence of what escapes figuration within the figure itself, the indiscernibleness (not the dialectic contradiction) of what is shown and un-shown,[60] the margin of unreality introduced in what is embodied, the concealing of what is displayed'. Among the film-makers who explore this 'elsewhere' of cinema, Narboni mentions Godard, Straub, Akerman and Luc Moullet (whose courageous, experimental *Anatomy of a Relationship* had just been released). The 'movies that matter' to *Cahiers* in 1977 are somehow caught between the Lacanian lure of the desiring gaze and the hidden seduction of denotation.

Having criticized cinema as the ideological apparatus of the bourgeoisie, having (often puritanically) campaigned for a certain 'militant cinema', *Cahiers* was now ready to explore and advocate diverse manifestations of authorship. Among these old and new objects of love were, in Europe, Godard, Straub, Marguerite Duras, Chantal Akerman, Joris Ivens and Marceline Loridan, Buñuel, Benoît Jacquot, André Téchiné, Eustache, Moullet, Pialat, Garrel, Wim Wenders, Fassbinder, Luigi Comencini, Marco Ferreri, Hans-Jürgen Syberberg, Werner Schroeter, Rudolph Thome, Raul Ruiz and Manoel de Oliveira, as well as former (or, in the case of Biette and Kané, current) collaborators of *Cahiers* like Comolli and Vecchiali; in the United States, still Robert Kramer and John Cassavetes, but also Scorsese, Coppola and eventually de Palma; a revisiting (or, in the case of Ozu, a discovery) of past works such as the films of Dreyer, Visconti, Fuller, Renoir, Sternberg, Cocteau, Grémillon, Mizoguchi, Tourneur; and also a new opening in the direction of non-Western film-makers: Youssef Chahine (although not until April 1980) in Egypt, Akira Kurosawa in Japan (see in particular Daney's article on *Derzu Uzala*, 'Un Ours en plus', in *Cahiers* 274, March 1977, reproduced in this volume) and Ousmane Sembene in Senegal.

Among these *auteurs*, 'Third Cinema' film-makers hold a very specific place, for they had already been written about during *Cahiers*'s Maoist years. However, the writing about 'Third Cinema' around 1972–5 was different from what was to be published later. At that time Third Cinema film-makers were, not unlike the 'working class', a figure of the Other as 'guarantor of truth'. A truth that was, definitely, elsewhere. A truth that, more or less, reduced to silence the petit-bourgeois that *Cahiers* writers were. So, while they showed a real enthusiasm for exploring Chilean, African and Arab cinema, they also displayed a sort of self-consciousness and modesty: the often fascinating interviews devoted to Helvio Sotto, Miguel Littin and Jorge Sanjines[61] or Mustapha Abou Ali,[62] Borhan Alaouie, the maker of *Kafr Kassem*,[63] Heiny Srour,[64] Sidney Sokhona[65] and Abdelaziz Tolbi (*Cahiers* 266–7, May 1976) were mostly focused on conditions of production, the film-makers' struggle with political and cultural powers, the political use of the film etc., and not on issues of *mise en scène*. At the same time, a number of texts on Third Cinema were written by Third World cinema writers – Ali Mocki/ Ali Akika on Algerian cinema,[66] Sidney Sokhona on African cinema (a text reproduced in this volume) – as if they were the only ones *entitled* to talk about their own cinema.

Of all these texts, Abdelwahad Meddeb on *Chergui* (*Cahiers* 263–3, January 1976) is the most significant and the most challenging, for it engages its *conditions of production as text*. Rather than being informative or didactic, it is a poetic, impressionistic analysis of a Moroccan film, *written by a Moroccan*. The subtlety of Meddeb's approach is that he posits himself as an insider/outsider in the space created by the film, a space itself complex, fragmented by history, by the multiplicity of the gazes that construct it. Meddeb is an insider in the Moroccan urban space, here Tangier, and can therefore appreciate the authenticity of its rendering by a Moroccan film-maker: 'Adventure films have accustomed us to Tangier as a criminal city used as a backdrop for stories of drug trafficking or spying. Here it is filmed from within, and shots of the architecture establish its component parts: Arab mazes and pompous provincial neoclassical cornices.' Yet within Tangier itself there are spaces of otherness, in which neither Meddeb nor the film-maker nor the protagonist are 'home', but in which Western viewers of the film (or the reader of *Cahiers*) could recognize themselves, which allows Meddeb to engage in a witty dialogue with the aesthetic choices of his colleagues at *Cahiers*. For this alien space is no longer the 'exotic' Tangier of adventure movies, but this 'villa on the heights of the city in whose garden there is a reception for foreigners, diplomats and very rich inhabitants of this other Tangier, analogous to the "white" and hermetic Calcutta in *India Song*'. The 'other Tangier' is determined by the power lurking in the off-screen space (colonialism as a historical phenomenon, exoticism as a Western mode of representation). Moreover, within the domestic sphere itself Meddeb, as a man, encounters another figure of otherness: the space reserved to women, such as 'the mausoleum of Sidi Charf, a place which, in the past, was only visited by women who built up their own power thanks to the magical qualities of the place. This amounted to the female eye of the town' – this last phrase also providing the title of the article. So the complex act of reclaiming the native space, the space of one's people, of one's culture, can be done only if this space is first acknowledged as lost, as *other* – in order to avoid the pits of barbarism and fundamentalism: 'We must become orphans in this specific area, through the use of the destructive knowledge of illusions and regressions', concludes Meddeb.

So by commissioning such texts *Cahiers* was doing more than 'opening up to the Other'; it was using this polyphony as a *mise en scène* of its own decentring, which could then be explored further in articles written by members of the editorial team. The opening lines of Toubiana's text on Littin's *Tiera prometida* (*Cahiers* 253, October–November 1974) are highly significant:

The Promised Land comes to us Europeans, for whom it was certainly not intended in the first instance, as an echo of Chile before the descent of the barbarians. It is a film of exile, which has been uprooted from the countryside and the *poblaciones* where it would have had a quite different impact from the one it has had here. We have the same affection for this film as we have for all exiles, and it inspires tremendous modesty in us. It is a film which is in every way exemplary and, provided we treat it neither as an exotic product nor as a universal model, it can help us to work towards the creation of a popular, militant cinema in this country.

However, the article is more than the expression of the critic's (acknowledged) unease in relation to the film. It becomes important for Toubiana to reinterpret it *in its original context*, as a film about the popular memory of revolutionary struggle *produced before the fall of Allende*, in other words in an optimistic context. A Pinochet is not the inevitable end for all struggles of popular liberation. From this perspective, the mouthpiece expressing the film's point of view is exactly the opposite of a Lacombe Lucien, doomed from the start (*we know* that the Germans lost the war and that collaborators were shot), a 'primitive and stupid character whom History exploits'. By giving the role of 'decoder' to an 'average person [who talks] about a historical process which he does not completely control and which sometimes even mystifies him', Littin takes a position against what Foucault calls 'The traditional processes of making heroes' in the writing of mainstream History (*Cahiers* 251–2, July–August 1974).

This question has been, from the outset, central to the notion of Third Cinema,[67] but it has also been of paramount importance in militant and post-militant cinema, under the guise of the 'positive hero'. In the second of his articles on 'the critical function', for example, Daney lingers on that question, which some considered old-fashioned. The positive hero is not an archaic term expressing the hard-core orthodoxy of a certain militant cinema, Daney stresses; one has to consider, on the contrary, that 'positivity is not the exception but the rule. *All* films are militant films. A film is always positive for someone.' So a 'positive hero' is simply a hero whose place in the fiction clearly determines whose interests he represents, of which class he is the mouthpiece. Hence the interest of the place of the protagonist in Littin's film: because he does not master the historical process he 'is transformed by the struggle in contact with the stereotypes and the signifiers that are contained in this struggle' (Toubiana). Similarly, in a companion article about the film, Bonitzer sees this process as defining a site of resistance which he analyses under the category of the Bakhtinian 'carnivalesque': 'a popular culture which is profoundly subversive . . . all the manifestations of which were savagely repressed . . . and which is now re-emerging in different forms, including the cinema'. Cinema is thus a double-edged sword – a powerful means of repressing popular culture through normalization, codification etc., but which also, *because it is a popular form*, expresses popular memory.

The opening of *Cahiers*'s pages to female writers such as Dubroux and Giraud was also a form of decentring. Significantly, these two writers' interventions were mostly at first on issues of militant cinema (Giraud), then on Third Cinema (Giraud and Dubroux – see in particular the latter's incisive review of Ousmane Sembene's *Xala* in *Cahiers* 266–7, June 1976, reproduced in this volume), then through reviews of specific films (*Numéro deux*, *Padre padrone*), and not, with one major exception,[68] on theory. The opening of the notion of *auteur* to female film-makers also followed another 'vanishing line', but in a direction opposite to that which had motivated interest in Third Cinema. It was no longer a question of content, of 'positivity', of the 'exemplary nature' of a struggle, but a question of form. In their reviews of *Jeanne Dielman* (*Cahiers*, 265, March–April 1976, in this volume) and *Je, tu, il, elle* (see note 49) both Dubroux and Narboni avoid explaining the films through the category of what Narboni terms, not without a certain contempt, 'the ideologies of the "specific female discourse" ... an *écriture* "specifically feminine", feminine *jouissance* working through artistic practices'. Dubroux sees the interest of *Jeanne Dielman* as a category of Freud's *Unheimlich*.

The return to the notion of *mise en scène* came about with Bonitzer's review of Duras's *India Song* (*Cahiers* 258–9, July–August 1976, in this volume), a text still oddly polemical in its attacks against the 'retro' fashion. In the spring the film was released, Parisian walls were covered with large advertising posters that quickly became an object of mild scandal and mockery in left-wing circles. Over a nostalgic image of the pre-Civil-War American South appeared the caption: 'They were decadent. They were racist. They were drinking *Gold Tea*.' Bonitzer accurately analyses the differences between Duras's masterful evocation of the colonial imaginary and that of the ad for a brand of iced tea, still carrying echoes of *Night Porter* and other fantasmatic projections. Through his insights, as well as those of a number of articles written about (or by) various film-makers at the time, one can draw the new outline of the situation of the *auteur* in *Cahiers* in the mid- to late 1970s. The quasi-perverse dyad linking the *auteur* and the spectator has undergone a fatal transformation. Two other terms had appeared, thus forming a new relationship that looked more like a rectangle. One of them was what had been variously termed the 'majority', the 'mainstream audience', which had its own desire and mode of functioning. What *Cahiers* writers had (sometimes painfully) discovered throughout the 1970s was not so much that they were not part of this majority but that they could not pretend to be constituting an avant-garde whose mission was to enlighten the 'general audience' (Oudart's 'Diffamations' is a masterful variation on this theme). The split was acknowledged, probably through an interview given by Jean-Marie Straub and Danièle Huillet,[69] later quoted in Toubiana's article on Godard's *Numéro deux*: 'I think we should also make films for minorities, because one can always hope that they will be, as

Lenin said, the majorities of tomorrow.' For Toubiana, the films of Straub and Godard construct their own spectators in these terms: 'Are we the possible spectators for these films, are we really that minority to whom these images are addressed. In which case, *how can we think of ourselves as a minority public against the ideology of the cinema which only thinks of the public in majority terms?*' (my italics).

The second term that appeared was a reformulation of the notion of the Other. It was no longer the Absent One of Oudart's quasi-architectural theoretical constructions, nor was it another name coined for the God-*auteur*. It was not, either, a category of people erected to the status of guarantor of the truth (the working class, the Palestinians). Rather – and this is where Bonitzer's insights (here about *India Song*) are, once again, dazzling – it was 'the residue' entirely generated by the dialectic between off-screen and on-screen space, where it is inscribed as 'the obsessive fear of something which cannot be handled by representation, by a historical discourse, by the tragic'. In *India Song* it is 'the song of the beggar woman from Savannakhet or the evocation of the lepers of Shalimar by the French vice-consul from Lahore'. As figures of otherness, the beggar woman and the lepers are 'completely out of shot . . . completely foreign, completely strange . . . Social parasites and rejects in real life, they are here literally the parasites and rejects of the narrative.' In *India Song* we have probably one of the most radical expressions of the fact that this sort of 'other' does not exist in the real world but is constituted by the process of film-making itself. So he can no longer be the guarantor of truth, but rather constitutes the locus of a crisis, which Daney analyses when retracing Godard's itinerary in his article 'Le thérrorisé':

> Godard's itinerary happens to point to a very concrete, very historical question, a question in crisis: that of the nature of what might be called the 'filmic contract' (filming/filmed). This question seemed to arise only for the militant or ethnographic cinema ('Ourselves and others'), but Godard tells us that it concerns the very act of filming.

So the consumption/crisis of cinema was now delimited by four parameters: the *auteur*; the spectator/cinephile; the 'majority'; and the 'Other' – linked to each other by way of transference, through the 'supposed knowledge' they are all assuming. Yet, as Deleuze noted in his landmark interview about *Sur et sous la communication* (*Cahiers* 271, November 1976), Godard's system (in so far as, Daney noted, 'it was this crisis that made him into a film-maker') rests entirely on the conjunction *and*: sound *and* image, man *and* woman, cinema *and* television, the gate of the factory before *and* after a day of work, the wife of the man sentenced to death before *and* after the execution, etc. The *and* is this 'stuttering' that will prevent our rectangle from solidifying into a system. For there is, floating in between, a fifth signifier, one that most *Cahiers* writers have been forced to take into account by the irruption of feminism in the cultural sphere, and it is woman.

Women, of course, can be *auteurs*: Duras, Akerman. Yet in the Godardian system, for example, the true relationship between woman and *auteur* is given by the conjunction *and*. Godard *and* Miéville. Yet this *and* betrays a fundamental inequality. Miéville is not to Godard what Gorin was.[70] 'It appears that a woman participated in making this film,' ironically writes Thérèse Giraud in her article on *Numéro deux* (*Cahiers* 262–3, January 1976). She is 'a "number two", she whom we see neither at the beginning nor the end of the film, reduced to the status of raw material, like celluloid, like something to talk about'.

In the same issue, Daney notes that the screen has become for Godard the place of a masochistic *mise en scène*, in which he is somehow condemned to repeat the 'correct discourse'[71] or the 'master-discourse' to the spectator/student. Yet the 'hidden truth' of this 'theoretical' masochism may be nothing else than sexual fantasy, for 'after 1968, this master-discourse is conveyed more or less systematically by a female voice. For Godard's pedagogy implies a division of roles and discourses according to sex.' In a short column that functions as a companion piece to his article Daney further describes Godard's 'strange feminism' as a 'perversion':

> He puts woman (voice, sound) in the place of what spells out the law (the 'correct thinking' whose phallic character is easily understood) and of what gives life . . . It is not certain that feminist claims will be satisfied with this 'place' men want no more, this 'power' they want to relinquish. It is not necessarily to the advantage of women, while man gets the benefit of masochism: he can become the director who stages how he wants to be punished, what kind of cruel mothering gives *jouissance*.

Woman, also, can be *spectator*, even though it seems that the category of cinephile does not really apply to her. Yet if porn somehow reveals the truth of both cinema and cinephilia, the position of woman becomes crucial. And in 1977 a film-text came to suture this position. In Eustache's *Une sale histoire*, the same story of voyeuristic obsession with the female genitals is told not only twice but *twice to women*. 'Why tell this story to women? There is obviously only one possible answer. To please them. Exhibiting the discovery of his "true desire" as "the truth of woman", the narrator offers as a gift, as a means of seduction, as a demand for love, his imaginary ego.'[72] What happens then is more complex. The female spectators are constructed by the film as *representing woman*. Put in the impossible position of being both the *recipient* and the *object* of this 'perverted desire', the women in the film react by 'not liking' what is told to them: 'What happens at this moment in [the women's] embarrassed faces is the *resistance of the real*, the resistance on the part of these women to assuming the imaginary being they are wanted to be.' Does this mean that the position of the female spectator is an impossible one? Or rather that its saturation, as complex as that of the (male) spectator theorized by Oudard, defined by an ever-changing vanishing line, was only imperfectly theorized by *Cahiers*?

For women are found, as well, in the third term of our equation, the 'majority'. This position is rather problematic because of *Cahiers*'s earlier refusal to consider feminism as a cultural front of its own, let alone to envision the specificity of women's culture, a direction taken by some feminist research in Britain. It strikes one, of course, as slightly silly, from a numeric point of view, to call women a 'minority' (likewise Asians, aware of their numeric superiority, are now either scandalized or amused to be listed as 'minorities' within the system of Western thought), but the concept of 'dominated ideologies' might be applied here. Except that it was not. Within the context of French leftist movements, women were more often than not taken as representative of a reactionary ideology of social stability and family value. And, as Daney correctly points out, for Godard, ultimately, woman is the Mother, an irrepressible, fascinating and frightening figure of power. Which makes it easier, eventually, to see women on the side of 'the majority'. The question, of course, as asked by Thérèse Giraud in the same issue, is how power is transmitted through 'other issues, unexplored and forgotten' which were not theorized or conceived as the locus of revolutionary struggle by post-May-'68 militancy: 'interior issues – the family, the body, sexuality – neglected and left in enemy hands, those of television, sentimental drama, porn cinema'. For Giraud, though, Godard fails in *Numéro deux* because, in his attempt to see woman as 'the other: that which he glimpses in the woman as different, as inaccessible to the law of his sex/phallus', he cannot help but 'reduce this other to his likeness, to the same'.

That the question of the majority is linked to the question of the Other is due to the fact that *Cahiers* writers perceived themselves as a 'minority'. (In fact, in an editorial written in 1978 by Daney and Toubiana, cinema is defined as 'a dominated medium, by television, of course, but also by the language of advertising'.[73]) The majority was the other, the enemy, the potential oppressor, the 'system', what they were standing against while theorizing its mode of functioning. The Other of representation, conversely, is both what is produced by a system of representation and what escapes from it. Which is why the Other is represented by a beggar woman or by lepers in *India Song*, or, in Godard's *Ici et ailleurs*, by dead Palestinians. This is why also, in any system, woman is an ambiguous figure of the Other.

The four-angle equation just circumscribed is not found *as such* in any article published in *Cahiers*, but it can be inferred from many of the texts written in the late 1970s. At that time, *Cahiers* seemed to put itself in a position of having a discourse on the 'crisis of cinema', while at the same time fostering a reflection that could allow the production/dissemination of filmic texts conceived as an answer to this crisis. In 'Le thérrorisé', Daney states that the ethical questions raised by Godard will retain currency 'as the traditional contract between the film-maker, the filmed and the film viewer, the contract established by the film industry (Hollywood), becomes ever more threadbare and the cinema as a form of mass culture for the family, a popular and homogenizing art, reaches crisis point'. Later, the acknowledgment of the deepening of the crisis was to lead Daney, who by then had left *Cahiers* and was writing for *Libération*, to stop writing about cinema. In a private conversation (Washington DC, April 1988) he said:

> The kind of cinema I defended was a single plane where you could find Straub on the one hand, and Hawks or Hitchcock on the other. This situation does not exist any more, audiences are parcellized, the people who go and see Hollywood films have never heard of Straub, the people who like Dreyer despise Hollywood, and it's no longer interesting to write for either of them.

In other words, the crisis forced the film critic to redefine himself either as 'ghettoized' (writing for a small, specialized readership of cinephiles similar to himself, another category of 'the same') or as a 'publicist' selling Hollywood and commercial cinema to a shapeless 'majority'. Maybe the question of criticism cannot be answered in relation to the public. Maybe, as Daney was to suggest later, the work of the critic should rather be considered as an 'open letter' sent to the film-maker, the element of a dialogue between two subjectivities, with film as a 'transitional object'. Thus criticism becomes a real *passion* – a passion of the idea, in the Hegelian sense, or an emotional passion. It is more like a dialogue between a son and his father (cinephilia has something to do with the constitution of imaginary filiations), or even between two lovers.

Two moments in Godard's *Passion* function as a metaphor. It is the story of an impossible love, and also the story of an impossible movie. Lovers, film-makers, producers, protagonists are constantly out of sync, running and screaming after each other, violently colliding into each other: it is a story of desire. From the depth of her frustration, Hanna Schygulla, beautiful, glamorous, cries to Michel Piccoli: 'I would have wanted to love you passionately!' As cinema would have said to the post-'68 spectator: 'I wanted to seduce you, to give you a scintillating array of fiction, romance, images and sound, but you kept on criticizing me, imposing impossible tasks on me, mercilessly deconstructing, along with the pleasure I was meant to give, my ideological unconscious.' And he, the cinephile, the critic, the film-maker, screams back at her, 'I too would have wanted to love you passionately!' Meaning: 'I wanted more from you. I wanted you to be the tool to reach a form of aesthetic and political absolute. I wanted pleasure, but also intelligence from you. I was criticizing you, tormenting you, demystifying you, to force you to disgorge the treasures you kept locked, concealed within yourself.' And they both failed, but they kept trying, and in the process made more movies and wrote more texts. The history of film criticism at *Cahiers* in the difficult years 1972–8, like the sexual impasse, like the psychoanalytic process, is the story of a permanently missed encounter in which subject and object were striving, sometimes painfully, sometimes cannily, often imaginatively, to redefine each other.

Notes

1 An abridged version of this text was translated as 'On Equal Terms – Analysis of a Television Programme', in John Caughie (ed.), *Television: Ideology and Exchange*, London, British Film Institute, 1978. 'Lou Sin' was an approximate French transcription of the name of the pre-revolutionary Chinese writer known in the West as either Lu Xun (People's Republic of China's new mode of transcription) or Lu Hsun ('traditional' mode of transcription, still used in Taiwan) and author of short stories such as *A Madman's Diary*, *The Story of A. Q.*, etc., that implicitly criticized the 'old society' in China and which were turned into films after the 1949 Revolution. Lu Xun was also a prolific essayist who accurately reflected on the crisis of civilization and identity undergone by China in the early twentieth century.

2 'The work, as it has been planned [in *Cahiers* 242–3] and done at *Cahiers* since, has repressed the specific contradiction for the sake of the main contradiction; the journal has become an organ of struggle in the cultural field, and no longer in the cinematic field' (Letter published in *Cahiers* 245–6, April–May–June 1973).

3 Serge Daney, *L'Exercice a été profitable, Monsieur* (posthumous collection of texts), Paris, Pol, 1993, p. 302. Daney modestly continues: 'For seven years, I felt like those burlesque heroes who try to land with all the cargo, without losing or forgetting anything, while they don't even have their pilot's licence!'

4 *Cahiers* 458, July–August 1992.

5 *La Rampe*, Paris, Gallimard, 1983; *Ciné-journal*, Paris, Cahiers du Cinéma, 1986, with a foreword by Gilles Deleuze ('the most beautiful gift I ever received', said Daney); *Le Salaire d'un zappeur*, Paris, Ramsay, 1988; *Devant la recrudescence des vols de sac à main*, Paris, Aléas, 1991; *L'Exercice a été profitable, Monsieur* was published posthumously in 1993.

6 These intellectuals (Guy Scarpetta, Jacques Henric, Stanislas Ivankov, Jacques Chatain, Pierre Guyotat) belonged mostly to the circle of *Tel Quel* that was to be intellectually close to *Cahiers* for the next few years. In the same issue one finds an extraordinary number of landmark texts (proof that Maoist influence was not that 'sterile', even if it led *Cahiers* to a hotchpotch of various levels of theory, credibility and gullibility). We find the first article written, by the Lu Hsun Group; Daney's and Bonitzer's criticism of Bazin's 'idealism' ('L'ecran du fantasme'); a text by Jean-Louis Schefer on Uccello; an enthusiastic (but later revealed as completely fantasmatic) description of the effects of the Cultural Revolution in the film studios in China by Joris Ivens and Marceline Loridan; the reproduction of a Chinese text on the development of revolutionary ballet; an article by Narboni on 'politics and ideological class struggle'; and the subtle, critical analysis by Oudart of Bresson's *Four Nights of a Dreamer* (the latter text is translated in *Cahiers du Cinéma 1969–1972: The Politics of Representation*, London, Routledge/BFI, 1990, Volume 3 of this anthology).

7 *Cahiers* 247, July–August 1973.

8 *Cahiers* 254–5, December 1974–January 1975.

9 Thérèse Giraud's first text, which dealt with the 'correct' and 'incorrect' use of 'Direct Cinema' (see note 33) and had nothing to do with feminism, appeared in *Cahiers* 250, May 1974. In the same issue was the first text by Jean-René Huleu (one of the founders of *Libération*), who was rewarded by having his name listed on the masthead of the next issue, though his collaboration was short-lived; while Giraud had to wait until June 1975 for a similar mention. Dubroux's first text was on

Chantal Akerman's *Jeanne Dielman* (*Cahiers* 265, April 1976, Ch. 26 in this volume). She was not listed as part of the editorial board until June 1977. Giraud, who wrote an original, furious, lyrical text on Godard's sexism in *Numéro deux* (Ch. 6 in this volume), left *Cahiers* in 1980. Dubroux left in 1985 and has since directed a number of films (all supported – with reason – by *Cahiers*): *Les Amants terribles*, *La Petite Voleuse*, *Borderline* and *Journal du séducteur*.

10 'the sacred, clandestine (vaguely pornographic) nature of cinephilia, but also, and above all, the fundamentally homosexual essence of this passion', 'Traquenards' (on Wim Wenders's *The American Friend*), *Cahiers* 282, November 1977.

11 'Contre la nouvelle cinéphilie', *Cahiers* 293, October 1978.

12 Antoine de Baecque, *Les Cahiers du Cinéma – Histoire d'une revue. Tome II: Cinéma, tours détours*, Paris, Cahiers du Cinéma, 1991.

13 Daney, *L'Exercice a été profitable*, p. 301.

14 These three texts appeared respectively in *Cahiers* 211 and 212, April and May 1969, *Cahiers* 223, August 1970, and *Cahiers* 225, November–December 1970. Both Oudart's text on 'suture' and the deconstruction of *Morocco* are translated in Volume 3 of this anthology. The collective text on *Young Mr Lincoln* has been translated several times, first in *Screen*, London, vol. 13, no. 3, autumn 1972.

15 *Cahiers* 240, July–August 1972.

16 *Cahiers* 248, September 1973–January 1974. *Les Aventures de Rabbi Jacob* (Gérard Oury, 1973): a comedy, starring the popular comic actor Louis de Funès, about an anti-Semite who disguises himself as a rabbi when he is inadvertently involved with an Arab terrorist.

17 'Le peuple et ses fantasmes', *Cahiers* 249, February–March 1974.

18 *Cahiers* 233, November 1971, is the last to offer the traditional 'list of films released in Paris' during the month.

19 In a short 'Note on R.-W. Fassbinder' by Daney, which still displayed some ambivalence towards the film-maker.

20 *Cahiers* 282, November 1977.

21 'Le Cru et le Cuit', *Cahiers* 323–4, May 1981.

22 Serge Daney, *Devant la recrudescence*, p. 112.

23 Ibid., pp. 230–1.

24 See Volume 3 of this anthology, p. 287.

25 *Cahiers* 264, February 1976.

26 See in particular Pascal Bonitzer, 'Off-screen Space' (*Cahiers* 234–5, December 1971–February 1972), translated in Volume 3 of this anthology.

27 This was of course an allusion to François Truffaut's legendary article (*Cahiers* 31, January 1954) in which he vehemently criticized the tradition of screenplay-based French 'quality' cinema (Delannoy, Christian-Jaque, Autant-Lara, Clouzot, Clément) to put forward his conception of the *auteur* (Renoir, Bresson, Tati, Cocteau, Gance, Becker, Ophuls, Leenhardt).

28 Laura Mulvey, 'Visual Pleasure and Narrative Cinema', *Screen*, vol. 16, no. 3, autumn 1975.

29 See in particular the works of Miriam Hansen, Anne Friedberg and Giuliana Bruno.

30 Daney, *Devant la recrudescence*, p. 131.

31 See in particular the influential article by Sarris in *Film Culture*, spring 1963.

32 Serge Daney, 'Après tout,' in *La Politique des auteurs*, ed. Jean Narboni and Alain Bergala, Paris, Editions de l'Etoile, 1984, p. 9.

33 The three instalments of Daney's text on 'The Critical Function' appeared as a contextual framework for two or three articles on specific films which in some way exemplified the problematic in the Daney text. The first segment (*Cahiers* 248, September 1973–January 1974) was followed by Jacques Aumont's attack on

Antonioni's *China* and Bonitzer's article on *Avanti* (Ch. 24 in this volume); the second (*Cahiers* 250, May 1974) introduced a theoretical text by Bonitzer on Louis Malle's 'retro' film *Lacombe Lucien* and Thérèse Giraud's polemical comparison of Malle's *Humain, trop humain* and Cinda Firestone's *Attica*; the third (*Cahiers* 253, October–November 1974) opens up towards Bonitzer's review of Buñuel's *Phantom of Liberty*, Daney's insight on Barbet-Schroeder's *Idi Amin Dada*, and Kané's text on William Friedkin's *The Exorcist*. These three articles are translated in this volume (Ch. 2). One has to add, however, that the first instalment of 'The Critical Function' was initially conceived as a two-part article, and only its first part is reproduced here. The second part, an analysis of the commercial failure of Allio's *Rude journée pour la reine* and of the effects of the dominant ideology on the spectator, appeared in *Cahiers* 249, February–March 1974.

34 See in particular the article of the same name he wrote in collaboration with Jean-Pierre Oudart in Volume 3 of this anthology.

35 Sigmund Freud, *Die Verneinung*, 1925.

36 'Au Nom du père – Viol en première page', *Cahiers* 245–6, April–May–June 1973.

37 Pierre Baudry, in his review of the film (*Cahiers* 231, August–September 1971), had denounced 'the absence of the working class', noting that 'the interviewees belong, for the most part, to the petit-bourgeoisie', and concluded that there was a 'repression of the discourse of the working class. No matter how severe this judgment seems now, it is quite coherent with the problematic of *Cahiers* in the 1970s intent on finding out 'who speaks?', 'what/who is missing?' and 'who is addressed?' in the filmic discourse.

38 *Cahiers* 271, November 1976, italics mine.

39 'Outside In Inside Out', in Trinh T. Minh-ha, *When the Moon Waxes Red*, New York and London, Routledge, 1991, originally published in Jim Pines and Paul Willemen (eds), *Questions of Third Cinema*, London, British Film Institute, 1989.

40 Of these film-makers, *Cahiers* later revised its judgment on Jean Eustache and Jacques Doillon and defended their work, starting with Eustache's *Une Sale histoire* and Doillon's *La Femme qui pleure* (albeit with a certain reticence towards the latter: in the special issue of June 1981, *Cahiers* 325, Alain Bergala said of Doillon that of the film-makers to emerge during the decade he was 'the most difficult to decide about . . . Will Doillon remain the director of one good film, *La Femme qui pleure*?' Yet Doillon's *La Vengeance d'une femme* was on the cover of *Cahiers* 427, January 1990). Eustache became a fully fledged member of the *Cahiers* family in the late 1970s, until his suicide in December 1981. In 1986 *Cahiers* published the screenplay of *La Maman et la putain* (1973), as well as a monograph on Eustache by Alain Philippon.

41 Richard Dyer, 'White', *Screen*, vol. 29, no. 4, autumn 1988; italics mine.

42 'Entretien avec Jacques Rancière: l'image fraternelle', *Cahiers* 268–9, July–August 1976.

43 Daney, *Devant la recrudescence*, p. 120.

44 *Cahiers* 266–7, May 1976.

45 See Jean-Claude Biette, 'Revoir *Wichita*', *Cahiers* 281, October 1977.

46 See 'The Name of the Author (on the "Place" of *Death in Venice*)', in Volume 3 of this anthology.

47 *Cahiers* 238–9, May–June 1972.

48 The mid-1970s was also the time when 'porno-chic' films like *Emmanuelle*, *The Story of O*, etc., hit French commercial screens and became a topic of conversation in mainstream cultural circles. See 'O et les veaux' (Oudart's review of *The Story of O*), *Cahiers* 260–1, October–November 1975.

49 'La quatrième personne du singulier', *Cahiers* 276, May 1977.

50 *Cahiers* 275, April 1977.

51 'L'orgue et l'aspirateur', *Cahiers* 279–80, August–September 1977, reproduced in part in Michel Chion, *La Voix au cinéma*, Paris, Cahiers du Cinéma, 1987.

52 Pascal Bonitzer, *Décadrages*, Paris, Cahiers du Cinéma, 1987.

53 *Cahiers* 236–7, March–April 1972.

54 *Cahiers* 279–80, August–September 1977, published a dossier on the work of Jacques Monory, with an interview and a widely illustrated theoretical text, 'La Trappe' by Serge Le Péron, which paid homage to Bazin.

55 *Cahiers* 258–9, July–August 1975.

56 The Sadean impulse of the *mise en scène* is particularly well analysed in Oudart's text on Bresson's *Four Nights of a Dreamer*, *Cahiers* 236–7, March–April 1972.

57 'For Pasolini . . . the *common people have a simple access to pleasure*, something that nothing or nobody can wear down. Conversely, the masters *desire to desire*. In vain. To sustain the fiction of their desire, they summon the proletarian body in the most violent way, to interrogate its secret (through seduction, prostitution, torture, question) by imagining it to embody a *jouissance* they have to regulate . . . In *Salò* the masters replay for themselves the spectacle of their everlasting failure, this time *in vitro*. As the film "advances", they end up destroying the very object of experimentation. The Sadean *mise en scène* is quite incapable of revealing this simple (disarming) secret: the access to pleasure' (Daney, 'Note sur *Salò*, *Cahiers* 268–9, July–August 1976).

58 See Giuliana Bruno's exciting analysis of the connection between anatomy lessons and the origins of cinema as a form of urban popular entertainment in her book *Streetwalking on a Ruined Map – Cultural Theory and the City Films of Elvira Notari*, Princeton, Princeton University Press, 1993, pp. 263 ff.

59 Lacan, 'The Gaze as Little A Object', in Alan Sheridan (ed.), *Four Concepts of Psychoanalysis*.

60 Untranslatable wordplay on *ce qui se montre* (what is shown) and *ce qui se dé-montre* (what is 'un-shown', but also what is demonstrated).

61 Respectively in *Cahiers* 249 (February–March 1974), 251–2 (July–August 1974) and 253 (October–November 1974).

62 *Cahiers* 247, July–August 1973.

63 *Cahiers* 254–5, December 1974 – January 1975.

64 *Cahiers* 253, October–November 1974.

65 A dossier on *Nationalité: immigré*, Sokhona's first film, was published in *Cahiers* 265, April 1976; his second feature, *Safrana*, was reviewed in *Cahiers* 272, December 1976; and an interview with the director was published in *Cahiers* 285, February 1978, alongside 'Our Cinema', an article by Sokhona about the current state of African cinema, translated in this volume, Ch. 18.

66 Respectively in *Cahiers* 248, September 1973–January 1974 and 251–2, July–August 1974 (Mocki), and *Cahiers* 266–7, May 1976 (Akika).

67 See in particular Teshome H. Gabriel, 'Third Cinema as a Guardian of Popular Memory: Towards a Third Aesthetics', in Pines and Willemen (eds), *Questions of Third Cinema*.

68 In *Cahiers* 273, January–February 1977, in a text titled 'L'être-ange' (an untranslatable pun, playing on the sound of 'the being-angel' and 'the strange one'), Danièle Dubroux analysed the 'domestic uncanny' in films such as Akerman's *Jeanne Dielman* and *Je, tu, il, elle*, Oshima's *The Realm of the Senses*, Ferreri's *The Last Woman*, M. Smihi's *Chergui*, Godard's *Numéro deux*, Cassavetes's *A Woman Under the Influence* and Bergman's *Face to Face*.

69 *Cahiers* 260–1, December 1975.

70 See Toubiana's assessment of the difference between *Vent d'est* and *Luttes en Italie*, on the one hand, and *Numéro deux* on the other, in his article on the latter film (Ch. 5

in this volume): 'There we were still dealing with the discourse of the other (Gorin perhaps), the historical and implacable, the grating super-ego . . . *Numéro deux*: how can a film-maker, a man, account for feminist discourse, how can male discourse . . . meet up with the discourse – one should also say *the voice or cry – of the woman?*' (italics mine). Obviously, the 'truth' that Gorin and 'woman' are guarantors for, as different figures of the Other, is *not* of the same order.

71 This phrase, which occurs in a few articles written in *Cahiers* at the time, has been directly borrowed from Lacan who, in his seminar *Encore* (in 1973), stated that 'thinking is on the side of the handle' ('La pensée est du côté du manche').

72 Bernard Boland's review of the film, *Cahiers* 284, January 1978.

73 *Cahiers* 285, February 1978. This issue also marks significant changes in the editorial organisation and visual presentation of *Cahiers*. Daney and Toubiana were still the two 'secrétaires de rédaction', but a 'comité de direction' was created, with Jean-Pierre Beauviala (an engineer based in Grenoble, who invented and marketed the Aaton camera), Daney, Narboni and Toubiana. The 'comité de rédaction' included Bonitzer, Comolli, Dubroux, Giraud, Kané and Oudart, as well as new-comers (or, as in the case of Biette, longtime fellow travellers whose association with *Cahiers* had stopped for a few years) Alain Bergala, Jean-Claude Biette, Bernard Boland, Jean-Paul Fargier, Jean-Jacques Henry and Louis Skorecki.

Part I

INTERVENTIONS AND CULTURAL POLITICS

1

EDITORIAL: *CAHIERS* TODAY

('Les *Cahiers* aujourd'hui',
Cahiers du Cinéma 250, May 1974)

Cahiers du Cinéma

We must return, once again, to the Avignon period and its aftermath.[1] Our need to do so derives from what is happening within the journal (what might be described as a 'rupture' of its unity). At the same time, a new situation (the establishment of a real cultural front) has arisen, one that is external to us but which nevertheless concerns us, and it is this that obliges us to say where we stand *in practical terms*.

A year ago, launching the project of a *cultural front* was an easy thing to do, easy 'in theory'. In the abstract, that unity of ours ran few risks; a pristine politics could co-exist quite happily with *unbridled politicism*. What mattered was that there should be no day of reckoning, no sanctions, no 'outside arbiter' to whom we had to be accountable. Then, at Avignon, that outsider appeared, disturbing our relative tranquillity with its questions. Who produces this journal? How and from what positions is it produced? What struggles does it reflect? What practices does it have in mind as a means of intervening on the cultural front?

Launching the project of a cultural front did not automatically mean leading it. The most common mistake, and the one that most impeded our project, consisted in a constant confusion between the *process of forming* the front and the process likely to give it direction. The dogmatists did not come out of it unscathed. We hope that they will bear it in mind, in other words that they will draw some lessons from it, for their own good and for ours.

A current of dogmatism within *Cahiers*?

Where did the idea of a cultural front originate? Even if it was not formulated in the 'manifesto' (*Cahiers* 242–3), it was implicitly written into it. At any rate, the system of tasks, practices and texts laid down in this manifesto was only a short step away from setting out the project of a cultural front. It was around this project that the Avignon school (August 1973) was held.

Contacts were made. On the one hand with particular groups identifying themselves as Marxist-Leninist (for it was already clear that this project of the cultural front could be conceived only within a process of liaison with and subordination to the Marxist-Leninist movement, even if that movement did not have – nor yet has – any project or practice on this front). And also with certain collective groupings of artists and cultural activists who subscribed broadly to our project. We say 'broadly', since it was more the general project (the *shorthand* cultural front) that motivated them rather than the real content that we were putting into it at that time. *And for good reason:* we did not come from the same place, we did not have the same history, and we were not speaking in the same terms.

There was, then, a meeting – now generally productive in various ways – between people (*Cahiers*) who were *already* theorizing a project, guided by Marxist-Leninist principles on the question of culture, and people who in fact, and by virtue of their *own identity*, were already making practical interventions, and in many cases long since, on the cultural front.

This was a meeting between a kind of *theoreticism* (the outcome of an abstract project; see 'For a Unified Intervention on the Cultural Front', *Cahiers* 247) and a kind of *empiricism* which was the outcome of practices of intervention that were still barely formulated but could well make a concrete contribution to evaluations and exchanges of experience. To all intents and purposes this meeting came about in Avignon. It marked out the terrain on which the debates unfolded, it fed a whole series of contradictions which exploded after the event. Those contradictions were redoubled and amplified through the intervention – and the intransigence – of certain Marxist-Leninist groups who were there.

The question of the 'direction' of the front

Let us go back to *Cahiers* 247 (preparing for Avignon). There we wrote:

> To locate the cultural front within a general perspective implies recognizing two different kinds of unifying process. First, the unification of comrades intervening on the cultural front within the perspective of setting up a *mass organization*. This unification must necessarily have a wide base. It must be articulated around a given number of general axes which are linked to the development of concrete practice according to particular sites of intervention (film, painting, theatre, cultural activism . . .), through both their separate characteristics and those they share – linked to the development of practices on other fronts. Second, the unification of the Marxist-Leninists, on both local and national levels, with the *political organizations*, a process articulated in a dialectical relationship with the unity between those

organizations – in that the cultural front entails a Marxist-Leninist political leadership.

It is not so much the two processes described that pose (that have posed) a problem, as their *articulation*. It is not enough to proclaim that a cultural front entails a Marxist-Leninist leadership. It still has to be justified, and justified in practical terms. And the least that can be expected of anyone (or any group) that publicly declares high principles is for them to be prepared *to win the right to be heard*.

These days, the simple fact of announcing Marxist-Leninist principles and their practical application . . . elsewhere (in China, for example) is not enough to convince just anyone of the justice of the ideas embraced in the name of those principles. The right ideas do not just fall out of the sky, even on to 'secondary' fronts of struggle. The great naivety of *Cahiers* was to believe that the existing Marxist-Leninist groups had enough (practical) experience on the cultural front to enable them to pose correctly the question of its leadership, but from a *perspective within its constituency*; or that the Marxist-Leninist groups did not have enough experience. In this case they would investigate what was happening, and listen carefully to what the most advanced collective groupings were saying. This would enable them to prepare the ground for a process – beyond Avignon – of setting up the way forward for the front.

Naivety on all fronts (if we may be excused for saying so)! The comrades who represented the Marxist-Leninist groups had neither the experience that could have made them 'teachers' nor any genuine desire to 'listen carefully' (as 'learners').

There remained a third position, which consisted in having their argument taken up by others, so that it might have more credibility and be more acceptable to all the participants in the school: to promote a way forward – *Cahiers* – which could take up the positions and the analyses of this or that component of the Marxist-Leninist movement.

We fell short (in both senses of the word) of playing that role of *pseudo-leadership*. It should immediately be made clear that it is not the method that we are judging or criticizing now, after the event. There is no question of taking up a moralistic, complaining stance in relation to the question of leadership. But this method reveals a particular conception of the role of revolutionaries in *mass organizations* and of the way in which they pose the problem of leadership within them. It was a conception that we shared, at the time of the manifesto and before Avignon.

The question of the journal's specificity

This question was constantly being asked at Avignon by the comrades who were already making interventions on the cultural front. There even appeared a *cleavage*, a false contradiction (false in the sense that it had no dynamic), between the practitioners on the one hand (who had come to talk about their experiences and were expecting us to talk about ours), and on the other hand those who were thinking *only* of the overall project, the theorization of practices and their systematization, those who were already thinking through the elaboration of a line of intervention on the cultural front.

The Italian comrades of the La Comune collective describe the latter as 'political commissars': those who set out the political line which others – progressive artists – *give shape to*, with the whole producing revolutionary works. Throughout the Avignon school we were perceived, quite rightly, as belonging to this category of militants. The *Cahiers* texts, from the manifesto[2] of no. 242–3 up to the text preparing for Avignon (no. 247), and including the text on 'the conjuncture' (no. 245–6), inevitably led us to play this role.

Given this critique, what matters is not to adopt a self-important posture, nor one of self-castigation: *it is necessary to put things right*. It has become essential, crucial, to refine our analysis of the conjuncture by clearly defining the place, the apparatus, the ensemble of practices out of which we can produce this analysis. In short, we had to – and we must – talk about ourselves, about the journal *Cahiers du Cinéma*. This cannot be done without (re)formulating certain problems. Probably the most important of these is the issue of our impact on the 'constituency' in which we are read, worked on and taken up critically. It must certainly be admitted that, given the dogmatic character of some of our interventions, of our texts, combined with a trademark that still weighs heavily upon us (an 'unreadable' journal, 'too theoretical'), this constituency was beginning to shrink dangerously.

Well, it is no mere coincidence that the two questions we have centred on throughout the whole of the past year, and particularly in the aftermath of Avignon, are the way forward for the front *and* the specificity of the journal. *Both questions are indissolubly linked*, and had to be correctly stated, or we should never be in a position to resolve them practically. If we have for some time privileged the first question, at the risk of falling into a kind of politicism (and of repressing the second question), it does not necessarily follow that we should 'make a complete U-turn' and now repress the first question.

Put schematically, that rules out considering the problem of leadership in abstract terms, in the interests of the *real* political principles, but in relation to the actual potential to be recognized – on our specific terrain – as one of the elements aspiring to leadership and participating in the struggle, and the debate, for leadership.

And this question arises *immediately*, at a time when the Marxist-Leninist movement is weak and divided, but while contemporaneously working-class struggles are advancing, either implicitly or *explicitly* (as in the case of Lip[3]), the issue of the artistic reflection of the new social relationships that are being constructed.

Let us also state something very clear and simple (which we insist on all the more as being something not yet arrived at by the militant comrades concerned with cultural questions): the way in which a mass organization is formed – and especially a mass organization intervening on the cultural front – is *different* from the way in which a vanguard organization is organized and built, with a call to the party.

We can put it more simply: within the same front a number of elements co-exist, a number of collective groupings of ideas and interventions. Whence an *ideological pluralism*. It goes without saying that we shall not accommodate ourselves to this pluralism. Pluralism does not entail the *absence of unifying principles* on the need for a cultural front, on the shared analysis of the ideological and political conjuncture, and *above all* on the system of practical tasks to be undertaken jointly.

To affirm this pluralism is to recognize that we have made a clear choice about the political-organizational character of this collective: we are not creating a cultural front belonging to any party, attached to one or other Marxist-Leninist group, with the role of elaborating the line of the group in question on cultural issues. Our project is a broad one, a unifying one, addressing itself to Marxist-Leninists, to revolutionaries, to progressists, to all those who in their militant practice, in their cultural practice (production/distribution), ask themselves the question: in whose interest?

Cahiers today

This short-circuit between the process of constituting the front and the process of leading the way forward (as if, having had the idea of this front, the business of leading it had fallen to us by right) has not been without its repercussions even on the functioning of the journal, the *Cahiers* apparatus. It functioned as a 'cadre school', as a 'political office', acting out the unification of all its members on the basis of a strategic analysis, and obliged to account for the least of its actions, the loss of the least of its members.

But it is as a journal (first specificity) making political interventions in the area of film (second specificity) that we had to be called to account.

At this moment the way the journal functions internally also resembles a front: in concrete terms, a group of contributors united on (and by) the project of a journal, a project linked to the more general one of the cultural front. Similarly, the ideological struggle within the journal is carried forward in the awareness that we are not a 'party journal' but an apparatus in the service of the struggles of the revolutionary movement, particularly in the area of film. The unity and ideological coherence of past and future issues of the journal will need to be measured not in relation to some hypothetical elaboration of a party line on intervention in cultural issues (which is something we are in no condition to undertake given our current strength), but on the basis of a single criterion: the part played by the journal in reinforcing the idea of a cultural front, and its will to reflect the ideological and political struggles being enacted on the site of its avowed intervention.

And now we come to the charge that has often been laid against us: that we are no longer a film journal but a political journal. It is difficult to deny that as we understood it the process of liaison with/subordination to the Marxist-Leninist movement was lived out, or else conceived, sometimes formulated, as the *renunciation* of any *anchorage* to a specific site, even the one by which we had been constituted: the cinema. In the interests of an abstract *politicism*, we ran the risk of cutting ourselves off from the 'constituency' of cinema and the struggles that were unfolding there. In the end our 'right to be heard' was becoming ambiguous. Political organizations and militants put their trust in our specialist expertise, while at the same time artists and cultural activists accepted our criticisms of them *in the interests* of politics (seeing us as political commissars). This cleavage, which was – and still is – a real one within the collective for the creation of a cultural front, was of our own making before we became its victims.

The need to be genuinely rooted in the 'constituency' (in the broad sense all of those who, whether within or outside the system, are involved in practices of production/distribution – on ideological bases close to our own) was revived and confirmed by the visit to France of Dario Fo and the collective *La Comune*, and by the lessons we could draw from the Italian experience.[4]

It was also by asking ourselves, concretely, the question 'How can we intervene? What should we privilege?' (journalism's own question) – every week in the context of the daily *Libération* – that we came to see ideological struggle as located not in a vacuum (of a conjuncture, a 'reality' made to our own design) but in the midst of what is actually happening; a struggle which takes on the enemy, determines what is at stake, and is mindful of where it is aimed at (the reader). This climb down off our high horse was salutary. In the first place, the ideological struggle developed from, or *in*, *Libération* (where we were far from being in a position of authority) forced us to tackle the issue of the alliances to be made with progressive film-makers and critics. And secondly this alliance assumed even greater urgency through the 'cinematic' conjuncture: the offensive of bourgeois, reactionary, fascistic films . . .

Given this situation, it was clear that *Cahiers* was not providing – no longer provided – an effective *support*, if only because of the time that elapsed between issues. It is simple enough for a film journal to declare its 'espousal' of the project of a cultural front, but it is obvious that it can 'espouse' nothing very much if it is not capable, from its own discursive position, of making a political intervention with regard to a film like *Les Chinois à Paris*.[5]

It is in the context of this *intervention* that we have to reformulate and rethink the question of 'theory'. For it was the complete abandonment of concrete intervention which resulted in theory being neglected, left to stagnate in disrepute. The articulation between theory and practice *in film* is still to be found. What we do know is that there is research to be done (historical research, for example), concepts to be forged (right now, for us, the relationships between statement [*énoncé*] and utterance [*énonciation*], realism and 'typage',[6] Brecht, Gramsci, etc.), but always bearing in mind their *reinvestment*, their interplay with practice. Which practice? The practice of ideological struggle (journalism, teaching), of course, but in particular the practice of the production and distribution of 'militant' films, films that support struggles, films that are themselves involved in struggle.

How to contemplate a *critical and theoretical* journal, if not in terms of its capacity to respond, with its own weapons, to the issues raised by the ideological conjuncture and the struggles going on there? At such a time, there is a need to synthesize, to condense, to move towards a greater degree of generalization, to have a global point of view. It is not a matter of rejecting this global point of view, but of making it the concern of all those who produce and promote films (and with *Cahiers* as *a site where it can be actively elaborated*).

As far as we are concerned, it is the production and promotion of militant films that must form the principal axis from which we can set about forging our weapons. For us (the journal and its editorial staff), it is on these issues that work and the struggle continue.

S.D. [Serge Daney] and S.T. [Serge Toubiana]

Postscript

In their latest, long awaited issue, our friends at *Cinéthique* put forward a number of criticisms of *Cahiers* and, more importantly, of the project of the cultural front with which we are concerned. To put it briefly, let us just say that the notion developed by *Cinéthique* displays a *judgmental* tone that speaks volumes about their assumed monopoly on Marxist-Leninist dogma. What it amounts to is this: 'By what right do you dare set up a cultural front, while Marxist-Leninists are neither united nor in any position to produce an analysis of this secondary front?'

For *Cinéthique*'s notion of the cultural front rests on an analysis of the weaknesses of the Marxist-Leninist movement. A very harsh analysis (p. 2):

> In common with the struggles opened up on new fronts since 1968, the cultural front has given rise to attempts at autonomous organization *because* [our emphasis] there is no Marxist-Leninist organization that has recognized how much the work of research and study around the class alliances with the proletariat needs to make if it is to achieve victory is implicit in the process of working out the political line.

One might be tempted to think that a movement which calls itself Marxist-Leninist and 'does not recognize' the question of class alliances has recognized very little. *Cinéthique* does not deny it. It is at this point, however, that *Cinéthique*'s critique of the Marxist-Leninist movement becomes irresponsible, since it is one that prohibits drawing any lessons at all from it. Even when it is wrong, the Marxist-Leninist movement, by its very nature, is still right. Moreover (p. 15):

Any attempt to organize the masses in struggle on the cultural front, on the basis of the concentration and systematization of the ideas of the 'intermediate elements' engaged in these struggles, can under present circumstances only produce two equally erroneous results: either it will hand over the leadership of the mass organization to the petite-bourgeoisie, or it will expose the present inability of the Marxist-Leninists to assume the leadership of such an organization, thus contributing to the *withdrawal* [*Cinéthique*'s emphasis] of Marxism-Leninism into a class fraction outside the solid base of the masses. *At the present moment* the Marxist-Leninists do not have the political means to apply on the cultural front a mass line that would serve the interests of the solid base of the masses.

In other words, provided that no one notices the weakness of the Marxist-Leninist movement! But how does *Cinéthique* analyse this weakness? Quantitative (not strong enough, but getting there) or qualitative (not quite correct, in which case some adjustments are in order)? That is a mystery. Unless deep within the movement, *Front Rouge* (which we learn at the end of a discreet paragraph on page 10 is the group with which *Cinéthique* almost certainly has dependent links) has radically new views on the subject . . .

The trouble is that *Front Rouge* has no interest in the cultural front, or rather that what does interest them about a cultural front is whatever has a direct relationship to the economic and to the reproduction of the labour force within the solid base of the masses (abortion, health, schooling). One assumes that art, culture, etc., are relevant only to the petit-bourgeoisie, while the masses have no cultural needs.

The role of a journal like *Cinéthique* is unclear in a project as workerist and economistic as that of the *Front Rouge*. Or rather it is not: it is to represent (in the sense of 'making representations') the need for a working-class leadership within the 'struggles on new fronts'. And to remind those who might be tempted to organize independently, on their own specific ground, without waiting for the green light, that this working-class leadership, even if it is impossible *at this moment*, is none the less the only correct one. In short, to restrain and ultimately to draw into its ranks.

It is also clear what this subordination implies: if the petite-bourgeoisie alone has cultural needs and problems, then in a strategy for alliance it would be correct for the Party (*Front Rouge* in the event) to investigate it. *Cinéthique* will be the instrument of this 'investigation' – an instrument all the more effective for being perfectly equipped to lecture and castigate, in a totally unproductive way, that petite-bourgeoisie which falls so short of perfection, and which *Cinéthique* itself has come out of.

Let there be no mistake, the cultural front can do without guard dogs.

Translated by Liz Heron

Notes

1 At the Avignon festival in July 1972 *Cahiers* organized a seminar on the theme of 'cinema and class struggle'. A 'manifesto' arising out of the seminar, 'Quelles sont nos tâches sur le plan culturel?', was published in November 1972 (*Cahiers* 242–3). In August 1973, again at Avignon, the 'Front Culturel Révolutionnaire' was launched, with a programme redefined by a series of texts published in the previous month (*Cahiers* 247), including 'Avignon 73: quelles sont les tâches de révolutionnaires sur le front culturel?' and 'Pour une intervention unifiée sur le front culturel'. These texts had been preceded in April 1973 (*Cahiers* 245–6) by an article entitled 'Les luttes dans la conjuncture', which argued that the struggle on the cultural front was inextricably associated with 'the general battle that has been waged, especially since the elections'. The 'conjuncture' included: 'the growing struggles since the elections' (in the factories, in the left-wing political movements and among high school students); 'the new tactics of the so-called Communists' (criticized as 'revisionists'); and 'the reaction of the bourgeoisie'.

2 Page 9: 'We must contribute whatever we can to the cultural education of the working class and its allies, make them aware of their own interests and what their tasks are, urge them to struggle for their own emancipation in this area (for without this their political and economic emancipation will be compromised, whether in the long or the short term).'

Page 12: 'The task of the revolutionary journalist is to assist in the education of the masses, make them aware of their own interests and what their tasks are, and urge them to struggle for their own cultural emancipation.'

Page 12: 'The cultural emancipation of the masses will be the work of the masses themselves, and the role of a journal like *Cahiers* must be – within its specific field – to contribute towards the organization and leadership of this struggle through the work of clarifying, analysing, educating and providing continuing stimulus. The journal as a tool of struggle on the ideological cultural front, in other words as a red base for the offensive to be carried into the midst of the masses and taken up by the masses themselves against bourgeois culture.'

These few quotations illustrate the 'professorial' aspect of the manifesto in *Cahiers* 242–3, the text which set out the journal's 'line' up to issue 247. This 'school-teacher' stance laid claim to the education of the masses on cultural issues, in the name of Marxist-Leninist principles, turning us into a self-proclaimed – but unrecognized – leadership, a red base for the cultural front. (Authors' note.)

3 Lip, a Swiss-owned watch factory at Besançon, was taken over by its employees in 1973 after it had been closed through bankruptcy.

4 Dario Fo: Italian dramatist whose plays, such as *Accidental Death of an Anarchist* (1970), use the format of farce to convey political comment.

5 *Les Chinois à Paris* (Jean Yanne, 1974) imagines a Paris invaded by the Chinese army, and the French all too ready to collaborate with a cruel, power-hungry enemy.

6 'Typage' is the idea, developed by Eisenstein, of using the physical characteristics of an actor to express the psychological essence of a film character. The actor thus represents both an individual character and a 'type', in Eisenstein's own words a 'social and personal biography condensed into physical form'.

2

THE CRITICAL FUNCTION

('Fonction critique', *Cahiers du Cinéma* 248, September 1973–January 1974; 250, May 1974; 253, October–November 1974)

Serge Daney

What form should our 'interventions' take? How has 'film criticism' been defined in *Cahiers*? (It is after all our main inheritance from the journal's past.) There have been two answers, two periods, two tendencies, the one hiding the other and both marked by a certain dogmatism.

First, the aesthetic criterion and the political criterion are given equal status. We assume that 'if there is something missing on the formal level there must also be something missing on the political level'. We remind those inclined to forget it that 'forms are not neutral', but this is just an excuse for not investigating their very real content, for not spelling out this content in political terms – we leave that to others.

Second, politics is 'the order of the day'. We no longer leave it to others to pronounce on political content. But we don't look any further than the scenario, and we limit ourselves to orthodox Marxist-Leninist theory, conceived more as an ultimate reference point than as a (critical) guide to action.

The difficulty, as one can see, is to think of the aesthetic criterion *neither as equal* (equivalent, analogous) to the political criterion *nor as flowing automatically* from it but as secondary. This is a very real difficulty and one which must be tackled. For example, by asking ourselves (which we have not done) apropos of progressive films, from *Z* to *State of Siege*[1] (for these are our primary concern), how we can criticize them *effectively*, how we can make them progress even further, and ourselves with them, how we can give concrete, straightforward support to those who are using these films today, whether through positive or negative example, in cine-clubs, youth clubs, etc.[2] A question which must serve as a guide for the 'film criticism' which we have neglected for too long. This text is simply a first attempt at setting the problem out. Others will follow.

To write about films (to 'intervene') is perhaps, in the last analysis, to establish how, for each film, *someone is saying something to us*. In other words it is to specify the relation between two terms: the *statement* (what is said) and the *enunciation* (when it is said and by whom).[3] People will say that's a truism. That every Marxist knows (it's the first thing they learn) that dominant ideas are those of the dominant class and that a film is a means like any other for the bourgeoisie to impose its vision of the world. But this knowledge remains dead, dogmatic, stereotyped and – as we have discovered – ineffective if we are unable to understand *how* it is imposed in particular films.

In this very journal we have tended for a long time to look for this 'how' in areas where no one, except on the mystical far left, was looking for it: in the basic apparatus, or in the structure of fiction or in the configuration of a cinema and the places it assigns. It is not that we were wrong, that all this is false and that all work along these lines must be abandoned. It's rather that by indicating obstacles which *seemed* to have to do with the very nature of the cinema, we were bound to have nothing to say when called upon to make a concrete 'intervention' in respect of particular films.

We urgently need to give ourselves the means, including the theoretical means, to *specify the exact relation that each film maintains between statement and enunciation* – above all, in borderline cases where the relation is unclear and where therefore the element of mystification is greatest.

This must be done for films where the statement predominates. In a documentary or a television programme, a discourse is presented, but it is so neutral, so objective, that it seems to be coming from no one in particular. We have to remind people forcefully, with examples to prove the point, that there cannot be disembodied statements, a timeless truth or an isolated, free-floating discourse.

And it must be done for films where the enunciation predominates. In a *film d'auteur* there is indeed a discourse, but it is spoken by someone who claims so much attention (the *auteur*) that it fades into the background. We must clearly remind people that behind the *auteur* and his rich subjectivity there is always, in the last analysis, a class which is speaking. And a class has objective interests, quite apart from the fact that any enunciation implies a statement. Let us note, in passing, that these two aspects can perfectly well co-exist, as in Antonioni's recent film on China.[4] An excess of neutrality (no one is speaking but something precise is being said) or an excess of subjectivity (someone is speaking and saying nothing): these are two *denials* which we ought to be able to recognize for what they are. This said, they are not symmetrical and they have to be fought against with different weapons: you wouldn't handle the false neutrality of the commentary in a television programme on Stalin in the same way as you would the false 'drifting' of Bertolucci's latest film.[5]

These are extreme cases. Between the two you have the mass of films that still go under the heading of 'critical realism', and among them the so-called 'progressive' films. The very expression 'critical realism' indicates how necessary it is for film-makers to think as much about their statements (realism) as about their enunciation (*critical* realism). Now, in these films (whether *R.A.S.*

or *Lucky Luciano*,[6] and you can be sure that there will be others), the dividing line between statement and enunciation is always mobile, shifting, unclear. This is what allows these films to function.

Let us take *R.A.S.*, for example. You have the time of the statement (1956; the Algerian war; the recalled soldiers) and the time of the enunciation (1973; France; the *loi Debré*: the 'army crisis' and the youth movement[7]). Even if the statement appears easily to predominate, you can't get away from the fact that each scene of the film is readable in both contexts, it can be read either way and the reader can choose. Let's be clear: it isn't this double reading which is awkward. A film on the French army during the Hundred Years War couldn't fail to be seen in the light of the army of Massu and de Joybert.[8] A double reading is not awkward: *it is inevitable*. What is problematical is the film-maker's relation to this double reading: this is what allows us, *in specific situations*, to distinguish between a reactionary, a progressive and a revolutionary film-maker depending on whether he denies it, whether he plays on it or whether he is truly responsible for it.

Permutations of the statement

Who says what? Where and when?

Nevertheless, for any class, in any class-based society, the political criterion comes first and the artistic criterion second.

Mao

Destroying an idea

We must get rid of a generally accepted idea according to which 'positivity' (the positivity of a message or of a hero) is of interest only to the propagandists, the party men, the big sectarian and Zhdanovian dinosaurs. It is nothing other than the outmoded and tedious consistency required of conscious heroes, clear messages, a precise political line; which makes it somehow edifying (in the religious sense) and, as they say, 'heavily didactic'. Instead of this, in 1974, bourgeois film-makers (Malle, Cavani, etc.) prefer to 'decode' the past, no longer even trying to prove anything at all. Fascinated by the inexplicable, they explain virtually nothing, being content – supported, valorized by a servile criticism[9] – to be 'daring' and show what was still hidden only yesterday (sex and politics and what passes for their privileged meeting point, fascism). Their courage is praised; people are grateful to them for not presenting things in black and white and for so pleasurably suspending judgment as they offer tragic dossiers of the kind that television is forever reopening: the Occupation, racism, fascism. Their positivity resides, if you like, in the fact that instead of generally accepted explanations they offer no explanations at all or else an overabundance of them. Too many explanations or too few.

We have no intention of replacing *their* 'ambiguity' (another fetish word) by *our* certainties, Marxist-Leninist or otherwise. To re-emphasize, in response to Malle, the truth and nobility of the Resistance (which he does not deny) or, in response to Antonioni or Yanne, the massive achievements of the Chinese people (which they fully acknowledge – just like Peyrefitte)[10] is a correct but defensive manoeuvre, the very minimum that has to be done. For ambiguity involves not a failure of knowledge or an uncertain knowledge (in which case it would be enough – armed with superior, indeed absolute knowledge – simply to fill in the gaps) but *another type of knowledge.* Malle and co. do not specialize in the inexplicable (despite their inner agonizing), but in the *inexplicit.* The inexplicit is not the opposite of positivity, it is one of the forms it takes (the dominant form, even).

In other words: each class possesses its own style of ideological struggle, its own way of putting across its view of the world, its (positive) ideas. Positive: that is to say, effective, easy to adopt and to put into practice. Bourgeois propaganda doesn't take the same form as revolutionary propaganda, any more than bourgeois information, or criticism, or art.

In short, we must destroy the idea that positivity is a limited concept or one left over from the past. It is not true that on the one hand you have the 'system' (art or commerce, art *and* commerce) and on the other 'militant' films (politics without either art or commerce). Positivity is not the exception but the rule. *All* films are militant films.

A film is always positive for someone

A class puts across its positive ideas, its 'natural' conception of the world. That means it puts its ideas into action (and in the case of the cinema into images) in such a way that they can be not only read and recognized but adopted and transformed into something else, into a material force, for instance. Take ideas like: 'Our motives are decidedly impenetrable', or 'There's something of the torturer and the victim in everyone, that's for sure' – two fashionable, retrostyle stereotypes. Their formulation may well be negative or ambiguous, but *from the viewpoint* of the bourgeoisie and its immediate interests they are nevertheless positive ideas.

And these ideas are all the more harmful for never being made explicit in the body of the film. It is the hypnotized spectator who 'freely' draws the lesson whispered in his ear, who cuts along the dotted lines he cannot see. The film's implicit discourse sends the spectator into a frenzy of interpretation which makes him or her forget the poverty and banality (sometimes the sheer stupidity: Cavani) of the lesson.[11]

But how is the question of positivity any different from that of meaning, of signification? The fact is that the question of signification, taken by itself, is a meaningless one, of no concern to anyone. In *Cahiers* itself, the battle cry has been: 'You don't see a film. You read it.' Fine. But this reading, this search for 'discrete elements' here, for bits of information there, wouldn't serve much purpose (except as fodder for academic rumination, as sustenance for semiologists) if one didn't know what it is that happens on the side of the receiver. The critic must be able to read a film: he or she must also know how the others, the non-readers, read. And there is just one way to find out: by inquiry. For it is a question not only of reintroducing the receiver into communication theory, not in the abstract sense (the general public) nor even in the concrete sense (a given social group or individual); but of remembering that the receiver is also something other than a receiver. *Just like the film he is seeing*, he is involved in the class struggle, he plays a part in it. And it is on the basis of this struggle, and the turns it takes, that the problem of positivity, as it affects all films, can be posed (for whom? against whom?); on the basis of this struggle too that one can begin to reply.

1974: Even for Pariscope, *there are political films*[12]

For whom? Against whom? We do not raise these issues out of dogmatism or a liking for clear-cut oppositions. For if the bourgeoisie never poses this question of positivity (if it did it would have to admit the class nature of its power), it is always coming up with answers. And especially so today. In 1974, all the way through[13] the system of film production and distribution, in France and also no doubt in Italy, right-wing film-makers have seized the initiative. Via all the reactionary, period-style films sympathetic to fascism (or just fascinated by it and therefore – and this is what gives cause for concern – incapable of *struggling* against it). Malle, Oury, Yanne and the rest have set themselves an ambitious task, politically, ideologically and indeed formally: to propose a new image, a new characterization of France and its inhabitants, the French, to represent on the screen the 'average Frenchman' and his two Others, the two objects of his increasingly obvious racism, those who are not French (foreigners) and those who are not average (those who are relegated to the margins). In other words: bourgeois ideologues and artists are working steadily to build a new image of the *French people.*[14]

As a result of this shift (the death of Gaullist ideology, the death of Pompidou, the crisis of a bourgeois humanist discourse in need of patching up), it is no longer enough to criticize mainstream cinema as one has done for years, taking it to task for 'abandoning the real', for neglecting certain subjects, for excluding or repressing others. It is no longer a simple question of repression. It is not enough to reproach bourgeois film-makers for not speaking of politics or sex or work or even History since *they* are the ones talking about these things today. The bourgeoisie can very well hold a (bourgeois) discourse on what, only yesterday, it still wanted to hide: it can film sexual debauchery if it keeps its monopoly over a normative (educational) discourse on sex. It can anchor its fictions in History if it has emptied the word of all content. That is how Malle's 'decoding' operation works (sex: *Le Souffle au coeur*; History: *Lacombe Lucien*; the working-class situation: *Humain, trop humain*).

'Progressive' film-makers are disconcerted by it all. To take an example: how do you explain the commercial success, at the same time, of two films like *Lacombe Lucien* and *Les Violons du bal*?[15] The fact is that they bring alive, for the public at large, a part of recent French history that has been veiled in secrecy or misrepresented for far too long. And yet these two films do not occupy the same ground, do not engage in any sort of struggle with each other. The humanist denunciation of racism in Drach's film would have to be aimed at a cinema which suppressed racism, which refused to speak about it, to have any impact. Even a purely abstract denunciation would then have some point, some urgency. But in the light of Malle's film it appears for what it actually is: humanitarian and ineffective. For what Drach must repress in the name of his abstract humanism (class contradictions). Malle allows himself the luxury of inscribing (Lucien, the illiterate peasant boy, etc.). Where Drach says nothing at all, Malle exaggerates. For it is obvious that the fact of inscribing such details doesn't make Malle (any more than the Kazan of *The Visitors*) a progressive film-maker: class contradictions, for him, are basically no different from other contradictions – they can always be overtaken and absorbed into a meta-physical overview in which they become accidents, particular (historical) instances of an a-historical split: the eternal ambiguity of 'human nature'.[16]

We have to recognize that fascist ideology (and this is one of its characteristics) *accepts* the existence of contradictions, of the class struggle (usually to deplore it, to move beyond it). *We have to know that today the struggle must encompass point of view as well as choice of subject.* As our Italian comrades of *La Comune* remind us: 'It is not enough to counter the false statements of the bourgeoisie. In and through our own statements we must convey a different view of the world.' For film-makers of all leanings, in this near-open battle, in their very craft of film-making, a single problem emerges: *How can political statements be presented cinematically? How can they be made positive?*

Statement/enunciation [énoncé/énonciation]

This cinematic presentation carries another name: enunciation. It consists in the articulation of two main terms: the *carrier* of the statements (who is speaking?) and the *terrain* on which they are brought into play (where and when and in what context?). A film's positivity (whose interests are served?) is based on the *nature* of the link between statement and enunciation. That is why criticizing a film doesn't mean shadowing it with a complicit or, as Barthes would say, *cosmetic* discourse. It doesn't even mean unfolding it or opening it out. It means *opening it up* along this imaginary line which passes between statement and enunciation, allowing us to read them side by side, in their problematical, disjointed relationship – and so not being afraid of destroying the false unity conferred on them in the 'present' of a cinematic projection.

There can be no statement without enunciation. This is the inescapable reality of all discourse, of all fictional films. It is what allows us to avoid the trap of a content-based criticism (a trap which lies in wait for militant criticism, one it falls into all too often). For a criticism of content which did no more than assess the truth (or falsity) of statements, which failed to examine the part they play in the film's organization, would be (and is) singularly lost for words, singularly ineffective (and quickly reduced to indignation or dogmatism) when required to intervene in day-to-day ideological struggles. 'Belief in the intrinsic force of the true idea' is not enough, was never enough to bring a (political or ideological) struggle to a successful conclusion. As Serge Toubiana reminded us, apropos of *La Villeggiatura*:[17] 'Just because a character makes some politically valid comment doesn't mean that the film's discourse, the author's discourse, has taken it over and is fully responsible for it.'

For what characterizes a discourse, a statement, is that it can be made, quoted, repeated, *carried* by anyone. The links between statement, carrier and terrain are not obvious and natural: we are always dealing with some *combination* of the three. In a future text, we shall try to describe some of these. The list is long and varied: statements can appear to have no carriers, or too many, they can be carried badly, they can be lost, stolen, hijacked, etc. But there is one of these combinations which we encounter all the time: when a statement that is (politically) true is taken over, carried, by its worst enemy on a terrain where it can have no impact at all.

One example (among thousands). Not so long ago the ORTF showed a short film on prisons. While the camera panned smoothly along the white walls of a model prison, the voice-over took up, in its own right and in its own language, a certain number of demands and problems expressed elsewhere (that is to say, everywhere except on television) by prisoners themselves. A content-based criticism will be satisfied with that and rightly see in it the effect – to be read into the film[18] – of the prisoners' real struggle without which the film would never have been made in the first place. But isn't it obvious to everyone that a film like this is *inherently* different from *Attica*?[19] The difference can be briefly resumed in the following way: not only are the prisoners in *Attica* the carriers of true *statements* which express the truth of this revolt, and every other, against the lies of those in authority, but the prisoners are also those for whom these statements are true (those who can appropriate them and mobilize them for *their* future struggles); they are the right people to be carrying them. Finally they are carrying them on a terrain (the yard that is occupied, filmed, transformed into a set) that they have built themselves, creating the material conditions for their enunciation and 'producing' a great film.

Anti-retro (continued)[20]

Two false couples

I would like to come back to *The Night Porter* and, in particular, to a scene that occurs towards the end of the film. In it we see the night porter (Max) meet his friends (Hans and co.) who, like him, are one-time Nazis gradually shedding their guilt – forgetting the past – and finding their place again in society. To be more exact, Max *appears* before them for – in this matter of his past, linked to theirs, a past in process of liquidation – there are things he must account for. The scene takes place at the top of St Stephen's cathedral in Vienna. Hans and the others are deadly serious; Max, on the contrary, is ironical and derisive. To cut short this interview which is getting him down and which, as far as he is concerned, is totally pointless, he tries a mock Hitler salute to which the others – reflex action or the return of the repressed? – respond, giving him just enough time to slip away.

At this precise moment in the film, we the spectators know a certain number of things about the night porter. We have seen him meeting up 'by chance' with his favourite victim, resuming relations with her, etc. Having been placed in the position of a voyeur (one more eye), we know things about Max that other people (Hans and the others, for instance) don't. We are in control of this story that is being told for us alone. Hans and his companions are wrong for two reasons: first, because they have been Nazis and are still Nazis at heart since they are still interested in power; and, second, because they don't see, know or guess anything of what is happening to Max, either in his head (inside him) or in his flat (his private space). They are doubly inferior for reasons which relate first to content and second to the *mise en scène* of this content in and through the fiction. We, on the other hand, are right for two reasons: first, because we are not Nazis; and, second, because we can observe and perhaps understand what is going on in the mad love between Max and Lucia. We are doubly superior first because we have a clear conscience and second because this clear conscience is reaffirmed in and through the fiction. Let us assume the existence of a law, one we had better know about, concerning the organization of fiction: a piece of fiction (the network of events seen, known or implied, everything that constitutes a film's internal knowledge) is not only an enigma for the spectator but also, in the imaginary space where they exist, for the 'characters' themselves, shadowy beings who also want to find out more, to see more.

This knowledge (about the film, within the film), this mastery, this clear conscience have their price. Let us come back to the scene on the cathedral rooftop. Between Hans, the neo-Nazi undergoing social recycling, and Max, the ex-Nazi who is willing – fairly romantically – to die for it, we simply have to choose. We will be (whether consciously or not doesn't really matter) in favour of the one who 'assumes' his Nazi identity and gets back in touch with his humanity[21] (Max), and against the one who represses himself as a Nazi and so continues to seem completely inhuman (Hans). We will be on the side of madness and humour and against stiffness and asceticism, with the victim (a torturer yesterday) and against the killer (a torturer yesterday *and* today). The whole film must, in a sense, culminate in this choice, make it seem natural, obvious to us. To refuse to make this choice (in the darkness of the cinema) is to refuse to see the film, to enter into it, to be one more eye. But as we know – and this is the point – the film is not short of spectators (336,107 admissions to 3 September 1974).

Not so long ago a television series, *Dossiers de l'écran*, devoted a programme (a film plus a debate) to Count Ciano.[22] The pretext was that the countess of the same name – daughter of Mussolini and widow of Ciano – had (finally!) accepted an invitation to participate. The film was Carlo Lizzani's feeble *Il Processo di Verona* [1962]. The question it raised was to what extent Ciano, a fascist but a germanophobe, had moved away from the Duce (who got rid of him). Already in the film, forced to choose between a Mussolini removed from the scene but all the more present for that and a Ciano who is indecisive, human, full of doubts and worries, the viewer could hardly not 'sympathize' with the less bad of the two, that is to say, with Ciano (just as he or she would no doubt have tended to 'sympathize' with Mussolini if the choice had been between him and Hitler). In the debate that follows, there is absolutely no mention of the Italian resistance. It's as if the main opposition is between Mussolini and Ciano, with the latter representing *from within fascism* everything in the Italian people which resisted fascism and fought against it. Let us add, for the record, that Ciano's widow, whose contribution to the debate is entirely frivolous, did nevertheless have the last word, stating that fascism (she admits: 'Perhaps I'm stupid') had been and continued to be the 'best thing for Italy' – an idea that P. Cardonnel has rightly protested against in a recent article in *Le Monde*.

Either/or

What do these two examples (Hans and Max, Mussolini and Ciano) have in common? *They make you choose* (you have to make up your mind) *the less bad of two terms* (chosen in advance from within the enemy camp). The main opposition (the real one, the one in relation to which you have to situate yourself) moves elsewhere, passing through one camp only, that of the enemy. Knowing which one, out of Hans and Max or Ciano and Mussolini (and one would guess that the list is endless, that these false couples are everywhere: Hitler can be set against Röhm, Nixon can be compared with Wallace, Guy Lux with Michel Droit,[23] *Pariscope* with *Ici-Paris*, etc.), represents *the lesser evil* becomes the only question that is asked and, very soon, the principal question. What is important is that, in this displacement of the opposition, the spectator has something to *gain*, something that has to do with the fulfilment of desire: a privileged view from above, a chance to step outside History, the right to enjoy the spectacle of contradictions between famous people and to choose between them. (This ties in with a whole conception of History 'for the people', *Historia*, etc.[24]) Nothing could be more fictional than this right that is conferred on the spectator by fiction. Manipulated, he or she joins the ranks of the televised housewife who recognizes (by touching them or smelling them, I can't remember) which of two piles of laundry is the whiter, not realizing that she is being made to perform twice over: by the ORTF and by a corporation like Unilever feigning – in her person – a competition all the more frenetic for being illusory.

We are saying: the spectator's knowledge is bought at a price, and the underside of mastery is submission. This submission doesn't come about only in the cinema: you choose between two presidents, two answers, two names, two washing powders within the same 'either/or' framework, failing to remember that you can refuse to choose between these two terms and insist on others that are more legitimate and more in line with your interests. For there is only ever one question, that of knowing exactly who is asking the questions.

Let us go a little further. A characteristic of bourgeois ideology is that it is for ever asking you to choose. A characteristic of the 'retro style' is that this choice is always situated inside the camp of yesterday's enemy (so that nothing has to be said about today's). Struggling against this twofold mechanism means not only criticizing the way in which the bourgeoisie in general poses its questions, but also finding another questioning system to put in its place. For this, two things are needed. First, a theory of what I shall call 'compulsory choice' (or arbitration). This would help us to detect the 'either/or' configuration everywhere it operates (elections of course[25] – questionnaires, surveys, opinion polls – *fiction*), and show us that it is a manipulatory, hence authoritarian technique. Second, what must be called (and not simply as a piece of wishful thinking) a definition of what constitutes the people's camp in France in 1974. Only in this definition can we even roughly trace a line from which we can start to learn to ask questions again – our own.

Compulsory choice

I must now answer a question that the reader must have asked him or herself. We know that *The Night Porter* is not seen by a 'spectator' aloof from the class struggle but in the main by a petit-bourgeois audience whose ideology and fantasies it echoes and supports (conferring on them, by way of a bonus, the dignity of the work of art). It is therefore dangerous to assume that a popular audience will react in the same way to this particular film as the intellectual petite-bourgeoisie. What is at issue is the social class of the audience. Two things follow from this. First, the mechanism of 'compulsory choice' is integral to bourgeois ideology. It becomes more specific when it is taken over, internalized by the different classes dominated by the bourgeoisie. According to whether it is experienced (taken over) by the petite-bourgeoisie or experienced (suffered) by the masses, it takes different forms – and a knowledge of these forms will depend on surveys still to be carried out, practical surveys into how films are actually received. Second, a further specification, relating to the particular medium of film: there is a *hysteria*[26] inherent in cinematic projection.

Arbitration

Let us come back to our two examples. The television programme on Ciano was not so much trying to make the viewers think as to get them to commit themselves emotionally. Let us suppose that a popular audience, even if the choices presented to it are not its own, comes down in favour of one side or another. This, travestied in the bourgeois presentation of sport, is the logic of the supporter. But it is also, when seen in its true light, that of commitment. The petite-bourgeoisie on the contrary – this is the very form its fantasy takes – internalizes both sides, both terms, and is for ever keeping the score. To take the sporting metaphor one step further, this is the logic of the referee. Acting the referee, for a class that is divided, hesitant, unsure of itself etc., is a means of preserving its existence, of giving itself, a little weight, a little meaning. To be a referee, to be an arbiter, you have to know the rules and be able to apply them. Legalism: taking the Other at his word, the Other: the bourgeois.

Two different *attitudes* are involved here. In the very excess of his commitment, the supporter may always see the feebleness of what he is supporting and redirect the excess in positive ways. The referee, on the other hand, is easily convinced of the importance of his role: without him, so he thinks, the game could not take place. He easily forgets that there is no referee for the class struggle.

This idea that the class struggle can be followed from a distance and pronounced upon, though completely false, is very much alive, even among the masses. Revisionism has a lot to do with it. You cannot with impunity present class confrontation in terms of a peaceful rivalry, you cannot ask the masses to choose, on the evidence presented to them, the *least bad manager* of bourgeois affairs, without making them more aware of the ideological hegemony of the petite-bourgeoisie (a hegemony in which the general idea of 'arbitration' is a principal element).

That is why it is no good saying to oneself, by way of reassurance, that *The Night Porter* is just a petit-bourgeois film. In the domain of the cinema, the assimilation of the dominant ideology by a popular audience means that the *auteur* film (thought, reflection, experimentation, a signature) can combine with the pornographic-film-set-in-a-concentration-camp, a 'popular' genre of which there are many recent examples, like *Camp spécial no.* 7 or *Uncle Tom* by the fetid Jacopetti. And this combination is precisely what we find in *The Night Porter*.

Hysteria

The fantasy of being the referee or arbiter (knowing the rules, applying them and, in this case, taking the Other at his word) goes with the *position* of the spectator. The hysteric is a prisoner of the discourse of the Other. And fiction relies crucially on the *desire for this discourse*. In letting the (desiring) spectators into the rectangle of light, it presents them with two Others (in the enemy camp) and forces them to choose the one whose discourse they will support and identify with. It's what Hollywood film-makers have always known. Take Hitchcock. What finer metaphor for the place of the spectator (for hysterical desire) than *North by Northwest*? A man (Cary Grant) is accidentally mistaken for another, an Other who is about to be killed. To save his skin he tries to become this Other. He is not successful; for the Other does not exist: he is a fictional character invented by the FBI as a bait for some spies (in the pay of the Soviets). It is Cary Grant (and not the Other he wanted to become) who ends up helping the FBI of his own free will. In the film, as in the reality which produced it, *fiction is a power structure*.

The people's camp

The fiction[27] we are talking about here, the kind that obliges you to make choices from within the enemy camp, must be fought against, and therefore understood. We have to be able to say why these couples, these choices, are false, why the really important opposition – yesterday as today – is not between Hans and Max or Ciano and Mussolini. There is, of course, no question of denying these oppositions, but it isn't tolerable, even in a film, that they should function as the main ones, and the point needs to be made urgently. There is also, of course, no question of denying that something can be learned, that there are lessons to be drawn from these oppositions, but 'teaching by negative example' simply doesn't work, is just an idle illusion, unless a positive alternative already exists in relation to which the negative can be situated, graded and criticized, and can provide valuable lessons. Now, the question of the positive alternative is always specifically, directly *political*. Where is the main dividing line in France, today? Where is the analysis of class in French society? These questions should not be thought too large or too general. In so far as film criticism aims to intervene politically in the ideological struggle, it must link up with what it considers to be the people's camp (always in the making through popular struggles), beginning from (but not limiting itself to) the particular place from which it speaks (the cinema).

For that, it is not enough to recite 'On a just resolution to contradictions among the people', to say with Mao that 'the notion of "the people" assumes a different meaning in different countries and at different periods of history'. Or to recall that there exist different types of contradiction and therefore different modes of resolution. These (infinitely true) principles are likely to prove irrelevant if they are made to function dogmatically. It was Mao who said: 'The dogmatic are lazy.' They are lazy if they do not consider what (or who) is involved and what is at stake in different kinds of contradiction. Fighting dogmatism means, for a film critic, facing up to a question that has become unavoidable: *in the name of what do I criticize?*

SERGE DANEY

Criticism in the name of what?

Let us return once again to our point of departure: the 'retro style'. Its 'merit' was to bring to light the weakness, the ineffectiveness, and even the mistakes of a criticism based on principles. A criticism that brings only moral disapproval into play. A criticism that reproaches Malle or Cavani for the philosophical assumptions of their films. These assumptions relate to the most hackneyed idealism. But precisely, the struggle against idealism is eternal (Engels). A criticism, finally, which consists in setting these films against 'historical truth'. For this truth is not a given. It can't be reduced to a formula like 'Gradually the French people recovered the desire to fight' (Foucault's example) or hollow stereotypes like 'The French people resisted heroically'. This truth needs a corpus that can be assembled and reassembled; the fact that the image of the French resistance, for example, is monopolized by Gaullism and the PCF [French Communist Party], and that there isn't another one, must not be repressed. Now that a rich literature is being published on this period, now that a man like Guingoin is finally publishing his memoirs, it's a question of saying: this image *can* be assembled, the image of a *maquis* organizing the people for the postwar period. It's time to say: that could be the subject of a film. And to add: our comrades in *Lotta Continua* have done it for Italy.

Film criticism in the name of what? In the name of something which is not given, but which exists in embryo, in the form of scattered elements that are repressed and disguised, impossible to recognize on occasion because they are differently coded. How can we build on these elements if we are not in a position to encourage them when they surface, to bring them back to life when they disappear? It is then, as we sift through the evidence, that principles come into their own, are truly useful, and that the experience of our Chinese comrades, for instance, becomes something other than a bleak recitation.

In the various individual confrontations of the class struggle, the enemy can score a point only if there is weakness on the other side. One such weakness is the absence of what might be called a *perspective of the left* on the analysis of fascism, one that is reasonably coherent and actively applied. Fascism poses two questions today: that of power as an exception (the departure from bourgeois democracy) and that of the eroticization of this power. On these questions the Marxist economic tradition, which has come down to us along with revisionism, has nothing to say. And what we know is that if this perspective of the left can be constructed, as it *must be*, it won't be in the name of some remote dogma, or even the endlessly repeated names of Brecht or Reich, but on the basis of what, today, in the practice of those who meet these questions in their struggle, already contains this construction.

Criticism would then become something more heterogeneous, something less settled than the simple metalanguage it is today. Neither a catalogue of what is beautiful (old-style cinephilia) nor an account of what is wrong (new-style dogmatism). For there are beautiful films that are harmful ('poisonous plants', as they say in China) and mistakes from which much can be learned. To criticize would be to specify, for a film or a mode, the precise *terrain*[28] on which it intervenes, the issue on which it adopts a position. You would no longer say: Malle is an idealist or Malle is an academic film-maker (though these statements are true). You would say: the real subject of *Lacombe Lucien* is the memory of popular struggles. From *his* point of view, that of an upper-class liberal, Malle is right: this terrain, deserted by revisionism, is still neglected; and there is hardly anyone in a position to make it productive (but there is *Le Peuple français*[29] in France, and in Italy Dario Fo).

From *our* point of view, we must build on everything that will help us establish a perspective of the left on popular memory (we must read, investigate, translate the considerable contribution of the Latin Americans, Sanjines, Littin, etc.).

This perspective of the left doesn't yet exist, it isn't there for us to apply. Often, it will even require translation. Let us return to the example of Malle's film and ask a simple question: is there anything today *in the cinema* (in this specific arrangement of images and sounds) that you could set against *Lacombe Lucien*? There is not. But in another area, itself heterogeneous (history? literature?) M. Foucault's work on Pierre Rivière provides a starting point, a possible counter-argument to Malle's theme of 'the primitive as plaything of a stupid history'.[30]

This argument has already been set out in the interview with M. Foucault. Let us return to it briefly. What is important for Malle? That Lacombe doesn't internalize anything or memorize anything, that he can be made to carry statements that he doesn't ever understand[31] and would be incapable of making in his own right? For Malle, Lacombe is a barbarian (who answers to nothing but nature, human and vegetable). For the revisionist Emile Breton, on the other hand, Lacombe bears witness to the 'confusion of certain social strata as yet incapable of producing for themselves a scientific analysis of the world' (*Nouvelle Critique*, no. 72). His development has therefore not progressed very far. The problem is: how can we think of Lacombe as anything other than a barbarian (who lacks humanity) or as underdeveloped (lacking knowledge)? When Foucault speaks about Rivière, what he emphasizes is that, if Rivière lacks knowledge, he doesn't lack discourse, *or memory*. Alienated doesn't mean a-historical.

The fact is that Malle poses (and resolves – for the bourgeoisie) a problem on which a *left* viewpoint can be established. The problem is this: how can you construct a piece of fiction (a story) from a perspective which does not imply an 'absolute knowledge' (of History)?

In Malle's system (to which, in this very journal, we had applied the term 'modernist'), the only person you could possibly contrast with Lacombe is not another peasant but a master – even if, cunningly, the master is unworthy (the schoolmaster in the film) or easily blamed (Malle since 1968). To get out of the system you have to ask another question (Littin's, for example, in this issue):

how can you accurately retrace a process from the viewpoint of those who do not master it fully, those who neither speak nor theorize?

This question is always going to require our intervention. That is the meaning of 'anti-retro'.

Translated by Annwyl Williams

Notes

1 *Z* (1968) and *State of Siege* (1973): films by Costa-Gavras, the first about a plot to murder a left-wing Greek politician, the second about the clandestine involvement of the CIA in Latin America.
2 Youth clubs: the publicly funded Maisons de la Jeunesse et de la Culture. (Translator's note.)
3 The statement and the enunciation: in French, *l'énoncé* and *l'énonciation*, a usage deriving from the linguist Emile Benveniste's distinction between the act whereby an utterance is produced (*énonciation*) and what is uttered (*énoncé*).
4 I.e. the documentary *Chung Kuo* (*China*), discussed by Jacques Aumont in *Cahiers* 248.
5 I.e. *Last Tango in Paris*. We have been unable to identify the television programme referred to here,
6 *R.A.S.* (Yves Boisset, 1973); *Lucky Luciano* (Francesco Rosi, 1973).
7 The *loi Debré*: a law which obliged students to complete their military service before the age of twenty-one. It was perceived by the left as a way of suppressing the student movement.
8 Jacques Massu and Marc de Joybert, French military leaders during the Algerian war. Massu was dismissed by de Gaulle in January 1960 for publicly opposing his policy of self-determination for the Algerians.
9 An example of 'impressionable' criticism: Bory (on Cavani): 'Where reason is powerless, where logic disappears, where morality is beside the point, where darkness, the unconscious, the unavowed and the unavowable hold sway, how can you analyse? It's better to show.' (Author's note.)
10 The reference is to Antonioni's documentary *Chung Kuo* (1972) and Jean Yanne's *Les Chinois à Paris* (1974). Alain Peyrefitte, French politician and writer, published a book on China in 1973. (Translator's note.)
11 This is what happens in advertisements where, as P. Bonitzer has suggested, the manipulation involved in the message appears less and less as a shameful conditioning technique but demands to be recognized, studied and *desired* as such. Advertising knows all about desire, and hence about the signifier. (Author's note.)
12 *Pariscope*: organ of the lumpen intelligentsia. Tries desperately to mimic Parisian intellectual debates. A Filipacchi publication. (Author's note.) The publisher Daniel Filipacchi had bought *Cahiers* in 1964. When he wanted to dispose of it in the aftermath of May 1968 and the magazine's politicization it was bought back from him.
13 It would be totally false to oppose the *film d'auteur* to the commercial film. This distinction exists but is of secondary importance. From *Lacombe Lucien* to *Les Chinois à Paris* via *Le Führer en folie* (Philippe Clair) it's the *same* ideological tendency that emerges. (Author's note.)
14 This does not happen automatically. A class, even when it is in power, takes a little time to find its ideologues, the people who will operate on its behalf in this or that situation. It too must work, or rather it must try to make something out of what it has inherited: in this case a certain tradition of French cinema (Pascal Thomas

claims to take his inspiration from Renoir) or a reassuring classicism (Malle, Granier-Deferre). The cinema too is returning to the past. But *acritically*. (Author's note.)

15 *Les Violons du bal* (1974): a self-referential film by Michel Drach, about his experiences as a Jewish boy in occupied France.

16 There are two ways for bourgeois ideology to ignore contradiction or do away with it. Either it sees it nowhere (universal harmony) or it sees it everywhere (universal contradiction). Malle chooses the second solution with a zeal and an application which give *Lacombe Lucien* an almost touching quality. One is tempted to announce, as in a film, in alphabetical order: collaborator/member of the Resistance, father/son, Jew/Gentile, law/desire, man/woman, nature/culture, peasant/bourgeois, torturer/victim, town/country, etc. You can say that he has simply overdone it and that these contradictions are not all on the same level. But that's where Malle succeeds in his sleight of hand: making us believe that he is being analytical. For him, not only are all the contradictions of the capitalist mode of production present, *but they are all fundamental!* It is not too difficult to see how, in these conditions, being unable to establish any kind of *hierarchy*, Malle and his heroes can never hope to understand anything. (Author's note.)

17 *La Villeggiatura*: a film by Marco Leto, reviewed by Serge Toubiana in *Cahiers* 249.

18 To read or write something into a film. This much bandied about phrase might benefit from being considered *historically*. For example: when Resnais's *Muriel* is shot, in 1963, the Algerian war, torture, are in effect forbidden topics in the cinema. To write this prohibition into the film, to import it in the form of an empty and all the more disquieting signifier ('Muriel' precisely) is a way of getting round the problem. That is what revisionist critics forget when they read anything into anything. Theirs is an accommodating reading of an inscription that poses no danger, no longer a ruse but a compromise, with film-makers (and critics) accepting that they no longer have to define themselves (their practice, their weapons) in the teeth of the restrictions imposed by a *political power*. (Author's note.)

19 *Attica*: a 1973 documentary by Cinda Firestone, focusing on the conditions at the Attica State Penitentiary in New York, which provoked a major prison riot. The film is discussed by Thérèse Giraud in the same issue of *Cahiers*.

20 Anti-retro: a reference to the interview with Michel Foucault in *Cahiers* 251, translated in this volume, Ch. 12.

21 There can be no 'retro style' without a discourse on human nature, without bourgeois humanism. And no such discourse without prior repression of class determinations. In Cavani's work, this takes the form of *neutralization*. It *had* to be the case that Max was socially dominant (linked to Nazi power) and Lucia a victim of this power (socially dominated), and the opposite had to be the case as well (Max a night porter and Lucia married into money). The 'human nature' effect is obtained by somehow inscribing the class struggle as a simple struggle for position, a game of musical chairs in which whoever loses wins. This can easily be proved *a contrario*: the story of *The Night Porter* played by a working-class couple would make people laugh (cf. Reiser, in *Charlie-Hebdo*) or bore the upper classes stiff. (Author's note.) *Charlie-Hebdo* was a weekly paper which used the crude simplifications of the comic-strip format to make social and political points.

22 Ciano was Mussolini's minister for foreign affairs. He was implicated in the coup which overthrew his father-in-law's regime, but was captured and shot by the renegade fascists of the shortlived Salò republic.

23 Guy Lux was a television entertainer and game show host; Michel Droit was a famous television journalist.

24 *Historia*: a glossy magazine edited by right-wing historians, which presented a popular, romantic view of history.

25 For which the electoral system is the ultimate model and guarantee. The late Murray Chotiner, a formative influence on Richard Nixon's political thinking, was of the opinion that people generally voted against something or someone, rarely for. Indeed, choosing the lesser evil has become the rule in American elections. The more the electoral apparatus is distanced from the people and from the real political life of the country, the more it has to highlight whatever little differences can still be found and make them sparkle in its own sphere (star system); a huge amount of energy, money and talent goes into it. The same could be said (minus the talent) of a particularly stupid ORTF programme, *L'Antenne est à vous*, where the Saturday-afternoon viewers are always voting: for one Western against another, for one cartoon against another, for one song against another. The point being that they should experience little differences as absolutely fundamental, and their vote as an act of world-shattering importance. (Author's note.)

26 And this hysteria cannot (cannot only) be exchanged for the illusory mastery that *knowledge* confers. The cinema makes use of knowledge, but only to refocus on the *belief* that lies at its heart. (Author's note.)

27 The famous argument that 'forms are neutral' depends on another: that there is only one ideology, the dominant one. Those two arguments, taken together, allow two others to be discounted: the argument that forms are not neutral, that they are themselves a form of action (in other words that they are linked dialectically to the ideologies which inform them), and the argument that there is something which resists the dominant ideology and which, for want of a better term, we must call working-class ideology. This ideology needs forms; it needs to know that fiction, for instance, is not an empty mould but a power structure, so that the question of its own power (its own ideological hegemony) can be posed. (Author's note.)

28 The 'real' subject is not the scenario or the theme. Determining the real subject means taking it over by force. You have to re-insert the film-object into a scene whose very existence it denies: that of the battle of ideas where no blow is lost, where no object stays empty for long. Taking it over by force: it is essential not to cut ourselves off from the ideological/political conjuncture. And this conjuncture isn't only what circulates as 'news', but what we can learn from popular struggles, provided we stay in touch with them (the famous 'cultural needs of the people': who could produce an account of 'Lip and the cinema'?). That means you have a foot in the apparatus (where struggles are taking place) and a foot in popular struggles (where the question of the apparatus is debated; cf. the cultural front). What is certain is that from the apparatus you can only see the apparatus. (Author's note.) For Lip see Ch. 1, note 3.

29 *Le Peuple français*, a journal of popular history launched over three years ago by a group of teachers. Published quarterly. (Author's note.)

30 See Ch. 12 in this volume.

31 Lacombe to Horn: 'My friends don't much like Jews.' By implication: I (nature) can't see the difference (culture). The whole film is in that statement. It would fall apart if Lacombe were just to say: '*I* don't much like Jews.' (Author's note.)

3

A PARTICULAR TREND IN FRENCH CINEMA

('Une certaine tendance du cinéma français', *Cahiers du Cinéma* 257, May–June 1975)

Serge Daney, Pascal Kané, Jean-Pierre Oudart, Serge Toubiana

After *Cahiers*'s (over)long silence on the subject of the French cinema, we are publishing this set of texts (which is not a single text but fragments of texts containing the seeds of texts to come) seven years after May 1968, at a time when French film-makers are beginning to wonder whether French cinema should be more firmly rooted in 'social issues' within the context of the existing system and of its rules and requirements. This therefore marks a return to social issues and to *naturalism* as a genre or a label, a way of filming and a world view.

On the basis of several recent films (which in the case of *Les Doigts dans la tête* and *Dupont Lajoie*[1] have been ideological mini-events), we attempt to define what is new in the French cinema and what the price of this novelty is. Naturalism remains the principal way of rendering what is in fact not 'natural' in society. Therefore what we would like to help to demonstrate is that naturalism (as a genre) is always related to the recourse to the *typical* (as an aesthetic problem), to *segregation* and to *racism* (considered as subjects and as ideological themes).

Naturalism and the recourse to the typical

It is often said that the French cinema is cut off from reality. In other words, little or none of what *really* happens in French society (the class struggle) is considered seriously or reflected in it. Instead, the French cinema offers irrelevant, pointless, petit-bourgeois and self-obsessed (the New Wave) images of a class 'which has no interest in realism'. This point of view may be crude but it is undeniable. But the question it raises is less one of realism than one of imagination. Because realism always requires a point of view (of reality and of the

73

'reality to be filmed', or the cine-reality) the questions it raises are political. But the imagination raises questions which concern what has never been seen, voyeurism and identification, the 'scoop' (cf. Boisset[2]) and the 'mirror stage'.

For it would appear that the gap this new 'trend in French cinema' has plugged is what one might call a 'crisis of specularity'. Broadly stated it amounts to this: the film-going public no longer has images of itself as a (French) people or a (silent) majority. The thing it desires above all is less a revolution in point of view than new views, new shots and the creation of a new supply of things that can be filmed. Film-makers who are working 'inside the system' urgently need to recharge their reserves of imagination rather than their signifying batteries (which is something the avant-garde ought rather to do) – their reserves both in the sense of a supply but also an enclosed area or territory. But what can be found in the bourgeois and petit-bourgeois reserves of imagination seven years after 1968?

S.D.

Naturalism is the sleight of hand game whereby those such as young people, immigrants and peasants, who were previously forbidden from making films, excluded from the national film community, and were never seen on the screen, are now suddenly included in fiction films (and in traditional fiction films) *as though* they had always been part of them. They are 'naturalized' in every sense of the word, recognized by the law, made normal, natural and legal, and accede to a sort of 'iconic dignity'. But what is glossed over in this process (which is the foundation of naturalism and its *raison d'être*) is how and why they *break into* the story. In the final scene of *Tout va bien* Godard, in anti-naturalistic manner, films the irruption of the 'new social actors' (young people and immigrants) into a scene which transforms a supermarket into a social theatre. This was a commercial failure for Godard but a success for naturalism, since the former films segregation while the latter presents the fantasy that it has been eliminated. Naturalism cannot exist without segregation.

S.D.

The remains of May 1968

In the memory of the petite-bourgeoisie of our generation May '68 was a general revolt against bourgeois institutions and an *overt* protest against their oppressive machinery.

It was a process whose scope was limited. It occurred, it took place, but it does not belong to serious history. The term 'events' suggests that May is a *romantic addendum* to bourgeois history.

It was a process which was neither politically organized nor strategically controlled, a kind of 'folly' as far as all organizational discourse is concerned.

It was a process which *burst* on to the scene. It was a conflagration of desire which has subsequently appeared to be the original feature in all political discourse concerning young people's movements, 'secondary' political fronts and any movement which appears uncontrollable. It is a distinguishing feature to which all other processes have to be related, not so much in terms of organization and political strategy (everyone is agreed that May '68 was not organized by any particular group) but *in terms of ethical and ideological values*. Since May, a certain intensity in revolt, a certain way of articulating demands, and a certain kind of practice have spontaneously been found among the 'dominated ideologies'.

J.-P. O.

Naturalism and the majority

What is the central issue in the critique of naturalism today? Is it 'modernity'? Is it the refusal to allow the natural to be the source of truth? Is it the need to reflect on the historical codes of realism? Is it the reading of the sign which has finally been freed from the analogical accretions of the image? It is perhaps the idea, adumbrated by Barthes in *Roland Barthes*, that the natural is always legal, and is always underpinned by a social majority. Naturalist films (such as those of Pascal Thomas) must elicit a reassuring and normative reading (yes, that's how it is, 'people' are really like that . . .).

Belonging to the majority is a matter of common forms of behaviour but never ideas (because this is supposed to be a natural, not an artificial community), something whose typical features cannot be exemplified because the typical is always *created in contrast* to something

The majority refuses to consider itself as a group. It is a group with no image of itself. It cannot therefore recognize itself unless it is not described as such, in unmarked images (which do not employ an *already* existing discourse). Such images are, above all, those of naturalism.

Naturalism, which is the form taken by the discourse of the majority, does not allow the majority to be described as in any way typical. But the majority sometimes wishes to describe *minorities*. These must not, of course, detract from the representation of the majority or call it into question. They therefore exist in the form of a closed, stilted and over-coded discourse which has no impact on the viewer – as a discourse of stereotypes. It would therefore appear that the stereotype points to power which is no longer operative, which is already dead – cf. the French Nazis in *Lacombe Lucien*, whom history has already buried, when confronted by a character who cannot be typecast. Boisset is quite as astute as Malle, and the use of stereotypes is the price he pays in order for his film to be 'effective'. As the representative of a social class which is gradually losing status, his Dupont Lajoie has unwittingly lost all his power. He becomes the naive mouthpiece for a racist discourse of which society – in this instance the spectator – disapproves but which in his little world has no name. He has moved from naturalism, a world in which names are not named, to the stereotype for which a name has to be found. The film shows precisely this movement. If Dupont were to succeed in avoiding this process of marking (through, for example, a more convoluted discourse) then the film's famous effectiveness would be diminished. What is sinful is not the thing in itself but the fact that it can be named as what it is, a disgraceful social value outside received opinion.

In this way the stereotype is not reflexive. The spectator must name it but the stereotyped subject must have no access to the name (otherwise it would not be available, it would not be the other which provides a negative definition for myself).

P.K.

Structural existence of the stereotype

There are two kinds of stereotype: first, the character of Schumacher, the bailiff in *Dupont Lajoie*; second, the son in *La Femme de Jean* who belongs to the 'new generation', or the 'hippie' in *Le Mâle du siècle*, or the average French people in *Mariage.*[3]

In the first case, the stereotype is embraced by the film. In the second, it is produced 'innocently' and it is we who name what has no name in the story. But one difficulty is that it might be considered arbitrary and gratuitous to identify these two kinds of stereotype. In this second case, is the 'stereotype' anything other than a simple, slightly contemptuous description, almost a statement of the obvious?

But in both cases we can see that the characters have the same function, which is to create a social category (which is apparently real but is in fact mythical) in which no spectator will recognize himself. How can this be done? By removing all power from the character. The puritanical and asexual bailiff aspires to a social order which is completely outdated, the son receives only a half-tender, half-severe parental look, the average French person is a coward. As for those on the margins of society, we immediately know that they seek no kind of power (and that is why they are tolerated, cf. Berri).[4]

Therefore, in addition to the subjective view (the impression that this has already been seen, or seen too frequently, that stereotypes are wearisome, don't make for enjoyment), a structural determinant is established. The typical characteristics of a stereotype cannot be claimed as their own by any social group that lives, and is conscious of its identity, inside the community.

P.K.

Naturalism and segregation

In *Le Voyage d'Amélie* (as in *Les Valseuses*) suburban hooligans, the new social actors, cease to be offered up to an ethno-sociological gaze. Their marginality is an indication to the audience that this is an image close to them and one they can almost use.

But the price of this naturalization is a new kind of segregation. The old lady is too dignified, the peasants are a backward and exotic tribe who for the first time are excluded by this new deal. In this way, when a representational space is opened up to a new social category in the cinema, a category which is eroticized and therefore prestigious, this is balanced by new forms of exclusion elsewhere: of the peasants (the great absentees from our cinema), of too average French people who can be forgotten without difficulty. Because they can be easily represented they have lost their imaginary potential and any figurative value-added.

P.K.

The stereotype is a trap. It is what is given to the viewer to recognize and discount at the first glance (the bailiff in *Dupont Lajoie*, the boss in *La Coupe à 10 francs*,[6] the collaborators in *Lacombe Lucien,* etc.). The stereotype is what you absolutely cannot identify yourself with. However, the stereotype has an important function because it allows attention to be diverted from the process of typecasting (Lajoie, Lacombe). It is the waste material from typecasting (because it is the corpse of typecasting) but also its backdrop, its negative limitation.

S.D.

It is true that the majority can be given a name. But within a discourse that must, by definition, be different from that of the majority: the stereotype of the 'average French person' with which no one identifies (the couples in *Mariage* or in *On s'est trompé d'histoire d'amour*[7] and the condescending and contemptuous descriptions of their narrowness). But it is also a political vision of a France composed of small and medium-sized businesses, so that the notion of majority is linked with the idea of a certain power, which is, for example, exerted against the apprentice in Condroyer's *La Coupe à 10 francs* or the bill poster in *Lo Païs*.[8]

P.K.

Modes of representation and power

Naturalism is therefore intimately connected with majority opinion, with legality, with implicit norms (it is 'encratic').

Typecasting breaks up the social body, it creates forms of exclusion and antagonism. It describes the lines of force which obtain in the social field today. For this reason its only mode of existence is that of the struggle to be recognized as a type within the work, a struggle for its difference to be named. It is not necessarily 'acratic' (not all differences are antagonistic) but it is at the very least 'paracratic' (it runs two risks: that of becoming dominant and ceasing to be different, of becoming imperceptible because transparent, and that of not deriving from any real power and so becoming a stereotype). Examples of types would be the bill poster in *Lo Païs* or Jeanne in *Rude journée pour la reine*,[9] both of whom start out in a similar 'natural' environment and gradually exclude themselves from it deliberately.

Stereotypes are lifeless typical characters who have become fixed and have entered the public domain (so that identifying them does not procure any particular autonomy, unlike the typical character). They can be talked about by everybody. They represented a power but they lost it.

P.K.

Party discourse and the language of the masses

The trend in contemporary French films (from *Lacombe Lucien* to *Mes petites amoureuses*[10]) is for social space and the range of bit-part players to be diminished. It is a trend which lends greater value to intimism and to the French 'quality tradition'. But these days its specific ideological purpose is to place history and politics in brackets. Malle succeeds in filling in the gaps in official history with a right-wing anarchist discourse, while Doillon places a different anarchist discourse in the interstices of dogmatic activism (his sensitive, spontaneous portrait of the daily lives of apprentices has nothing to do with class consciousness). Condroyer, meanwhile, speaks in a more radical (but also more naive) and ultra-subjective way about alienation (so that there is no connection between the disappropriation that his hero feels in relation to the body and what others, even his friends, might say about it).

In *Les Doigts dans la tête* this leads to a miniature May 1968 reconstituted in a single room (the Bohemian or student setting connotes the marginality of these young rebels by reference to images from the nineteenth century), and in *La Coupe à 10 francs* to the Bressonian closed space of the factory, though it is an ouvrierist Bresson placed in an almost medieval context in which revolt must take quasi-mystical form.

But what would happen if the revolt of these characters, these young workers disguised as petit bourgeois, took collective shape, and if they encountered other workers, if there was an explosion of the closed space of fiction which excludes them from any class group as well as from any collective statement (and condemns them to the role of objects in the bourgeois imagination)? At that point the films would cease to function as sources of individualism and subjectivism. The characters would be recognized as carrying elements of a different ideology within a struggle and within the perspective of a mass debate made concrete by the number of different voices discussing work, trade unions, the political parties and so on. Instead of which Doillon and Condroyer's blind mistrust of (militant) political metalanguage leads the former to avoid the depiction of any political situation and the latter to enclose his character in a scene of mythical struggle to the death, so as to preserve their individuality.

In other words, how to articulate the discourse of the party apparatus and the language of the masses, the organizational point of view and the existential

78

position? Is this a question avoided by these films? It is. But this question raises the issue that the films are there in order to provide no answer.

J.-P. O.

The New Wave of the 1960s continually filmed (and typecast) individuals who had been placed on the edge of 'society' or the 'world' by chance, their own arrogance or the malice that surrounds us. With *Pickpocket*, Bresson provided the *ideological and formal* model for the *mise en scène* of these fringes of society. He furnished the ideological model by making the heroes of his films characters, such as a pickpocket or a saint, who were least susceptible of recuperation (unless by an all-seeing God). And he provided the formal model by filming the gaze which nothing in the world or out of the frame (which amounts to the same thing) could satisfy or *suture*. Bresson invented the means which allowed the confrontation between the actor-object as rebel and the subject-*auteur* as beneficiary of his rebellion to be fetishized. The means to enjoy what the other allowed to escape. 'Model. You tell him what gestures to make and what words to speak. In return he gives you (and the camera records) a *substance*' (*Notes sur le cinématographe*).

French cinema around 1975 records something different. Its problem is not that some person or thing has been completely excluded from it but that various groups have been relatively privileged. These groups include the Party, the group, the gang and the family – all collective entities whose voices are heard in various ways. Small and medium-sized businesses (Sautet, Goretta), petty criminals (Blier, Vergez, Duval, Le Hung), the ghetto of the petit-bourgeois family (Thomas, Boisset), or the great family of the Party (Simon). What these groups have in common is that they are all defensive; they neither struggle nor rebel but try to pull together with the minimum damage to themselves. The Bressonian approach described above is still used but it has become generalized and commonplace. Cf. *La Coupe à 10 francs*.

S.D.

What is a poster? An image in which everything is carefully weighed; which has neither the arrogance of a slogan nor the 'chance quality' of everyday life. The problem the poster poses (both for those who create it and for those who look at it) is the way it incorporates what can be shown, doxa in action, encoding as it is taking place. The poster is always *a compromise formation*, based on the principle of homogenization. For example, a political or electoral poster will be the most appropriate means for representing class alliances. *Il pleut toujours où c'est mouillé* is neither more nor less than the sum total of what the PCF [French Communist Party] must take account of today in its strategy and also have represented or presented in images.

It must show the revolt (of those on the edge of society, the obstinate refusal of André the peasant and the woman schoolteacher); it must also reabsorb these images immediately. Jean-Daniel Simon films what occurs in between *acting out* and taking the Party card, so he needs short bursts of rebellion. A bitter class struggle has to be mimicked (and there must be blood) but no class enemy must be clearly designated (so fascist bully boys are needed). The apparatus of repression such as the police and ideological apparatuses of bourgeois domination such as television or school must be filmed and shown, but they must, above all, not be criticized as apparatuses. 'Leftism' must be taken into account (in the character of the schoolteacher) but it must be reduced to a flaccid and snobbish mixture of 'new ideas' and sexual engagement. That's what a poster is. A collection of pledges which give rise to a series of little tableaux.

S.D.

The three powers

All films mobilize certain values. But for whom? *For a majority of viewers or for a social majority?* Can the cinema audience be identified with a social milieu?

For militant cinema there is a need to produce such divisions and to distinguish between audience and milieu so as to gain a majority among the audience in order to fight the social majority. (But how can this be done? Since Brecht, or even before Brecht, we have known that this is not automatic.)

For naturalism, on the other hand, there is no such distinction (nor indeed are there any risks, since neither the power the film exercises over the viewer nor the power of the bourgeoisie is ever visible in naturalist films).

To take one example, in *Vincent, François, Paul et les autres*[11] power of course remains disguised. This is because the ideology of the film is exactly consonant with a real but declining power in France today (that of small businesses). Therefore there is no typecasting in the majority camp. The boss of the small company, the intellectual and the good employee belong to universal humanity, as in the end does the former Communist. The same ideology and the same class are dominant inside the cinema and outside it. But then the boss of a big company drives up in a Rolls to visit the factory that he is going to buy from the bankrupt Montand. And suddenly we are in the realm of the caricature or the stereotype. So that the point is within the cinema to take power away from something which, outside the cinema, has not yet gained total power – international capitalism.

Let us now turn to the third kind of power, which is both the most obvious and the most disguised by the transparent cinema of diegesis (the story, the signified). Making the story obvious could present a problem for the progressive cinema (and it was something which, for example, all Nouvelle Vague cinema repressed). Even today, naming a power when it is a reactionary form of power which is supposed still to divide French people (Pétainism, Gaullism) appears to be a courageous move which connotes the left.

The Pétainists and French Nazis named in *Lacombe Lucien*, the small businessman who is so sure of himself in *Les Doigts dans la tête*, the secret services under De Gaulle in *L'Attentat*, all point to forms of power. But in these films it is as though naming them was the equivalent to demonstrating their existence, as if a (progressive) point of view implicitly and automatically accompanied these 'tableaux'. But we know that this is not the case. That is why such representations of power have little effect, because they are always representations without meaning, preceding the film's discourse about power. Thus Malle shows the collaborators but also wants to persuade us that one of them is more than a collaborator or something other than a collaborator . . .

For the progressive cinema the problem is that representing power may reinforce the distinction between the cinema audience and the social milieu. Costa-Gavras's film *Section spéciale* was a great disappointment on this score. In it Pétainism is not a metonymy for power today but a great metaphor for the contradiction between the individual and society. There is therefore no difficulty in uniting the audience both against an abstract power, which it is practically impossible to get outside (the resistants do not take part in the contradiction which is presented), and against a concrete situation which is today largely discredited by history.

P.K.

The woman as educator

In *Il pleut toujours*, what renders a woman's desire acceptable and filmable is the fact that she can make use of her knowledge of her desire. The 'leftist' schoolteacher brings some cosmetics to the peasant's wife and sex education to the village children. This enables her to act as a seducer and to demonstrate her sexual liberation. In this way a new character is created, a new stereotype which will undoubtedly recur (see Liv the Swedish girl in *Les Doigts dans la tête*): the woman as educator. Puritanism is the inevitable result of this. The liberated schoolteacher will be accused of not wearing a bra by the most reactionary characters in the story; the viewer laughs at them, forgetting that all he will see of the teacher is an artistic nude back.

Revisionist fiction must be chaste. But like all fiction it needs superfluous desire, some excess to make it advance. The full might of Union Populaire deployed against a few monopolies needs something from outside (such as desire or violence) to be captured, filmed and fictionalized and made to demonstrate its strength and cohesiveness, its capacity to embrace everyone. This is a defensive spectacle.

S.D.

Segregation and racism

Militant criticism is disarmed by *Dupont Lajoie*. This is because the way the film struggles against anti-Arab racism is by permitting racism against fools, thus exacerbating the contradiction between the intelligent and the stupid petite-bourgeoisie which is ultimately the same as the contradiction between the intellectual and the non-intellectual petite-bourgeoisie. This is a firmly rooted and very French tradition, from the *Canard Enchaîné* to today's *Charlie-Hebdo*.[12] Foolishness is most spontaneously revolting because (as Barthes points out) it is fascinating.

Militant critics (usually petit-bourgeois intellectuals) are confronted with a contradiction which is by no means new. On the one hand, they know (History teaches them) that they must prevent this non-intellectual petite-bourgeoisie from tilting to the right and becoming the agent of creeping fascism. On the other hand, they find the greatest difficulty in associating themselves with social strata whose support they wish to secure but whose members they tend to despise (a caricatural example of such contempt is to be found in what the magazine *Foudre* wrote about *Les Valseuses*).

In addition, the film does not assist militant criticism. It can offer no positive alternative to the average French person. The film's anti-racism is purely defensive, that of non-average French people – the policeman, the Italian, the person repatriated from North Africa and the young man.

S.D.

The film *Dupont Lajoie* appeals to a wide public, as Yves Boisset has attempted to do since he began making political films. As far as this particular film is concerned, we should ask whether it has aroused public concern or whether the concern already existed and was waiting to be expressed in such a work, waiting to welcome and embrace what it says, to graft on to it its own language and to see in it a reflection of its own ideological preoccupations.

S.T.

Absence of point of view

Dupont Lajoie is produced by the situation it describes. The film and the pro-filmic material already have an uncertain and imaginary relationship. How do we know this? Even during the shooting no one knew who wanted what. The actor Mohammed Zinet was shot, hotels refused to give rooms to Arab actors, racists congratulated Boisset and told him that people like him were what was needed. There was a mirror relationship between reality and the film, as there was between the film and its audience. The only question really put to the viewer is that of his or her identity: I (we) am (are) like this/other people (not me) are like this. Certainties wavered on both sides of the mirror.

S.D.

Progressive cinema

This is a label which has been empty of meaning for a very long time. It must be recognized that present-day French cinema has not been created by those whom orthodox and militant terminology calls progressives. Such a term described the fellow travellers, left-wing intellectuals and humanists who were still bourgeois and who preferred to become involved with noble causes. Progressive sometimes meant that they themselves could 'progress' (and perhaps become revolutionary artists) and sometimes that although they themselves had incurable limitations they could nevertheless help others to progress a little. A recent typical example of a progressive film-maker is Costa-Gavras. However, a problem arises today because of the fact that it is men like Boisset and Curtelin, neither of whom (but especially Curtelin) can be said to come from that particular progressive stable, who have carried forward the positive project of making an anti-racist film. What should *Dupont Lajoie* be judged against? Should it be judged in relation to a great film which is equally popular but less ambiguous, which can mobilize the masses and is politically irreproachable, against a great 'progressive' film? Such a film does not exist. And Boisset's film asks why it does not exist. We should therefore be asking ourselves not what ideology the Boisset–Curtelin project subscribes to (an ideology which at best tends towards that of anarchism), but why their film occupies an area of ideological struggle which the cinema which we label progressive has abandoned either because it is weak and worn out or because it has simply given up. This is why there is no point in taxing Boisset with lack of perspective or simplistic analysis. In the same way, militant critics overdo things when they give 'critical support' to the film for want of anything better. It so happens that a film such as *Dupont Lajoie* can accuse-attract-impugn its audience without any help from the critics.

S.D.

The risk and the norm

In the end, racism as a theme belongs to the doxa. Everyone has opinions on it, it is a subject which belongs to everyone and everyone ignores or pretends to ignore the fact that it is a subject which cannot avoid stereotypes but which secretes and creates them.

As far as the cinematic apparatus is concerned, 'racism' is also a paradoxical, daring, risky and powerful subject, all of which can be explained by the chronic depoliticization of French cinema. Thus Boisset's film succeeds in having things both ways. Its strength is that it functions within the doxa, feeding its language and its opinions which it both challenges and reinforces, and gives it a stage, an extra performance, a series of images in which its divisions and petty paradoxes can be played out at leisure. But as well as acting within the doxa, the film divides the audience by showing the limits and the margins of the cinematic apparatus.

The audience emerges from the cinema deeply divided. There are those for whom it is (mainly) a film against racism and who will use it as an additional weapon, an extra proof in their anti-racist argument. But in this case who is the enemy? Against whom can this point of view be mobilized? Against another section of the audience by appealing to the contradiction between the intelligent and the Poujadist petite-bourgeoisie? This class fraction (which makes up the audience for *Dupont Lajoie* and for whom the film was made) will take the film at face value as a comedy of manners, up to a certain point, because the second part of the film must provoke a response from the audience. When racism no longer remains an idea but becomes something to be put into practice, when some people (the same kind of people as those in the cinema) try to exclude others in a way that marks the bodies and affects the lives of those who are the victims (through rape, pogrom or manhunt), a new kind of racism occurs against the film itself. This is the risk incurred by a film such as *Dupont Lajoie* when it claims to show the French an accusatory and traumatic image of themselves. There is segregation in the cinema and this is the aim of the film. But what arguments does the film offer anti-racists and how does it help them to transform other people's trauma into a new awareness?

S.T.

Trickery or marketing?

It will be said – to justify Boisset – that you have to play tricks with the apparatus. That is a fair comment and an influential argument. But it presupposes that one cannot do more than the apparatus allows; that one is somehow outside it and only becomes involved under certain conditions. *We must not confuse marketing the apparatus and the stratagems of some progressive film-makers!* Unfortunately, these conditions are often imposed by the apparatus. The opposite rarely occurs. The positive question is: under what conditions can a left-wing film-maker work according to the rules of the artistic apparatus? It is often posed negatively: at what cost and with what compromises does a film-maker agree to work within the financial, fictional, etc., rules of the film art market? Theoretically this question remains where Brecht left it. Can any advance be made on what he wrote if we are satisfied simply with going over the same theoretical ground? Above all, is it possible to ask such a question purely from the Art point of view, taking into account only artistic conditions (the state of artistic techniques, as Brecht would have said) but without making any link with more general ideological and political conditions and the particular and changing way in which such ideologies and policies think or do not think through the way they are reflected in or have an impact on artistic practices? *We must, at one and the same time, politicize the question of artistic stratagems and introduce aesthetics into political questions.*

Left-wing film criticism – it does exist – often gives up when it comes to such issues and is simply content with pointing to the marks of politics which it is able to discern in films, ideologems which the apparatus points to just as such criticism does.

S.T.

Boisset's great skill

Boisset does not move outside his particular genre, he simply 'politicizes' it. By making the first part of the film into yet another jarring comedy on the pitiful exploits of the average Frenchman, he invites the audience to enjoy the satisfaction of the usual game (of seeing themselves filmed) – self-mortification (for being so stupid). This is a well-worn formula (cf. Claude Berri). But by pursuing the logical consequences and the underlying truth of the first part into the second part the viewers are trapped by their own habits of viewing and punished by their own mistakes. Trapping the viewers is what interests Boisset (as it does all film-makers strongly influenced by Hollywood) much more than condemning racism as such which is a noble subject that appeals to people's consciences. In this respect, he works very differently from so-called 'progressive' film-makers. They always pretend to be talking not to an audience but to a collection of consciences gathered together in a cinema (like a jury). In so doing they find it hard to accept that they too are creating entertainment, whereas Boisset takes the audience into account – indeed, that is all he takes into account.

Stupidity and blindness

It is dangerous to talk of stupidity (of *Dupont Lajoie* as a crusade against idiots). As we know, one can talk of stupidity only from a safe place – that of intelligence, to which access depends more on grace than on struggle. This leads to elitist talk which represses the question of power (power is always in some way stupid and *this* is not how you fight against it) as well as the question of point of view (what does it mean when a viewer speaks with an intelligent or enlightened point of view?)

Should we therefore adopt the Brechtian term of reference and speak of blindness? Blindness has the advantage of not implying a value judgment of a given and therefore immutable state of 'human nature'. In itself it represents a questioning or a shifting of the question from: 'Who is stupid (or blind)?' to 'Who benefits from stupidity (or blindness)?'

It can lead from there to 'some' awareness. But we still have to show what causes blindness. Without that, didacticism can degenerate into the merely contemptuous (though this is denied) representation of a member of a class (generally the petite-bourgeoisie). This is, for example, the case in Bertucelli's film *On s'est trompé d'histoire d'amour*, in which a couple, consisting of a middle manager and a switchboard operator, are submerged in an ideology. Blindness quickly degenerates, just as stupidity does, into a state from which nothing, apparently, will allow them to emerge, neither 'politics', which is totally absent from the film, nor their social practice, which is innocent of all conflict, struggle or solidarity. There is nothing positive, except implicitly with the need for someone to see things clearly for them, instead of them, and to teach them to live better (a position which the 'aware' viewer and the film-maker

85

adopt). By contrast, in *Rude journée pour la reine*, there is an attempt to give material form to things which alienate, such as the press, television and family values. In that film the description of blindness can be combined with a real love for the characters because the image of what would be their 'truth' is presented throughout the film. This could show the way out of the ideologism specific to the genre (of its deconstructive and purely critical aspect).

Blindness provides a respite from stupidity. It allows its end to be glimpsed in class consciousness. But can this be *shown*? Can we get beyond the Brechtian problematic of consciousness-raising or does this constitute an impasse for the whole 'ideological criticism' movement?

P.K.

Is *Dupont Lajoie* a film about the racism of the French, a film about stupidity, or a film which invites us to despise the petite-bourgeoisie? We need first to decide what racism and stupidity are.

(1) Are they a lack of intelligence, generosity, tolerance and humanity?

(2) Do they consist of a large dose of bourgeois ideology, egotism and paranoia with fascist tendencies?

(3) Are they to do with sex, with an inability to conceive of relationships with other people or to imagine that those who are different can experience the same form of desire as we do?

If (1) is the case all classes must face this problem, the division crosses all social milieux but, according to Boisset, working-class groups especially because of their living conditions and their promiscuity.

If (2) is the case, then not all social classes have the same *objective* disposition in relation to the problem. Good divisions must be exploited from a particular point of view (Brecht) and class alliances and the critique of racism must be thought through. We therefore cannot get round the fundamental question of how practically to be militantly anti-racist, and this completely overturns the dominant fictional discourses (the way we think that characters in fiction are positive, the way we allow victims of racism to speak).

If (3) is the case, then we are all involved and any show of understanding of others can be attributed to a denial based on liberal humanism. Racism becomes an almost natural reaction, an ineradicable component of the subject, the place in which everything the subject represses is concentrated.

S.T.

Practical racism

It is not enough simply to recall the many sources for racist ideology, whether they are economic, religious, sexual or political, nor to state the way it is articulated with the arsenal deployed by bourgeois ideology to maintain its domination. Beyond – or rather starting from the basis of – moral considerations racism poses a political problem which is precisely *the way it relates to politics*. At what point does racism change from being an ideological practice, a moral attitude towards a different community, into a directly political intervention, a power struggle between two groups or two communities by questioning the responsibility of the state and the government?

To what extent can it be said that the everyday practice of racism which turns it into a mass ideology *prefigures* civil war in a developed society, that is, the direct confrontation between social classes and open conflict or rupture between different fractions of the same class?

Boisset's argument (which bears an astonishing resemblance to Liliana Cavani's in *Night Porter*) that 'racism is dormant in every one of us' cannot take account of the mechanisms which trigger racist actions and gestures. Instead of making the racist gesture something typical or exemplary in a negative way, Boisset makes it seem natural. It is because a member of the community, Carmet, *cannot own up to his sexuality*, and because each of the members of this community might similarly be led to acknowledge their own disturbed sexuality (Tornade and Peyrelon), that a nexus of repressed intensity is created and they defend themselves collectively in order to repress this admission. The racist is paranoid and Boisset's film permits such a reading. Racism, however, is not *simply* paranoia.

We have to explain how racist ideology – and its agents – can gain ground, become implanted in discriminatory practices, in military interventions, going further than the state whose role, in times of civil peace, consists in regulating and pacifying conflicts; that is, in making conflicts acceptable to the various classes. But the *desire for racism* and for exclusion is not deterred by illegality, it takes that risk (Schumacher, man of the right). The contradiction is that racist ideology adores the law. In the community in which the law is obeyed the racist is profoundly normative, the Other cannot be tolerated, nor can the law of the Other. But the self-control of racism waits for the opportunity to explode, to break through the framework of the law and to give free rein to its desire for murder.

Whilst being ultra-normative racist ideology is, at the same time, deeply *illegitimate*. It transgresses the role of the state, it places itself *outside the law*, overtaking the ideology of consensus which it attempts to break up. Racism does not immediately need the backing of an apparatus because it secretly lies within every bourgeois apparatus. It is a supplement which is biding its time, waiting for the moment when it can contaminate the whole fabric of the dominant ideology.

However, *the state is not innocent and this must be demonstrated by anti-racist politics*. There are at least two reasons why it is not innocent. It is responsible for the material organization of the segregation of classes, social strata and ethnic groups, and the source of the many forms of segregation linked to the development of capitalism. The second reason is that it tolerates 'excesses', it does not impose consensus, so that the image of the state as conciliator quickly becomes a deception.

S.T.

Militant anti-racism

Anti-racism finds it extremely difficult to constitute an area of political intervention. We can easily understand that it can be summed up as a humanist, moral, progressive position. But what is its objective? The racist objective exists and it consists in increasing segregation, claiming supremacy for one group over another and denigrating those who inhibit this supremacy. Anti-racism is above all defined by being anti. It is against something and therefore finds it difficult not to be defensive. Anti-racism is triggered not by repression but by its opposite, and in order for it to go on to the offensive it needs to attach itself to a collective project, a common (altruistic and collective) struggle, a common desire which disturbs the blinkered unconscious (and which also works on consciousness). Thus it is difficult to change the field of struggle and hard to ask a film such as *Dupont Lajoie* to do this for us. However, perhaps it does at least help us to think about this question.

S.T.

Stereotype + naturalism = typecasting?

The real 'hero' of *Dupont Lajoie* is not an individual but a trio of average Frenchmen, a little collectivity that is very tight-knit (they go on holiday together) but not very homogeneous. The film is extremely skilful in not erasing the differences among the three men, and if these differences are looked at closely they can help to explain how, by means of what appears to be but is not in fact a paradox, naturalism inevitably secretes its 'opposite', which is typecasting.

In order for the character of Lajoie to achieve a degree of exemplarity (to incarnate the typical 'average Frenchman who is racist because repressed'), he has to be placed between the two extremes or boundaries, inherent in all naturalist cinema, of the stereotypical and the atypical, the caricatural and the natural, or in this case the bailiff Schumacher and Tornade the women's underwear sales representative.

Schumacher, who is the guardian of the moral order, wishes to know nothing about desire (see his first appearance in the film). He wears his castration like a medal and his (racist) language as a substitute. Despite the fact that he is the only 'ideologue' in the film, the only character to think of racism as a policy, the only person to remain monolithic throughout the film (as is characteristic of the stereotype), what he says is not believed by the viewer precisely to the extent that he takes no account of the sexual basis of racism. By contrast. Tornade, who is the least spontaneously racist of the three, succumbs only under the influence of suffering, and only with regret. He has no special language but a kind of common sense and good health which, right from the beginning of the film, we are shown as being associated with a 'normal' and occasionally very active sex life. He thus embodies 'good' human nature and is the most resistant to typecasting. And if he fails to understand what is happening (the racism) this is because, in contrast to his counterpart Schumacher, he is not repressed enough.

There remains Lajoie to occupy the middle ground between the stereotype who lacks a fully rounded personality and the character who is not typical (and who cannot therefore on their own offer any fictional appeal). Lajoie fulfils a very precise role, which is that of repression, a role which is decisive in the sense that the possibility of the return of the repressed gives rise to the possibility of fiction and therefore to the film. Lajoie's unwanted or 'misplaced' desire is necessary for the story to unfold. Boisset is not the only film-maker to make the return of the repressed the motor of fiction and the hidden cause of all catastrophes (though he did so in *R.A.S.*). It is a fictional device typical of Hollywood (in Hitchcock and Kazan) and has recently been used by Malle, Cavani and so on. There is no fiction without desire or without a perspective on desire. But one condition is imperative for this device to work; and that is that there should be space *only* for the viewer, who must be the sole beneficiary, the privileged witness. On this point Boisset does not spare us: not only does the viewer witness the rape but the victim is always seen through Lajoie's eyes (and has no filmic existence outside his gaze). It is up to the viewer, and only the viewer, to stick the label racism = repression on to something which everyone else (racists like Schumacher and anti-racists like the policeman or the Italian) merely sees as sexual excitement.

S.D.

Imagination and racism

We lack a theoretical framework within which to talk about racism and, more generally, about any phenomenon of social segregation (of which racism is only the most flagrant aspect). In order to understand such a phenomenon perhaps we should follow the line of current commonplaces such as: 'We've got nothing against such people but we wouldn't want our daughter to marry one of them . . .'

This points to the fact that it is the family which serves as the principal ideological means of segregation in France, especially in social categories whose identity is created by groups of families and in which the organization of the family, family relationships and the couple constitute the typical basic traits of their identity (this is primarily true of the middle classes or the petite-bourgeoisie).

Racist discourse is constituted on this basis and is embodied by organizing the differences perceived in others (in this case other ethnic groups) into systems of opposition in relation to the characteristics which are typical of their own identity or of their 'specular image'. This is brought out, for example, in *Rumeur d'Orléans* (1969), in which the account of the imaginary kidnappings of women organized the fictional subversion of the institution of marriage (with the migration to the Orient, erotic bargaining, prostitution, polygamy), achieved through stereotypes of oriental or 'primitive' sexuality. How does such a discourse work in practice? In this film, as *fantasy*. Bourgeois racism fantasizes sexuality, the couple and the family. It unleashes fantasies about the migration of women outside marital institutions, subverts the rules of matrimony and invents new ones.

For such fantasies to be set off some (real or imaginary) attack must be made on an element which is fundamental to the social fabric (families). All it requires is for a few schoolchildren to be absent from school and to come home later than usual (as was no doubt the case in Orléans).

But this is merely the general ideological underpinning of our racism, its commonplace form. And it is precisely this commonplace which is depicted in *Dupont Lajoie*, which integrates the specular image of the petite-bourgeoisie and the middle classes – which are to be seen in all recent films on 'middle France' (composed of a group of families) – into an ideologically racist scene in which all the families on holiday confront a small group of Arabs who have no family, no women and therefore no children and whose relationships and sexuality are therefore problematical.

But it is completely misleading to the extent that it opposes a sexist discourse which claims to fight racism ideologically (thus: the bourgeois family is the source of repression, and repression is the cause of racism – you are racist because you are repressed) to the commonplaces of racist ideology (and fantasy) by moving them from one side to the other (you are obsessed with the idea that the Arabs are going to take your women, but you will rape your neighbour's daughter).

In fact we do not for one moment get away from the racist imagination. As Boisset depicts it, racism is fantastic, irrational and cannot be appropriated. The viewer is deprived of all reference to its concrete ideological mechanisms and its everyday manifestations. He comes out of the film either scandalized or speechless.

As an ideological event such a spectacular demonstration of the commonplaces of racism resembles *Night Porter* (the cliché this time is that Nazism is erotic). In both films the narrative is organized to show a fortified position on to which there bursts a scandal which affects the mythology of the viewer who is not directly involved in racism or fascism: *reality is worse than what you imagined but it is also exactly as you imagined it* (the ideology of the *fait divers*).

J.-P. O.

The film too readily lets the characters get away with what they do. The people who are in positions of power are completely outside the fiction, lawgivers who are ultimately neutral. The state administers the law (badly). Yet again, the policeman has the greatest awareness and the most humanity. The two people who are against the racist attack are not French and do not provide the viewer with an alternative point of view within the fictional framework. The young man (Lajoie's son) uses the racist episode to settle his own scores with his family. In doing so he takes a small step forward and one can only wish him luck. Finally, there is the Arab worker's attempt at revenge, at the end of the film. This closes the circle, suspends the fictional narrative, but cannot be assumed or accepted by any fictional character or by any member of the audience. The reason for this is that it represents the return of the dominant fictional economy: we agree to make a film 'about racism' that half a million people in Paris will pay to see, provided that it does not offer a positive alternative or give any assistance to the establishment of a different point of view.

S.T.

Translated by Jill Forbes

Notes

1 *Les Doigts dans la tête* (Jacques Doillon, 1974); *Dupont Lajoie* (Yves Boisset, 1974).
2 Yves Boisset's films of this period were glossy political and social thrillers such as *Un Condé* (1970) and *L'Attentat* (1972).
3 *La Femme de Jean* (Yannick Bellon, 1974); *Le Mâle du siècle* (Claude Berri, 1975).
4 Berri's work includes several films on Jewish themes, including *Le Vieil Homme et l'enfant* (1967), an evocation of his own childhood as a Jewish boy in Occupied France.
5 *Les Valseuses* (Bertrand Blier, 1974).
6 *La Coupe à 10 francs* (Philippe Condroyer, 1975).
7 *On s'est trompé d'histoire d'amour* (Jean-Louis Bertucelli, 1974).
8 *Lo Païs* (Gérard Guerin, 1973).
9 *Rude journée pour la reine* (René Allio, 1973).
10 *Mes petites amoureuses* (Jean Eustache, 1974).
11 *Vincent, François, Paul et les autres* (Claude Sautet, 1974).
12 Satirical weeklies. *Le Canard Enchainé* gained an international reputation for its political lampoonery. *Charlie-Hebdo*'s style was much broader.

4

ROUND TABLE ON CHRIS MARKER'S *LE FOND DE L'AIR EST ROUGE*

('Table ronde sur *Le Fond de l'air est rouge* de Chris Marker', *Cahiers du Cinéma* 284, January 1978)

Jean-Paul Fargier, Thérèse Giraud, Serge Le Péron,
Jean Narboni, Serge Daney

JEAN-PAUL FARGIER: I often feel very close to the feeling of Marker's film in so far as it is, I think, the film of a generation. That is, ten years – 1967 to 1977 – and what took place from the point of view of the Revolution, witnessed by a generation which passed through Stalinism and who were militants before me. I feel myself very close to this sensibility, to its re-examination of Stalinism, its despairs and disillusionments.

THERESE GIRAUD: The film aspires to be a collage of different moments but in fact I find it highly linear in construction. What is examined is the idea of collective memory, of rediscovering a legacy in the present. The vision of history presented at the beginning of the film is there right up to its end.

FARGIER: I believe it to be a highly personal film, the film of someone who says 'we' because he feels himself in sympathy with a dozen or so people with whom he lived through those years, people such as those we hear on the soundtrack: Signoret, Montand, Périer and also Régis Debray . . . But I quite understand that we will not agree, that it will not have the same resonance for others . . .

SERGE LE PERON: These voices – so well known, coded, and immediately resonant – have a curious status in relation to those ten years. They are effectively the voices of a generation before ours and are made to appear as if they speak right from the heart of that generation while at the same time saying that this was never really so. And it's this that troubles me about the film, the idea of attributing a kind of paternity to the children of May '68, the 1960s generation. There is a deep ambiguity in the film. The 'we' address makes it appear as if these voices had all been part of this era –

92

body and soul, and with all the faith that this implies – while they were already, because of the ideology of the left and the status it offered intellectuals for example, outside of it. It's as though they believed in a sense of history but never in the events when they happened; as though they knew in advance that things were always going to go badly.

JEAN NARBONI: We ought to talk about the film and the effect of an event that it produces. What is it that contributes to this effect? The scale and scope of the film, its duration, the madly ambitious side of the project – a balance sheet, a summing-up – the research that went into it, the quality of its documents, and of course Marker himself as a sort of reference figure, as a guarantee of integrity in the area of political cinema. And the critics have noted the film's difference from its predecessors in Marker's work: the relative abandonment of over-elaborate stylistic effects, the less oppressive role of the commentary, the questioning of the provenance of the images, etc. The only question I would pose is whether this film is not simply a refinement of Marker's system. Is it not a matter, ultimately, of a fairly outmoded film arising from an old-fashioned concept of politics *and* history *and* film?

FARGIER: What's new, I think, is that one is constantly confronted with a game of ping-pong, with the reactions of ideas and sensibilities. Sometimes we agree with them, sometimes not. Sometimes we believe that a particular discourse expresses the film's point of view, then a little further on it is contradicted. There is here a sort of game of juggling with discourses. For example, the sequence where the film-makers are in a cutting room, discussing the as it were unequalled importance of Marxism-Leninism. Immediately afterwards we cut to Castro on the cult of the book. It's put here as a critical comment on the abstraction and dogmatism of the argument of the people in their cutting room. A little further on, there will be several sequences showing Castro's evolution and Castro himself being criticized. Another example: Marchais[1] and Elleinstein are shown in a way such that the contradictions in the Communist Party over Chile are made apparent. First Marchais says, 'Chile is proof that we can succeed in France'; then, when Chile has returned to a dictatorship, Marker shows a television clip of Elleinstein saying, 'Chile can never be taken as an example, we've never suggested that.'

NARBONI: Of course, there are layers of argument in the film. But its overall organization ultimately produces a *single* argument which the commentary of course never states but which is subtly there for the viewer to infer, which I take it is as follows: 'It is impossible to consider or to practise a politics that doesn't go via the Communist Party (French or otherwise).' From start to finish the film hammers away at this one idea – 'Criticize the Communist parties all you like, give them no credit, reform them, advise them but whatever else, if you don't go via them, there's no hope.' The whole film is focused round the question of the Party, that's its centre. And what's the result? For me it's that the film can incorporate only elements, movements and forces that are themselves part of this question, that cannot be considered other than as a part, even a contradictory part, of the question of the Communist parties. Marker leaves it in the air; he cannot accommodate any of today's political forces which dismiss all this, which no longer even resent or despise the Communist parties, knowing that it's all happening elsewhere; forces that are no longer haunted, truly haunted as Marker is, by the Party question and the question of 'Where do I position myself in relation to it?'

And it's precisely those forces which are the most original and lively in politics today that the film can't take account of – all the demands for a 'civil society', the radicalism of the Italian movements, the independence movements, the ecologists (Europeans, and not just the Japanese, which is too easy), who are displacing the old oppositions, the old political dualisms, and also women (seen otherwise than they are at the end of Marker's film) . . . I'm not even talking about the absolute and shameful silence about the Palestinians, which relates, though only partly, to what I've been saying. For me, all this is indicative of the film's old-style politics. There's practically no sign of today's new movements.

GIRAUD: If he doesn't mention the Palestinians it's because his film is ultimately Eurocentrist, even if he's talking about Latin America, at a time when there's no problem about making a connection with France. At this moment, the main problem of the left is how to be a Communist without being Stalinist. It's this problem that dominates the whole of the film's second part. Having shown the phenomenon of the street demonstrations, a little too Che-Guevara-style, in May '68, Marker doesn't show anything of the post-'68 period. He represents '68 with a police cordon, a CGT[2] cordon on one side, the leftist marshals on the other, and between them an empty space to be occupied, a kind of junction point to be located. And from here he rewrites history, returning to this question as the motor of the whole story.

FARGIER: Even if there are more and more people today who are no longer involved with it, you can't avoid bringing up the problem of the Communist parties, who are still on the political scene. With the slide into vulgar Marxism, for example, they have an increasing amount of power in a lot of areas. To my mind, it's important to come back to all this, especially if it's a road you've travelled a lot. If Marker doesn't show what's happened in Italy, it may be because at the time he was finishing the editing (which he had started three years earlier). He has another way of switching track, of opening up a space other than that of the Communist parties, and that's the cats sequence. 'Cats are never on the side of power.' It's a way of saying a great many things . . .

NARBONI: I'm not suggesting that we ought to stop thinking about the Communist parties, Stalinism and so on. I'm saying that such thinking could maybe lead us in another direction, whereas the film does this in order to *come back* to this question, and to make us come back to it. This is the way it's organized, like the way television debates are structured. No matter that opinions differ or clash about a subject or a problem or an issue, the important thing is that the debate *produces this subject* as an indisputable subject for debate. I'm blaming Marker not for not including shots of what happened in Italy, but for not taking account of the spirit of those events. In fact, this is the film of a spiritual adviser, a morose instructor of the Communists and the traditional left, hoping to fill the empty space between the two contingents that Thérèse Giraud was talking about, the space between the finally destalinized, democratized Communists and the 'serious', non-devout, non-sectarian left.

FARGIER: Maybe there is something of that in the film, but it's not only that. Because there is also the permanent obsession, the permanent agonizing over how to make a revolution, how to change the order of things without causing a massacre. The film is caught up in the same dilemma as we are. The first image is from *The Battleship Potemkin*, the screaming woman on the Odessa steps, overlaid with the voice of Signoret saying that this image evokes memories for her. And the final image is of animals in the desert, blasted to death by a helicopter. Two images of death.

LE PERON: The film gives the impression of being the same old story. What's said about the last ten years could have been said about the world in the 1930s and 1940s, especially in the USSR. The limitation of people like Marker, Signoret and Desanti[3] – people who are now doing the thinking about the left, revolution, Marxism etc. – is a post-Stalinist masochism which they don't want to leave behind. Ever since Sartre's *Les Mains sales* perhaps, we've had fragile, outstretched hands, hands cut off, which recalls Jean-Louis Bory in the *Nouvel Observateur* saying, 'I'm one of those who think that hands grow again.' It's thinking about the decade to come in the same way as the one that has passed. It's imprisoning us within an ideology which, if no longer expressed in the form of a violent, dogmatic, openly didactic voice-off (which is really prehistoric), precisely because of the tone of voice of the people speaking, permeates the film all the more. Even if it's not a lesson, it's an invitation to start again.

FARGIER: You make it sound as though all these questions couldn't crop up again, couldn't still demand to be answered. They're extremely persistent, all these questions about the problem of the Communist parties! Personally, I like hearing these voices and everything they carry over from that period.

LE PERON: I don't agree. It's a way of recoding the past, but it's possible to see things differently, in a way that's not necessarily 'historical-materialist' or 'dialectical-materialist'. And this issue isn't even raised in the film. But it's a current of thought that's still running today.

SERGE DANEY: I haven't seen the film, but let me butt in here. From the outset you've put two questions without putting them. Is the film linear or not? Is it a monologue or not? Is there a single discourse involved or several? And a subsidiary question. Are the voices of Signoret and others the voices of actual experience or are they rather the voices we've heard in all films of the left, *La Spirale*[4] included?

GIRAUD: I think it simply comes down to the problem of enunciation. The 'we' and the 'I' involve actual experience, but at the same time that side of things marked by the whole Stalinist period doesn't appear, as you say. Marker doesn't place his enunciation; instead, he pretends to have an alternative one, the one that belongs to a new generation which starts with Vietnam, May '68 . . . And this is presented as though it were untouched by all these problems. It's a sleight of hand to make these problems reappear, completely unchanged, as if they were something new, something purified.

FARGIER: Even so, they're not so different from us! They were of their time – Vietnam, for example.

LE PERON: Yes, but theirs was an interpretation of the events that did not correspond with what was really going on. When the Vietnamese were fighting, as Signoret says, they were saying 'Peace in Vietnam!', not 'Victory to the NLF!' But that was what was involved and about to happen: the victory of the NLF.

GIRAUD: I find myself feeling utterly frustrated, deprived, not as an individual subject but as a historical subject caught up in different tendencies which may not have been very well managed, but that's how it was, and the mistakes are also important – the too much and the not enough. Marker deals with everything in a flash. It all works at the level of metonymy – one image for the whole. Look, this is Vietnam, there it is! It's an old comrade with all his experience and that's how it works for people.

FARGIER: Often, what he shows is what he's filmed himself . . .

NARBONI: This question of metonymy is important and perhaps we'll come back to it when we talk about how the film is pieced together, the way it's structured. In any case, as far as linearity and a single voice are concerned, I think that for all its confusions and bifurcations and so on, in the final analysis the film is wholly preoccupied with a 'dialectical', directional, completed, teleological idea of history, of the 'clock of world history' kind. Except that it could represent something like the 'negative moment'. The title of the film is clear enough: *Le Fond de l'air est rouge*. A classic piece of socialist thinking of the type that sees every illness as the dawning of a cure, every setback as a potential advance, every collapse as a rebuilding, etc. In what way does this film differ from a unanimist[5] fiction such as Rancière defined it, where the question is how to make the perspectives *converge* on a fiction of the 'we're coming from here' type? This is the *subject* of the film. And the more contradictory positions there are at the outset, the more oppositions to absorb, and the more benefits to be had when this convergence is put in place. It's hardly surprising that Bory should put the finishing touches to this work of negativity when, after the comment about weak hands and hands cut off, he adds, 'but hands will always grow again' etc. The film demands this conclusion. And Richard Roud is absolutely right when he says in the press book for the film that Marker is attempting to unify voices that were previously discordant.

FARGIER: You're right, but at the same time the opposite also applies: it's clever, crafty and I'd even say perverse. The question that also arises is: what are you allowed to despair of today? The sequence with the cats shows a wish to locate a somewhere else where these questions would no longer have to be asked.

LE PERON: It's also a matter of interpellating the grass-roots militant communist. We are carried along by the sense of history, and we know that this sense of history can lead us into terrible disasters – anyway, there is a contradiction in wanting to make a revolution since one day the revolution will be in power and power is a bad thing, etc. There's no suggestion of a break with all this, a break that was made by May '68 and many other things that have happened since.

The reverse side of the film, its positive face, might be *Milestones.*[6] In this case, we never see a real collective enunciation, something which through its *écriture*, its fiction, might offer the possibility of saying 'we'.

FARGIER: There are other things that strike you in the film, the way it brings together different voices, the way it lets us hear two very separate discourses which suddenly sound the same. For example, Allende's speech to the factory workers when he asks them, 'Why aren't you involved in politics?' Every leader's ritual chant to his subjects: get involved, get involved. Then there is the Rateau sequence where the militants say, 'There are only a few of us, why aren't the others involved? We have to convince them.'

LE PERON: But Allende is hardly an evil power figure . . .

FARGIER: Precisely. Suddenly you sense the exhaustion of a discourse that you credit with good sense and which is now completely empty. The film has no answer for these impasses, but it sets them up.

DANEY: After seeing the film, did any of you change your ideas about these ten years of history?

NARBONI: As far as I'm concerned, no, not really. Yes, there are some moments that are very powerful, striking, even overwhelming. The secret reunion of the Czech Communist Party, the American pilot in Vietnam, Allende's daughter . . . They provide new 'supporting evidence', but they don't really change the case, in terms of the way you think about politics.

LE PERON: Except as regards May '68 perhaps, where the argument was, 'The great thing about May '68 was that everyone was talking' – and where he's been cruel or smart enough to show us that there was a lot of rubbish said then. For instance, the fellow who says, 'I don't know if I can go on with you because I was on the barricades', and then suddenly explains how you make a revolution. Also Vilar at Avignon . . .[7]

GIRAUD: An image, for Marker, works like a word, an abstraction, and from there he completely remakes grammar, he has no problem in crossing boundaries. There's a quite spectacular example of this, which starts at Rateau. Someone mentions the death of Pompidou, and suddenly we leave Rateau and find ourselves at Notre-Dame, with Nixon, then we go on to the cats, then to Japan . . . What bothers me about this is that it always works by presuming a prior knowledge. I mean, if you haven't followed the main line of militancy, the line of the leftist leaders (Vietnam, Che, '68), you're all at sea. And Marker isn't getting through to anyone here, either those who were there or those who weren't.

FARGIER: What interests me above all is the personal interrogation of the images. I find the sequence where he says 'You never know what you're filming' very affecting. You think you're filming a trooper and you're actually filming a counter-revolutionary.

NARBONI: That said, I find the treatment of Castro a little too much 'you never know what you're filming'. Yes, one knows the place Castro has in Marker's life, but there are still moments when you have to say no. Castro's speech on Prague is one of the most contemptible and twisted things I've ever heard in politics. You remember it? 'Yes, of course the Soviet stance is morally indefensible, but politically . . . And what should the Czech people do? Of course they should not accept this, but we must be careful: if they rebel, aren't they going over to the CIA camp, joining the enemies of socialism? And can the USSR stand by and watch the dismantling of people's democracies? No, no, no, I tell you no.' This is a ghastly mix of precautionism, denials and distortions. Well, of course, we see this awfulness in the film and that's good. But then at the end it's all made up for, blurred, forgotten, because in the USSR Castro bumps into microphones that won't bend. Everyone laughs, and we're on Castro's side against those naughty, stiff Soviet microphones. A gag makes us imagine all kinds of heresies about Castro, and the trick's done, the speech about Prague is forgotten. For someone like Marker who's been knocked sideways by Prague and who shows this throughout the start of the film's second part, it's a bit too much of a conjuring act, a balancing act.

LE PERON: Here's the disillusionment, the despair — the intense desire to preserve the imagery of the left, socialism and the sense of history.

NARBONI: How does Marker link up the images, make this imagery work? Through analogies, metaphors, metonymies, associations — it scarcely matters. The film's foundation, its generating formula, is the colossal analogy of its opening, with *Potemkin*. Since Marker likes both metaphors and cats, one could say: in the dark night of repression all cats are grey. All these shots of repression around the world gathered round the Odessa steps. After that the film can only spread out, open up, stretch out this structure with facile and shaky associations.

FARGIER: But these equivalences are questioned. The idea of death as a unifier (we're always finding ourselves behind funeral processions – like the Overney sequence and many others) – this is questioned.

GIRAUD: Marker concludes the sequence on May '68 by moving on to Ireland and elsewhere, the idea being that the same thing happened everywhere. Maybe. But a few days previously I'd heard Schmidt[8] on television saying, 'Baader[9] is not a German phenomenon, there are also the Palestinians, the Basques, the Corsicans, the Irish.' All this to say that Germany had nothing to do with it, that it was a sign, a curse of the times that had come down from above, and nothing could be done about it – the modern plague. I'm putting these two sounds and images together. From the point of view of an 'I', a subjectivity – it's my own vision and I have every right to be a poet – it comes down to an argument that blocks all differences, levels everything down, and says, 'This is the meaning of history.' This depends on a terrorism of experience – I was there, I was everywhere – that we should really put an end to. He's acting as a classical historian, in fact – on the basis of a supposedly all-inclusive knowledge, a position of superiority (it's his speciality), he sorts through, rearranges and manipulates the documents, rewrites History. He says 'I', granted, but it's already the 'I' of the historian who's seen everything with his own eyes but is still interested because there's material in all this . . .

FARGIER: But why can't you grant Marker the right to think differently from you, to think for himself and others? Why don't you want to hear an argument other than your own? You should make your own film, from your own documents and with your own vision of ten years of history. I think this film reflects a subjective despair, and that's one of the reasons it's interesting.

NARBONI: I'd like to return to analogy and association as they work in the film. Godard, for example, works far more through metamorphoses than through metaphor, but it's also true that in *Ici et ailleurs* he sets up rhymes, likenesses, comparisons (the word 'popular' as it relates to Hitler, Thorez, Lenin; the use of the raised hand by all three of them, etc.). But just as it's the *'et'* in *Ici et ailleurs* which interests him, in these comparisons it's less the terms compared that concern him than the *how*. When he replaces one transparency with another it's the gesture of 'I replace' that counts. And when he says 'How is it?', you can be sure that whatever the reply – if he gives one – it's never 'It's self-evident.' What's troubling about Marker isn't that this metaphorical process is there but that it's made natural, erased as such. Hence the extraordinarily simple switching from one sequence to another – for instance, linking a shot of the CRS[10] at Cerizay to an act of repression in Ireland in order to introduce women. I'm not using the primitive Marxist line – 'Ho, ho, watch out, he's not analysing the specific differences between the Cerizay struggle and the Irish women's struggle' – I'm saying that in film terms it's too easy, ultimately very like the Marker of old, and it makes for political confusion.

LE PERON: It's like Ulrike Meinhof[11] and the old woman in the ghetto. It's the relationship of the images that causes the problem. For example, Marker appears to think that all movements, all violence, all demonstrations are alike. When you see them all linked together, and you can recognize them (which he doesn't make easy), you see that it's not all the same, as when during the left-wing demonstrations you see people running, zooming off like missiles. In terms of manipulating cinematic images (images in movement), there are things he should have been interested to show – different movements of the same general kind (demonstrations, women, etc.). There were fantastic things to bring out in the immobility of Prague, everything stopping for a moment, people saying we've had enough of the sense of history, we're stopping, we're opposing it with the craziest things (our bulk, our inertia, as Baudrillard has said).

You still have the idea of a pre-composed soundtrack, even if it is an intelligent and subtle film.

GIRAUD: How do we explain (I'm sticking to this) that he doesn't mention the Palestinians, even though at the very last moment he's found a way of situating the women's movement, for example? In the first place there's an answer outside the film, which is that history is also being made over there, even if it's less immediate for us, and it's being made in terms that are of absolutely no interest to him – he doesn't want to know. Hence the total exclusion of the Palestinians, even as dead bodies, even when he's talking about Munich.[12] And there's also the fact that if he had mentioned them, then in terms of his wholly associative method he would have had to talk about them and he couldn't do that. It's not within our compass, which is to say that it partly passes us by, that there's no readily available discourse to be had there, no well-framed images all ready to taken in.

NARBONI: I'd like to say, finally, that this is a very 'Editions Maspéro'[13] film (and François Maspéro has a role in it). It's the 'Maspéro spirit', with the whole range of contradictory positions that are found in Maspéro publications, but nothing else. And without underestimating the importance of this work, I'd also say that in the last few years the newest political thinking has also come from elsewhere – from Editions de Minuit, Gallimard, Seuil, 10/18, Flammarion, etc. – and there's no trace of that in this film.

Translated by Chris Darke

Notes

1 Georges Marchais, leader of the French Communist Party from 1972.
2 CGT: Confédération Générale du Travail, the powerful Communist-led trade union.
3 Dominique Desanti, leftist writer.
4 *La Spirale*, a film by Armand Mattelart, discussed by Serge Toubiana in *Cahiers* 265.
5 The literary theory of *unanimisme*, developed by Jules Romains, asserted the interdependence of a given social group. It arose out of a shortlived experiment in communal living when in 1906 a group of French writers (notably Georges Duhamel),

artists and musicians set up in a house in Creteil, near Paris, where they grew their own vegetables, operated their own printing press, etc. Cf. the similar movement established by William Morris in Britain. The revolutionary Marxist Jacques Rancière was interviewed in the *Edinburgh Magazine*, no. 2, 1977.

6 *Milestones*: see Chs 10 and 11 in this volume.

7 Jean Vilar, founder of the Théâtre National Populaire, which every summer took its repertoire to Avignon.

8 Helmut Schmidt, Social Democrat chancellor of West Germany, 1974–82.

9 Andreas Baader, co-leader (with Ulrike Meinhof) of the West German urban guerrilla group, the Red Army Faction.

10 CRS: the French security police, notorious for their uncompromising tactics during the May '68 'events'.

11 Ulrike Meinhof: see note 9.

12 Munich: i.e. the terrorist attack on the Israeli team at the 1972 Munich Olympics.

13 François Maspéro was the proprietor of a bookshop, 'La joie de lire', and the publisher of political writers such as Frantz Fanon. His influence on *Cahiers* had been decisive in terms of its political stances, particularly over the Algerian war. See Antoine de Baecque, *Cahiers du Cinéma: Histoire d'une revue 2, 1959–1981: Cinéma: tours détours*, Paris, Cahiers du Cinéma, 1991, p. 169. (Translator's note.)

Part II

PERSPECTIVES

5

A MATTER OF CHANCE

('Le hasard arbitraire', *Cahiers du Cinéma*
262–3, January 1976)

Serge Toubiana

It's through the reactions of the critics that we begin to see what's unacceptable in *Numéro deux*: continuity and repetition.

Godard had been silent for some time, and the film world, the critics, had few complaints. The cinema's bad conscience was saying nothing, had calmed down, in exile far from Paris, far from the places where films are made and discussed. In this latest film, by going back to the beginning, with a new enthusiasm for video, and amateur actors with strange accents, Godard continues to pose the same questions. What is an image? Just an image, but what else?

And there's nothing the critics find more boring than when something, a film, a voice in a film made within the system, questions itself ad infinitum, poses the same question over and over again. What does it mean to *make films*? What are you doing if you refuse to play the cinema's game, if you can't take it for granted like everybody else? Godard is, if you like, the little cog in the big wheel that Lenin talks about in connection with revolutionary culture, but one that, instead of contributing to forward movement, throws you out of gear, forces you back to your starting point, to the original question: what is the practice of film-making?

One understands the critics' qualms when faced with this type of question. It says that the desire to be inscribed in a history of the cinema is wishful thinking; it completely undermines any belief in the progress of cinematic art; it rules out the evolutionary view according to which the cinema, from Lumière to Rivette, has forged its own past, its own background, its own reservoir of forms. The cinema has no past, and therefore it has no future: we have to return to the starting point of art (destruction precedes construction, says Mao, and any artistic revolution requires artistic destruction, that's to say, the destruction of myths).

There must therefore be regression, and the idea of the cinema's non-progress, non-advance, must somehow be inscribed. Godard takes on Gutenberg and printing. There was a before-printing and an after-printing, a before-Gutenberg and an after-Gutenberg. He encourages us to think about everything that printing has destroyed and look for 'the crimes committed by the news media'.[1] To consider how it was that social relations could do without printing and what the repercussions were on the imaginary and the symbolic.

But is there a before-the-image and can there be an after-the-image? Can the image and the photo be passed by, can they be forgotten? Can one imagine social relations without the image, without film, or new social relations without new images, without a new way of looking at images?

Before you imagine, you have to destroy: in *Numéro deux* the image is smaller than the screen, it carries with it its black border which frames it and announces the colour of death. It has in tow that part of itself which will be for the spectator the tomb of his eye (as Serge Daney says), that black strip which forces the image to occupy less than the whole field of vision, to play with the eye's imaginary plenitude, its insatiable capacity for enjoyment, so as to draw it along into death. *Numéro deux* is a filmic catastrophe for the spectator's eye which doesn't know what to do with the screen.

'The unbelievable is what you don't see' (Ferré[2]), and the image is what you see and what you imagine; but how can what you see be described? Usually, what you see is day, and light; and what you don't see is night and anything that's outside your field of vision. Here day is night and night is day (Ferré). Things are reversed: the image is light, life, and it is also darkness, death. It is *both* in an atmosphere of violence, it is the river and its banks, and the river grown impatient of its banks.

The unbelievable is also this: how can a film-maker invest his whole life (and the spectator a moment) in something, an image, of which we can't even say where it comes from, or where it is going, and whose duration is so illusory ('before I was born, I was dead', writes the little girl)?

We are living in a period of image techniques, where everything the spectator invests in the image, in film, with his eye, his brain and also his body is not invested elsewhere, that's to say in social relations without images, in communication.

To go to the cinema is to try to sidestep social relations in favour of imaginary relations, to relate to oneself alone through an imaginary and phantasmic other, to immerse oneself in the religion of the metropolis — the narcissistic relation of self to self coinciding with the period in which imperialism is reaching the point of total collapse.

The final phase of the Gutenberg era is the word inscribed on a screen, electronically, in the black frames of *Numéro deux* as on airport screens. The letters, the words follow on from each other mechanically — between one letter and another, how many millions of images per second! — automatically, without our being able to see the hand that starts the machine, that programmes it. It is an image of the arbitrary, of a hidden power, a power which it never occurs to anyone to criticize: one which has no counter-field because it is not inscribed in the field itself.

The Gutenberg era in its final phase – the complete opposite of the world of small businesses[3] – is the antechamber of the image, it is writing-and-image (the titles are no longer titles but title-images), or something that goes beyond the image, a new image that would break the frame of the imaginary and deprive the spectator of any imaginary: an image that is arbitrary and a matter of chance.

Godard stages the relation between statement and despotism: if the film-maker consents for the first time to be filmed, to film himself, to appear in the field, it means that he too consents to being stated by the image, written by it; he gives his body to the image as one gives one's body to science, accepting that it will be dissected and that on it the marks of death will be inscribed. Statement in the cinema is the contract signed between Gutenberg and what comes after (television), a contract between discourse, the text (the old) and how it appears in filmic representation. No film-maker is as blunt in staging the violence of this contract, and the fact that it is unacceptable above all to the spectator's eyes, in the concrete sense that it hurts your eyes and has an unsettling effect.

A film made with new equipment and the latest techniques will say nothing more than a film by Lumière. It can just about say things differently. In *Numéro deux* Godard is perhaps looking back: no longer do we find the grand Marxist-Leninist discourse of *Vent d'est* or the grand theory of *Lotte in Italia*. There we were still dealing with the discourse of the other (Gorin, perhaps), the historical and implacable, the grating super-ego: how can a petit-bourgeois film-maker, an artist, encounter or give an account of May '68 and left-wing ideas?

Numéro deux: how can a film-maker, a man, account for feminist discourse, how can male discourse (that of the technician, the one who makes the images, who has the filmic know-how) meet up with the discourse – one should also say the voice or cry – of the woman? And how can discourses co-exist in the illusory democracy (democracy = coexistence + struggle) of a sound-track and an image-track, where the truth of the other's discourse is conveyed in the images and via the sounds without it being possible for a man, for an '*auteur*', to assume responsibility for them.

Contradiction: the discourse of truth (the woman's revolt, the actress's revolt, *her lesson*) depends for its presentation on an outdated apparatus of production and power, an apparatus made for other truths, and that causes anguish. A discourse that has its own language comes face to face with another language, film-language or image-language. 'Wordplay is a word slipping on something, it's language and then after all it was love that taught us language, that had a hand in the process, at least – which explains the slipping, the short-circuits, the interferences . . .' (Godard): short-circuits between the language (of the woman) that teaches us *love* and the image (of the man) that teaches us *desire*.

This relation of reciprocal self-teaching between woman and man, between sound and image, this suggestion of being back at school (the image-blackboard), unthinkable without masochism and violence, can always be seen at work in Godard's films.

Godard speaks *differently* about this and that, has a different way of discussing the topics that everyone discusses. *Numéro deux* falls back on the family, daddy, mummy and the others, the children, the old people. The family — the ideological apparatus within reach, and therefore within reach of the camera and easy to aim at, the easiest to criticize on the basis of one's own experience because it's the closest, but also the hardest to handle because you can't separate yourself from it. Precisely the apparatus for washing your dirty linen. To make a film about how you wash your dirty linen in the family is to represent social relations within the couple: you find that already in *Tout va bien*, along with the idea that it can be done in front of history, during the strike and with the working class, or at least not against it. You also film the family to say that the cinema is a family, one big family in which Rivette and Verneuil are brothers at loggerheads, in which pornography and culture do battle with the same weapons and on the same stage. Godard, in *Numéro deux*, is washing the cinema's dirty linen, settling his account with pornography or the Rivette genre, cleaning up the tape, settling accounts with what all films have in common, the obscenity of the image.

Taken live, which does indeed refer to living flesh, not the essence of things, just the skin, the tape, the surface. Something is extracted for someone's profit, the mechanism of surplus value comes into play: when someone takes something from someone else and gives it back in the form of an image, a film, a piece of merchandise which the other person can't recognize or appropriate. The mechanism is more complicated than that since there is more than one beneficiary: it's the film-maker, it's art in general that is reproduced with its differences, it's the spectators for whom the films are made.

Cinema is the participatory art *par excellence*. Hence, *for us*, a difficulty: how can you say that such and such a film is reactionary when it rests on a consensus that Straub's films or those of Godard don't enjoy? Cinema is the art of majorities, or at least that's how the bourgeoisie thinks of it.

That is where a film like *Numéro deux* defies the dominant cinema: is a minority cinema which is not a ghetto cinema possible? (Straub: 'I think we should also make films for minorities, because one can always hope that they will be, as Lenin said, the majorities of tomorrow', *Cahiers* 260–1[4]). Is it possible to film majorities or majority problems along 'minority' lines (for Straub, Corneille, Bach, Brecht, Schoenberg: universal culture; for Godard, the family, the couple, television, adverts: daily life)?

At the same time, *Numéro deux* and *Ici et ailleurs* force us to ask ourselves (as spectators): are we the possible spectators for these films, are we really that minority to whom these images are addressed? In which case, how can we think of ourselves as a minority public against the ideology of the cinema which only thinks of the public in majority terms?

What *Numéro deux* and *Ici et ailleurs* ask us to do is to disentangle the notion of spectator activity, of the spectator at work, to make our vision sharper – avoiding the pitfalls of semiology, the distortions of any would-be scientific approach – so as to recover the true logic of the cinema which consists in looking and doing, in listening and recognizing images and sounds, *working all the while on our own account.*

Translated by Annwyl Williams

Notes

1 Toubiana's text is accompanied by a cutting from *Le Parisien libéré*. Below a photograph of the murdered Pasolini, the paper comments:

A poet and a talented writer as well as a film director, Pier Paolo Pasolini cut a dashing figure alongside Maria Callas. Looking pale in the glare of the lights, this Marxist-in-a-sports-car casts a scornful look over the 'bourgeois press' to whom he is presenting, somewhat pretentiously and against a background of national flags, his film *Medea*. It is his consecration. And yet it is the only film he will ever construct around a star. He prefers to use attractive young men and women, or even animals, to film frolics from which homosexuality is rarely absent.

Did he doubt his talent to the point of courting scandal to make his mark? Or was he deliberately trying to poison the society he rejected? His second film resulted in legal proceedings. For the third, he received a prison sentence . . . He had just finished *The 120 Days of Sodom* [*Salò*], based on the Marquis de Sade. He was found yesterday morning near the beach at Ostia as this butchered, bloodstained, unrecognizable corpse.

Divine retribution? Immanent justice? In fact, quite simply, he was beaten to death by a young hooligan of seventeen (his emulator?) who confessed to having finished him off by running him over with his own sports car . . . Whether it was divine retribution or impromptu bludgeoning, the director of *Pigsty* would certainly appear to be the victim of forces he unleashed among young people whom he encouraged, via the written word and the image, to indulge in sick pleasures.

Toubiana comments:
'The crimes committed by the news media.' For example, with Pasolini's death, what does death become? How can the crime not be questioned? What has been done for his death to enter our homes, our heads, every morning (as we read *Le Parisien*) and every evening (through the voice of the television newsreader), without any questions being asked of us, without it even being possible for this death to keep its disturbing quality?

Because he writes screenplays, we are told that the artist can die like the characters in his stories.

Because he doesn't live conventionally, we are told that the artist becomes completely isolated, bringing down upon himself forces of hate that know no limit.

Because he criticizes the society in which he lives, we are told that it's normal, at a given moment, for this society to lynch him.

You have to denounce crimes, and the crimes committed by the news media which match them; you have to make the machinery grind down, take the images out of their frames, bring in others in their place and interfere with the voices, to reinvent the screen.

2 Léo Ferré, songwriter and singer, whose songs feature on the soundtrack of *Numéro deux*.

3 'Small businesses': the French is 'PME', i.e. Petites et Moyennes Entreprises. The PME federation aims to encourage efficiency and modernization in the traditionally conservative world of small businesses in France.

4 In a presentation of the text of Straub's *Moses and Aaron*.

6

RETURN OF THE SAME

('Retour du même', *Cahiers du Cinéma* 262–3, January
1976)

Thérèse Giraud

After May '68, Godard gets down to a problem: how to make political films
politically? How to integrate consistently within the film the question of
where the images come from? And, step by step, to combat the effects of the
dominant ideology in cinema as in politics.

This was a philosophical reflection, too abstract, too theoretical. An overly
intellectual working method, too Parisian. Godard journeyed back to the
provinces: away from the head and towards the body.

For Godard comes up against a problem. Beyond the issue of political commitment such as it was being expressed – both by himself and more generally
– are other issues, unexplored and forgotten; issues that had created their fair
share of disillusionment in post-'68 militant circles: interior issues – the family, the body, sexuality – neglected and left in enemy hands, those of television,
sentimental drama, porn cinema.

A change of direction: to start no longer from theory but from the man.

Sex and politics

Take one: *Tout va bien*. A woman's hand on a man's penis. An image not from a
porn movie but from a photograph. The photograph as an object of discussion
and argument, a nucleus (one of several?) of the contradiction between the man
and the woman who are otherwise addressing the problems of their own political commitment.

A photograph of an erect penis grasped by a woman's hand; the photograph
and the sex as an exhibit: this is.

But a photograph within a film, alongside a film – another place, another
time.

Take two: *Numéro deux*. The issue of political commitment is no longer
addressed alongside that of sexuality; it is a commitment starting from and

111

about sex. Addressing the issue of sexuality in political terms takes centre stage. Being neither a sex movie nor a political film but a shattering of the divisions imposed by media imagery; within the place where these images speak – the family.

Speaking politically about the issue of sex; resituating sex in its social cell, the family.

Starting from an imprisonment . . .

The family, as the product of sex, of sexual relationships (non-relationships), of conjugal love, a product which reproduces itself and is obliged endlessly to reproduce itself. Production and the relations of production.

The family: where the children are taught that what happens when mother and father are alone in bed is the two sexes kissing, that this is love, this is how they learn to speak.

This is what it is all about.

But the children, despite this rote-learning, see only buggery, rape and deaf, dumb, blind violence. They see one who, from the outside, ejaculates and fills the other who receives within, absorbs and swells.

Overproduction.

It goes in from all sides and does not come out. Forced in, blocked. Blocked up as in buggered. Buggered by the sex, up the arse, in the mouth (the rote-learning), by the ears (the headphones).

Starting from this imprisonment, therefore showing it as that of the family, of woman. With the man's sex designated as the guilty party. Lacerating bourgeois forms of representation to talk about sex: didactic images, imposed by an absence of fiction, music and drama. Images which are imprisoned by darkness and off-screen sound. Sublimation, escape, projection into a fictional elsewhere – all these are denied the spectator, who is forced to see things for real. In place of the love that is sublimated as much through pornography as through sentimental drama, to show instead bodies side-by-side, bodies that don't connect, that collide, that do each other harm.

The reality of things in imposed, imposing images, but images without the possibility of transformation. An enclosed, hermetic, blocked up film.

Here are images, a chain of images, *just* images.[1] Locked up in the dark. Is this the darkness of ideology? And where do these images come from? This is the question to which Godard has always forced himself to respond and which finds a response here in the shots at the beginning and the end of the film, two shots that bracket the film, that are no longer just images, where the ideological darkness has vanished and they fill the screen. They are the relations of production: it's me, what's-his-name, master of my work, my equipment, my celluloid, who has made all this, who has organized it in space and time.

It is I who manipulate the sounds and images.

His image: of man.

His image: of woman. Placed at the centre of the film. The dynamic of the contradiction between man and woman.

It appears that a woman participated in making this film, in the construction of these images. It's a film by two people. This 'number two', who we see neither at the beginning nor the end of the film, is reduced to the status of raw material, like celluloid, like something to talk about.

I'm speaking in her place, because she cannot speak yet, for lack of the means of production, of knowledge of the language of cinema.

I'm speaking in her place, still . . . Making speech for her; taking power for her, the power of cinema and its images.

For the machine that allows him to speak, which he speaks from, is not solely the one that we see, that he shows us (controlling the means of production), but is also the one that we don't see, being hidden by the other.

His sex, concealed, unacknowledged, shameful.

The film's centre, recalling *Tout va bien*, except that here all is far from well, the sex here is never erect, never wants to be erect. A refusal to function, a state of retention, a voluntary castration but one for which it seeks to revenge itself.

Because it functions all the same, it ejaculates elsewhere, in the images, in his speaking. It functions as the phallus.

Castration and vengeance.

A hermetic film, full, blocked, like the woman and his image of the woman. In the same way as the only sex worthy of the name is that of the man.

A film congested with sex, just as Godard is congested by his own sex, like a man who discovers how it works but doesn't know what to do with it, either with his sex or with its discovery.

So he shows it.

He shows it and shoves it into us all over the place – in the mouth, up the arse, in the ears – redoubling reality, its reality. I say what I see.

It is a film about phallocracy.

He imposes it upon us again . . . in sadistic impositions and initiatory rites, just as the worldly grandfather imposes on the little girl the headphones and Ferré's[2] melancholy, just as the parents impose their initiatory discourse on love, as Godard number one imposes the recital of *A bout de souffle* on the children of number two.

For the man has the sex, a privilege which starts to weigh heavily on some, such as Godard (a consciousness whose origin is concealed, just as his partner is concealed, as finally is the origin of these images: is not the ideological darkness to be filled by the words of the woman, by her images, and would one thus see less sex?), but he has only this. But not *only*; he also has all that is permitted by his sex, all that resembles him – the desire for power, the problematic of power and impotence which he cannot get away from, the desire to possess, to crush, to enclose the other in a film, in a succession of words and images.

The other: what, in the woman, he glimpses as different, as inaccessible to the law of his sex/phallus.

This other which he reduces to his same.

He mutilates the sex on the sole condition of mutilating the woman's body, of rigging it out in the same desires, the same functions: veneration of the penis, violence of the penis.

Woman alone: congested (with sex), lamenting, or masturbatory violence, the search for liberating ejaculation, only the sex uncovered, its body absent, veiled.

The woman's word – filled with his sex or around his sex, in masturbating it.

The mutilated body of the woman, transformed into a penis, an extension of his that engorges no longer. Return of the same.

We never speak of the violence on the banks that enclose the river. Me, I speak of it and it makes me understand your violence. Your violence, my violence: the phallus sees only itself.

Perhaps women will never know how much men hate them. No doubt it was for this reason that Godard made his film (and not their film). To enclose them once again within the objectivity of his discourse on sex, in another image of woman, but one marked by a troubled male conscience, an image of death. To exclude the other, the unsexed other, the other words that for him don't exist, to which he refuses existence and life.

His image of woman: bloated, congested by the sex, the eternal victim. Or the woman-penis.

Because men hate women to such an extent that they would like them to hate them as much in return, in the same way, with the same weapons. This would perhaps be the war in which male violence could explode without shame or guilty conscience . . . Is this sex war that men dream of more than women perhaps lying somewhere behind this film?

But this would again be a form of sublimation, and that is excluded: the images are stopped before anything – the slightest element of fiction, of projection – can occur.

Closing off any such opening; imprisoning it; a sealed, hermetic film. And facing it, facing his images, Godard imagines himself as the grandfather (as Ferré?) who, under the table, can no longer get it up, and above it no longer has the words with which to speak of his life and its struggles.

Life, its struggles left behind him. The desire for solitude, for death.

War or withdrawal; death, anyway.

The impotency of the phallus facing life, the struggle for life.

Dichotomies:

The dichotomy of the retention of sex but its discharge nonetheless through the words and images.

The dichotomy of the retention of music (sublimation), but its oozing through all the cracks in the film, bursting in liberation over the final image.

The music of Ferré: glancing towards solitude, glancing towards death. A glance towards cinema.

Withdrawal?

The final image: hands, sick and hesitant, on the levers.

114

Sick of these sounds and images, too unbearable, without hope of transformation.

Hermetic images, sealed and closed; fine as a way of speaking about others, of speaking theoretically about theory and practice.

But it's simply too much torture to speak of oneself, of one's melancholy and one's anguish.

There is here the question of a limit; the limit of a cinema, the limit of a man's talking about himself, of truly saying 'I', of giving up just a little bit of power.

Translated by Chris Darke

Notes

1 Giraud is making reference to Godard's famous maxim from *Vent d'est* (1969): 'Ce n'est pas une image juste, c'est juste une image' (literally, 'It's not a just image, it's just an image'). (Translator's note.)
2 Ferré: see Ch. 5, note 2.

7

THEORIZE/TERRORIZE (GODARDIAN PEDAGOGY)[1]

('Le thérrorisé: pédagogie godardienne', *Cahiers du Cinéma* 262–3, January 1976)

Serge Daney

Learning, retaining

May '68, as we know, confirmed Godard's suspicion that the cinema was, in every sense, a 'bad place', at once immoral and inadequate. A place for facile hysteria, for the eye's filthy roving, for voyeurism and magic. A place where, to use a metaphor that was once all the rage, one came to 'sleep in the picture bed' [*dormir dans le plan lit*], to get an eyeful and in fact to see nothing at all – to see too much and to see it badly.

The doubts cast by May '68 on the 'viewing community' – a community that secretes more images and sounds that it can see and digest (the image flashes by and disappears) – reached the generation that had invested most in it, that of the self-taught cinephiles for whom the cinema had taken the place of school and family, the generation of the New Wave, brought up in the *cinémathèques*. From 1968 Godard was to react by pulling out and retracing his steps: from the cinema to school, and then from school to the family. Regression? Why couldn't one say 'regressionism'?

In 1968, for the most radical – the most left-wing – element among film-makers, one thing is certain: you have to learn to get away from the cinema (from cinephilia and obscurantism) or at least forge a link between the cinema and something else. And to learn you have to go to school. Not so much the 'school of life' as the school of film. That was how Godard and Gorin came to transform the scenographic cube into a classroom, the film dialogue into a recitation, the voice-off into a lecture, the shooting into a practical, the film topic into course headings ('revisionism', 'ideology') and the film-maker into a schoolmaster, tutor or supervisor. School thus becomes the 'good place', the place that gets you away from the cinema and closer to the 'real' (a real awaiting transformation, of course). It's the place which has brought us the films of

116

the Dziga-Vertov group[2] (and already, *La Chinoise*). In *Tout va bien*, *Numéro deux* and *Ici et ailleurs* the family apartment has replaced the classroom (and television had taken the place of the cinema), but the essential remains. The essential: people giving each other lessons.

We need look no further to explain the extraordinary mixture of love and hatred, of rage and irritation, the moans and the groans that Godard's 'cinema' – pursuing a fairly tough Maoist line, initially – proceeded to unleash. Had Godard been 'recuperated by the system', people would have forgiven him a lot (even today, how many people are still indignant at the idea that he won't give them another *Pierrot le fou*?). Had he become totally marginalized, an underground figure happy with his underground status, they would have rendered him discreet homage. But what can they do with a Godard who continues to work, to teach and be taught, whether people come to see his films or not? There's something in Godard's pedagogy that the film world – the film world especially – won't tolerate: the fact that it is addressed to no one in particular.

Godard's pedagogy. School, as we were saying, is the 'good place' (the place where you make progress, the place you're bound to get out of) in contrast to the cinema (the 'bad place' where you regress and where your chances of getting out are nil). Let's take a closer look and pursue the analogy.

First, school is more than anywhere else the place where you are allowed, indeed encouraged, to confuse words and things,[3] to remain in ignorance about what links them, to postpone having to think about it until later (is there anything to vouch for the truth of what we are taught?). School means nominalism and dogmatism.

Now the *sine qua non* of Godard's pedagogy is this: you must never question the other's discourse, whatever it is. You must take it literally, unthinkingly. You must also take it word for word. Godard concerns himself only with things-already-said-by-others or things-already-said in the form of established statements (quotations, slogans and posters, jokes and stories, words on a blackboard, newspaper headlines, anything at all). Statement-objects, little monuments, words taken as things: learn them or not as you prefer, take it or leave it.

Things-said-by-others have the status of a *fait accompli*: whatever else, they exist, they consist of something. Their very existence rules out any attempt to reconstruct behind, before or around them the domain of their enunciation. Godard never asks any questions of the statements he receives – where they come from or what makes them possible, or what guarantees they offer. He never queries the desire they betray and at the same time conceal. His approach is anti-archaeological in the extreme. It consists in noting what is said (about which nothing can be done) and immediately looking for the other statement, the other sound, the other image which might counterbalance this statement, this sound, this image. 'Godard' would simply be the empty space, the black screen where images and sounds would co-exist, cancel each other out, recognize and point to each other – in short, struggle. More than 'who is right?' and 'who is wrong?', the real question is 'what could we oppose to that?' The devil's advocate.

Hence the malaise and 'confusion' with which Godard is often reproached. He always replies to what the other says (asserts, proclaims or recommends) by what *another other* says (asserts, proclaims or recommends). There is always a big unknown quantity in his pedagogy, and this is because the nature of the relation he entertains with his 'good' discourses (those he defends) is ultimately uncertain.

In *Ici et ailleurs*, for example, a 'film' based on images brought back from Jordan (1970–5), it's clear that the film's self-interrogation (the way in which it dissociates 'here' and 'elsewhere', images and sounds, 1970 and 1975) is possible and intelligible only because, early on, the syntagm 'Palestinian revolution' already functions as an axiom, as something that can be taken for granted (something already-said-by-others, in this case by Al Fatah), something in relation to which Godard doesn't have to define himself personally (and say not just 'I' but 'I'm on their side') or mark his position in the film. He doesn't have to make his position, his initial choice – for the Palestinians, against Israel – acceptable, convincing or desirable. The logic of school, again.

Second, school is more than anywhere else the place where the master doesn't have to say where his knowledge and his certainties come from.[4] And on the other hand it's the place where the pupil cannot reinscribe, use or put to the test the knowledge imparted to him. Before the master's knowledge, and after the pupil's knowledge, is a blank, a no man's land, a question that Godard will have nothing to do with, the question of how knowledge is appropriated. He's only interested in (re)transmission.

And yet in every pedagogy there are values, *positive* contents, to be communicated. Godard's pedagogy is no exception. Every single one of the films made after 1968 latches on to (and distances itself from) what one might call – without any pejorative nuance – a 'correct' discourse [*discours du manche*]. Let's recapitulate: Marxist-Leninist politics (the Chinese positions) in *Pravda* and *Vent d'est*; Althusser's lesson on wrong notions of ideology in *Lotte in Italia*; Brecht's lesson on 'the role of intellectuals in the revolution' in *Tout va bien* and, more recently, snatches of feminist discourse (Germaine Greer) in *Numéro deux*. Correct discourse is not a discourse in power, but it's a discourse that *has power*: it is violent, assertive, provocative and fully constituted. Correct discourse changes hands, so to speak, but it always comes from above and is quick to lay blame (things to be ashamed of, in turn: being a cinephile, being a revisionist, being cut off from the masses, being a male chauvinist).

But Godard is not the conveyer – still less the originator – of these discourses which he asks us to believe in (and submit ourselves to). His role is more like that of a tutor [*répétiteur*]. A three-term structure is then established, a little *théâtre à trois*, where the master (who is after all only a *tutor*) and the pupil (who only repeats) meet up with what has to be repeated, the correct discourse to which master and pupils are subjected, if unequally, and which bullies them.

The screen, then, becomes the place where this bullying is experienced and the film its staging. But in this arrangement two questions are completely ignored: how the correct discourse is produced (in Maoist terms: where do correct ideas come from?) and how it is appropriated[5] (in Maoist terms: what is the difference between true ideas and correct ideas?). School is not of course the place for these questions. The tutor appears as a modest and at the same time tyrannical figure: he makes the pupil learn a lesson which doesn't arouse his own curiosity, and to which he is himself subjected.

After 1968 this master-discourse is conveyed more or less systematically by a female voice. For Godard's pedagogy implies a division of roles and discourses according to sex. Man speaks but woman makes the speeches. The voice that reprimands, corrects, advises, teaches, explains, theorizes and even theorizes/terrorizes is always a woman's voice. And if this voice begins to speak about women's issues, precisely, it adopts the same assertive, faintly declamatory tone: the opposite of the naturalistic experience and concern. Godard doesn't film a revolt that can't speak for itself, that hasn't found its language, its style, its theory. In *Tout va bien* we see the character played by Jane Fonda move very quickly from dissatisfaction to a kind of theoretical explanation of her dissatisfaction (one that Montand doesn't understand). There is nothing at all before discourse, before things-said-by-others.

Third, for the master and for the pupils, each year brings with it ('back to school') a re-enactment, a repetition of the first time, a going back to the beginning. To the time when nothing was known, when the blackboard was empty. So that school – the place of the *tabula rasa* and the blackboard on which nothing remains for long, the gloomy place of permanent transition and waiting for things to happen – is an obsessional, non-linear place, closed in on itself.

From his very first films Godard has shown an extreme reluctance to 'tell a story', to say 'at the beginning, this happened' and 'at the end, that'. Getting away from the cinema was also getting away from this obligation, well formulated by old Fritz Lang in *Le Mépris*: 'You always have to finish what you begin.' A basic difference between school and the cinema is that there's no need to please or to flatter schoolchildren because school is compulsory. The state insists on schooling for every child. Whereas in the cinema, to hold on to your public, you have to give them things to see and enjoy, tell a story (spin a yarn): hence the accumulation of images, the hysteria, the calculated effects, the retention and the discharge, the happy ending – the catharsis. The privilege of school is that it retains its pupils so that they retain what they are told; the master retains his knowledge (he doesn't say everything) and punishes the bad pupils with detention.[6]

Keeping and giving back

School was therefore the 'good place' only because, as the place of endless deferral, it allowed you to retain the maximum number of things and people for the longest possible time. For 'to retain' means two things: 'to keep back' but also 'to delay', 'to defer'. You keep an audience of pupils to delay the moment when they might move too quickly from one image to another, from one sound to another, see too quickly, come to premature conclusions, think they're done with images and sounds when they have no idea of the complexity, the seriousness of what is involved in the ordering of these images and these sounds.

School allows you to turn cinephilia back against itself, to reverse it like a glove, taking all the time you need. This is why Godard's pedagogy consists in for ever coming back to images and sounds, pointing to them, matching them, commenting on them, putting images within images and sounds within sounds, criticizing them like so many insoluble enigmas: not losing them, keeping them in sight, *keeping them*.

A masturbatory pedagogy? No doubt. It has as its horizon, as its limit, the enigma of enigmas, the sphinx of the still photograph: it is what defies the intelligence that can never exhaust it, what holds the look and the meaning, what fixes the scopic desire: actively retains it.

For the place from which Godard speaks to us, from which he addresses us, is certainly not the secure place of a profession or even a personal project. It's somewhere in between, even a between-three, an impossible place that embraces the photograph (nineteenth century) and the cinema (twentieth century) and television (twenty-first century). The photo is what retains once and for all (the corpse to work on). The cinema is what retains for a moment only (death at work). Television is what retains nothing at all (a fatal spilling out, a haemorrhaging of images).

Thus Godard's advance on other manipulators of images and sounds has to do with his complete disregard for any discourse on the 'specificity' of the cinema. You have to see how he finds a place on the cinema screen for both the still photo and the television image, how he quietly fits them in (the cinema's only specificity now consisting in – provisionally? – receiving images that were not made for it, in allowing itself to be taken over by them: *Numéro deux*), to understand that Godard goes beyond any discourse on the specificity of the cinema, whether the spontaneous discourse of the spectator (that's what the cinema means to me), or that of those professionally involved (that's how you make films) or that of enlightened academics (that's how the cinema works).

The cinema, as we were saying at the outset, is a bad place, a place of crime and of magic. The crime: that images and sounds should be *taken* (torn, removed, stolen, extorted) from living beings. The magic: that they should be exhibited in another place (the film theatre) for the pleasure of those who see them. The one who benefits from the transfer is the film-maker. That's where the real pornography lies, in this change of scene: it's literally the ob-scene.

People will say: these are moral questions, of the sort addressed by Bazin, and what's more, this type of symbolic debt can't be repaid. Indeed. But Godard's itinerary happens to point to a very concrete, very historical question, a question in crisis: that of the nature of what might be called the 'filmic contract' (filming/filmed). This question seemed to arise only for the militant or ethnographic cinema ('Ourselves and others'), but Godard tells us that it concerns the very act of filming. Is he exaggerating? One can't seriously think that this is one of those questions that can be resolved with good will and pious hopes (for the good cause – the artistic masterpiece or the correct militant action). It is going to arise and is bound to become more pressing as the traditional contract between the film-maker, the filmed and the film viewer, the contract established by the film industry (Hollywood), becomes ever more threadbare and the cinema, as 'a mass, family, popular and homogenizing art', reaches crisis point. Godard speaks to us already about this crisis, because it was this crisis that made him into a film-maker. But it's already a question of pornographic films (*Exhibition*) or militant films (*Un simple exemple*). A question of the future.

For Godard, retaining images and his audience, pinning them down in a sense (as butterflies are cruelly pinned down), is a despairing activity, and a hopeless one. All his pedagogy wins for him is a little more time. To the obscenity of appearing as the *auteur* (and the beneficiary of filmic surplus value) he has preferred that of displaying himself in the very act of retention.[7]

The impossibility of moving on to a filmic contract of a new sort has therefore led him to keep (retain) images and sounds, not knowing who to give them back to. Godard's cinema is a painful meditation on the theme of restitution, or better of *restoration*. To restore is to give back the images and sounds to those from whom they were taken. It is also to commit them (a truly political commitment) to producing *their own* images and sounds. And so much the better if this forces the film-maker to change his way of working!

A film in which this restitution-restoration takes place, at least ideally, is *Ici et ailleurs*. Who can these images of Palestinian men and women that Godard and Gorin (invited by the PLO) bring back from the Middle East, these images that Godard keeps to himself for five years, be given back to?

To the general public eager for sensation (Godard + Palestine = scoop)? To the politically aware anxious to be confirmed in its orthodoxy (Godard + Palestine = good cause + art)? To the PLO who invited him, allowed him to film and trusted him (Godard + Palestine = weapon of propaganda)? No, not even the PLO. So what does that leave?

One day between 1970 and 1975 Godard realizes that the soundtrack has not been translated in its entirety – what the fedayeen say in the shots where they appear has not been translated from the Arabic. And he realizes that basically there would have been few complaints (everyone would have accepted the superimposition of a voice-over). Now, Godard tells us, these fedayeen whose speech has remained a dead letter are themselves awaiting death, as good as dead. They – or other fedayeen like them – died in 1970, assassinated by Hussein's troops.

Making the film ('You always have to finish what you begin') then amounts, quite simply, to translating the soundtrack, making sure that people can hear what is said; or better, that they listen to it. What is retained is then released, what is kept is given back, but it is too late. The images and the sounds are given back, just as tributes are paid, to those to whom they belong: to the dead.

Translated by Annwyl Williams

Notes

1 A wordplay (*théorisé/terrorisé*), characteristically Godardian, which is of course impossible to render in English.

2 Dziga-Vertov group: a loose association of film-makers and political activists, set up by Godard in collaboration first with Jean-Henri Roger and later with Jean-Pierre Gorin, with the aim of making films collectively. The group's films include *British Sounds*, *Pravda*, *Lotte in Italia* and *Vent d'est*.

3 In *Numéro deux*, words *are* things. In between the rare moments where they make sense, the orange letters [in some prints of the film the letters are white] inscribe in the heart of the black screen only the enigma of their form: hieroglyphics. Meaning becomes no more than a particular instance of non-meaning, just as life is a particular instance of death – and a fairly uncommon one at that. Who *wants* these images, these sounds, these letters? Who *is letting* us see, hear or read them? Certainly not an *'auteur'* (origin and property). Godard is, in the most modest sense, a manipulator. (Author's note.) In the original text this and subsequent notes are unnumbered marginal comments by Daney, integral to the text.

4 The role of the educator has become, over the years, suspect and joyless. But there was a time when it was desirable. Jacques Rancière reminds us that Althusser's teaching was aimed in the first place at the 'regeneration of leaders through theory' ('leaders' = those of the French Communist Party). To which he rightly adds: 'You could therefore say, stretching the point a little, that the political model assumed by this problematic was the very model of the educator's philosophy: enlightened despotism.' A position of power that implied two possible relations: either the party leaders had to become philosophers, and that's what Althusser was trying to achieve, or else the philosophers had to become party leaders, and that was what happened with the Union des Jeunesses Communistes (Marxistes-Léninistes). (J. Rancière, *La Leçon d'Althusser* [Paris, Gallimard, 1974], p. 106). (Author's note.)

5 Appropriation is (inversely) a key notion for militant cinema, it's what makes it a militant cinema in the first place. Something that smacks of the command, the instruction, the demonstration – and always the example – has to be passed on. Film is merely the element in which opaque signifiers are 'set alight' to become organizing, transforming signifieds. A lesson is recited, directed at those whose lesson it is (that's didacticism) whereas an example is followed (appropriated).

To follow an example is to make it one's own, to pass directly to the stage where *an* example is adapted to *a* concrete situation. The example is necessarily transformed and even travestied. Who would be bold enough to say that they know how experiences of struggle are communicated (other than 'parties' small enough to create their reality and keep a tight rein on first-hand accounts and other forms of communication – the logic of the mass educator, again)?

To make militant films is to accept this dispossession, to recognize that the process of appropriation always involves an element of travesty. Godard's refusal to 'make' militant films (when he says, after 1968, that 'production determines diffusion') becomes easier to understand. For the only thing he would be happy to have appropriated (and therefore to have taken away from him) is the burden he carries alone, his relationship to images and sounds, the love-hate-reflection he devotes to them. (Author's note.)

6 Godard's leftism means bringing down the barriers. Between private life and public life, work and leisure, the stage of History and the behind-the-scenes of daily life. But it's a sad, super-egoistic, moral leftism: private life becomes public (and the bed a theatre: *Tout va bien*, *Numéro deux*), leisure time (wasted in going to the cinema) becomes working time (seeing the film is work, work for the eye and the ear). Godard makes 'a whole history' out of daily life. Making love, going to the cinema: hard labour. (Author's note.)

7 To sum up: the photograph retains once and for all (but what does it retain if not the real as impossible?). The cinema receives a syncopation of images and sounds only to lose them again – they are taken *here* and given back *elsewhere* (and in the meantime there is this duty, this imposition, which consists in retaining them, keeping them back: like school, or constipation). Television never retains anything. Images and sounds file past (march past, parade in line, like soldiers) at the bidding of an anonymous power. As the passageway for this diarrhoea of images and sounds, television is the other horizon of Godard's 'cinema': the place where things are for ever being churned out mechanically, the place which isn't concerned with morals (choice, bad conscience), which knows only two possibilities: it works/it doesn't work. A (horrible) passageway, meeting place, eating house (bring your own food!).

'The psychotic's body appears, if you like, as an inert cylindrical surface, a kind of screen where imaginary productions are inscribed without giving rise to a meaning effect. It can keep nothing, retain nothing, appropriate nothing. It can receive nothing from . . . give nothing to . . . conceive of nothing for itself. It lays itself open to constant manipulation. But this way of putting it is misleading: it gives the psychotic's body the status of a self-reflective subject ("it lays itself open"). It would be better to say: it is "laid open" (by everyone and no one).' Denis Vasse, *L'Ombilic et la voix: Deux enfants en analyse* (Paris, Editions du Seuil, 1974), p. 94. (Author's note.)

8

ON *SUR ET SOUS LA COMMUNICATION*: THREE QUESTIONS ON *SIX FOIS DEUX*[1]

('A propos *Sur et sous la communication*: Trois questions sur *Six fois deux*', *Cahiers du Cinéma* 271, November 1976)

Gilles Deleuze

1. *We are asking you for an interview because you are a 'philosopher' and we would like a text of this kind, but above all because you like and admire Godard's work. What did you think of his recent television programmes?*

Like many people I found them powerful. They made a lasting impression on me. I can tell you how I think of Godard. He's a man who works very hard, and it follows that he is completely alone. But this loneliness is not the common sort: it's filled by a huge assortment of things. Not dreams, fantasies or projects, but actions, things and even people. It is a many-faceted, creative loneliness. It's what lies behind Godard's ability to operate powerfully on his own, but also as part of a team. He can deal on equal terms with anyone, with big organizations or the powers that be, with a cleaning lady, a manual worker or the insane. In the television programmes, Godard's questions are always straight. They trouble us, the viewers, but not the people they are addressed to. He speaks to the insane in a way which is not that of a psychiatrist or that of a fellow madman or someone pretending to be one. He speaks with workers without being a boss or another worker or an intellectual or a film director with actors. This is not because he can switch his manner to suit the occasion, because he is a skilful operator, but because his loneliness somehow opens him up to anyone and everything. In a way, it's always a question of stammering. Not of stammering in your speech, but of stammering in language itself. You can only be a foreigner, generally speaking, in another language. Here, on the contrary, it's a question of being a foreigner in your own language. Proust said that good books are necessarily written in a kind of foreign language. It's the same thing for Godard's programmes: he has even perfected his Swiss accent for this purpose. It is this creative stammering, this loneliness, which makes Godard so powerful.

Because, as you know better than I do, he has always been alone. Godard has never achieved real success in the cinema, as some would have you believe, those who say: 'He's changed, his later films are just not worth watching.' They are often the same people who hated him from the start. Godard has kept up with everyone, and moved ahead, but instead of taking the paths that might have led to success he has followed his own zigzag line, actively pursuing its underground course, forever changing direction. The fact remains that, in the world of film, people had more or less succeeded in condemning him to his solitude. They had confined him to a particular area. And here he is taking advantage of the holidays, of a vague appeal to creativity, to occupy six times two programmes on television. It's perhaps the only case of someone who wasn't had by television. Usually, the battle is lost in advance. People would have forgiven him for putting his films in context, but not for making this series which strikes at the heart of television's concerns (interviewing people, getting them to talk, showing images from elsewhere, etc.) – even if no one pays any attention to these things any more, even if all discussion of them is stifled. It was inevitable that many groups and associations would be offended: the statement issued by the Association des Journalistes Reporters-photographes et Cinéastes is typical. Godard has at least resurrected the hatred. But he has also shown that television can be differently 'filled'.

2. *You haven't answered our question. If you had to lecture on these programmes . . . what ideas did you perceive, or feel? How would you explain your enthusiasm? We're not denying the importance of other considerations, but let's set them aside for the moment.*

All right, but ideas, having an idea, this is not a question of ideology but of practice. Godard has a nice formula: not a true image, just an image [*pas une image juste, juste une image*].[2] Philosophers should say that too, and practise what they preach: no sound ideas, just ideas [*pas d'idées justes, juste des idées*], because *sound* ideas are always ideas which conform to dominant meanings or established slogans, they are always ideas which verify something, even if that something is in the future, even if that future is revolutionary. Whereas 'just ideas' corresponds to what is in the making in the present, it's a stammering of ideas, something that can only be expressed in the form of questions, questions of the sort which tend to be difficult to answer. Or else which show something utterly simple and obvious.

Working along these lines, there are two ideas in Godard's programmes that are constantly overlapping, coming together or separating from one segment to the next. It's one of the reasons each programme is divided into two: as in primary school, you have the two poles: lessons on 'things' and lessons on language. The first idea concerns work. I think that Godard is for ever questioning a vaguely Marxist schema that is by now all-pervasive: you posit some fairly abstract notion like 'labour-power' [*force de travail*] that is bought or sold in conditions which imply a fundamental social injustice or, on the contrary, make for a little more social justice. Now Godard poses very concrete questions; he shows images which lead us to ask: What exactly is being bought and sold? What is it that some are prepared to buy and others to sell, which is not necessarily the same thing? A young welder is prepared to sell his welding skills, but not his sexual potency by becoming the lover of an old woman. A cleaning lady is perfectly willing to sell hours of housework, but not the moment when she sings a snatch of the *Internationale*. Why? Because she can't sing? But if she were paid to speak, precisely, about what she can't sing? And inversely, a watch-maker asks to be paid for what his specialized knowledge allows him to do while refusing payment for the work he puts into his home movies, his 'hobby', as he says; but the images show that the actions involved in watch-making and film editing are remarkably similar – he could be doing the same thing. But no, says the watch-maker, there's a big difference in what I put into it, my movies are a labour of love, I wouldn't want to be paid for them. But, then, what about the film-maker or photographer who is paid? And even more to the point, what is the photographer himself prepared to pay? In some cases, he will pay his model. In other cases, he will be paid by his model. But when he photographs torture or an execution, he will pay neither the victim nor the executioner. And when he photographs sick, injured or hungry children, why doesn't he pay them?

Guattari[3] was reasoning along similar lines when he proposed at a meeting of psychoanalysts that the person being psychoanalysed has as much right to be paid as the psychoanalyst, since the latter's contribution is not exactly a 'service' – there is rather a division of labour, two types of work that evolve together but not along parallel lines: the psychoanalyst's work of listening and sifting, but also the psychoanalysed person's work on the unconscious. Guattari's proposal appears to have gone unheeded. Godard is saying the same thing: why not pay the people who watch television, instead of making them pay, since they do a job of work and render a public service in their turn? The social division of work implies that, in a factory, those who work not just on the shop-floor but also in offices and research laboratories get paid. If this were not the case, why shouldn't the workers themselves be responsible for paying the draughtsmen who design what they make? I think that all these questions and many others, all these images and many others, tend to destroy the notion of labour-power. To begin with, the very notion of labour-power arbitrarily isolates a single sector, cutting work off from its relation to love, creation and even production. It turns work into an act of preservation, the opposite of a creative activity, something which involves reproducing consumer goods and its own power, in a closed exchange. From this point of view, it matters little whether the exchange is fair or unfair, since there is always selective violence in the act of payment and mystification in the very principle which leads us to speak of labour-power. It's in so far as labour can be separated from its pseudo-power that very different production flows – highly divergent ones, of all kinds – could be directly related to money flows, independently of any mediation by an abstract force.

I am even more confused than Godard. And so much the better, for what's important are the questions Godard asks, the images he shows and the feeling the viewer may have that the notion of labour-power is not innocent, that it can't be taken for granted, even and especially from the viewpoint of a social critique. This goes a long way towards explaining the reactions of the French Communist Party and of certain trade unions to Godard's programmes, even if there other more visible reasons for their disapproval – Godard has questioned this holy notion of labour-power . . . And then there is the second idea, which concerns information. Once again, language is presented to us as essentially informative, and information as essentially an exchange. And once again, information is measured in abstract units. But it is doubtful whether the school-teacher, when she explains a procedure or teaches spelling, is passing on information. She is telling the children what to do; she deals, rather, in commands. And syntax is given to children, like tools to workers, for producing sentences that conform to the dominant meanings. When Godard says that children are political prisoners, the phrase must indeed be taken literally. Language is a system of commands and not a means of information. On television: 'Now for some entertainment . . . the news will follow shortly . . .' In fact the hierarchies of information theory need to be reversed. Information theory implies a maximum of theoretical information; then at the opposite pole it puts pure noise, interference; and between the two, redundancy, which detracts from information but puts it on a higher level than noise. It's the other way round: at the top you should put redundancy as the transmission and repetition of orders and commands; below that information, always a minimum requirement if commands are to be understood. And below that? Well, there would be something like silence, or stammering, or a cry, something which would flow under redundancy and information, which would make language flow and still make itself understood. To speak, even if you are speaking about yourself, is always to take someone's place, someone on whose behalf you claim to speak, and to whom you refuse the right to speak. Séguy[4] has his mouth open to transmit orders and commands. But so does the woman whose child has died. An image is represented by a sound, like a worker by his delegate. A sound assumes power over a series of images. And so, how can you ever speak without giving orders, without claiming to represent something or someone, how can you make speak those who don't have a right to speak, and acknowledge the value of sounds in the struggle against power? That's what it must mean, being like a foreigner in your own language, tracing a kind of flow line in language.

These are 'just' two ideas, but that's already a lot, a huge amount; just two ideas contain many things, and other ideas. So Godard questions two current notions, that of labour-power and that of information. He doesn't say that information must be truthful or that labour-power should be well paid (those would be sound ideas). He says that these notions are dubious. He writes FALSE beside them. He has said for a long time that he wished he could be a whole production department rather than an author, and a television news editor rather than a film-maker. Clearly he didn't mean to say that he wanted to produce his own films, like Verneuil; or acquire a position of power in television. The purpose, rather, would be to assemble pieces of work, instead of measuring them against an abstract force; to juxtapose sub-informational items, all the open mouths, instead of relating them to an abstract information taken as a command.

3. *If those are Godard's two ideas, do they coincide with the theme that is constantly developed in the programmes, 'images and sounds'? So that the lessons on things, the images, would relate to work and the lessons on words, the sounds, to information?*

No, the coincidence is only partial since images must also contain information and sounds work. Certain sections can and should be cut in several ways which only partially coincide. To try to reconstitute Godard's version of the image–sound relation you have to tell a very abstract story, in several episodes, only to realize in the end that this abstract story was simplest and most concrete in a single episode.

First, there are images, even *things* are images, because images don't exist in your head, in your brain. It is the brain, on the contrary, that is just another image. Images are constantly acting on other images, reacting to them, producing and consuming. There is no difference between *images, things* and *movement*.

But, second, images also have an *inside*, or certain images do, and are experienced from the inside. These are subjects (cf. Godard's statement about *Deux ou trois choses que je sais d'elle* in the anthology published by Belfond, pp. 393 ff.). There is indeed a *gap* between the action these images are subjected to and the reaction they produce. It is this gap that gives them the ability to store other images, that is, to perceive. But what they store is only what interests them in other images: to perceive is to abstract from the image what doesn't interest us; there is always *less* in our perception. We are so full of images that we don't see those outside us for what they are.

Third, on the other hand, there are sound-images which appear not to be privileged. And yet these sound-images, or some of them, have an *underside,* call it what you like: ideas, meaning, language, expression, etc. This is what gives them the power to take over or capture other images or a series of other images. A voice presides over a set of images (Hitler's voice). Ideas, acting as commands, are made concrete in sound-images or soundwaves and tell us what should be interesting us in the other images: they dictate our perception.

There is always a central 'rubber stamp' which normalizes images, removing from them whatever it is we're not supposed to see. In this way, and thanks to the gap previously mentioned, we become aware of two currents (as it were) running in opposite directions: one which goes from outside images to perceptions, the other from dominant ideas to perceptions.

And so, fourth, we are caught in a chain of images — each in its place, each being itself an image — but also in a web of ideas acting as commands. From then on, what Godard does with his 'images and sounds' goes in two directions at once. On the one hand it's a case of making outside images full again, so that we don't perceive less, so that our perception is equal to the image, so that images have nothing taken away from them; which is already a way of struggling against this or that power and its rubber stamps. On the other hand, it's a case of dismantling language in its power-seeking role, making it stammer in the soundwaves, breaking up any set of ideas that might claim to be 'sound' ideas so that we are left with 'just' ideas. Perhaps these are two reasons, among others, why Godard makes such novel use of the *static shot*. It's a little like what some present-day musicians do: they establish the sound equivalent of the static shot, thanks to which *everything* in the music will be heard. And when Godard shows us a blackboard on which he writes, it isn't an object that is there to be filmed; the blackboard and the writing become a new televisual resource, as it were an expressive substance that is given a current of its own in relation to other currents on the screen.

This whole abstract story in four episodes has a science-fiction quality. It corresponds to our present-day social reality; and curiously, it coincides on a certain number of points with what Bergson was saying in the first chapter of *Matter and Memory*. Bergson is generally considered to be a perceptive but outdated philosopher. It would be nice if cinema and television could give him back his novelty (he should be on the IDHEC[5] syllabus, perhaps he is). The first chapter of *Matter and Memory* develops an amazing conception of photography and of cinematic movement in their relation to things: 'The photograph, if photograph there be, is already taken, already developed in the very heart of things and at all the points of space, etc.'[6] That is not to say that Godard is going back to Bergson. It would be more the other way round, with Godard not even reanimating Bergson so much as finding snatches of him along the way, as he reanimates television.

4. *But why are there always 'two' in Godard? You have to have two before you can have three . . . right, but what does this 2 mean, or this 3?*

You can't be asking that seriously. You know very well that it's beside the point. Godard is not a dialectician. What matters in his work is not 2 or 3 or any other number, but *ET* [AND], the conjunction *ET*. The use of *ET* is the most basic thing. It is important because our thought systems tend to be modelled entirely on the verb 'to be', *EST* [IS]. Philosophy is littered with discussions about the judgment of attribution (the sky is blue) and the judgment of existence (God is), their reducibility or irreducibility. But it's always the verb 'to be'. Even conjunctions are measured against the verb 'to be', as can be seen in the syllogism. The British and the Americans are virtually alone in having liberated conjunctions and reflected on relations. Only when you make the relational judgment independent from all others do you realize that it gets everywhere, works its way into everything, affects everything; *ET* is no longer even a particular conjunction or relation, it brings in all relations; there are as many relations as *ET*s and *ET* doesn't only put all *relations* into the balance, but being, language, etc. The *ET*, '*et . . . et . . . et*', is precisely a form of creative stammering, a foreign usage of language, in contrast to its dominant, conformist usage based on the verb 'to be'.

Of course, *ET* represents diversity, multiplicity, the destruction of identity. The factory gate is not the same when I go in and when I go out, or when I walk past it, being unemployed. The convict's wife is not the same before and after. Only diversity and multiplicity can fully escape being drawn into aesthetic collections (as when you say 'one more', 'one woman more' . . .) or dialectical schemas (as when you say 'one leads to two, which leads to three'). For in all these cases what is retained is the primacy of the One, hence of being, which is deemed to multiply. When Godard says that everything can be divided into two, and that a day is morning *and* evening, he is not saying that it's one or the other, or that the one becomes the other, splits into two. For multiplicity is never in the terms themselves, however numerous they may be, nor in their sum, or totality. Multiplicity is precisely in the *ET*, which doesn't belong to the same order as elements or groups.

Neither an element nor a group, what is *ET*? It's Godard's strength, I think, to live and think and to show the *ET* in a very new way, and to give it an active role. *ET* is neither one thing nor another, it's always in between, on the frontier, for there's always a frontier, a line along which things run or flow, only it's invisible, because it's the hardest thing to see. And yet it's on this line that everything happens, that the future is made and that revolutions are conceived. 'The strong are not those who occupy either camp, it's the frontier that is strong.' Giscard d'Estaing, in a lecture on military geography delivered recently to the army, made the sad observation that the more stable things become on the level of the big groups, between East and West, the USA and the USSR, global entente, rendezvous in space, worldwide police operations, etc., the more they become 'destabilized' on the North/South axis. He cites Angola, the Middle East, the Palestinian struggle, but also all the disturbances that threaten 'regional security', hijackings, Corsica . . . Running from North to South there will always be lines that will deflect the groups, an *ET, ET, ET* which each time marks a new threshold, a new direction for the broken line, a new definition of the frontier. Godard's aim is 'to see the frontiers'; that is, to show what cannot be seen. The convict *and* his wife. The mother *and* the child. But also images *and* sounds. Or again, the watch-maker's gestures on the production line *and* at the editing table: an invisible frontier separates them, which is neither the one nor the other but which draws them both into a divergent evolution, into a flight or a flow in which it is not clear which one is in pursuit of the other or to what end. A whole micro-politics of frontiers, as against the macro-politics of the big groups. At least we know that that's where it's all happening, on the frontier between images and sounds, at the point where images become too full and sounds too loud. That's what Godard has done in *Six fois deux*: passing this active, creative line six times between the two, making it visible and taking television with it.

Translated by Annwyl Williams

Notes

1 In fact, there are four questions, the second question reformulating the first.
2 The pun is of course lost in English. See Ch. 6, note 1.
3 Félix Guattari collaborated on a number of books with Gilles Deleuze, notably *L'Anti-oedipe: capitalisme et schizophrénie*, published in 1972 (translated as *Anti-Oedipus: capitalism and schizophrenia*, Minneapolis, University of Minnesota Press, 1983).
4 Georges Séguy, Communist leader of the powerful trade union, the CGT.
5 IDHEC: Institut des Hautes Ecoles Cinématographiques, the leading French film school.
6 Henri Bergson, *Matter and Memory*, trans. N. M. Paul and W. S. Palmer (London, Swan Sonnenschein, 1911), p. 31.

9

FAMILY, HISTORY, ROMANCE
(extract)

('La famille, l'histoire, le roman', *Cahiers du Cinéma* 260–1, October–November 1975)

Louis Seguin

The opening paragraphs of *The Eighteenth Brumaire of Louis Bonaparte* are especially important (and, like Marx's other political commentaries, are nowadays neglected for reasons which might well be investigated): in them Marx sketches out a theory of the historical imaginary. He describes not the Freudian 'family romance', as brought into play in Straub's *Chronicle of Anna Magdalena Bach*,[1] but what might be called 'historical romance', the romance that is told not by subjects but by classes, and one class in particular, the bourgeoisie.

Marx splits the problem into two. Quoting Hegel, he repeats the remark that 'all facts and personages of great importance in world history occur, as it were, twice'.[2] He continues: 'He [Hegel] forgot to add: the first time as tragedy, the second as farce.' The bourgeoisie gives itself a theatre and degrades it.

'Men', said Marx, 'make their own history.' Then he corrects himself: to say that they 'make' it is misleading:

> But they do not make it just as they please; they do not make it under circumstances chosen by themselves, but under circumstances directly encountered, given and transmitted from the past. The tradition of all dead generations weighs like a nightmare on the brain of the living. And just when they seem engaged in revolutionizing themselves and things, in creating something that has never yet existed, precisely in such periods of revolutionary crisis they anxiously conjure up the spirits of the past to their service and borrow from them names, battle-cries and costumes in order to present the new scene of world history in this time-honoured disguise and this borrowed language. Thus Luther donned the mask of the Apostle Paul, the revolution of 1789

to 1814 draped itself alternately as the Roman Republic and the Roman Empire, and the revolution of 1848 knew nothing better to do than to parody, now 1789, now the revolutionary tradition of 1793 to 1795.

Ideology re-enters the field. It is also, in this case, a practice (and not an instrument), a transitory one which serves as a disguise and is then discarded, which cannot easily be exchanged. 'Roman phrases' had contributed to the 'task of [the] time', the setting up of 'modern *bourgeois* society'. 'Unheroic as bourgeois society is, it nevertheless took heroism, sacrifice, terror, civil war and battles of peoples to bring it into being.' 'Passion' had to be maintained 'on the high plane of great historical tragedy' while 'the bourgeois limitations of the content of their struggles' had to remain concealed.

Marx insists on the 'heroism' of these circumstances, of this evocation of the past, only to set it against its opposite, its 'parody', its 'ghost' as employed by the second bourgeois Revolution, that of 1848.

It is important, for what follows, to understand that what Marx places in the field of ideology (whereas Freud was analysing his own case history, his body, himself as 'subject') is not a mechanism. Ideology (the point has been made often enough) is not a tool made by a class, but its manifestation: the discourse it holds and the law it imposes upon itself. Roman imagery was a way of resurrecting the 'universal' model of Roman law.

To summarize:

- The ideology of the ancient world (or at least of the past) appears in times of historical 'crisis'.
- It is, like Freud's 'feeling' [his 'warm feeling of affection' for his friend R, in the dream where his friend R is his uncle], 'false and exaggerated'.[3]
- It belongs to the order of fiction.
- It is, by definition, transitory and anchored in time.

In spite of its biblical reference *Moses and Aaron* did not fall from heaven, either for Schoenberg or for its producers Straub and Huillet. When Schoenberg begins to write his opera, straight off, without a draft, without any preliminary work, during his holidays at Lugano (he is then a teacher at the Musikhochschule), and dates his first pages 17 July 1930, he seems to be embarking on a race against time, against history. In his letter of 8 August 1931 to Alban Berg, he speaks of the enormous difficulty of his undertaking, the libretto and the music proceeding hand in hand, according to a method which, he says, ought to be recommended to all composers of opera, a target of twenty bars a day which he fails to meet given the effort demanded by the text and the choruses. He explains the hurry in a way which owes nothing to the traditional enthusiasm of genius: 'I want to try very hard to get the opera finished before going back to Berlin'.[4] If the work remains unfinished, this is not for vague reasons that would support the idealist fable of the drama of creation, but because he is overtaken by events. Exile will soon remove him from Berlin where Hitler is about to take power, anti-Semitism about to be unleashed. *Moses and Aaron* is indeed a work of 'crisis', and its reference to the past, its exaltation of the Theocracy and the Promised Land correspond exactly to what Marx says about the 'high plane of great historical tragedy'.

Moses and Aaron is also, of course, a theatrical work. A few months previously, between 15 October 1929 and 14 February 1930, Schoenberg had written, on commission (another, directly economic form of the temporal pressure of history conceived not as an absolute of fatality but as a dialectic of circumstances), his *Accompaniment to a Cinematographic Scene*, whose three sections, as Straub insists in another of his films, carry the subtitles 'Threat', 'Danger' and 'Catastrophe'. For a musician who was always thinking about the staging of his works, the concept of 'catastrophe' is not confined to the everyday meaning of 'great disaster' – it spills over into its original, theatrical meaning of 'final and paramount event of a tragedy, a drama'. It is an extreme form of the *peripeteia*, understood as a 'sudden change in fortune in drama'.

We are dealing with 'reflection' and, as the Althusserians would say, with a 'mirrorless reflection', one which does not appeal to the copy or the model or to mechanical reproduction but, as Dominique Lecourt says in *Une crise et son enjeu*, to 'what is realized in the historical acquisition of knowledge'. The 'respectable disguises' and 'borrowed words' are not a reply – not even a deformed or allusive one – to a history which exists beyond deformation and allusion; they are part of History, they are themselves historical options. Replying to Bazarov, the author of *Essays on Marxist Philosophy*, Lenin accused him of substituting 'for the question of whether things exist outside our sensations, our perceptions, our representations, that of how exact our representations of "these same" things are'. He continues: 'to be more precise, you *mask* the first question with the second.' Straub and Huillet's work occupies the area of the 'mirrorless reflection', the theatre of historical 'romance'. It is thus opposed to those who preach total submission to the work and what it says, as well as to the over-literal interpretations of the conductor Michael Gielen, for whom Aaron is the positive hero of the opera, the mouthpiece of a historical materialism strangely confounded with political realism (see on this topic Gramsci's notes on Machiavelli), while Moses is the idealistic advocate of a mystical theocracy – a curiously anti-Brechtian hypothesis, since it reintroduces the concept of a model that the spectator has to identify with (only in a new way).

Straub and Huillet's production, as I say, does not fall from heaven. It has its own tradition, its own 'romance'. The last shot of *Othon* links up with the first shot of the commentary on Schoenberg's *Accompaniment to a Cinematographic Scene*, where the scene returns to the music to develop the twilight concept of 'catastrophe', displacing it from the rise of Nazism to the contemporary threat of imperialism. This displacement avoids repetition, nostalgia. Straub and

Huillet refuse to meditate; they are concerned only with the 'crisis', the moment when History gives way, when the balance tips, in a movement which owes nothing to fatality (and besides, since then the Vietnamese people have overcome their oppressor), but is its knowledge, its science.

Brecht's *Die Geschäfte des Herrn Julius Caesar* then become *History Lessons*. But here the link is misleading: the Roman 'signifiers', the map and the statue, which serve to make the connection are 'false and exaggerated', they are fascist copies, the residues of fascism's 'historical romance'. By the same stroke, eternity is eliminated, the myth of the cyclical recurrence of History. The difference is indicated in the first shots of *History Lessons* which hollow out the gap between History and its fiction, between the return to the past and the lesson to be learned. *History Lessons* refuses historicism. The suppression of the story of Rarus, the freed slave, and its replacement by 'meaningless' trips through a non-symbolic Rome without a past, repeats in another register the irony which Brecht attached to the tale. In Straub and Huillet's pedagogy, as in Brecht's, questions open only on to other questions, truths on to other truths, the discourse of one class (and its interpreters: bankers, lawyers, writers) on to that of another (peasants).

What happens at the end of the text-chain and at the end of the production-chain?

For Schoenberg, anticipating the production is not a practice but a barrier to be erected. Less a question of proposing ideas than of ruling them out; of persuading people that any production at all will be impossible. As he says in his letter to Webern:

> It was a very great deal of work [. . .] getting the scene 'Dance round the Golden Calf' worked out properly. I wanted to leave as little as possible to those new despots of the theatrical art, the producers, and even to envisage the choreography as far as I'm able to. [. . .] Anyway, so far I've succeeded in thinking out movements such as at least enter into a different territory of expression from the caperings of common-or-garden ballet.[5]

The indications of position scattered through the libretto – which either keep the characters at a distance from one another or make them move around one another, or again (as at the beginning of Act II, Scene 3) suggest an invasion – seem to work so as to obstruct, to empty and at the same time to fill up the traditional space of representation. Schoenberg defies the Italian-style proscenium theatre. He does his best to make his opera 'unplayable' in it. To the crisis he introduces into ideology, one that reflects the contemporary historical crisis, he adds another, more its reflection than its double, a crisis in theatrical practice.

The production he proposes is a denial of the opera; Schoenberg proceeds 'as if' the 'historical romance' of the Jewish people, at the dawn of their persecution, were impossible to recount. In Freudian terms, the 'latent content' of the work is censored by a 'manifest content' whose paradoxical role, in the theatre, is to 'prevent interpretation'. Or again (to quote Marx), he refuses to behave like 'that mad Englishman in Bedlam who fancies that he lives in the times of the ancient Pharaohs and daily bemoans the hard labour that he must perform in the Ethiopian mines as a gold digger'. Schoenberg refuses his own 'folly'. As he is about to speak (and not just to write, to compose, to play a part in the composition, precisely), he makes sure that he has nothing to say. Moses is an operatic hero who does not sing. The 'Sprechgesang' negates the opera from within. *Moses and Aaron* is a work of self-denial, and this self-denial is not a tragedy of creation and impotence, but a 'desperate' attempt to stay in equilibrium on the moving edge of the 'crisis'.

René Leibowitz, in his book on Schoenberg – in which he notes the political implications of *Moses and Aaron*, seeing them however as incidental and fortuitous – writes:

> Of his first two works, *Erwartung* and *Die glückliche Hand*, we were able to say that they were not so much operas as attempts to radically renew the lyrical tradition. The comic opera *Von Heute auf Morgen*, on the contrary, marks a return to a more traditional view of the lyrical work. Schoenberg is basically trying to master a tradition which he had previously subjected to 'radical doubt' and which cannot be 'superseded' (in the Hegelian sense of the term) without being preserved ... Finally, *Moses and Aaron* attempts to preserve, and at the same time supersede, the form of the grand historical opera (in this case, biblical), and this results in what seems to me to constitute the most complete synthesis within the lyrical tradition.

This thesis is interesting in that it offers an exemplary formulation of the idealist approach (in which contradictions are resolved in a higher unity) which 'traditional' productions of *Moses and Aaron* will adopt. Leibowitz makes the common and by no means innocent mistake of twisting the meaning of the untranslatable 'Aufhebung' which combines the *preservation* and the *elimination* of the Hegelian dialectic too closely for the French language; he gives the word its more banal, a-dialectical meaning, vulgarized by 'existentialist' psychology, i.e. the effort of the individual to transcend his situation. This transcendence leads once again (as does every aspect of idealist aethetics) to the ever-present subtext of impassioned creativity and the unfinished work that will underpin productions of *Moses and Aaron* for forty years.

From the first performance of 'Dance round the Golden Calf' in Darmstadt in 1951, under the direction of Hermann Scherchen,[6] to the latest performance, strangely, in French in 1973 at the Paris Opera, under the direction of Rolf Liebermann and Raymond Gérôme, via the famous Zurich performance, under the direction of Rosbaud, productions of *Moses and Aaron* repeat the same discourse, are based on the same principle. The principle amounts to getting rid of Act III, of which only the libretto had been sketched out in New York in 1935. The discourse is exemplified in an interview with Raymond Gérôme, published in the journal *Harmonie* in 1973, before the 'French' performance. The production is enclosed in a psychological/mystical problematic in which the dialectic of the 'Aufhebung' is related not even to full-blown classical idealism but to precision of feeling: 'The difficulty for the performers is to match their feelings, their view of the character, with what the music imposes on them. For one of the basic themes of *Moses and Aaron* is *doubt*, and the music succeeds admirably in conveying the characters' hesitations.' Raymond Gérôme has, as he says, a 'conception of the work': 'It strikes me as extremely significant that Schoenberg left his work unfinished at the very point where Moses despairs of this "Word which deserts him" ' (a misunderstanding of the German text, hardly accidental!). 'It's a kind of acknowledgment of the bankruptcy of the thought/speech/action dialectic [*sic*].' The production becomes little more than the technical challenge 'to make the 165 members of the chorus evolve'. Technique fills up the gaps, the 'fatality' of History.

And so Straub and Huillet begin not by following the properly cinematographic tradition of the musical and moving back the walls of the stage-cube, widening and deepening it, but by choosing *another* space. The cube is replaced by an elliptical arena and, by the same stroke, the 'historical romance', the telling of the story, is put back in its place of origin which is the public place, the forum, of the 'civic festival'. The Roman identity of this new location, however discreet, weighs on the operation. Its archaeology ties in with the biblical reference. The political spectacle is referred to its Jacobin model. It offers a new 'history lesson'. 'National education' (by which one should understand not the apparatus, but literally the education of the nation), says the conventional Rabaut Saint-Etienne,

> demands circuses, gymnasia, games and contests open to all, national festivals, a spirit of friendly competitiveness among people of whatever age or sex, the imposing and delightful spectacle of human society brought together; it requires open spaces, access to the countryside and to nature; that is how moral behaviour acquires the status of law. A revolution can occur in festivals and in the heart, as has occurred already in living conditions and in Government.

These Jacobin festivals must as always offer an exemplary spectacle, or rather, they are the privileged locus of the exemplary. In Grégaire's report to the Convention of 16 Prairial year II [4 June 1794], we read that 'true Republicans only have to be shown the good; they do not need to be told what to do'. Education works through persuasion; it invites people to imitate the paradigms of virtue and heroism. Fundamentally anti-Brechtian (or rather, offering a political spectacle in the pre-Brechtian mode), the festivals play on the identification of spectator and model. Their metonymy is synchronic: they impose an ever new environment, an insistence. Boissy d'Anglas: 'Public institutions must be the true education of the people, but this education can be useful only if the institutions are associated with ceremonies and festivities, or rather if they are themselves ceremonies and festivities.' Renée Balibar, in her book on *Le Français national*, has shown how these celebrations, these 'spectacular diversions', were aimed at making their participants submit – in various ways, through the systematic use of a common, literary language, for example – to the rising ideology of the bourgeoisie. But of course, Straub and Huillet's anachronistic and critical displacement has a quite different function.

The civic festival in *Moses and Aaron*, Jewish and/or Roman, is no sooner replaced in its original location than it is perverted. The symmetry and permanence of politics, of the spectacle and the festival, are called into question. The mirror disappears from the reflection.

First of all, the relations between hero and chorus are inverted. By enclosing them in the same circularity (which the panoramic shot of Act I, Scene 1 describes and repeats), Straub and Huillet turn the choir-mass away from its traditional role of respondent (to the hero) and relay (towards the spectators). To be more precise, they give this enclosure a new meaning: it is no longer a question of reproducing the 'feelings' of the characters and inscribing these meanings in a space, but of first describing the space that determines them. Straub and Huillet's production emphasizes separation and confrontation; it reiterates, on its own level, in and through its theatre, a fundamental principle of Marxism-Leninism as formulated by Althusser: 'In order for there to be classes in a "society", the society has to be *divided* into classes: this division does not come *later in the story*; it is the exploitation of one class by another, it is therefore the class struggle, which constitutes the division into classes.'[7]

Schoenberg in his opera had suggested a grotesque, painted disguise for Cecil B. De Mille, and this creates an additional obstruction. As for Straub and Huillet, they pick up and develop Lang's practice in *Die Nibelungen* – obvious despite lengthy concealment to anyone who sees the films again today – which established a contradiction, a dialectic, between the hieratic and the unspeakable, the geometric and the formless, the heroic figure and the demoniac (the dwarfs of *Siegfried*, the barbarians of *Kriemhild* and, more generally, trivial indications of one sort and another, what Lotte Eisner calls the 'multiplication of little comic touches'). It is no longer a case, as Gielen tried to maintain (although the 'scandalous' nature of his statement is productive in its way), of deciding whether Moses or Aaron is right, and of going against custom, but of playing one hero against another, the second against the first. It is a case, first of all, of sending them back – in perpetual confrontation, as in the high-angle shots which, in the angle of the framing, distinguish between the prophet and the demagogue, wordlessness and eloquence – to their ideological space which is that of closed discourse, of the formal hypothesis and of magic reduced to trickery. It is then a question of abolishing this link between illusion and the flow of speech by opening it up to popular intervention. The excesses of the people, the 'demoniacal', as in Lang but this time explicitly, upsets the orderliness of the festival. The adoration of the golden calf lays open the immaculate field of logic to darkness, bloodshed and abjection, to the stampede of the peasants and their flocks. The history lesson of the 'civic festival' is dissipated, dismantled, torn apart under the pressure of another lesson, which is no longer that of formal correctness, the individual and the model, but the 'wild' lesson of confrontation and invasion. The confined space of the festival is burst open. The song of freedom escapes from the civic theatre and unfurls, in the lyrical *peripeteia* that is a cause for popular rejoicing, against the background of the Nile valley.

The natural decor is no longer restricted to Rabaut Saint-Etienne's 'countryside', but on the one side to an arid land, hemmed in by walls and mountains, and on the other, to the discovery of a limitless horizon. At the same time, the 'romance' [*roman*] rediscovers its Bakhtinian vocation. It is no longer a monologic murmuring of the exemplary but its dialogic transgression. Straub and Huillet's production puts back into place, 'on its feet', in freedom, a dialectic enclosed, restricted, until then in the to and fro, the symmetry of a problematic. They give 'historical romance' back to Romance and to History.

The reinstatement of the Third Act, quite apart from being a challenge to the dominant ideology of ill-fated creativity, is absolutely necessary to this new production which gives power to the people. When Moses finally triumphs over Aaron, when the man of words is crushed under the weight of History, we find ourselves in a new, shapeless, indeterminate place, in a wasteland which is 'all [the heroes] have left' after the people have smashed the walls of the arena that contained them. The triumph of theocratic monarchy, which Schoenberg does not at all reject, is accorded its historical logic but also blurred by a paradoxical appeal to the nomadic existence (Moses is a king without a kingdom); it is condemned to shapelessness and impermanence, to an uncertainty which in the end can be read only in materialist terms.

The systematic use of 'Sprechgesang' is also, with Günter Reich's help, more than a subterfuge, more than just a clever way of compensating for the absence of music. It is a political gesture. Leibowitz provides an excellent summary of the commonplace view:

> Moses, the thinker, the powerful bass voice given over from start to finish to 'Sprechgesang'. This vocal mode *symbolizes* [my emphasis] the character's *introversion*, his constant struggle to express his thoughts, formulate his vision. Aaron on the other hand, the man of action, is conceived as the typical tenor of lyrical drama, a noble and heroic figure with brilliant, flowing lines that symbolize the character's 'extroversion' and his sometimes superficial strength.

The rest, the 'less important roles', says Leibowitz, are relegated to the accidental, the decorative, the ornamental. This tautology of the psychological/

mystical 'interpretation', in which the inexpressible and the expressed relate monotonously to each other and which recourse to a vulgarized psychoanalytical vocabulary does little to hide, is all the more unacceptable because it denies the originality of 'Sprechgesang'. This had appeared thirty years earlier in the *Gurrelieder*, and was described by Leibowitz again, rightly this time, as a way of 'transcending' (the Hegelian concept of denial/transcendence is already there) the 'classical drama–music dualism', or alternatively the no less classical 'recitative–arioso' opposition. 'Sprechgesang' displaces ('aufheben') the opera's historicism, its division, precisely, between action and meditation, episode and ode; its neutrality does not relate it to any and every space, but to another space, another scene and another music that is not so much 'out of phase' or, as a superficial knowledge of Brecht might suggest, 'distanced', but turned back on itself, returned to the 'dialogism' of the romance which produced it. The musical space is divided up into three levels and two oppositions. 'Sprechgesang' is opposed not only to the lyrical but also, and this time along with it, to what an idealist commentary reduces to silence, which is the song of the people, its complexity (Schoenberg himself acknowledges this), its savagery (the golden calf scene) and its enthusiasm, that is to say, literally, its 'fury'. The concreteness of the singing, which Straub and Huillet underline through the concreteness of the outdoor performance and its noises – the resonance of the open air and the sound of footsteps, bells ringing, people shouting – triumphs over this scene that splits open under the weight of it all. After that, there is room only for the return of 'Sprechgesang', neither words nor music, nor both, corresponding to the indeterminate, unresolved nature of the 'crisis': a residue of idealism which transgresses it because it no longer implies the (psychological) history of desire but the (materialist) desire for History.

Between the *Chronicle of Anna Magdalena Bach* and *Moses and Aaron*, Freud and Marx, 'family romance' and 'historical romance', the Promised Land and the theatre of 'crisis', there are too many links for us to be satisfied with the simple concept of reversibility. Politics, 'historical romance' are already there in Freud and in Bach, where domesticity is only a pretext, successful and provisional, for withdrawing from a world which, no sooner expelled, returns to invest it. It is Marx who brings together the fictional motives and motifs. And the symmetry is only an effect of this bringing together. My own 'intervention' might have proceeded in the opposite direction, retrospectively. It might have spoken of 'historical romance' and dialectical materialism apropos of the *Chronicle*, and then used the notion of 'family romance' to explode the psychologism of *Moses and Aaron*, denouncing its classical reliance on the father figure, on *Oedipus* and Reich. But this reversal would have done no more than exploit the link after the event by 'rewriting History'. It would merely have substituted coincidence for intersection and contradiction. And it is not a question of chance, or ingeniousness, but again, of connections and contradictions that are a feature of the cinematic production. Straub and Huillet's cinema is one from which you cannot escape because neither Straub nor Huillet escapes from the cinema, because for them (see the interview in *Cahiers du Cinéma* 258–9) it is a practice. Unlike a cinema which prides itself irrationally on a faked 'expenditure', which spends non-existent money and is generally wasteful, a cinema which protects itself from this loss only by the derisory accumulation of effects to demonstrate mastery, they present, stage, an expense of another kind, a new economy akin to the new method of analysis of which Marx says, in his preface to [the French edition of] *Capital*, that 'it had not previously been applied . . .'. All that I have tried to do here is, partially at least, to follow it.

Translated by Annwyl Williams

Notes

1 The first part of Seguin's article was devoted to this earlier film and to the part played in it by the concept of 'family romance' as developed by Freud. I have glossed the French text here to clarify the distinction. (Translator's note.)

2 Quotations from *The Eighteenth Brumaire of Louis Bonaparte* are taken from: Karl Marx and Frederick Engels, *Collected Works*, vol. 11 (London, Lawrence & Wishart, 1979), pp. 103–5. (Translator's note.)

3 S. Freud, *The Interpretation of Dreams*, trans. J. Strachey (Harmondsworth, Penguin, 1976), pp. 221–2. Strachey translates: 'ungenuine and exaggerated'. (Translator's note.)

4 *Arnold Schoenberg Letters*, ed. E. Stein, trans. E. Wilkins and E. Kaiser (London, Faber & Faber, 1964), p. 151. (Translator's note.)

5 Ibid., pp. 152–3. (Translator's note.)

6 Not, as in Seguin's text, Rolf Liebermann.

7 'Reply to John Lewis', trans. G. Lock, in L. Althusser, *Essays in Self-criticism* (London, NLB, 1976), p. 50. (Translator's note.)

10

ROUND TABLE: *MILESTONES* AND US (extracts)

('*Milestones* et nous: table-ronde', *Cahiers du Cinéma* 258–9, July–August 1975)

Pascal Bonitzer, Dominique Villain, Serge Daney, Jean Narboni, Serge Le Péron, Thérèse Giraud, Serge Toubiana

The interior point of view

PASCAL BONITZER: I think we should start by saying that this is a film we liked as much for its subject as for its technique and its referent. It's a film that reflects a phenomenon which can be seen everywhere, here in Europe, in France, as in the USA – the ebbing away of the great movements and acts of opposition that came into being following May '68. It gets to grips with this phenomenon, which is of concern to us, and makes it the starting point of its montage: it is a film by two film-makers, Robert Kramer and John Douglas, who were part of that movement, along with people, actors and characters, who were also part of it. And on a broader level it's also a film which attempts to understand the historical movement in its present situation, starting from the concrete situation of the United States now and in particular from the resounding defeat of American imperialism.

And instead of taking issue with that politics, Kramer and Douglas have done something quite different, which is what I think excites us about the film. They have fashioned a portrait of the interior of what is represented, not by the politics of oppression, of American imperialist aggression against other peoples and especially against the people of Vietnam, but more precisely of what is represented for us today by the resistance of these peoples, their struggle, and in general the struggle of all minorities oppressed by American imperialism. I think that's where we have to start from, this method of approaching history not from the global point of view or from a global understanding of what imperialist oppression represents, but on the contrary from the point of view of the resistance, the struggle, the daily life of the oppressed, with the many faces of these oppressed peoples. Because we have here both the 'oppressed of the exterior', if one can put it that way, who are the Vietnamese, and the 'oppressed of the interior', who are the blacks, the American Indians – all those who are marginalized by the system.

DOMINIQUE VILLAIN: I'm not sure I quite agree with what you're saying, because I don't find in the film the *struggle* of minorities against imperialism in the usual sense of that word.

BONITZER: No, what I mean is that I think what's interesting about the film is that it's not at all made on the classical principle of militant films, which is to show aggression on one side and resistance on the other (if I said that, I expressed myself badly), or power on one side and struggle on the other side. No, this film assumes the existence of the oppressed, lets them talk, shows them from the inside.

VILLAIN: But that's precisely what I don't quite follow, because I don't see that the Vietnamese, the blacks or the American Indians are shown resisting. I think this relates more to the Americans, the main characters in the film – the 'leftists' – in the way their faces and bodies are shown. For example, the pregnant woman who says in close-up: 'America is grinding me down, wasting me'. And for her, America is also the genocide of the Indians, racism etc. Whereas we are only shown blacks in the film in photographs of slaves in chains, and not at all in the present moment of 'struggle'.

SERGE DANEY: What seems to me to be important is that this is in no sense a film of *denunciation*, when one might expect politicized, radicalized people like Kramer and Douglas to attack the enemy, to attack the injustices, the abuses, the atrocities, as for example in *Hearts and Minds*, which is the prototype of the kind of progressive film whose function is to attack the enemy in their midst, American imperialism as it is also manifested within America. The important thing about Kramer and Douglas's film is that since it is not a film of denunciation, it is really organized from *within*. And I think we have to say that this is what makes it an event for us at *Cahiers*, because of course it was *Ice* that prompted the debate that marked our political radicalization – our backing off from the French Communist Party (even if we were still looking at the film from the outside, in an extremely formalist way). Both for Kramer and for us some time has passed, and now for both of us there is a kind of standing off, something that makes for a moment of reflection, maybe the loss of certain illusions but in any case a firmer anchorage, a steadiness that allows both Kramer and ourselves to begin to think about something that will be *our* history. The whole film is made from the inside point of view of people who have lived through that history. At a time when we are starting to see films which explicitly or implicitly take what we call 'leftism' as their subject, whether it's the leftism of today or the older historical versions (I'm thinking of the Taviani brothers' film), it's important to note that there are two approaches to this. There is one which involves – as with *Allonsanfan*[1]

143

– taking a line on something you have never been part of, like the Taviani brothers, who are revisionist film-makers fascinated by leftism as a source of subject matter and method; and on the other side there is the Kramer–Douglas film, which is a story of people learning about things but putting them to good use, thinking about them, talking about them among themselves, in other words giving themselves a way of thinking about their history and not just giving it to others to think about. This could also be interesting in relation to what we might have said in *Cahiers* about militant cinema and especially about *Histoires d'A*,[2] about what we called a *collective statement*. How might it function, how could it be adapted to talk about its own history? And then how could it be filmed?

BONITZER: I'd like to go back to the comparison you made with *Hearts and Minds* so that I can clarify what I was saying just now. There is in fact a fundamental difference between a film like *Hearts and Minds*, which if you like is talking about the same thing – the reality of Vietnam for America – and the Kramer–Douglas film. *Hearts and Minds* is a liberal film that represents current trends in the USA, such as you might see reflected in the *New York Times* – it's the point of view represented by Kennedy's former adviser Ellsberg, with his sentimental moralizing. The argument of *Hearts and Minds* comes down to this: how wrong we were, how blind we were, how stupidly anti-Communist. Kramer and Douglas's point of view is altogether different. It's not at all the liberal's bad conscience about American imperialism, heart bleeding when it sees the wrong it has done; it's rather a testimony about something that exists both on the inside and the outside of the United States, and which consciously marks a radical demarcation line between these positive, populist forces and the aggressive force of American imperialism, the power of the state. The film testifies to the present condition of these forces, what unites them and connects them. It represents this by (from the point of view of) the way it is put together, by the enactment of its fiction. And that's the point of view it is made from – it's not just another film about American bad conscience, about one more negative aspect of the reality, it's about the positive existence of forces which are asserting themselves, trying to assert themselves, the different minority groups.

JEAN NARBONI: I have the feeling that what is beginning to take shape in these initial interventions is what one might call an 'interior' or 'inside' point of view, as opposed to a point of view which talks about things, which is outside them, in order to expose them, to describe them or even to valorize them. I think this is an extremely important factor in Kramer's cinema, going beyond the relationship of the films to their subject matter, and connecting with the way in which we ourselves talk about them. This is something that has always struck me. Every time we go to see a Kramer film, and we talk about it afterwards and say a little about how we respond to it, we find it impossible to adopt an outside point of view on these films. We're completely inside the problems they pose; there is something in these films that we find very familiar, and at the same time there's also something very far removed from us. They are both very close to us and also very American. And I think that when Kramer said in his *Le Monde* interview, 'We've tried to keep close to the spirit of Vietnam', if we take that literally it can give us a lead on how in fact his films function in relation to their subject, their audience and, even more than the audience, those who find themselves wanting to hold on a little to the spirit of Kramer's films. In any case, from *In the Country* through *The Edge*, *Ice* and now *Milestones* and the films by the Newsreel team, this is something that has always struck me.

SERGE LE PERON: Yes, there is something that strikes a chord with us here. And that is that contrary to what you might feel, however you might approve of or sympathize with or politically support films like *Hearts and Minds*, I think what strikes us particularly about *Milestones* is its refusal to take a 'balanced' approach, with all that that word implies: a period of history has passed, let's see why, let's turn back to the past, and so on. What's interesting about this film is that while it is certainly telling us about a period that is over, it constantly refers that period to the present; at every moment in the film, and particularly because the relationships between the people we see in it are highly developed, it's showing us a movement, it's reflecting on a period in movement, what has carried through from that period to the present and for the future. It doesn't look at that period with a bad conscience, because the film-makers were active during it, indeed they were its participants. They have set out the testimony of someone who lived through that period positively and who in the end has emerged from it as a winner, someone who has come out of that period strengthened, and has managed to connect it to what one might call, historically and spatially, the 'other America': the kind of positive approach which existed then, which lived through the events in a different way, and which now finds itself strengthened by the victory of the Vietnamese people over imperialism.

[. . .]

'Being American': genocide

NARBONI: [Talking of 'America'] Something Kramer said in *Le Monde* is striking: the fact that in *Milestones* they tried to reflect on what *being American* means. All the internationalist themes of national and other minorities etc. which were in *Ice* and *The Edge* also appear in this film, but in addition, as an explicit theme, there is an interrogation of what America is – the process of the setting up of the American nation, with a clear sense that America was founded on a genocide, a crime. Some words were used just now – pioneers, radical, first time – and what the film has is this

145

double movement: what it means to create something for a first time, in relation to a blood-stained beginning – everything they buried, everything they liquidated, everything they exterminated: the American Indians.

BONITZER: In fact, these are the film's American roots, and also what connects it – though in opposition – to the American cinema, which in its most popular forms at least set out to misrepresent and conceal this past, this genocide, this original crime. The Western has had no other function for some considerable time. Compared with European cinema, American cinema – as made in Hollywood – has had this particular characteristic of being a historical cinema which is constantly returning to the founding of the American nation-state; and for years all these stories have been so many misrepresentations, lies, masquerades about American history. In recent years there have been liberal fictions, of the *Soldier Blue* kind or Arthur Penn's films, about the massacre of the American Indians. But it's one thing to say we massacred the Indians, and quite another thing to say we are of the same flesh and blood as the Indians given the power structure that was erected on their massacre, their bones. From this point of view, in fact, the Kramer–Douglas film breaks new ground because for the first time they are saying just this: that this is not the White Man disguising himself as an Indian, as in Sam Fuller's *Run of the Arrow*, it really is the Indian speaking, it actually is the American who is also an Indian and who as an Indian can only rebel.

VILLAIN: Talking of the American Indians, I'd like to mention the use of space in the film and how that space, which in a way resembles the space we've seen in Westerns, is at the same time completely different. You feel that they are still there, still occupying this space. I was particularly struck by this, and it's also true for all the other spaces in the film.

BONITZER: Indeed, and it's because the film is also intervening at a moment when the American Indians are beginning to speak again, as Indians, which has not happened for a very, very long time. The incident of Wounded Knee which is referred to in the film is historically an inaugural event.

DANEY: It's true that for some time now alternative Westerns have been made, *Little Big Man* for example. But the Kramer–Douglas film is saying something different: we are like the American Indians. That is not the only thing it says, however, because it is also saying: we are Whites. And a problem arises here, a very important one for the question of the collective statement: *the place you are speaking from.* I mean, up to what point do the film-makers consider themselves authorized to speak in the name of others, American Indians, blacks, etc? How do you not take their place and at the same time record their existence, their oppression, their resistance? How do you show the importance of their resistance so that it is included in the film and not distorted? It struck me that in a film where people are talking all the time, there is a moment when the talking stops, which is throughout the long sequence about the blacks, the movement of the blacks, where the images are fairly shocking but remain silent about repression. One feels that they should be there, but at the same time one does not have the right to speak in their place.

[. . .]

Confiscated memory

THERESE GIRAUD: I think the place the blacks, the American Indians and the Vietnamese have in the film comes principally from the film-makers' own approach to this, in terms of the way they see the movement developing.

SERGE TOUBIANA: To give a partial answer to Thérèse's point, I admit that I'm reading the film more in terms of its particular context in America and in terms of what it allows us to think about – which we don't think about in France – and that is a certain way of speaking politically, of having a dialogue with oneself and with others. And if we go back to the idea of a pioneering movement – the idea that it's a radical movement, and that since the last war it is the first wave of the movement that incorporates blacks, young radicals, and perhaps other social classes and other races – then behind all this there is also the idea that in the United States there is no instrument which might claim to be the memory, living or dead, of the struggles of the century. Whereas in France, and I think in every European country, with the possible exception of Germany, for concrete historical reasons, the Communist parties have assumed this right of being (generally in a defunct sense, though that has still to be proved) the site and the embodiment of all the traditions, all the layers and strands, of anti-imperialist and anti-capitalist struggles waged by the people. And if we're talking about revisionist parties, there's a vast system of confiscating the memory and the tradition of struggle.

All right. In this context we should have to talk about the Algerian war, which in concrete terms was not an issue for us, at least for those of us who were politically active in 1968, or only a very minor one. It's not an issue for us now because we see Algerians in the street every day, we talk with them, we've been politically active with them; it is only in this sense that the question of the Algerian war has come up again for us, has made our generation think of the past. For people who are a little older, this may work differently, traumatically if they were involved in it, heroically if they deserted or helped the FLN. As for the French Communist Party, it has nothing to say about the question of the Algerian war; perhaps out of shame for what it did, perhaps because it can't revive it as an issue after ten years. Maybe it's the same with the Resistance, or 1936,[3] or many other things. Which means that we, as young revolutionaries or young progressives, cannot inscribe ourselves within any militant past. The only connecting link we have is Marx, Lenin, Mao. We know that there are, or were, struggles; we know that there is a Marxism, and it serves revisionists as much as ourselves and certain university technocrats; we know, in other words, that there is a body, to which we feel ourselves tied, or committed or aligned, and which is a body of doctrine. This is what explains why, in some ways, we are politically relatively cut off from the struggles and traditions and social classes which historically have an interest in revolt – I'm thinking of the working class. And this is also why you sense that in the United States, precisely because they do not have this body of doctrine to enframe and cover them, and also because they are the first, they feel themselves more accountable for their future struggles and their actions, much closer to their ideals.

NARBONI: As regards these apparatuses which confiscate memory, one thing it's important to note is the way in which it is the apparatuses themselves that reinstate memory, and the way that people who were not involved talk about these apparatuses, something that struck me in relation to the question touched on in the 'Forum on History'[4]: Is the Algerian war part of our History? What strikes me is precisely the difference in tone between the writings emanating from the Party and the writings of people who were not involved and who waged the struggle from the outside. For instance, in the statements by militants in the book *Voyage à l'intérieur du Parti Communiste* the argument is greatly different from the way in which, say, the Sartrians talk about this. When Charby and Maschinot talk about the war in Algeria in *Le Reflux*, something reminds us of Kramer. What also struck me is that in his interview in *Le Monde* the third thing Kramer said was: we're a little bit existentialist here, in a proprietorial sense. I think there is something that might be investigated here, around this idea: the involvement of individual subjects in struggles, the *incorporation* of the struggles waged by peoples within a personal problematic, as opposed to the discourse of apparatus where the 'lived experience' of militants serves only as an anecdotal support to the Story of the Truth which this apparatus embodies.

[. . .]

A cinema of denotation

DANEY: To come back for a moment to the film as object, first of all it should be said that we don't know much about the way the film was made, or how it is going to be distributed, seen and responded to in the United States. But if we're talking about the way the film works formally, I think it is important to note that, outside of the shots in which they appear, we never know who the characters we see are or what they do. It's impossible to reconstruct an exterior for the film, a kind of foundation, a reserve, from which the film's shots could be set apart. And yet these shots, as they are, are not abstract or enigmatic, shots which make us want to know more about each of the characters. Here again, we find what we were saying just now about intimacy; there is no suggestion here of something being hidden behind what we see which the camera is helping to force out. On the contrary, everything contained in the shots *functions as information*, and I think this is a film in which there is no wastage. There is, it's true, an enormous lee-way in the sense that it's a very long film and it takes its time, the time of the people who are living in it, but all the elements here function as infor-mation, as *denotations*. There is a minimum of connotation, no uncon-trolled connotation. For me, this brings me back to a question I ask myself equally of Straub, of Kramer, or of Alaouié[5]: what is this cinema that tries to let you detail everything you see on the screen, everything you can iden-tify, and which as a result makes it in a way difficult to follow, because you have to get inside it, you can't let yourself stay on the sidelines? The oppo-site of advertising films, in fact . . .

GIRAUD: What you're saying is very important, especially about the difficulty of following it. I certainly found the film a bit hard going, particularly at the beginning, and it takes quite some time to get used to it, you really have to hang on to it, because for three and a half hours you're watching a suc-cession of people coming and going, interacting with each other, and you can't say who they are, you don't know what is determining all these com-ings and goings, you can't latch on to anything else. This links up with what we were saying before, the fact that there is no referential discourse in this film: you can never say that if someone says this and does this, that's because previously he did that, he was like that. And finally, it's quite hard going because it forces us to step outside ourselves and listen to what is being said, actively listen – see what's really behind it all, what it means, what always needs to come through, what's going on under the surface. In the end, it's listening in the Maoist sense of that word, listen-ing for what is new, the seeds of the new. And as I see it, the film works a bit like a lesson, a moral lesson with the birth at the end.

BONITZER: Going back to what Serge Daney was saying, it's true that Kramer isn't at all intrigued by intimacy. In so far as this is a cinema which plays the realism game, and which therefore has some connection with classical European *cinéma-vérité* – although in this case the characters are involved in a fictional, dramatic framework which completely excludes the place of the observer – it doesn't make any attempt to emphasize personal intimacy, as in *Chronique d'un été* for example, which tries to bring out the interiority of people. In this case, people's experience is expressed in a much more gen-erous way.

NARBONI: I think this is because in *Milestones* there are two kinds of component, and the biggest mistake one could make in respect of a film like this would be to link it with '*cinéma-vérité*' or 'candid eye' etc. On the one side, we have all these very precise details, all the things that seem to be caught

head-on, as they come, the fragmented bits, the big close-ups, the sublim-
inal shots, the staccato editing. And on the other side – which is not at all
the symmetrical reverse of the first side, but what one might call its unifying design – we have an *architecture*, a form of open-ended thinking
which is musical, progressively spacious, and belongs with the kind of cinema that is more structured, more abstract, in the best sense of that term:
the films of Dreyer, Godard, Mizoguchi, to which indeed Kramer is always
referring. It's this architecture, this serial composition which in my view
completely frees those aspects of the film that seem to belong to *cinéma-
vérité* from the stiffness, the slightly tasteless, slightly *indiscreet* intimacy
from which that kind of cinema is only rarely free. There is no other way I
could describe the feeling I had about a film which, while it always keeps
to the level of everyday experiences, as it unfolds increasingly acquires this
spaciousness, this dimension of a broad universe.

BONITZER: Yes, in the Kramer–Douglas film there *isn't* the kind of opposition
you had in the 1960s between a montage cinema that was a cinema of
manipulation – manipulation both of minds and material – and a cinema
of real life which took life as it unfolds in front of the camera's eye. There
isn't that opposition here; you get the accidents of life as the camera
records them, and also the editing works in such a way as to give the
material a musical form and a much broader and much more collective
perspective in the way it brings together very different things, spaces,
places, people that are generally heterogeneous.

LE PERON: That said, as regards this particular approach to editing, I had a
problem with the film. We've said that this is our kind of cinema, a collective statement, but in itself it misses something of the individual
nature of the different relationships we watch in the film. For instance, the
problems and failures of living in a community and the transformation of
the couple relationship are raised, certainly, but there is a kind of communal contentment, happiness, tenderness showing through it all which is
perhaps a little too noble.

GIRAUD: That's why I said before that Kramer and Douglas are taking up a
position in the film about the far left in America. The far left is not like
that, a single unity; and one senses that there are a lot of problems, that
things are on the move in every sense, and it's here that Kramer and
Douglas are intervening, forcefully, to point to the way forward, as you
were saying. What they're doing is showing all these possible objectives
and confronting them by setting them off against one another, working on
them in fact, working on what is germinating, in the process of being
transformed, as one works clay to make a pot.

DANEY: Coming back to the film, there is certainly no fiction there, in the sense
that there is no fictional *investment*, but at the same time there is something evolving in the film, and that is a birth. The approach the film takes
is to ensure that no one event steals the limelight; and here Jean Narboni

is right to talk about Dreyer in respect of narrative economy, and we certainly should not let the film pass as a sort of absolute and faithful mirror. Because the approach it has is the theme of rebirth, which involves dealing with the objective problems set for the people in the film only to the extent that they talk about them themselves, and in the terms in which they talk about them, and so not as 'problems'. Which means that the only thing that's going to happen in the film is something one sees being prepared for, and the scene of the birth at the end is what happens to *everybody at the same time*. So there's no place here for individual problems, except perhaps for the story of the GI and also the story of the work-bench, and that's interesting because it reinstates the problem of the working class, the problem of their being outside.

TOUBIANA: We've been trying to talk about the film, and in the end we've not said a great deal about it. But something touched me deeply after the screening: everyone got up and Jean shouted out, 'It's not finished!' There was the shot of the waterfall after the birth and then the people in the film said nothing, and we also said nothing. One didn't know what to say after seeing this film. As regards the collective statement being made, the 'we' who are debating the film, we are in a very awkward position as an audience in the cinema. We ask ourselves what we are doing watching a film like this in a cinema, and we immediately want to find the people with whom we can form a collective, to say how we can respond to the film, share in it, define our personal relationship to its ideas so as to bring them to life, our relationship to a collective in which we are included; we want to form an audience collective, a collective which makes use of the film. It's a film that disturbs us in our passive position as individual spectators.

Translated by David Wilson

Notes

1 *Allonsanfan* (1974), directed by Paolo and Vittorio Taviani, a film about the betrayal of a revolutionary leader following the 1816 restoration of the monarchy in France, which was criticized for its political equivocation. See Pascal Bonitzer, 'Les yeux stériles', in *Cahiers* 260–1.

2 *Histoires d'A* (1973), a militant film about abortion, banned in France for a year. See *Cahiers* 251–2 and 253–4.

3 '1936': i.e. the Popular Front coalition of left and centrist parties in France which came to power in 1936.

4 In *Cahiers* 257.

5 Borhan Alaouié, director of *Kafr Kassem*. See Ch. 22 in this volume.

11

THE AQUARIUM (*MILESTONES*)

('L'aquarium (*Milestones*)', *Cahiers du Cinéma* 264, February 1976)

Serge Daney

There is a risk of seeing in *Milestones* just another bleat for some kind of American conviviality. Our own round table[1] is a little romantic about a film which is very far from being that (romantic). If we can, let's change the record.

Nasty experiences

In *Milestones* there are two *agonizing* moments, two rips in the film's fabric — agonizing because absolutely unforeseeable. The first is when Gail, the young woman who works in an all-night café (which looks like a seedy place), is assaulted by a sexual maniac ('I want you to suck me'). Speechless with horror, she is only saved by the intervention of the blind man who has been alerted by the noise (John Douglas, the film's co-director). The second moment is when Terry, the demobbed GI, finds himself *alone* in the street (after a long meal, a moment of truth when he reveals his wish to join the – male – community which is very willing to accept him) and meets someone (a friend?) who asks him to take part in a 'no risk' break-in. The break-in goes wrong: Terry is killed, shot by a cop.

What Gail and Terry have in common is that they are at a turning point in their lives, about to enter into new associations and so eliminate a bit of their past (Gail wants to leave her job and her boss, Al, who desperately wants to keep her; Terry wants simply to live again, far from Vietnam). Had the film been this post-leftist pastoral which we're all rather anxious to see (and what a relief it would be!), it would have included some beautiful, indelibly moving moments of mutual support and solidarity. Nothing of the kind. What Gail and Terry are going through (and the latter loses his life in the process) is more akin to a *rite of passage* (a difficult passing through, a passage through a void, a final examination, etc.).

A fabric doesn't keep warm

When we discussed *Milestones*, we talked about a (large) family, a community, an alternative party, a people's camp, a collective statement, etc. Reassuring words. It seems to me that the cast of characters (or rather the 'bodies' that speak) in *Milestones* creates neither a fresco, nor a chronicle, nor a document, but a *fabric*. A fabric seen under the microscope, and seen to be held together as much by the spaces between it as by its fibres. A lacunary tapestry. Quite the opposite of a house, a warm place or maternal protection. A fabric is not made or undone just like that, at will (even goodwill): it spreads, getting progressively larger, with inevitable knock-on effects (the turning back and forth of a relentless boustrophedon[2]). The newly woven material meshes with (and is meshed into) what has already been woven. Human relationships don't knit together with complete dependability; they are tied together over an empty space, on a wire and without a net. To fall through the meshes of the net, *to pass through a void*, is to die, to die from a nasty experience.

For the militants of *Ice*, the nasty experience was emasculation. In *Milestones* the nasty experience is something that is never mentioned again in the film: the reality of sexuality (Gail), the reality of death (Terry). In both cases, violence. Nothing to do with a return of the repressed; what returns here is what has been *denied*. We don't wish to know anything about the violence which *is* the American reality and which, like the banks which enclose the river in *Numéro deux*, threatens and sometimes overlaps the narrow path paved by the *Milestones*. A return to reality, reality as a trauma.

The real: what doesn't come twice

To continue the textile metaphor. From what material is the film woven? From long rolls of actual experience, where what one person says finds an echo in what another person hears? The sea-green naturalism of the 'as if you were there (with them)' kind? Quite the opposite. You only have to stop listening to the soundtrack to be confronted by what, in the images, *has nothing to see*.

Nothing to see (as said to a crowd to move them away from an accident: there is nothing to see) = nothing in common = nothing to look at. The heterogeneity of the images disregards suture, and off-screen space, that reserve fund of perceptions. An omnipresent camera, continuous speaking, are there *for real*, and from this – the pattern woven from them – there is no way out. Likewise for the collective, there is nothing to see, nothing to meet. No one sees it and it sees no one (not for nothing is there a blind man at its centre). Has it been noticed that in *Milestones* you can cross America without seeing anyone? Anyone from the other camp, the other America, the non-marginal, middle, contented America.

What you do come across, through a couple of moments of inattentiveness, lurking among the shots – and which the weaving, if it is too slack, lets you

153

glimpse – are the scattered elements of a kind of improvised universe: erratic images, cruel inserts – desert sand, ripples, a waterfall, but also the flame of a burner, red-hot stones, a placenta, fish (maybe dead). The insert in *Milestones* is the site of a passage through a void, the fixed point of the propelling force of death (a return to the inanimate, the organic – what moves but is not human). For Kramer, the insert is the site of pleasure (as with blackness in Godard): the place where the *whatever* of the real appears.

What might the *real* actually be in cinema? Not the referent or the effect of the real, but the real of which Lacan tells us (*Tuché et automaton* in *Séminaire*, book XI, p. 54) that it is 'the encounter as it may be missed, as in essence it is the missed encounter'.

Undoubtedly, something shown to be *unassimilable*. Images which are presented but which will not be re-presented. There will be no time to take it in: it is not the imaginary, then. There will be no chance to lock into the writing [*écriture*]: it is not the symbolic, then. The real: what doesn't come twice. It is precisely what happens to Gail and Terry: they are very close to the dangerous edge (*The Edge*) of the loom, the point where the encounter may be fatal because it occurs (and is filmed) only once.

The tribe weaves

And the encounter is only so bad because *Milestones* (as Jean-Pierre Oudart rightly says in his poem![3]) is conceived *from and within a process of segregation*. As much and more than a documentary about the dissolution of the American left or an invitation to universal love, the Kramer–Douglas film is: *what forms a tribe?* And how is this tribe formed from its own visual representation? A question posed by the film-makers without an ounce of humour, and a question that we tended to blur in our round-table discussion, in the name of a Marxism-Leninism that may have become exotic (American) but is still comprehensible, even if it is always purring away. Might we want to weigh up what is nevertheless the evidence: segregation is the truth of America, the shadow cast by its democratist ideology, the soil which gives us the mishmash of *Milestones* and the Manson gang, the Weathermen and the Jesus people? Ghettoization: the final stage of imperialism.

So it should be said that *Milestones* is the anti-*Nashville*, since the special, staggering thing about Kramer and Douglas's film is that *they know no more than their characters but out of what they do know they want to put together a defensive wall and mark out a future*. Instead of which, in the name of the several light years ahead that the artist-as-witness-to-his-time Robert Altman has over his contemptible creatures, his ridiculous Southern zoo, *Nashville* reassures us (us: the right-thinking opinion-makers of the New York and/or Parisian left) about these 'worthless others', this system of worthless stars.

A tribe? If so, can we just as easily speak about 'new social relations'? Maybe, but provided that we see what this *Milestones* tribe is weaving together: a kind of *ethnological masquerade* (will we finally realize that the truth of ideology, its very reality, is masquerade, fancy dress?), the image of primitiveness: trying out the land and denial of other tribes – the new Indians. Of course, it's a paranoid tribe and, as Schreber[4] said, it is lop-sided: no chiefs (except for a blind guru who makes hardly any impression on the narrative); no common work, hardly any rites. Almost all of them simply find themselves in front of a huge aquarium, a metaphor both for the film's space and for Karen's body (the waters of birth: the waterfall *after* the film ends, when the audience itself has already got up from *their* seats to leave their aquarium – the cinema). A tribe with two or three age groups eliminated: has it been noticed that we don't meet anyone in this film who is, say, fifteen or forty-five?

Not telling lies

What holds the tribe together? What does it consist of? A glob of spittle, we might say. Words heaped on words. Careful, though: the lie, I mean the *deliberate* lie, is forbidden. The film's incurable lack of humour (which makes it, unlike the appealing *Nashville*, a largely troubling experience) arises out of this prohibition. And in what I'm saying – if I have any sense of humour – there is the hint of another discourse, a different one: one that is hostile, opposed, which I have to come to terms with. This other discourse is completely missing from *Milestones*: refused, deferred, in parentheses. What's being said in *Milestones* has a quite different function: it's the weaving itself, it's – that most important word – the *survival* of the tribe. To lie would be to endanger the community. (For some Eskimos, the material conditions of survival are so perilous that speech, rarely expended, has to be truthful, a lie being for them both a luxury and a crime.)

Loss of sight

Our round-table discussion has a flaw: we scarcely mention the film's *form*. Now, there is a limited number of organizing principles for the images and sounds in *Milestones* (as indeed in *The Edge*, *Ice* or *In the Country*). If the film breaks irreparably with all forms of naturalism, it's because it only films – in the most natural way – situations involving *loss of sight*. The whole film is a never-ending piece of *fort–da*. A lightweight camera loses sight of the person it was framing a moment ago only to find him again in a space that was only 'off' for the blink of an eye. Those lost from view are rediscovered. Fathers and sons, mother and daughter *re*-establish contact, *re*sume, *re*new their relationships. And those who were in prison, the out-of-sight by definition, get out. A conversation between Peter, released from prison, and John the blind potter: 'How old were you when you went blind?' – 'What do you remember?' In *Milestones* there is one and only one division of labour: *those who are filmed talk about those* (and about what) *who are not*. A rough and ready means of dispensing with off-screen space. The outside, as we have seen, is the interpolation of an insert. Everything happens *inside* an aquarium, in which the fish take turns to put on a bit of a performance at the edge of the mirror-glass-screen. Sole message: we exist.

But, you'll say, this is forced labour! Yes. A tribe can't allow itself to lose a single one of its members – even from sight!

Translated by David Wilson

Notes

1 See Ch. 10 in this volume.
2 Boustrophedon: lines reading alternately from right to left and from left to right, as in some ancient inscriptions.
3 'Pour *Milestones*', in *Cahiers* 262–3.
4 Dr Paul Schreber was the subject of one of Freud's most celebrated 'case histories'. Daney is making a playful reference to paranoia.

Part III

THEORY AND HISTORY

12

ANTI-RETRO

('Anti-rétro: entretien avec Michel Foucault', *Cahiers du Cinéma* 251–2, July–August 1974)

Michel Foucault in interview with Pascal Bonitzer and Serge Toubiana

Lacombe Lucien, The Night Porter, Les Chinois à Paris, Le Trio infernal, etc.[1] These films, whose avowed aim is to rewrite history, are not an isolated phenomenon. They are themselves inscribed into a history, a history in progress; they have – as we are sometimes criticized for saying – a context. This context, in France, is the coming to power of a new bourgeoisie, of a fraction of the bourgeoisie along with its ideology (Giscard, president of all the French; a more-just-and-caring society etc.), its conception of France, and of history. What goes by the name of '*après-gaullisme*' is also an opportunity for the bourgeoisie to rid itself of a certain heroic, nationalist but also anti-Pétainist and anti-fascist image, which was still reflected if not by Pompidou, at least by de Gaulle and Gaullism. Chaban's electoral defeat marks the end of this heroic, exaggerated and somewhat grotesque image (cf. Malraux) of recent French history.[2] Something else is beginning to be written and represented: that France wasn't all that anti-fascist, that the French couldn't have cared less about Nazism, that anti-fascism and the Resistance were only ever, precisely, this derisory image of Gaullist 'grandeur' which is now showing its false nose.

What is emerging is a cynical ideology: that of big business, of the multi-national and technocratic culture that Giscard represents. The French, it is thought, are ripe for this cynicism (cynicism of the ruling class, disillusionment of the exploited classes): a cynicism illustrated, on the screen, by the phenomenon known as the 'retro style', i.e. the snobbish fetishism of period effects (costumes and settings) with little concern for history.

This false archaeology of history had to be denounced in all its implications and all its effects. A true archaeology had to be – has to be – put in its place: the popular memory of struggles (of all forms of struggle) which has never really been able to speak – which has never had the power to do so – and which must be revived against all the forces which are constantly bent on stifling it, on silencing it once and for all.

No one was better placed to situate the question and to spell out its implications than Michel Foucault, whose work systematically uncovers what the official text represses, what lies forgotten in the damnable archives of the ruling class. We hope that the interview that follows may open up new avenues of research.

P.B. and S.T.

CAHIERS: Let's take as our starting point the journalistic phenomenon of the 'retro style'. One might simply ask: How is it that films like *Lacombe Lucien* or *The Night Porter* are possible today? Why are they so immensely popular? We think there are three levels that ought to be taken into account. First, the political conjuncture. Giscard d'Estaing has been elected. A new type of relation to politics, to history, to the political apparatus is being created, one that indicates very clearly – and in a way that is plain to everyone – the death of Gaullism. We therefore have to see, in so far as Gaullism remains very closely associated with the period of the Resistance, how this manifests itself in the films that are being made. Second, how can bourgeois ideology be mounting an attack in the breaches of orthodox Marxism – call it rigid, economistic, mechanistic, whatever you like – which for a very long time has provided the only grid for interpreting social phenomena? Finally, where do militants fit into all this, since militants are consumers and sometimes producers of films?

What has happened since Marcel Ophuls's film *The Sorrow and the Pity* is that the floodgates have opened. Something which until then had been completely suppressed, that is to say banned, is being openly voiced. Why?

FOUCAULT: That can be explained, I think, by the fact that the history of the War and what happened before and after the War has never really been inscribed in anything other than wholly official histories. These official histories are basically centred on Gaullism which, on the one hand, was the only way of writing that history in terms of an honourable nationalism and, on the other hand, was the only way of casting the Great Man, the man of the right and of outdated nineteenth-century nationalisms, in a historical role.

It boils down to the fact that France was exonerated by de Gaulle, and on the other hand the right – and we all know how it behaved at the time of the War – found itself purified and sanctified by de Gaulle. Suddenly the right and France were reconciled in this way of making history: don't forget that nationalism was the climate in which nineteenth-century history (and especially its teaching) were born.

What has never been described is what happened in the very depths of the country from 1936 on, and even from the end of the First World War to the Liberation.

CAHIERS: So, what has perhaps been happening since *The Sorrow and the Pity* is that the truth is making its return into history. The question is whether it's really the truth.

FOUCAULT: That has to be linked to the fact that the end of Gaullism has put a stop to this justification of the right by de Gaulle and the episode in question. The old Pétainist right, the old collaborationist, Maurrasian and reactionary right which camouflaged itself as best it could behind de Gaulle, now considers itself entitled to produce a new version of its own history. This old right which, since Tardieu, had been disenfranchised historically and politically, is coming to the fore again.[3]

It supported Giscard explicitly. It no longer needs to wear a mask, and so it can write its own history. And among the factors that explain Giscard's current acceptance by half the French (plus two hundred thousand),[4] one mustn't forget films like those we're talking about – whatever the film-makers actually intended. The fact that all that has actually been shown has allowed the right to re-form along certain lines. In the same way that, inversely, it's the blurring of the distinctions between the nationalist right and the collaborationist right that has made these films possible. It's all part of the same thing.

CAHIERS: This piece of history is therefore being rewritten both in the cinema and on television, with debates like those on *Dossiers de l'écran* (which chose the theme of the French under the Occupation twice in two months). Film-makers considered to be more or less on the left are also apparently involved in this rewriting of history. That's something we have to investigate.

FOUCAULT: I don't think things are that simple. What I was saying a moment ago was very schematic. Let me continue.

There's a real battle going on. And what's at stake is what might be roughly called *popular memory*. It's absolutely true that ordinary people, I mean those who don't have the right to writing, the right to make books themselves, to compose their own history, these people nevertheless have a way of registering history, of remembering it, living it and using it. This popular history was, up to a point, more alive and even more clearly formulated in the nineteenth century when you had, for example, a whole tradition of struggles relived orally or in texts, songs, etc.

But the fact is that a whole series of apparatuses has been established ('popular literature', cheap books, but also what is taught in school) to block this development of popular memory, and you could say that the project has been, relatively speaking, very successful. The historical knowledge that the working class has about itself is becoming less all the time. When you think, for example, about what the workers knew about their own history at the end of the nineteenth century, and what the tradition of trade unionism – using the term 'tradition' in its full sense – represented up until the First World War, it amounted to something pretty substantial. That has been gradually disappearing. It's disappearing all the time, although it hasn't actually been lost.

Nowadays, cheap books are no longer enough. There are much more efficient channels in the form of television and cinema. And I think the whole effort has tended towards a *recoding* of popular memory which exists but has no way of formally expressing itself. People are shown not what they have been but what they must remember they have been.

Since memory is an important factor in struggle (indeed, it's within a kind of conscious dynamic of history that struggles develop), if you hold people's memory, you hold their dynamism. And you also hold their experience, their knowledge of previous struggles. You make sure that they no longer know what the Resistance was actually about . . .

It's along some such lines, I think, that these films have to be understood. What they're saying, roughly, is that there has been no popular struggle in the twentieth century. This statement has been formulated twice, in two different ways. The first time immediately after the War, when the message was a simple one: 'The twentieth century, what a century of heroes! Churchill, de Gaulle, all those parachute landings, airborne missions, etc.' Which was a way of saying: 'There was no popular struggle, *that* was the true struggle.' But no one, as yet, has said directly: 'There was no popular struggle.'

The other, more recent way – sceptical or cynical, as you wish – consists in opting for statement pure and simple: 'Well, just look at what happened. Did you see any struggles? Can you see anyone rebelling, taking up arms?'

CAHIERS: There's a kind of rumour that's been going round since, perhaps, *The Sorrow and the Pity*. Namely: the people of France, in the main, didn't resist, they even accepted collaboration, they accepted the Germans, they swallowed the lot. The question is what that really means. And it does indeed seem that what is at stake is the popular struggle, or rather people's *memory* of it.

FOUCAULT: Exactly. That memory has to be seized, governed, controlled, told what to remember. And when you see these films, you learn what to remember: 'Don't believe everything you were once told. There are no heroes. And if there are no heroes, that's because there's no struggle.' Hence a kind of ambiguity: on the one hand, 'there are no heroes' positively debunks a whole mythology of the war hero in the Burt Lancaster mould. It's a way of saying: 'War isn't that at all!' Hence an initial impression that historical untruths are being stripped away: finally we're going to be told why we don't all have to identify with de Gaulle or the members of the Normandy–Niemen mission, etc. But hidden beneath the phrase 'There were no heroes' is another phrase which is the real message: 'There was no struggle.' That's how the process works.

CAHIERS: There's something else that explains why these films are successful.

They make use of the resentment felt by those who did indeed struggle against those who did not. For example, in *The Sorrow and the Pity* people active in the Resistance see the citizens of a town in central France doing nothing, and recognize this response for what it is. It's their resentment that comes across more than anything; they forget that *they* struggled.

FOUCAULT: What's politically important, to my mind, more than this or that film, is the the fact that there's a series – the network that's made up of all these films and the place they 'occupy' (no pun intended). In other words, what is important is the question: 'Is it possible, at the present time, to make a film that's *positive* about the struggles of the Resistance?' And of course you realize that it isn't. The impression you have is that people would find it a bit of a joke, or else, quite simply, that no one would go and see it.

I quite like *The Sorrow and the Pity*. I don't think it was a bad thing to have done. Perhaps I'm wrong, that's not what matters. What matters is that this series of films corresponds exactly to the fact that it is now impossible – as each of the films emphasizes – to make a film about the positive struggles that may have taken place in France around the time of the War and the Resistance.

CAHIERS: Yes. It's the first thing they say if you criticize a film like Malle's. 'What would you have done instead?' is always the reply. And of course we don't have an answer. The left should be beginning to have a point of view on this, but in fact it has yet to be properly worked out.

Then again, this raises the old problem of how to produce a positive hero, a new type of hero.

FOUCAULT: The difficulties don't revolve around the hero so much as around the question of struggle. Can you make a film depicting a struggle without making the characters into heroes in the traditional sense? It's an old problem: how did history come to speak as it does and to recuperate the past, if not via a procedure which was that of the epic, that's to say, by telling its own story in the heroic mode? That's how the history of the French Revolution was written. The cinema proceeded in the same way. The strategy can always be ironically reversed: 'No, look, there are no heroes, we're all worthless, etc.'

CAHIERS: Let's come back to the 'retro style'. The bourgeoisie has been relatively successful from its own point of view in focusing attention on a historical period (the 1940s) which highlights both its strong and its weak points. For on the one hand that's where the bourgeoisie is most easily unmasked (*it* laid the ground for Nazism and collaboration), and on the other hand that's where today it tries to justify, in the most cynical way possible, its historical attitude. The problem is: how can we produce a positive account of this same historical period? We – that is, the generation that took part in the struggles of 1968 or Lip.[5] Is this the point on which we should go in and fight, with the idea of possibly, in some way or another, taking the ideological lead? For it's true that the bourgeoisie is on the offensive as well as on the defensive on this question of its recent history. On the defensive strategically, on the offensive tactically since it has found its strong point, the thing that enables it best to manipulate the facts. But ought we simply – defensively – to be re-establishing the historical truth? Ought we not to be finding the point which, ideologically, would take us into the breach? Is this automatically the Resistance? Why not 1789 or 1968?

FOUCAULT: As far as these films are concerned, I wonder whether something else couldn't be done on the same topic. And by 'topic' I don't mean showing struggles or showing that there were none. What I'm thinking is that it's historically true that among ordinary French people there was, at the time of the War, a kind of refusal of war. Now where did that come from? From a whole series of episodes that no one talks about, neither the right because it wishes to hide them, nor the left because it does not want to compromise itself with anything that goes against 'national honour'.

During the First World War, after all, some seven or eight million lads were conscripted. For four years they had a terrible life, they saw millions and millions of people dying around them. Back home in 1920, what did they have to look forward to? A right-wing government, total economic exploitation and finally, in 1932, an economic crisis and unemployment. How could these men, who had been packed into the trenches, still be in favour of war during the decades 1920–30 and 1930–40? In the case of the Germans, defeat rekindled their nationalist instincts, so that this distaste for war was overcome by the desire for revenge. But when all is said and done, people don't like fighting bourgeois wars, with the officers involved, for the gains involved. I believe that was an important phenomenon in the working class. And when, in 1940, you have men driving their bikes into a ditch and saying, 'I'm going home', you can't just say, 'What a bunch of cowards!' and you can't hide it either. It has to be seen as part of the whole sequence. This disobeying of national orders has to be traced back to its roots. And what happened during the Resistance is the opposite of what we are shown: that's to say that the process of repoliticization, remobilization, the taste for struggle was gradually revived in the working class. It slowly began to revive after the rise of Nazism and the Spanish Civil War. What the films show is the reverse process: after the great dream of 1939, which was shattered in 1940, people just give up. This process did indeed take place, but within another much longer process which was moving in the opposite direction and which, beginning with the distaste for war, ended in the middle of the Occupation with the realization that there had to be a struggle. As for the theme 'There are no heroes, everyone's a coward', you have to ask yourself where it comes from and what it grows out of. After all, have there ever been any films about mutiny?

CAHIERS: Yes. There was Kubrick's film (*Paths of Glory*), which was banned in France.

FOUCAULT: I believe that this disobedience in the context of national armed struggles had a positive political meaning. The historical theme of Lacombe Lucien's family could be picked up again if taken back to Ypres and Douaumont . . .[6]

CAHIERS: Which poses the problem of popular memory, of its own particular sense of time, which doesn't correspond at all to the timing of events like changes of government or declarations of war . . .

FOUCAULT: The aim of school history has always been to show how people got killed and how very heroic they were. Look what they did to Napoleon and the Napoleonic Wars . . .

CAHIERS: A certain number of films, Malle's and Cavani's included, tend to abandon any attempt to deal with Nazism and fascism historically or in terms of the struggle they provoked. Instead of this, or as well as this, they hold another discourse, usually a sexual one. What do you make of this other discourse?

FOUCAULT: But isn't it quite different in *Lacombe Lucien* and *The Night Porter*? Personally, I think that in *Lacombe Lucien* the erotic, passionate aspect has a function that's fairly easy to pinpoint. It's basically a way of reconciling the anti-hero, of saying that he's not as anti-heroic as all that. If all power relationships are indeed distorted by him, and if he renders them ineffective, by contrast, just when you think that for him all erotic relationships are similarly warped, a true relationship is discovered and he loves the girl. On the one hand there is the machinery of power which leads Lucien more and more, from the puncture onwards, towards a kind of madness. And on the other hand there is the machinery of love which seems to be following the same pattern, which seems to be distorted and which, on the contrary, works in the opposite direction and re-establishes Lucien at the end as the beautiful naked boy living in the fields with a girl.

And so there's a kind of fairly facile antithesis between power and love. Whereas in *The Night Porter* the problem is – in general as in the present conjuncture – a very important one: it's that of the love of power.

Power has an erotic charge. And this brings us to a historical problem: how is it that Nazism, whose representatives were pitiful, pathetic, puritanical figures, Victorian spinsters with (at best) secret vices, how is it that it can have become, nowadays and everywhere, in France, in Germany, in the United States, in all pornographic literature the world over, the absolute reference of eroticism? A whole sleazy erotic imaginary is now placed under the sign of Nazism. Which basically poses a serious problem: how can power be desirable? No one finds power desirable any more. This kind of affective, erotic attachment, this desire one has for power, the power of a ruler, no longer exists. The monarchy and its rituals were made to evoke this kind of erotic relation to power. The great apparatuses of

Stalin, and even of Hitler, were also created for that purpose. But this has all disintegrated and it's clear that one cannot love Brezhnev or Pompidou or Nixon. It was perhaps possible, at a pinch, to love de Gaulle or Kennedy or Churchill. But what's happening now? Are we not seeing the beginnings of a re-eroticization of power, developed at one derisory, pathetic extreme by the sex shops with Nazi emblems that you find in the United States, and (in a much more tolerable but equally derisory version) in Giscard d'Estaing's attitude when he says, 'We'll march along the streets in suits shaking people's hands, and the kids will have a half-day holiday.' There's no doubt that Giscard fought part of his electoral campaign not just on his physical presence but also on a certain eroticization of his personal self, his elegance.

CAHIERS: That's how he projected himself in an election poster, the one where his daughter is facing him.

FOUCAULT: That's right. He is looking at France but she is looking at him. Power becomes seductive once again.

CAHIERS: That's something that struck us during the election campaign, especially in the big television debate between Mitterrand and Giscard; they were on quite different territory. Mitterrand seemed like a politician of the old school, belonging to an old-fashioned left. He was trying to sell *ideas*, themselves dated and slightly quaint, and he did so with great dignity. Giscard on the other hand was selling the idea of power as if he were marketing a cheese.

FOUCAULT: Even quite recently, you had to apologize for being in power. Power had to be erased and not show itself as such. That was, up to a point, how democratic republics functioned: the problem was to render power sufficiently insidious and invisible so that it became impossible to get a hold on what it did or where it was.

Nowadays (and in this de Gaulle played a very important role), power is no longer hidden, it is proud to be there and actually says: 'Love me, because I am power.'

CAHIERS: Perhaps we should speak about the fact that Marxist discourse, as it has been functioning for some time, is somehow unable satisfactorily to account for fascism. Historically speaking, Marxism has accounted for the Nazi phenomenon in an economistic, determinist way, completely ignoring what was specific to the ideology of Nazism. You can't help wondering how someone like Malle, well enough in touch with developments on the left, can play on this weakness, fall into this gap.

FOUCAULT: Marxism defined Nazism and fascism as 'the open terrorist dictatorship of the most reactionary fraction of the bourgeoisie'. This is a definition completely lacking in content, and one which lacks a whole series of articulations. What is missing in particular is the fact that Nazism and fascism were made possible only by the existence within the general population of a relatively large fraction willing to take on and be responsible for a certain number of state functions: repression, control, law and order. That, I think, is an important aspect of Nazism. The fact that it penetrated the general population so deeply and that some power was effectively delegated to certain people on the margins. That's where the word 'dictatorship' is both generally true and relatively false. When you think of the power an individual could possess under a Nazi regime from the moment he joined the SS or became a Party member! He could actually kill his neighbour, appropriate his wife and his house! That's where *Lacombe Lucien* is interesting, because it shows that side well. The fact is that, contrary to what one usually understands by dictatorship, that's to say the power of one individual, in a regime like that the most detestable, but in a sense the most intoxicating, part of power was given to a large number of people. It was the SS man who had the power to kill and to rape . . .

CAHIERS: That's where orthodox Marxism breaks down. Because this implies that there has to be a discourse on desire.

FOUCAULT: On desire and on power . . .

CAHIERS: That's also where films like *Lacombe Lucien* and *The Night Porter* are relatively 'strong'. They can handle a discourse on desire and power in a way that *seems* coherent.

FOUCAULT: In *The Night Porter* it's interesting to see how, in Nazism, the power of one man was taken up by many people and put to work. That sort of mock tribunal they set up is fascinating. Because from one angle it begins to look like a psychotherapy group, but in fact its power structure is that of a secret society. It's basically an SS cell that has re-formed, that gives itself legal powers different from and in opposition to the power at the centre. We have to remember how power was dispersed, how it was invested within the population itself, we have to remember this impressive displacement of power that Nazism brought about in a society like German society. It is untrue to say that Nazism was the power of the big industrialists continued in another form. It wasn't the power of the top brass reinforced. It was that too, but only on a certain level.

CAHIERS: Indeed, that's an interesting aspect of the film. But what seemed very questionable to us was that it seemed to be saying: 'If you're a typical SS man, that's how you behave. But if on top of that you have a certain "notion of expenditure", that's the formula for a great erotic adventure.' So the film never abandons the idea of seduction.

FOUCAULT: Yes, it's like *Lacombe Lucien* in that respect. For Nazism never gave anyone a pound of butter, it never gave anything but power. You have to ask yourself, if this regime was nothing other than a bloody dictatorship, how on 3 May 1945 there were still Germans fighting on to the last drop of blood, if these people were not attached to power in some way. Of course, you have to take into account all the pressures, denunciations . . .

CAHIERS: But if there were denunciations and pressures, there must have been people to do the denouncing. How did people get caught up in it all? How were they ever conned by this redistribution of power in their favour?

FOUCAULT: In *Lacombe Lucien*, as in *The Night Porter*, this excessive power that is given to them is converted back into love. It's very clear at the end of *The Night Porter*, with the recreation around Max, in his room, of a kind of concentration camp in miniature, where he is dying of hunger. There love has converted power, super-power, into total powerlessness. Roughly the same reconciliation occurs, in a sense, in *Lacombe Lucien*, where love takes the excess of power by which it has been trapped and converts it into a rural nakedness miles away from the Gestapo's shady hotel, miles away also from the farm where the pigs are being killed.

CAHIERS: Are we then perhaps beginning to explain the problem you were posing earlier: how is it that Nazism, which was a puritanical, repressive system, is now universally eroticized? Some kind of displacement takes place: a problem which is central and which people don't wish to confront, the problem of power, is bypassed or rather completely displaced towards the sexual. So that this eroticization is really a displacement, a form of repression . . .

FOUCAULT: The problem is indeed a very difficult one and it has not perhaps been sufficiently studied, even by Reich.[7] How is it that power is desirable and is actually desired? The procedures through which this eroticization is transmitted, reinforced, and so on, are clear enough. But for it to happen in the first place, the attachment to power, the acceptance of power by those over whom it is exercised, must already be erotic.

CAHIERS: What makes it all the more difficult is that the representation of power is rarely erotic. De Gaulle and Hitler weren't exactly attractive.

FOUCAULT: That's right, and I wonder whether in Marxist analyses one doesn't sacrifice a little too much to the abstract character of the idea of freedom. In a regime like the Nazi regime, it's quite clear that there's no freedom. But not having freedom doesn't mean that you don't have power.

CAHIERS: It's on the level of the cinema and television, television being entirely controlled by power, that historical discourse has the greatest impact. Which implies a political responsibility. It seems to us that people are increasingly aware of it. For some years now, in the cinema, there has been more and more talk of history, politics, struggle . . .

FOUCAULT: There's a battle going on for history, around the history that's now in the making, and it is very interesting. People want to codify, to stifle what I have called 'popular memory', and also to propose, to impose a grid for interpreting the present. Until 1968 popular struggles had to do with folk tradition. For some they had no connection at all with anything going on in the present. After 1968 all popular struggles, whether in South America or in Africa, find an echo, a resonance. No longer can this separation, this sort of geographical *cordon sanitaire*, be established. Popular struggles have become not something that is happening now, but something that *might always happen*, in our system. And so they have to be set at a distance once again. How? Not by interpreting them directly – you would only lay yourself open to all the contradictions – but by proposing a historical interpretation of popular struggles from our own past, to show that in fact they never took place! Before 1968, it was: 'It won't happen, because it only happens elsewhere'; now it's: 'It won't happen, because it has never happened! Even something like the Resistance, the stuff of so many dreams, just look at it . . . Nothing there. An empty shell, completely hollow!' Which is another way of saying: 'In Chile, don't worry, the peasants don't give a damn. In France too: a few troublemakers and their antics won't affect anything fundamental.'

CAHIERS: For us, the important thing when one reacts to that, against that, is to realize that it's not enough to re-establish the truth, to say, about the Maquis for example, 'No, I was there, it didn't happen like that at all!' We believe that to conduct the ideological struggle effectively on the kind of terrain that these films lead into you have to have a wider, more comprehensive system of references – of positive references. For many people, for example, that consists in reappropriating the 'history of France'. It was against this background that we spent some time on *Moi, Pierre Rivière* . . . because we realized that in the end, and paradoxically, it helped us to explain *Lacombe Lucien*, that the comparison brought out a number of things. For example, one significant difference is that Pierre Rivière is a man who writes, who commits a murder and who has a quite extraordinary memory. Malle's hero, on the other hand, is presented as a halfwit, as someone who goes through everything, history, the War, collaboration, *without building on his experiences*. And it's there that the theme of memory, of popular memory, can help us to make the distinction between someone, Pierre Rivière, who uses a language that is not his and is forced to kill to obtain the right to do so, and the character created by Malle and Modiano[8] who proves, precisely by not building on anything that happens to him, that there is nothing worth remembering. It's a pity you haven't seen *The Courage of the People.*[9] It's a Bolivian film, which was made for the specific purpose of providing an exhibit for a dossier. This film, which can be seen everywhere except in Bolivia, because of the regime, is played by those who actually took part in the real-life drama it recreates (a miners' strike and its bloody repression) – they undertake to represent themselves so that no one will forget.

It's interesting to see that, on a minimum level, every film is a potential archive and that, in the context of a struggle, one can take this idea one step further: people put together a film intending it to be an exhibit. And you can analyse that in two radically different ways: either the film is about power or it represents the victims of that power, the exploited classes who, without the help of the cinematographic apparatus, with very

169

little knowledge of how films are made and distributed, take on their own representation, give evidence for history. Rather as Pierre Rivière gave evidence, that's to say, began to write, knowing that sooner or later he would appear before a court and that everyone had to understand what he had to say.

What's important in *The Courage of the People* is that the demand actually came from the people. It was through a survey that the director first learned of the demand, and it was those who had lived through the event who asked for it to be memorized.

FOUCAULT: The people create their own archives.

CAHIERS: The difference between Pierre Rivière and Lacombe Lucien is that Pierre Rivière does everything to enable us to discuss his history after his death. Whereas, even if Lacombe is a real character or one who might have existed, he is only ever the object of another's discourse, for purposes that are not his own.

There are two things that are successful in the cinema now. On the one hand, historical documents, which have an important role to play. In *Toute une vie*, for example, they are very important.[10] Or in films by Marcel Ophuls or Harris and Sédouy, when you see Duclos waving his arms about in 1936 and in 1939, these scenes from real life are moving.[11] And on the other hand, fictional characters who, at a given moment in history, compress social relations, historical relations, into the smallest possible space. That's why *Lacombe Lucien* works so well. Lacombe is a Frenchman under the Occupation, someone very ordinary who stands in a concrete relationship to Nazism, to the countryside, to local government, etc. We have to be aware of this way of personifying history, of bringing it to life in a character, or a group of characters who, at a given moment, stand in a privileged relationship to power.

There are lots of characters in the history of the workers' movement whom we don't know about: lots of heroes in the history of the working class who have been totally repressed. And I believe that something important is at stake here. Marxism doesn't need to make any more films about Lenin, there are more than enough already.

FOUCAULT: What you are saying is important. It's a characteristic of many Marxists today. They don't know very much about history. They spend their time saying that history is being overlooked, but are only capable themselves of commenting on texts: 'What did Marx say? Did Marx really say that?' But what is Marxism if not another way of analysing history itself? In my opinion, the left, in France, is not very interested in history. It used to be. In the nineteenth century you could say that Michelet represented the left at a given moment. There was also Jaurès, and then a kind of tradition of left-wing, social democratic historians (Mathiez etc.).[12] Today that has virtually dried up. Whereas it could be an impressive movement of writers and film-makers. There was of course Aragon and *Les*

Cloches de Bâle,[13] which is a very great historical novel. But it doesn't amount to much, if you think of what that could represent in a society whose intellectuals are, after all, more or less steeped in Marxism.

CAHIERS: Film-making brings in something new again in this respect: 'live' history . . . What relation do American people have to history, now that they see the Vietnam War every evening on television as they eat their supper?

FOUCAULT: As soon as you begin to see images of war every evening, war becomes utterly accepted. In other words, extremely boring – you would certainly prefer to watch something else. But once it becomes boring, it's accepted. You don't even watch it. So what do you have to do for this news, as it appears on film, to be reactivated as news that is historically important?

CAHIERS: Have you seen *Les Camisards*?[14]

FOUCAULT: Yes, I liked it a lot. Historically it's beyond reproach. It's a beautiful film, it's intelligent, it explains so much.

CAHIERS: I think that's the direction film-makers should be taking. To come back to the films we were talking about at the beginning, another problem that must be mentioned is the confused response of the far left to certain aspects of *Lacombe Lucien* and *The Night Porter*, the sexual aspect especially. How might the right take advantage of this confusion?

FOUCAULT: On this subject of what you call the far left, I don't really know what to think. I'm not even sure whether it still exists. All the same, a huge balance sheet has to be drawn up for the activities of the far left since 1968: the conclusions are negative on the one side and positive on the other. It's true that the far left has been responsible for a whole lot of important ideas in a number of areas: sexuality, women, homosexuality, psychiatry, housing, medicine. It has also been responsible for the diffusion of modes of action – which continues to be important. The far left has been important in the kinds of action it has taken as well as in the themes it has pursued. But there is also a negative balance in terms of certain Stalinist, terrorist, organizational practices. And there is equally a misapprehension of certain currents running wide and deep which have just resulted in thirteen million votes for Mitterrand, and which have always been neglected on the pretext that that was just politicking, party politics.[15] Any number of aspects have been neglected, notably the fact that the desire to defeat the right has for some years, some months, been a very important political factor among the masses. The far left didn't have this desire because its definition of the masses was wrong and because it didn't really understand what it means to want to win. To avoid the risk of having victory snatched away it prefers not to run the risk of winning. Defeat, at least, can't be recuperated. Personally, I'm not so sure.

Translated by Annwyl Williams

Notes

1 *Lacombe Lucien* (Louis Malle, 1974); *The Night Porter* (Liliana Cavani, 1973); *Les Chinois à Paris* (Jean Yanne, 1974); *Le Trio infernal* (Francis Girod, 1974).
2 Jacques Chaban-Delmas, French Prime Minister from 1969 until 1972, when Pompidou dismissed him. Giscard d'Estaing won the presidential election following Pompidou's death in April 1974. André Malraux had been de Gaulle's controversial Minister of Culture.
3 Maurassian: Charles Maurras (1868–1952) was a right-wing writer and journalist of the Third Republic. André Tardieu (1876–1945), journalist and politician, was premier of France three times. From 1936 he was a strong critic of the Third Republic.
4 Giscard won the May 1974 presidential election by a narrow margin (51 per cent of the votes).
5 Lip, a watch factory at Besançon, was taken over by its employees in 1973 after it had gone into liquidation.
6 I.e. to the First World War.
7 Wilhelm Reich (1897–1957), Austrian psychoanalyst who controversially expounded the relationship between power and sexuality. His theories of personal sexual liberation were paid eccentric homage in Dušan Makavejev's 1971 film *WR: Mysteries of the Organism.*
8 Patrick Modiano, novelist and co-scriptwriter of *Lacombe Lucien.*
9 *El coraje del pueblo* (Jorge Sanjines, 1971). Alternative English title: *The Night of San Juan.*
10 *Toute une vie* (*And Now My Love*) (Claude Lelouch, 1974).
11 André Harris and Alain de Sédouy scripted and produced *Français, si vous saviez* (1972), a documentary analysis of Gaullism and the role of French politicians in the two World Wars and the Algerian war, described by Marc Ferro as 'a settling of scores with de Gaulle'.
12 Jules Michelet (1798–1874), French historian, noted particularly for his monumental *Histoire de France* and his seven-volume *Histoire de la Révolution.* He lost his academic appointments by refusing to swear allegiance to Louis Napoleon. Jean Jaurès (1859–1914), French writer and founder of the Socialist Party. Editor of *L'Humanité*, which he helped found, until his assassination in 1914.
13 Louis Aragon (1897–1933), poet, novelist and essayist, an early Surrealist who later became a Communist. His novel *Les Cloches de Bâle* was translated by H. M. Chevalier as *The Bells of Basel* (London: Peter Davies and Lovat Dickson, 1937).
14 *Les Camisards:* René Allio's 1972 film about a Protestant revolt in 1702 which engaged in a guerrilla campaign in the Cévennes against the forces of the French Catholic state. The film's parallel with the Vietnam War was unmistakable.
15 The Socialist François Mitterand narrowly lost the May 1974 presidential election. (He won the 1981 election.)

13

I, PIERRE RIVIÈRE, HAVING SLAUGHTERED MY MOTHER, MY SISTER AND MY BROTHER . . . BY RENÉ ALLIO

('Moi, Pierre Rivière, ayant égorgé ma mère, ma soeur et mon frère . . . de René Allio', *Cahiers du Cinéma* 271, November 1976)

Jean Jourdheuil, Serge Toubiana, Pascal Bonitzer, René Allio, Pascal Kané, Michel Foucault

The texts which follow are intended as contributions to a new dossier – on the important film which René Allio has based on Pierre Rivière's memoir.[1] We begin with several short pieces written by the scriptwriters during their collaboration. Michel Foucault's comments are transcribed from an interview with Pascal Kané which appears in Kané's short on Allio's film.

The everyday, the historical and the tragic

The film will deal with a case of parricide in the nineteenth century (1835, to be precise) in a French province, Normandy. It will therefore show the daily life of the country, agricultural work, the role of the village notables (the priest, the magistrate), the way in which people of different ages spend their time (children, adults, old people), etc. And yet the dramatization of everyday life is not its *raison d'être*; our aim is not to paint a picture of country life and manners.

Everyday country life is of interest in this film in that it leads to a triple murder. One might therefore be tempted to speak of a dramatization of the news item, bearing in mind that this notion is already restrictive. The news item is strictly speaking what a murder like the one which concerns us is reduced to by the press, by the legal system. On the other hand, it wouldn't be too far off the mark to say that it is in the dominated classes (the peasantry, the working class), where basic conflicts cannot be acted out in language, that such basic conflicts find their resolution in the news item.

In the case which concerns us we will therefore attempt to show what, in the life and behaviour of the main characters, resists reduction (the reduction to the news item which the judicial and medico-legal machinery is bound to produce) . . . And what resists reduction, that *excess* that the judges and doctors cannot explain, one might (to be brief) call passion, a passion for life, for truth, for the absolute: a double passion, that of the mother, that of the young Rivière.

And so, this film focuses on more than one thing: daily life, the news item, passion (the tragic). I am not thinking of the tragic as a literary genre (ancient Greek tragedy or French seventeenth-century tragedy) but rather, if you like, of the essence of the tragic in its historical implications, as described by J.-P. Vernant:

> The tragic turning point thus occurs when a gap develops at the heart of social experience. It is wide enough for the oppositions between legal and political thought on the one hand and the mythical and heroic traditions, on the other, to stand out quite clearly. Yet it is narrow enough for the conflict in values still to be a painful one and for the clash to continue to take place.[2]

The tragic passions here (of the mother, of Pierre Rivière) are not therefore ahistorical, but historically situated at the moment when the judicial, medico-legal and psychiatric institutions, while having already virtually established their dominance, have not yet managed to fully override the chaotic disorder of popular myths and customs, notably in the country areas of Normandy.

Michel Foucault must take the credit for uncovering the various procedures whereby in the eighteenth and nineteenth centuries a new order – that of the bourgeoisie – was established (cf. *Madness and Civilization*, *The Archaeology of Knowledge* and more recently his Collège de France seminars on medico-legal practices), and for establishing a 'genealogy' of the disciplinary apparatuses which weave the web of oppressions not only in the sense of external limits to the behaviour of individuals but also as a chain of internal obstacles, inhibitions, internalized norms, etc.

Foucault's work, in that it marks a break with the 'rationalist', 'scientific' conception of the Human Sciences modelled on nineteenth-century forms of the physical sciences or 'Natural Sciences', produces something like an X-ray of the actual and latent forms of those crises which involve, historically speaking, a decisive shift, a reorganizing principle. Of course, this 'genealogical' work does not deliver (or aim to deliver) some positive body of knowledge that we – through cinematic means – would only have to repeat and vulgarize. We have to appropriate not so much the results of Foucault's work as its genealogical and paradoxical procedure. If we appropriate only the results of Foucault's

174

work, we miss what's essential: the everyday/historical/tragic quality of life caught in its movement (and in its pace) as something that can still affect us.

These three things at stake: the everyday, the historical and the tragic are moreover not foreign to the purposes of René Allio's previous films. In *La Vieille Dame indigne* everyday experience did not exclude paradoxical reversals; *Rude journée pour la reine* showed how aspirations on the historical scale were stifled by the demands of everyday life; and in *Les Camisards* the focus was on history: the historical failure of a popular uprising, part military and part religious struggle, saw individuals having to return to an impossible but necessary routine. What should be new with *Pierre Rivière* is the way in which the everyday, the historical and the tragic are linked up.

Jean Jourdheuil

The one who knows too much

Here it is a question of writing and of memory, with writing, for Pierre Rivière, being a particular way of fixing memory down, his own very strange way of speaking, of holding a discourse on his act, and in a sense repeating it. Of all the ways in which he recapitulates his act, whether in writing, speech or memory, none aims to diminish the significance of his gesture, none is a denial – a form of self-criticism so dear to the law. All on the contrary make Pierre's attitude, his attitude to his project, even stranger, hence more abnormal. For parricide to be the most odious of crimes, the murderer must also be of all murderers the most insane, hence the most hardened, the most marginalized, someone of whom one can say that he has nothing to lose and nothing to gain, not even his life, even if he is unfortunate enough to be granted it by a jury.

Pierre is a 'case' who teaches the law a few things about itself – the law, thinking it knows everything about the deviants it habitually deals with, judges and locks away, comes up against one such person who prevents the code from codifying, the norm from normalizing, the law from being applied, someone who tells them in a way: 'You see, you don't have an answer to everything.' On either side, *in either camp*, conscience and reason progress through failure, through that which (him who) from the outside poses the limit-question, the question of the limit, holds a mirror up to society, shows it its own reflection, saying in addition: 'It is you who made me into that – the monster you call a monster is all the more monstrous for living in your midst, for having been born and brought up among you.' The strange is all the more strange and terrifying when it appears almost normally, side by side with the normal, and even without there being any clash. This strangeness, this madness has an offensive quality in that it delivers blows and poses questions, forces the law and the law courts to defend themselves, the press to defend the law, psychiatry to come to its aid and the state to appear as such; majority views have to be repeated, restated and dissolved, on the admission that nothing is eternal.

And it is in these social rejects that the machinery is shown up for what it is, despotic and hateful: for crime makes the apparatuses speak and, in speaking, they speak of themselves, finding a pretext for appearing on stage in a pompous, ridiculous, laughable way. And what can Pierre Rivière oppose to this masquerade in fancy dress, this authoritarian and bureaucratic production, but his own: with the help of a prolific memory and the sharpness of his observation, he dreams up scenarios, period reconstructions, large-scale historical metaphors in which he plays the leading roles, transforming himself into legendary heroes. What he offers, in short, is an imagination at work, one whose work introduces embarrassment and disarray into the material order just as much as into the symbolic order, that of representation. Massacring cabbages? The boy must be crazy!

Strange, mad, supremely intelligent or hopelessly retarded, Pierre Rivière is all these things at once, and the spokesmen for the bourgeoisie don't mind contradicting themselves on the matter. But what is at issue in this psychological battle, this play of labels and contradictory characterizations, is also perhaps the status of knowledge as it is beginning to be cultivated in the rural areas by and through the church. Pierre had a great aptitude for studying and writing, as the priest will testify. But he is also a determined autodidact, one who is already learning about life in his own way, finding his way alone in the world of ideas and discoveries. He is an inventor, he dreams of new machines, a self-propelling carriage or an instrument for churning butter, he is familiar with great voyages and adventures, he makes up stories, he has a sense of his own place in history.

He knows more than a young peasant is expected to know, he knows too much for what the village can offer him. Already one imagines him writing letters for his father or reading the letters his father receives. His sister Victoire, on her side of the family, does the same for the mother. But isn't that already too much power in the hands of children? In the country, the child is still the monster, the monster being as much the one who is too intelligent as the one thought to be not intelligent enough. And Pierre Rivière manages to combine the two, both for the law and for the village, which in general doesn't recognize the prodigy. He doesn't grow up in harmony with the village, his development runs alongside or against it. He belongs to the village even as the village cannot recognize him. He utterly transgresses the laws of the village and of the family through an excess of knowledge, a surfeit of violence and imagination.

Serge Toubiana

The powers of falsehood

Pierre Rivière has secretly declared war on the powers of falsehood, which are female and find their embodiment in his mother. They corrupt whatever they approach, even at a distance. The female beast, which undermines everything that is just and proper, everything that is true, must be destroyed. The mother is false: she lies, she acts, she mimes (sorrow for example). It is because the father is 'true', because he really feels what he says he feels, and because he always tells the truth, that he is in danger of succumbing. And Pierre who does not speak – who writes – will in turn resort to lies, secrecy and dissimulation to triumph over the forces of untruth. The crime will be the means whereby truth, justice and male honesty are avenged; the billhook, as it cuts through the corrupting layers of a misleading drama production, will be the instrument of this vengeance. Then the truth will shine through, the court will provide Pierre with a platform and death will confirm his martyrdom; from that moment on his ideas will spread far and wide, reaching the manly spirits still waiting for their liberator.

But that isn't what happens at all. Long before the murder, Pierre's position is ambiguous. He too thinks along theatrical lines (not only does he hate his mother, as a man might hate a wild animal, but he despises her as a producer might despise an actress who goes over the top). He too disguises himself to carry out the murder. But it is above all the murder itself which falsifies the whole sequence of events. Even the project itself involves something wrong, misleading: the killing of the younger brother, intended to deceive the father, to falsify the meaning of Pierre's gesture, to evoke the father's horror and not his thanks. Pierre, in order to reveal the truth, has therefore chosen disguise and double meaning; his gesture, instead of being clear, is a model of ambiguity, marking him as a criminal and at the same time as a dispenser of justice. Instead of being a triumph for the truth, it unleashes the powers of falsehood and pretence. Scarcely has he committed the murders than Pierre no longer recognizes himself in what he has done, no longer understands what he sees. Reality, in the form of the corpses, comes as a violent blow to his imaginary constructions. The meaning is lost. Pierre will enter the dock not as the tribune or heroic dispenser of justice he had wanted to be, but as a ridiculous figure, someone who happens to have committed a cruel, clumsy and senseless act. He is ashamed. It is not so much the reality of his crime that overwhelms him as its irremediable falsity in relation to the (ideological) truth he believed in (the threat posed by the reign of women to the order of the world): a truth rendered derisory and illusory.

This falsity does not only overwhelm Pierre. It contaminates everything, corrupts everyone, and no one knows what to make of it. Pierre is a false madman, a false criminal, one or the other, or both. He is absolved of responsibility for his crime, having been made to bear responsibility for it, but no one will go so far as to say that he is not truly responsible for what he has done. The commutation of the sentence doesn't make sense: if Pierre is a criminal, he should be sentenced to death; if he is insane, he should go to an asylum – life imprisonment is neither one thing nor the other. For Pierre, this is the hardest thing to bear, it gives concrete form to the meaninglessness, the horror of his position. He wants to be dead, that is to say, punished as a criminal. He thinks he is dead (or does he?), which is to say that he is mad: he hangs himself, at once a madman and a criminal, or neither: we see with what cowardly relief the papers report the circumstances of his suicide as a confirmation of his madness. At last! This whole affair has a name, an identity, a cause. But even in the relief, a doubt persists.

The trail of destruction is thus extended: the false is to be found at the heart of journalistic 'truth', psychiatric 'truth' and the 'truth' of penal law.

Pascal Bonitzer

The theatre of battle

The narrative is punctuated by movements which have a theatrical quality, although they don't seem to refer to and follow exclusively the conventions of the theatre. One can't help thinking of another, no less codified set of movements, those pertaining to war.

The mother descending on La Faucterie, alone and unencumbered, to harass the father and force him into battle. The father conducting his raids of reprisal on Courvaudon, never alone, always with a horse and cart, to carry things away and secure them.

It is worth thinking for a moment about these tactics; like all tactics, they tell us a lot about the position and respective forces of either party. What gets them moving (and what moves them), as a Courvaudon neighbour so rightly says, is their attachment to property ('Was she not as attached to her property as he to his?'),[3] but there is already a fundamental difference: the mother can think only of defending her property, and even then she only possesses half of it. The father, on the other hand, is concerned with getting more. He begins with the annexation (which the mother doesn't really accept), and has every intention of continuing. At the beginning, the mother is therefore on the defensive and doubly disarmed: because she is a woman and because of the original contract which makes her over, along with her 'value', to one who has the law, social custom and public opinion on his side, the boss in law and according to custom: the father.

And so there is only one tactic that she can adopt if she doesn't want the annexation to go ahead: she has to take the initiative, resort to trickery, shift the ground of the debate, literally as well as metaphorically, keep getting it started all over again in some other way. She also needs language, exaggeration, dramatic entries, all the resources of the theatre and of guerrilla warfare for getting the money spent (guerrilla warfare also has its theatrical aspects: it is often a case of creating an illusion).

So the father cannot move ahead and pursue his project. He, in his turn, must defend what he has. The situation is reversed, he can no longer think in terms of acquiring more property, he must first accept the mother's deliberate spending and make sure that his own position does not get any worse.

This translates into two responses: first of all he braces himself, tries to stand firm, to hold his ground, not to give in – which forces the mother to intervene once more, to engage in new forms of harassment – and then, from time to time, when the spending or the anguish of having to spend can't be contained, the raid on Courvaudon, the reprisal, several people arriving together, with the horse.[4]

The mother, since she is always on the attack, never stays still, never allows us to focus on anything for very long, so that when Pierre describes her, we never see her working (although we know from the father's reactions that she does her bit, making butter, selling it, pruning, gardening and helping with the harvest, like a careful proprietor). She is always in movement. And the only time we see her staying quite still, never to move again (her interrupted work in the background), is when she is dead, stretched out on the kitchen floor and described by the magistrate.

The father on the contrary, in his efforts to resist, to play the impregnable fortress, usually stays put. What can a peasant in his position do? He works: and indeed, Pierre always shows him busy at something, against the décor of some well-defined place of work. The sense of the father's capacity for work is conveyed so strongly that even the reprisal raid on Courvaudon strikes us less as a risky undertaking, a movement or a journey, than as a job of work! And it is carried out as such. If in spite of this there is some movement at the end, it is precisely because the mother decides to bring it about through work of her own, which is full of surprises.

The mother conducts an inventive campaign, sure of her rights, confident of victory, full of disdain for her dull adversary. The father stubbornly pursues his cumbersome tactics, with the mentality of a victim. He is afraid of her and is always looking to other people for help. It is not surprising that he loses the war in the end. The only thing that saves him, in spite of himself, is the kamikaze attack of Pierre Rivière.

René Allio

Theatre of the father and the mother

It is remarkable how the relations between the father and the mother find their spatial expression in displacements which belong to the conventions of the theatre. 'Entrances and exits', separations, reunions: almost all their movements correspond to this pattern, which functions as in the most conventional genres – opera or *théâtre de boulevard* – making their relationship into a performance, quite literally.

The mother's whirlwind arrival at La Faucterie, after each clash: she comes to set the father off again, appearing all of a sudden at the house or in a field, bursting in on a scene already in progress (a meal, haymaking, cider-making), thoroughly upsetting it, as if from the wings or like some grotesque jack-in-the-box. For these entrances she often wears the costume best suited to the 'scene' she is about to play (she appears 'as a beggar woman', 'going to market', 'as a tearful mother', and so on)! She is always alone.

On the Courvaudon scene the father acts as the mother does on that of La Faucterie, but we perceive *his* entrances less in terms of physical movement than as snatches of dialogue, endlessly repeated, a series of automatic responses. He and the mother go over the same ground again and again, to the point of exasperation, in their one area of common interest: money, possessions.[5]

The exits, as in the theatre, mark the end of each scene, while also preparing us for what will follow. They hold things in suspense, the character who has just left the stage (the mother especially) standing just out of sight in the wings, ready to intervene once more to keep the action going.

In this written scenario (if not in the décor, which in this case is almost always the place of work), in this way of occupying space, in these comings and goings, one cannot but recognize, almost exactly reproduced, the characteristic movements of a highly conventional genre, so-called 'boulevard' theatre – a theatre of marital infidelity – whose conventions merely translate the basic conflict which works on the bourgeois family from within, the debate over who owns the essential commodity: the wife.

René Allio

Calibènes[6]

Pierre Rivière's obsessional side. The project's appeal, it seems to me, has a lot to do with this. *Pierre Rivière*, the film, may lead us to speak differently about topics we have often sought to raise in the cinema and elsewhere. In a way which takes Pierre as a model and which, when all the reflection, all the analysis, all the criticism is over, will allow our own obsessions to become engulfed in the abyss it opens up. 'Calibènes'. Is that not also a film? Is it not also for us what those invented machines were for Pierre, machines which he wanted to be the product of his imagination only and which would allow him to communicate with other people, when he himself had never had the knack of living in society?

Pierre's gesture is a perfect metaphor for the act of artistic creation: it is another, highly intense, life-and-death way of expressing violence within, and rationalization all about. Art is another such means of expression – although from our own particular standpoint (science and reason!) we are all too often inclined to forget it – one where the unconscious knows what is being said at least as well as us and where life itself is at stake (some would of course dismiss such a statement as 'subjectivist'); art is a means of expression of that sort, and not the kind that consists in defining a topic, 'something to say', in advance, bringing only one's rational faculties into play, a programme that one then only has to execute by putting one foot after the other along the anticipated route – but never putting one's foot in it, never putting a foot wrong.

And without a prior notion of 'content', without having done all the thinking in advance, I can already find possible meanings for the film in the memoir, in the first-hand accounts, in the texts of those who have proposed interpretations, in Foucault's approach. All that is quite enough, I don't need anything else. What interests me this time is not in the first instance what there is to say or what *has to be said*, but that these words that were said and these events that took place over a century ago, and which are recounted in detail by Pierre Rivière, make me feel today that I also want/need to make an entirely new instrument, tragic in its way, 'to distinguish myself': a 'calibène'.

Is it possible to meet up with Pierre Rivière in the *present-day landscape*? In other words, can the story be recounted and represented *accurately* (with period costumes, objects of the time) but in present-day locations, not just fields but also towns and villages? The risk of this approach (it seems to me) is that you end up with a flat imitation of Pasolini, or something which in its very 'distancing' would begin to approach the commonplace.

René Allio

Interview with Michel Foucault

CAHIERS: May we begin by asking you what interested you about the publication of the dossier on Pierre Rivière and more especially what you see as interesting in the fact that it has now been made into a film, at least in part?

MICHEL FOUCAULT: For me the book was a trap. You know how nowadays people are forever talking about delinquents, their psychology, their unconscious, their drives, their desires, and so on. There's just no end to what psychiatrists, psychologists and criminologists have to say on the topic. Now this discourse on delinquency goes back about 150 years, to the 1830s. So here was a splendid case: a triple murder, dating from 1835, and on this murder we had not only all the documents relating to the trial but also an absolutely unique first-hand account, by the criminal himself, who left a memoir over a hundred pages long. And so, publishing this book was, for me, a way of saying to all those experts in psycho-whatever (psychology, psychoanalysis, psychiatry): you've been around for 150 years and here's a case that belongs to the period of your birth. What do you have to say about it? Are you any better equipped to talk about it than your nineteenth-century colleagues?

And I can say that, in a sense, I won; I won or I lost, I'm not sure, since of course my secret desire was to hear the criminologists, psychologists or psychiatrists holding forth on this Rivière affair in their usual, insipid manner. But they have been literally reduced to silence: not a single one of them has spoken up to say: 'This is what Rivière really was: I can now tell you things that couldn't be said in the nineteenth century' (except for one silly woman, a psychoanalyst, who insisted that Rivière was the perfect illustration of Lacan's paranoia . . .). Apart from her, nobody spoke. And what this shows, I think, is that present-day psychiatrists are as much at a loss to explain this case as their nineteenth-century counterparts; they have nothing to add. But this said, I have to admire their prudence and lucidity in deciding not to engage in their own discourse on Rivière. And so I won my bet or I lost it, depending on which way you look at it . . .

CAHIERS: But more generally, isn't it difficult to be analytical about this sequence of events, about its focal point, which is the murder, and also about the character responsible for it?

FOUCAULT: Yes, because I think Rivière's own account of what he did goes so far beyond, or is at least so resistant to any possible analysis, that there is nothing you can say about this central point, this crime, this gesture, which can even begin to match it. It's a phenomenon for which I can't see any equivalents in the history of crime or of discourse: a crime accompanied by a discourse so powerful and so strange that the crime doesn't in the end exist any more, can't be pinned down, by the very fact of what is said about it by the criminal himself.

CAHIERS: How then do you see your position, if analysis isn't possible?

FOUCAULT: I didn't say anything myself about Rivière's actual crime, and again, I don't believe anyone can. No, I think he has to be compared to Lacenaire, who was his exact contemporary, and who committed minor crimes by the handful, shamefully, ignominiously and on the whole unsuccessfully, but who managed by writing about them, very intelligently, to transform these crimes into real works of art and the criminal, that's to say himself, Lacenaire, into the supreme artist of criminality.[7] That was another *tour de force*, if you like: he managed for decades, for more than a century, to give an intense reality to acts which were basically nasty and despicable. There was nothing very admirable about him, as a criminal, but the splendour and intelligence of his discourse lent consistency to his behaviour. Rivière presents us with something quite different: a truly extraordinary crime re-enacted in a still more extraordinary memoir, so extraordinary that the crime ceases in the end to exist – and that's what happened, I think, in the mind of his judges.

CAHIERS: Are you in agreement then with the approach in René Allio's film, which tends to emphasize the idea of the peasant class taking language into its own hands? Or had you also thought of this before?

FOUCAULT: No, I hadn't. Allio must take the credit for this, but I'm completely in agreement, because if you reconstruct the crime from the outside, with actors, as if it were a criminal event and nothing else, I think you miss the point. On the one hand you have to situate yourself inside Rivière's discourse – the film had to be a film of the memoir and not a film of the crime – and on the other hand this discourse of a peasant lad living in Normandy in the 1830s had to be set against what the discourse of the peasantry might have been at that time. Now what could be closer to this than the speech, the voices of the present-day peasants living in the same place; and 150 years on it's basically the same voices, the same accents, the same raw, clumsy words that relate the same thing only barely transposed. The fact that Allio has chosen to commemorate this act in the same places and with almost the same characters as 150 years ago means that the same peasants repeat the same gestures in the same locations. It was difficult to reduce all the apparatus of the cinema, all the apparatus of the film, to so little and to have done that is truly extraordinary, and quite unique, I think, in the history of the cinema.

What is also important, I think, in Allio's film is that it gives the peasants their tragedy. Basically, until the end of the eighteenth century, the peasant's tragedy was still, perhaps, hunger. But from the start of the nineteenth century, and perhaps still today, it was, like every great tragedy, the tragedy of the Law, of the Law and the Land. Greek tragedy is about the birth of the Law and the mortal effects of the Law on men. The Rivière affair takes place in 1836, that is to say twenty years or so after the *Code Civil* had come into effect: the peasant's daily life is subject to a new law, and he has to struggle in this new legal universe. The whole Rivière drama is a drama of the Law, of the Code, of the Land, of marriage, of possessions . . . And it is always within that tragedy that the peasant world must move. What is important, then, is that present-day peasants are made to play this age-old drama which is, at the same time, that of their own life: just as Greek citizens saw their own city represented on the stage.

CAHIERS: What, in your view, might be the effect of present-day Norman peasants being able, thanks to the film, to remember this event, this period?

FOUCAULT: As you know, there's plenty of literature on the peasantry; but a peasant literature, some form of peasant expression, is harder to come by. Here we have a text written in 1835 by a peasant, in his own language – that of an only just literate peasant. And this gives present-day peasants the possibility of acting out, in their own way, this drama which represents their own coming into existence, not so very many years previously. And looking at the way in which Allio makes his actors work, you probably noticed that in one way he was very close to them, that he explained things at length and was tremendously supportive, but that in another way he gave them a lot of latitude, so that their language, their pronunciation and their gestures might be truly theirs. And if you like, I believe that it's politically important to give peasants the opportunity of playing this peasant text. Hence also the importance of outside actors to represent the world of the law, the lawyers, the barristers . . . all those people who belong to the town and who have basically nothing to do with this very direct communication between the nineteenth-century peasant and his twentieth-century counterpart that Allio has managed to bring about and which, up to a point, he has enabled these peasant actors to bring about.

CAHIERS: But isn't there a danger that they will find their voice only through such a monstrous story?

FOUCAULT: There was a potential danger, certainly; and Allio, when he began to talk to them about the possibility of doing the film, hesitated to tell them what it was really about. When he did tell them, he was very surprised to see that they took it all in their stride, and that the crime wasn't in any way a problem for them. On the contrary, instead of becoming an obstacle, it was a kind of space where they were able to meet, speak and get a whole lot of things off their chests – things that preoccupied them in their daily lives. In fact, instead of inhibiting them, the crime tended rather to liberate them. And had they been asked to play something that was closer to their daily lives, to their current concerns, they might perhaps have felt more fictional, more theatrical, than with this kind of distant and slightly mythical crime which provided the perfect cover for them to be themselves.

CAHIERS: What I had in mind, rather, was a slightly unfortunate parallel: at the moment it's very fashionable to make films about the sinfulness, the depravity of the bourgeoisie. Was there not a risk of falling into the trap of the indiscreet violence of the peasantry?

FOUCAULT: And linking up with the tradition of appalling representations of the peasant world, as in Balzac or Zola . . .? I don't think so. Perhaps for this very reason that the violence is never made concrete or theatrical. What you are aware of in the film are degrees of intensity, things going on below the surface, barely translated into words, distant rumblings, repetition, a multi-layered depth – but violence as such doesn't exist . . . The idealization of peasant violence and abjection that you seem to fear doesn't happen. That's how it is in Allio's film, but that's also how it is in the documents, in history. Of course, there are a few frenetic scenes, the parents fighting over the children, but these scenes are not very frequent and above all what comes through is always how refined, how sensitive, how subtle even, these people are in their wickedness, often how delicate. So that these characters are not at all like those wild and completely unrestrained animals that you find in a certain kind of literature on the peasantry. Everyone is terribly intelligent, terribly astute and, up to a point, terribly restrained . . .

(Interview by Pascal Kané)
Translated by Annwyl Williams

Notes

1 *Moi, Pierre Rivière, ayant égorgé ma mère, ma soeur et mon frère . . . Un cas de parricide au XIXe siècle présenté par Michel Foucault* (Paris: Gallimard/Julliard, 1973); English edition trans. F. Jellinek (New York: Pantheon, 1975; Harmondsworth: Penguin, 1978). Allio's film was made in 1976.

2 J.-P. Vernant and P. Vidal-Naquet, *Mythe et tragédie en Grèce ancienne* (Paris: Maspero, 1972); trans. J. Lloyd (Brighton: Harvester, 1981), p. 4.

3 *I, Pierre Rivière . . .*, p. 94.

4 There are only two episodes where the horse has something to do with their interaction when it is the mother who has just scored a point and the father bitten the dust: these are the two journeys back from the lawsuits, when the father has had to consent to giving in or paying, when they are travelling home alone, once in the trap and the other time on horseback, moving through the countryside together, for once at the same time and at the same pace. (Author's note.)

5 So much so that the mother, in the heat of battle, when she should be finding some new tactic, just sends back the same old refrain ('I want my land back'), like a boomerang. (Author's note.)

6 'Calibène' is the name given by Pierre Rivière to one of the machines he invents, or dreams of inventing: the 'calibène' is for killing birds (see *I, Pierre Rivière . . .*, pp. 31, 37, 103).

7 Pierre-François Lacenaire (1800–35), a well-educated petty criminal, was guillotined for a double murder. His unfinished memoirs were published in a Russian magazine edited by the young Dostoevsky, who was interested in Lacenaire's views on crime and punishment. See Oliver Cyriax, *Crime: An Encyclopaedia* (London: André Deutsch, 1993), pp. 218–19.

14

DEFAMATIONS (FRAGMENTS).
PRETEXT: *KARL MAY*
BY H.-J. SYBERBERG

('Diffamations [Fragments]. Prétexte: *Karl May* de
H.-J. Syberberg', *Cahiers du Cinéma* 266–7, May 1976)

Jean-Pierre Oudart

Yesterday

A fascinating film. In the first place because of its subject, the portrait of a
writer, the author of popular exotic novels at the end of the nineteenth century
in Germany. This exotic literature, which starts to proliferate in Europe at this
time, arrives with colonialism and the rise of racism – carried along on the
same currents from which ethnographic research in part emerges. Half-dreamt,
half wild imagining, this is a discourse on the Other, the other race, the other
ethnicity. But it is equally a discourse on the sexual pleasure of this Other, no
less enigmatic than female sexual pleasure, another privileged subject in the
literature of the time.

As regards the social position of those who were writers, the film orients
itself in such a way that its historical references remain enlightening about the
paradoxical situation of the artist at the heart of bourgeois societies today. It
extends its interrogation (and one has rarely seen a less didactic film) to consider what is attributed to the writer in order to make him an object of scandal. Attributions such as: knowledge of the sexual pleasure of the Other, an
access to it and indulgence towards it that regularly brought defamations rain-
ing down on him. The fact is that defamation is the great political and criminal scandal to bring artists and their bourgeoisie into conflict, and that it is the
price the writer has often paid for putting the fascinating sexual pleasure of the
Other into writing, and into stories, provided that the writing does not create
too many unsettling resonances within the bourgeoisie's own ranks, or that it
does not flagrantly call into question the order of things.

As for Karl May, in the truly Kafkaesque labyrinth of judicial proceedings
which he is caught up in throughout the film, the aspect ceaselessly and relent-

lessly pursued by his accusers concerns the extent to which his writings truly possess him. They want to know everything, the whole truth, and because of this they launch all-out accusations concerning his sexuality, his texts, their referent: before writing his successful works had he not, in his youth, written pornographic novels? Is it certain that he visited the regions he described, or, rather, did he post letters from abroad in order to create a trail of red herrings? Had he himself written certain pages, deemed licentious, or had they been editorial additions? Had he had a homosexual relationship with an Indian, the hero of one of his books?

So many strands to the enigma of a personality, and it is of course the fact that they don't mesh that constitutes the scandal. For how, in that case, can you know everything about the artist's pleasure?

Evidently, this is elusive knowledge; what imprisons the bourgeois myth of the divinely inspired artist is an effect of the historical development of signifying practices which determined that their products appear, in the market place, as divided – divided by what their development has been able to contribute to supposition, fabulation and defamation by way of access to the pleasure of an Other. In the case of exotic literature, to an 'Other' ethnicity; in the case of ancient and medieval literature (retro *avant la lettre*) to people of olden times – an Other again evoked, invoked, called forth through dream, wild fantasy, drugs (an Other that had yet to name itself the unconscious).

We have continued to attribute to the bourgeois artist an ulterior motive. Attributions made in the name of his artistic practice [*écriture*], imbued as it is with the solemn musings of current public debate on other societies and with the permanent moral crisis of his own society. An ulterior motive made concrete in his writings, either as a delight taken in the (more or less unavowable) sexual pleasure of the Other or in his conjuring up of it for himself. Such are *the divisive effects of artistic practice* that sometimes one can barely conceive of their impact and social repercussions when it is not literature but painting that is involved. Consider, for example, the scandal of Manet, the painter whose bizarre daubs, when compared to those of Academy painting, would not have appeared quite so different to the naked eye if it were not that their pictorial accentuation made them appear dedicated less to the masters whom Manet portrayed than to those painters (Hals, Velázquez, Goya) whose tones he too ostentatiously celebrated. This is the *stroke* of scandal, of paintings whose pleasure had neither value nor worth for the spectators but which none the less generated a spiteful resentment, of the evil eye of the bourgeoisie turned against an artist suspected of not venerating their values and of ridiculing them.

From this it transpires that the defamation of which the artist was made the object was never entirely carried by such and such an exhibit through which he came to be accused, when it was his writings that, materially, gave him form. I am reminded of Manet, and of the madness of the Empress's gesture in whispering 'Olympia . . .'.[1]

But equally, of course, the artist can go along with such defamation only excessively, to adorn himself with his writings as though they were gaudy plumage.

Today

Let us now leave Karl May as he is shown in the film's final images: the defamed artist (and now cared for by a woman), surrounded by the trophies of his travels and clothed again in his exotic finery. These are images well suited to pander to the spectator's cult of what might be called the 'marginal' – either the diverse modes of pleasure that develop on the fringes, in the folds and the pores of a social system whose processes of internal segregation (achieved on a grand scale in the USA) channel and in large measure contain the rebellions that one would be wrong to underestimate, as regards the potential for resistance that accumulates there.

Resistance, rebellion, pleasure: we are bound to place ourselves in their knots and their networks. There are no 'second fronts' of struggle and we shall have to accept the consequences: breaks in ideologies and politics, fractures in theory. There is for us (at least for me) no longer anything in common between the discourse of what we call political economy, the mapping of the capitalist organization of pleasure – of which Lacan reminds us that 'an economic science inspired by Capital does not necessarily lead to its use as a revolutionary potential' – and what psychoanalysis has laboriously worked on during three-quarters of a century as an approach to the investment of desire; no common ground except in the treatment of the apparatuses (of production or otherwise) as bodies, as the assembly of bodies and networks whose pleasure depends materially on their functioning and which closes off, censors, represses the others, precipitating the processes of segregation which find no anchorage in the discourse of Marxism.

Elsewhere

Why is it that so-called socialist countries (the USSR) undertake such a violent censorship of cultural products as apparently inoffensive, politically speaking, as abstract painting for example? Because, a sociologist might say, a painting can become a flag. Yes, but does not the outrage provoked in such societies (and there have been worse) have something to do with such products fundamentally evoking a means of access to another pleasure? One that has nothing in common with that to which the workers, installed in their system of state production, accommodate their desires and labours in a morality of the common good which is paid for by concentration camps and psychiatric hospitals? These are not works of common sense, they cannot fall within the realm of the common good, they are censored. And they are defamed as much as possible.

Here

Closer to home, still following this train of thought *of a pleasure that politically divides artistic practice*, if there exists a film-maker who is defamed and insulted it is Godard with *Numéro deux*. And what does the outrage consist of? Godard gets straight to the point in two ways.

First, by closing off the pleasure of spectators (of the left), by disconnecting his images from the tissue of good sense which might have sustained it. He does not seek to point these images of political leaders, factories and couples in the predictable direction of progress — progress through knowledge, revolt, power. Man and woman might be taken on the road to feminist revolt; factory and couple might lead to Communist Party familialism; Mitterand plus factory plus family to a common Social Programme. Woman plus man plus factory might paint a glowing portrait of a sociological interpretation of the relations between the sexes, etc.

Second, by indicating that he, as the film-maker, is holding on to this obstruction and systematically turning it in the opposite direction.

Some people are outraged by this tactic, and start bandying about terms like control and contempt — and, worse, accuse him of dishonourably enjoying it. However, who takes pleasure from such outrage, if not governments? Who is contemptuous, if not the apparatuses that, in their universalist discourses, merge the terms? And who controls, if not the film-makers producing such fare as *Vincent, François*, and the Others?[2] At the very least those who, in the eyes of many, rejoice in their 'good sense'.

Here and elsewhere

It is very difficult these days to give written form to a pleasure that does not pander to such good sense. Those who risk it are neutralized through defamation when they come close, or through story-telling when they remain distant — exotic. *Milestones* has managed to get *Positif* twittering in their attempt to attribute to this tale — however unremittingly the film itself contradicts it through its own construction, through the difficulties which mark it, like the scars of memory (memory of the living, not the dead) — bodies moored to a story which is close to us because the film, the writing, places them in a realm of pleasure that relates — to what precisely? Not in swimming in the waters of a risky historical common sense, nor in going against the current (underground), nor in contradicting on principle (*Milestones* does not contradict *Nashville*), but in marking the lines of a resistance to imperialist America, lines no doubt as fragile as the bodies that trace them.

Still

Trial by defamation, it never ceases to be spelt out — and, above all, to be staged. Remember the death of Pasolini, and recall how the fascist press, during his lifetime, fed on its own vilifications: homosexual and left-wing thinker – left-wing thinker and international artist – international artist and homosexual. Such couplings are certainly not indifferent: they worked to feed the worst parasitical fantasies of bourgeois society through those it continues to repress, imprison or kill. And to convert these interior acts of segregation into the idea (the offensively delirious idea) of a threat from outside, shadowy and omnipresent, of which Pasolini, among many others, could be the living exhibit.

But why, when his death was announced, this barrage of insults, these unbridled articles accompanying the last photographs of him? What is the association of this image with these blatant insults other than the return of the repressed figured by the silent, terrifying photographs of the dead of the Paris Commune (cf. Serge Daney, 'Un tombeau pour l'oeil', and Serge Toubiana, 'Le hasard arbitraire'[3]), here arranged as a Sadian staging of the final act of the trial of a corpse that it was necessary to resurrect, to summon back to life, in order to feed again the readers' pleasure, to perpetuate it until it acknowledges (under the cloak of moralism) that he died the death he was looking for, the death he desired. That is to say, the death which the fascist spectators could enjoy as a spectacle, by inventing a character of accomplice-executioner to incorporate into the scenario of their imaginings of Pasolini, as regards pleasure – as in the final chapter of a pulp novel.

Translated by Chris Darke

Notes

1 Manet's *Olympia*, with its unabashedly nude figure of a reclining woman, outraged contemporary French society.
2 Scenes from Claude Sautet's *Vincent, François, Paul et les autres* (1974) can be seen playing on a monitor in the opening sequence of Godard's *Numéro deux*. Oudart is making a pun on the title of Sautet's film and the idea of the 'Other'.
3 'Un tombeau pour l'oeil', *Cahiers* 258–9; 'Le hasard arbitraire', *Cahiers* 262–3, translated in this volume, Ch. 5.

15

CINEMA AND HISTORY

('Cinéma et histoire: entretien avec Marc Ferro',
Cahiers du Cinéma 257, May–June 1975)

Marc Ferro in interview with Serge Daney and Ignacio Ramonet

Everything recorded on film since the beginning of the century (micro- or macro-history, factual or otherwise, documentary or fiction) today forms a considerable archive stored in the warehouses of *cinémathèques*, in television networks, in private collections and in people's memories.

For a long time the relationship between peoples and their past – their memory – was difficult to distinguish from their relationship with this archive (their 'filmic memory', in a sense). Naturally, this saw the creation of a kind of mass cinephilia. The apparatuses that now have a privileged access to our archive have, at the same time, the possibility of intervening in this relationship with the past, of shaping it. This is precisely what is happening with the educational tools with which the Hachette–Pathé group has undertaken to serve up History in audiovisual segments.

This is not without problems, which for present purposes have been assembled under the rubric 'Cinema and History'. Problems such as:

- How does the recourse to filmed (rather than written) documentation explode the traditional field of historical research? How can it contribute to reviewing (or reinforcing?) the dominant conception of History as it is taught?
- Is to 'historicize' filmed documents, to confer on them the dignity of historical documents, achieved at the price of a certain suppression of any political perspective, either the one in force at the time of the recording of the images or the one present today in the way they are read and used – hence at the price of a certain *depoliticization*?

In order to start answering these questions one needs to interview one of the few people who have asked such questions of themselves in a *practical* fashion. We start with Marc Ferro, responsible for the films produced by Hachette–Pathé (*Images de l'histoire*), a historian turned film-maker.

CAHIERS: First, at what point did people with cameras start to film events 'live' around the world? Second, at what point did the images obtained in this way begin to form a 'stock' of images? What are the relationships between the formation of this stock and different political powers? Third, at what point did these images start being considered as 'documents', as 'historical proofs', even as 'weapons'?

MARC FERRO: All these problems appeared simultaneously, but they did not develop at the same pace. The first great burst of enthusiasm takes place with the 1914–18 war. Certainly since the end of the nineteenth century cameras were already filming people and events, notably anything that related to the ruling families. Queen Victoria's jubilee in 1897 was given extended coverage, as were various activities of the young Wilhelm II. One of the first political acts caught on camera was the suicide of a suffragette who threw herself under the King's horse at the Ascot Races, in 1907, I think.[1] Was it accidental that the camera was present? As for the political use of film, this dates right back to the very beginnings of film: in 1901 the British in Shanghai reconstructed a terrorist action by the Boxers. Clearly a loyal subject of Her Majesty could not trust these individuals.

Propaganda films of this type mushroomed during the 1914–18 war through the impetus of army film units. Private companies also contributed. However, the camera's principal function was to record reality, and the enemy's armament in particular. To this end, for example, the Germans had automatic cameras installed in the trenches, some of which captured unforgettable images of French or British soldiers being cut to pieces by machine-gun fire.

However, one has the impression that, even if after the war there was a simultaneous development in the industrialized countries of the cinema of newsreel and reportage, the function of cinema had yet to be analysed seriously, which explains the disparity of such efforts and their relative independence.

This also has to do with the status of cinema in society at the beginnings of the twentieth century. On the one hand, following on from its origins, it is considered a piece of avant-garde machinery for the well-informed and the technicians. It is seen as an instrument that records movement and everything that the eye can't retain. On the other hand, film is completely ignored as a cultural phenomenon. Produced by a piece of machinery, like photography, it was thought to be neither work of art nor document. It is significant that newsreel items never had any name attached to them other than that of the company that produced them. The cameraman did not belong to the ruling society, the world of the clerks. He was only a 'messenger', a messenger of images. Thus produced – an orphan – the image was good only for prostituting itself to the people; in cultivated society and among people of distinction the cinema was an entertainment for the underclass.

The contempt in which the ruling classes have long held the image has precise causes which we have analysed elsewhere.[2] We should note that the inferior[3] status of the image, its subordination to the written text, ruled it out for a long time as an object of the law. An orphan, beyond the pale, the image was necessarily wild. It could not express an opinion and was politically neutral. In fact if, as we know, moral censorship has for a long time kept an eye on the images rather than the texts of films, political censorship has gone the other way. Even in 1940, the Swedish government explained that in screening German and British newsreels at the same time, but *without sound*, they were observing their neutrality.

The Soviets and the Nazis were the first to take on cinema in all its complexity, to analyse its function and to grant it a privileged status in the world of knowledge, propaganda and culture. They were building two counter-societies and had nothing but contempt or hatred for the cultural policies of the leaders from whom they had taken over. They were the only ones to mention the name of the cameraman in newsreel credits. The image-messenger now had a right to a written mention; his practice now became a document, a work of art, in any case a work of some description.

Trotsky and Lunacharsky certainly saw the role that cinema could play as a weapon of propaganda. 'We must control it', Trotsky wrote. Lunacharsky[4] himself made a film dating from 1918 which demonstrated the necessity of reconciling the enlightened bourgeoisie with the working class. However, being intellectuals themselves and analysts of texts, of arguments rather than images, the Bolsheviks remained clerics and the cinema did not really concern them. Lenin wanted films to be 'educational', which indicates the very limited place that cinema occupied in his imagination. In fact, the Soviets did not really take control of cinematic production until around 1927–8, when Stalin fulfilled Trotsky's wish. The first *Pravda* editorial devoted to cinema dates from the release of *Chapayev* in 1934; film became as much an object of prestige as an instrument of propaganda. In the functioning of the Soviet system it remained well behind the text, the written word; it was hoisted up to the status of important, but not privileged, cultural object. The Nazis alone privileged film. Because they were plebeians with no access to other culture? Whatever the reason, for the Nazis the cinema was not just an instrument of propaganda, after they took power. It played the role of disseminating information and gave them a parallel culture. Goebbels and Hitler spent entire days at the cinema, and when Goebbels oversaw the production of a film, such as *Jud Süss* for example, he actively participated at all levels of production and not only, like Lunacharsky, as a screenwriter.

The Nazis were the sole ruling power of the twentieth century whose imagination, for the most part, derived from the world of the image.

CAHIERS: Could you tell us a little more about your films for Hachette–Pathé?

FERRO: The production of these films made me think about the function of history, about the nature of the genres that it employs and about the link that exists between the choice of themes developed and the techniques involved. Things that are not always obvious when one is writing a book appear very starkly during the production of a film; for example, the glaring contrast between the history of the historians and history considered as a society's preserved inheritance. We don't consider one as being more legitimate than the other; each has its function. Only, the production of a film demands that a specific genre be adopted, a place chosen in which to treat such and such a problem.

Take, for example, three films produced for Pathé and Hachette in the series *Images de l'histoire*. Having to make a film on the Algerian problem[5] it seemed impossible to adopt a so-called objectivity, a 'scientific' approach. In choosing to analyse an aspect of the problem, the rebellion of a colonial subject, it was possible to define the colonial regime, to explain the causes of the confrontation, its inescapable character; in short, to reconstruct in full the argument and behaviour of an insurrection. To ask questions of the merits or legitimacy of this argument or behaviour is a separate task. The work of reconstruction was the priority; before the machinery of the state – French or Algerian – was able to erase what shreds of this past remained; and before institutional history could file this argument on the computer and obliterate its very existence.

The coherence of the theme dictates the choice of images: the film does not show Algeria as the French would see it, with its roads and schools, but as the Arabs would see it, with its internal frontiers of garrisons and barracks that isolated the opulence of French Algeria from the wretched poverty of Arab Algeria. The treatment of the sound also follows this approach, with the noises and fanfares overlapping the images of the colonial system; the flute is identified with a growing national awareness, at first hesitant but by the end overlapping even the diving planes.

In making a film about Germany under Hitler[6] it seemed useful to ask a single question: how did Germany become Nazi? The choice of this question indicates the perspective adopted, which is at once historical and sociological. Also, from a sample of witnesses, the production attempts to give a sense of the process of identification with Nazism prior to 1933, and then with Hitler's regime. As with the film on Algeria, this production is also a reconstruction. It was very difficult to get Germans to talk about this period of their past, and so it was necessary to preserve the tracks of their evidence before they were erased completely. Some of the films in *Images de l'histoire* start from this approach, while others privilege a particular perspective or interpretation, such as the film about a colonial rebellion or the one on the problem of the American blacks in which it is only the blacks themselves who speak.[7]

The film on the 1914–18 war is very different; in one sense it's more the film of a historian of the *Annales* school[8] who would seek to set the argument of the images against the argument of texts. Here, the perspective on History takes the form of this confrontation. The texts are the assertions of politicians, sabre-rattling strategists. The images represent the tragic counterpoint of a deluded society. Again, these images are shown – with the help of Pierre Gouge – in such a way that they never have the appearance of being History, and this allows us to go beyond the image alone. Like the emphasis on texts in Marx and in the *Annales* school from Bloch to Braudel, the argument which is presented here attempts to go further than the level of appearances, beyond the experience of the everyday.

CAHIERS: The 'retro fashion'. Where does this generalized interest in History come from?

FERRO: I believe that the 'retro' fashion is linked to the general questioning of ideas and certainties that is the mark of our times. Let's say that, in this respect, the watershed was the Khruschev report on the functioning of the Communist parties and the official Marxist analysis of societies. Soon, with the development of the audiovisual, the parallel culture in its turn called into question the legitimacy and validity of conventional behaviour and knowledge. This parallel culture has disseminated information and, from the ensuing confrontation, has revealed the inconsistency and incoherence of individual or collective attitudes: a man of the 'left' could be an absolute tyrant at home. It became increasingly clear that the morality of governments and censors was a mask created to disguise their own perversion . . .

But within this general re-evaluation one thing certainly holds good, that fascism is evil. Some have wanted to see this for themselves because it seemed to them that, whilst this was undoubtedly true, things weren't perhaps as simple as they appeared. This is a lonely, though dangerous, approach in a world where fascism is clearly still with us.

Contrary to the *Cahiers* critic Pascal Bonitzer, with whom I usually find myself in agreement, I greatly appreciated Louis Malle's approach in *Lacombe Lucien*. It seemed to me less ambiguous than Visconti's.[9] Malle does an admirable job of showing that when a society functions in the way that ours does it will produce individuals like Lacombe Lucien. It's a profound critique which questions an entire discourse on fascism; an analysis to follow through, but who's taking it up?

Enterprises like this cause distinct reverberations because our society wants absolutely to know how it functions, and traditional knowledge is in place and alert, in order to prevent this happening. Now, History ought to produce a response to this; but often, when it is in the service of institutions, History settles – even in the guise of a 'scientific' approach – for simply disseminating dreams. It too often neglects to explain the present, a tendency to which one can attribute the admittedly shortlived ground swell of sociology. It is imperative that History becomes an active, operative science.

CAHIERS: Faced with these documents and the (party political) apparatuses that use them for their own ends, what is the place of the historian?

FERRO: The historian's primary task is to restore to society the History which the institutional apparatuses have dispossessed it of. To question society, to begin to listen to it — to my mind, this is the primary duty of the historian. Instead of settling simply for using archives, it is equally important to create them and to contribute to their setting up: to make films about and to ask questions of those who have never had the right to speak and be a witness. The duty of the historian is to dispossess the apparatuses of the monopoly they have assumed, of being the only source of History. Not satisfied with dominating society, these apparatuses (governments, political parties, the Church, trade unions) mean also to be its conscience. The historian must help to make society aware of this mystification.

The second task consists of confronting the different discourses of History and, through this confrontation, discovering an invisible reality. Happily, the *Annales* historians and Michel Foucault are working on this. For my part, I am trying to discover the analytical methods applicable to contemporary History which, because of our perspective on it, is more difficult to study. Film has been a great help in this case, fiction as much as so-called documentary. In fact, I don't believe that frontiers exist between different types of films, at least to the historian for whom the imaginary is just as much history as History.

Translated by Chris Darke

Notes

1 This event actually took place in 1913, not 1907, and the race (the Derby) was at Epsom, not Ascot; the suffragette was Emily Davison. She did not commit suicide, as Ferro suggests, but died four days later from her injuries.

2 In *Annales* (Économies-Sociétés-Civilisations), 1973, 1. (Authors' note.)

3 Although the French text has 'supérieur', the context implies 'inferior'.

4 Anatoli Lunacharsky was the Soviet Commissar for Enlightenment from 1917 to 1929, with overall political responsibility for cinema. He also scripted a number of films, mostly popular melodramas.

5 *Algérie 1954*, co-direction M.-L. Derrien, 15 minutes. (Authors' note.)

6 *Comment l'Allemagne est devenue nazie*, co-direction M.-L. Derrien, interviews by Rebecca Lewerenz, 16 minutes. (Authors' note.)

7 *Du Ku Klux Klan aux Panthers Noires*, edited by Michel Brasier, documentation by M.-F. Briselance, 15 minutes. (Authors' note.)

8 The school of French historians, notably Marc Bloch and Fernand Braudel, associated with the journal *Annales d'Histoire Économique et Sociale*, which promoted a research-based view of history radically different from that of the event-centred approach.

9 I.e. Visconti's grandiose vision of Nazism in *The Damned* (1969).

16

DEFRAMINGS

('Décadrages', *Cahiers du Cinéma* 284, January 1978)

Pascal Bonitzer

The entire Renaissance science of perspective – the encounter between painting and Euclidean optical geometry, the miraculous submission of figures to mathematical idealism – has a profoundly equivocal meaning, as Panofsky noted in *Perspective as a Symbolic Form*:

> We are justified equally in conceiving the history of perspective as a triumph of a sense of reality, constituting distance and objectivity, as much as a triumph of the desire for power that inhabits man, negating all distance: a systematization and a stabilization of the exterior world as much as an enlargement of the personal sphere. Must artists necessarily restrict themselves to employing this ambivalent method? Must the perspectival disposition of a painting organize itself around the point effectively occupied by the spectator [. . .] or, conversely, must the spectator adapt himself and his responses to the disposition adopted by the painter?

Among the theoretical debates opened up by the last of Panofsky's alternatives, he cites the question of distance (long or short) and of the obliquity, or not, of the point of view. By way of an example Panofsky opposes Antonello da Messina's *St Jerome* – painted in deep perspective and situating the point of view at the painting's centre, a construction which holds the spectator 'outside' the scene – to Dürer, whose short perspective and oblique view produce an effect of intimacy and give the impression of 'a representation determined not by the objective laws of architecture but by the subjective point of view of a spectator happening on the scene'. In a way, then, the reduction of distance and the obliqueness of point of view 'snatch' the spectator into the painting's interior.

Classical painting pushed the effect of the spectator's seduction by its apparatus even further than this, but at the price of a numbing 'centrifugation' of composition. And it is the look that implements this 'centrifugation' (I have no other term for it). Dürer's St Jerome is bent over his writing table, making the spectator a voyeur of his meditation. But if he had his head raised and was looking, what would then be happening? The painting that most famously plays with this effect is, of course, Velázquez's *Las Meninas*,[1] which portrays a scene whose principal participants are situated beyond the painting, in the very space of the spectator. Their image is murkily evoked in the deep background in the mirror placed at the painting's perspectival vanishing point (an image, needless to say, of Philip IV of Spain and his wife); but what renders them so present, so necessary to the scene, is that the looks of all the characters in the painting are directed towards them, posing as they are for the self-portrayed painter. I will not dwell on the general implications of this portrait, which have been analysed by Michel Foucault in *Les Mots et les choses* [*The Order of Things*]. I want only to emphasize the arrogance and audacity of this supreme seduction which forces the spectator to believe that the scene extends beyond the boundaries of the frame, holding him in this space as well as pushing him beyond it, which multiplies the power of the representation to evoke in it the unrepresented, if not the unrepresentable, and opens up an unlimited space to him.

In perhaps no other work – of the classical period, at least – are the respective positions of the artist and the sovereign staged in a manner so intriguing, so tense, so dramatic as they are here (making of the anonymous spectator the fascinated witness and the drama's arbitrator). Doubtless Velázquez is not saying much more here than he appears to be saying, and the deployment of such skill and daring is not making a statement about the tension between the humility of the courtier and the mastery of the artist. The portrait is not, if it ever was, this manic reduplication of the visible; it is also a conjuring up of the hidden, a game of truth with knowledge and power.

The unmastered space of modern art is similarly replete with lacunae, with solicitations of the hidden and the invisible. However, the game has been complicated, or rather, made more obscure, while simultaneously becoming simplified, plainer. In painting today, Cremonini, Bacon, Adami – or certain hyper-realists, Ralph Goings, or Monory (there are multiple examples) – put these concealments, this deframing, very much into play, making the painting the place of a mystery, of a suspended, interrupted narrative, of a question eternally without an answer (the Surrealists did so too, but for the most part without subtlety). I should like to concentrate on the process that I call, for want of a better term, deframing.[2] It involves something quite different from the 'oblique view' of classical painting. Take Cremonini, for example. His bathrooms, lovers' bedrooms, train compartments (*Les Parenthèses de l'eau, Posti occupati, Vertiges,* etc.) appear to me more interesting, or in any case more enticing, than the *Cavaliers* and *Boeufs tués* of his early canvases, precisely because of the unusual angles, the limbs suggestively truncated, the inadequate reflections in clouded mirrors, which haunt these later paintings. It is true that the partial invisibility of the decors and characters here, and in direct contrast to *Las Meninas*, has no importance as regards the identity and real faces of these characters. Here we have anybody, anywhere: the average man or woman, the person in the crowd. Nevertheless a sense of mystery, of fear, of semi-nightmare, takes hold of the spectator. It has been remarkably little noted how, in this case, painting quotes, or appears to quote, cinema.

After all, was it not cinema that invented empty shots, strange angles, bodies alluringly fragmented or shot in close-up? The fragmentation of figures is a well-known cinematic device, and there has been much analysis of the monstrosity of the close-up. Deframing is a less widespread effect, in spite of movement of the camera. But if deframing is an exemplary cinematic effect, it is precisely because of movement and the diachronic progress of the film's images, which allow for its absorption into the film as much as for the deployment of its 'emptiness effect'.

For example, a woman stares wide-eyed with horror at a sight that she alone sees. The viewers see, on the screen, on the canvas, the woman's expression of horror, the direction of her look, but not its object, the cause of this horror, off-frame. I am reminded of a canvas by the writer Dino Buzzati portraying a woman screaming, apparently naked, caught as a half-length figure in, I believe, a window-frame, or even in the conventional panel of a cartoon strip, her eyes fixed on something unknown, situated, from her look, nearby and at about the height of her knees. Written on the canvas, just as in cartoon strips, a caption underlines – with perfect sadism – the enigmatic character of the thing in question with a banal enquiry ('What's making her scream like that?' – I don't recall the text exactly). In the painting (it would of course be the same for photography), the enigma is clearly destined to remain suspended, like the expression of horror on the woman's face, since there is no diachronic development of the image. In cinema, on the other hand (and in cartoon strips, which follow the same principle), a reframing, a countershot, a panning shot, etc., can – and therefore in a way must, if the director doesn't want to be accused of deliberately prolonging the viewer's frustration – show the cause of this horror, answer the question that the truncated scene raises for the viewer, in fact answer the challenge of this gaping hole: fill it, produce the satisfying semblance of a cause, so that, to put it another way, the viewers can really experience the horror. Suspense consists in varying this satisfaction, in order to feed it.

Any solution of continuity clearly calls for a repairing, a putting together again. At this point, it might be noted that this solution of continuity is twofold: narrative and scenographic. The two shots do not overlap one another. The second is produced by the first, in the sense that making of the frame [*cadre*] a masking [*cache*], thus the setting up of an enigma, is necessarily to get the story rolling.[3] It falls to the story to fill the hole, the *terra incognita*, the hidden part of the representation. In Buzzati's painting, as in all paintings, the responsibility for the story falls to the spectator since the painting can only initiate. It is no accident that one of the rare film-makers to relentlessly muti-late the body through his framing, systematically and unrepentantly to 'break' the space – and here I mean Bresson rather than Eisenstein – delights in think-ing of 'cinematography' in terms of painting (cf. his *Notes sur le cinématographe*). Through their deployment of unusual and frustrating framings Antonioni, Duras and Straub are likewise painters. They introduce to the cinema some-thing like a non-narrative suspense. Their scenography of lacunae is not des-tined to resolve itself into a 'total image wherein all the fragmentary elements fit together' as, conversely, Eisenstein desired ('Montage 1938').[4] There is here a tension that persists from shot to shot and which the 'story' does not elimi-nate: a transnarrative tension arising from the angles, framings, choices of objects and temporal durations which highlight the insistence of a look (as does, in an erotic fashion, Buzzati's canvas), wherein the practice of cinema is intensified and concentrated on a silent interrogation of its own function.

Deframing is a perversion, one that adds an ironic touch to the function of cinema, painting, even photography, all of them forms of exercising the right to look. In Deleuzian[5] terms it needs to be said that the art of deframing, the displaced angle, the radical off-centredness of a point of view that mutilates the body and expels it beyond the frame to focus instead on dead, empty zones barren of decor, is ironically sadistic (as is clear in Buzzati's painting; I would also like to cite the drawings of Alex Barbier which appeared – too infre-quently – in the weekly magazine *Charlie*). Ironic and sadistic inasmuch as its off-centre framing, as a rule frustrating for the spectator and disfiguring for the 'models' (Bresson's term), is the response of a cruel mastery, a cold and aggres-sive death-drive: the use of the frame as a cutting-edge, the living pushed out to the periphery, beyond the frame (for example, the lovers' embrace in Cremonini's *Vertiges*), the focusing on the bleak or dead sections of the scene, the dubious celebration of trivial objects (such as the sexualization of wash-basins and bathroom implements, again in Cremonini), highlight the arbi-trariness of this curious directorial gaze, one that perhaps delights in the sterility of its point of view.

Perhaps. For such a look has only a ghostly existence, after all. The look is not the point of view. It would be, were it to exist, the pleasure of this point of view. It is the peculiarity of the point of view that presupposes it, the pecu-liarity implied in the deframing, since what I call deframing, perhaps improp-erly – the deviant framing, which has nothing to do with an obliquity of point of view[6] – is nothing other than this very peculiarity. This peculiarity draws attention to itself because at the centre of the painting – as a rule occupied in classical painting by a symbolic presence (for example, the mirror image of the sovereign and his consort in *Las Meninas*) – there is nothing, nothing is hap-pening. The eye that is accustomed (educated?) to focus immediately on the centre, finds nothing and turns back to the periphery where something still flickers, on the point of disappearing. A *fading* of representation, which also often finds itself reflected in the figures and the themes of the said representation; the empty cars and deserted drugstores of Ralph Goings, the demented carcasses of Francis Bacon, the blind, corpse-like figures of Cremonini,[7] the crossed-out eyes of Monory. The irony is in coldly showing, coldly telling the deathly truth.[8]

This control-fixation in a space lacking control, this obsession with the place of the master, very often correlative with a hysterical neo-mastery (hyper-realism), certainly have something sinister and unpleasant about them, even in their allure. It is this mortifying side of deframing that is painful and without humour. Photography, for example, which is the art of framing and deframing *par excellence* (a slice of life caught hot or cold in a snapshot or a composition), is an art basically bereft of humour, devoted to irony, to accusation.[9]

Now cinema, in this respect, presents more possibilities, perhaps because of the movement that governs it and the events that it is obliged to produce. Events in cinema, anything that confounds the frame, always take a humorous form: the gag — that is to say, the non-tragic catastrophe, which belongs neither to the beginning (sin) nor to the end (punishment) but springs up in the middle and proceeds by repetition — is the prototypical cinematic event. There is a potential for *upsetting* the point of view or the situations which belong specifically to cinema. In Godard's work, for example, what is important is neither framing nor deframing, but what shatters the frame, like the video tracings on the surface of the screen, lines and movement that deceive any controlling immobility of the look. The significance of the still shots in *Six fois deux* is not the apparent sadism of the static frame, but the *duration* that here combines with it to produce vocal and gestural events. In this sense deframing is not divisive, fragmentary (it is so only from the point of view of a long-lost classical unity) but, on the contrary, a multiplier, a generator of new arrangements.

The sadistic irony of off-centre framing can — as shown in Jean Eustache's moral fable *Une sale histoire* — always tip the decor upside down in a masochistically humorous fashion. The great ironist, the master — but who never showed it — was Hitchcock, one of whose statements Truffaut summarized thus:

> There is something to which all film-makers would have to admit, which is, in order to achieve a realistic interior to a planned frame, it would be necessary eventually to accept a great unreality in the surrounding space: for example, a close-up of a kiss between two characters who are supposed to be standing will perhaps be obtained by placing the two characters on their knees atop a kitchen table.[10]

(See also the entire passage on *Psycho* in the same chapter.)

What gives the story of Picq/Lonsdale its attraction, and makes Eustache's film an ethical-theoretical cinematic lesson, is the hole being at ground level and the voyeur having to press his cheek against the floor tiles, with his hair in danger of trailing in pee. Its humour is in the cheerful confession of the *work* that this posture has cost him, and to have derived from it that feeling of dignity towards the word on which the film ends, twice over.[11]

Translated by Chris Darke

Notes

1 Velázquez's *Las Meninas* is also referred to by Jean-Pierre Oudart in his 'Notes for a Theory of Representation', translated in Volume 3 of this anthology.
2 Bonitzer's term *décadrage* is here translated as 'deframing', following Lynne Kirby, who provides a valuable analysis of Bonitzer's work on the relationship between cinema and painting in her article on his volume of collected essays, *Décadrages: peinture et cinéma* (Paris, *Cahiers du Cinéma*/Editions de l'Etoile, 1985). See Lynne Kirby, 'Painting and Cinema: The Frames of Discourse', *Camera Obscura* no. 18, September 1989, pp. 95–105. (Translator's note.)
3 The Bazinian distinction between frame [*cadre*] and masking [*cache*] is well known. 'The outer edges of the screen are not, as the technical jargon would sometimes seem to imply, the frame of the film's image, but a masking which can show only part of reality. The frame polarizes space inwards, while what the screen shows us is regarded, on the contrary, as something that extends indefinitely out into the world. The frame is centripetal, the screen centrifugal' ('Painting and Cinema', in *Qu'est-ce que le cinéma?*, II, p. 128). There is nothing to add to that, except that the two properties can mutually corrupt each other, as Bazin shows elsewhere. (Author's note.)
4 Eisenstein's 'Montage 1938' is translated in Michael Glenny and Richard Taylor (eds), *S. M. Eisenstein, Selected Works: Volume 2: Towards a Theory of Montage* (London, BFI Publishing, 1991), pp. 296–326.
5 Gilles Deleuze, French philosopher and writer, whose article on Godard's *Six fois deux* is translated as Ch. 8 in this volume.
6 On the obliquity of point of view and the suturing of the spectator's subjective position in classical cinema, see Jean-Pierre Oudart, 'La Suture', in *Cahiers* 211 and 212. (Author's note.) The essay is translated as 'Cinema and Suture' in Volume 3 of this anthology.
7 Althusser has commented (*Cremonini, peintre d'abstrait*) on the blindness and indifference of the faces in Cremonini's work, and on the strange absence that haunts them. 'A purely negative absence, that of the purely humanist function that is refused them, and that they refuse; and a positive, determined absence, that of the structure of the world which determines them, which makes them the anonymous beings they are, the structural effects of the real relations that govern them.' A little later in the same article, Althusser adds: 'He can "paint" this abstraction only on the condition of being present in his painting in the form determined by the relations he paints: in the form of their absence, which is in this case in the form of his own absence.' This should be understood, I assume, as the refusal of any specular, narcissistic idealization. The curious thing is that this refusal leaves a trace, a conspicuous absence (conspicuous at least to Althusser, to the extent that he sees it as intensified). One can equally see it in an 'absence' which also bars the canvas to heavy lines that counter pictorial depth, like the pure inscription of the flat, fading subject, of the 'discourse of knowledge' in which Althusser tends to place Cremonini's pictorial statements, and which is simply this very same absence. (Author's note.)
8 Bonitzer coins the word 'cadavérité', a play on 'cadavérique' (cadaverous) and 'vérité' (truth). (Translator's note.)
9 For the oppositions irony/humour, sadism/masochism, see Gilles Deleuze, *Présentation de Sacher-Masoch* (Minuit, 10/18), and Gilles Deleuze and Claire Parnet,

Dialogues (Flammarion), especially pp. 83–4. As regards photography, I am thinking of, among others, an album of de luxe erotic photographs by Helmut Newton, *Femmes secrètes* (Flammarion, 1977), and of a telling hesitancy in the tone of the preface: 'Newton's eye is inhuman, cold, and really rather cruel. There is no warmth to temper the humour his work is steeped in, and yet humour – or perhaps it would be more appropriate to speak of irony – is given free rein here.' And a little earlier: 'These women, always of striking physique, are nevertheless subjugated in Newton's world to his controlling eye, and are transformed into symbols whose erotic attraction is stripped of humanity – they are no longer people, but personae.' This is, of course, a special case. As regards the ironic and accusatory function of photography, I am thinking more generally of journalistic or militant reportage, as well as portrait photography (Avedon, for example). (Author's note.)

10 In *Le Cinéma selon Hitchcock*, Paris, Seghers, 1983, p. 296. Translated as *Hitchcock*, 1984.

11 Eustache's *Une sale histoire* consists of two short films which tell the same story, the recollections of a male voyeur in a women's lavatory. The first (with Michel Lonsdale) is shot as a fictional story, the second (with Jean-Noël Picq) in documentary style, Eustache's aim being to interrogate the 'truth' of reality, and of fiction.

17

COLD SEX (ON PORNOGRAPHY AND BEYOND)

('Le Sexe froid: du porno et au delà',
Cahiers du Cinéma 289, June 1978)

Yann Lardeau

The medium is the message. The message is the massage.

McLuhan

Art Press: 'Pornography delivers an extraordinary realization. Recall how in '68 it took strikes, barricades, speeches and paving stones for it to begin to register that *everything is political*. Censored, proliferating and intensified, pornography is going to start to make us glimpse that *everything is sexual*.' *Le Sexe qui parle* is the title of a film. Is pornography still speaking to us? Has it ever – on whatever occasion – spoken about sex?

In *La Volonté de savoir*,[1] Michel Foucault shows how, historically, the sexual mechanism is structured around the techniques of confession, and particularly from the confession ritual following the Council of Trent.[2] 'The significance,' he wrote, 'is in sex having been constituted as a wager of truth.' And again: 'Truth does not belong to the order of power but it shares a founding moment with liberty: just as these are themes traditional to philosophy, so a "political history of truth" would have to return to demonstrating that truth is neither by nature free nor a slavish delusion, but that its production is entirely traversed by relations of power. The confession is an example of this.'

Pornography, by nature demagogic, is entirely swallowed up in this strategic (political) order of the problematic of truth and freedom – of the liberation of a truth that will also be the truth of this liberation – in this field that produces power and the trap of its subversion, which confers on pornography its true meaning. It is in this metaphysical dialectic of truth and freedom (which always intensifies, within its wager, the strategic complicity of knowledge and power) that, since its emergence, the object 'sex' has always occupied a nodal position, the latter defining in fact the principle of the former's reality, so completely that, outside this field, it no longer has meaning (strictly speaking, it does not exist). It is the mechanism of sexuality as a field of knowledge and power (on which Sade once confronted the Church) which pornography tirelessly, repetitively, makes us see – this mechanism in its coded reality. A veiled truth to be uncovered, a violence buried in the silence of a secret which it is necessary to reconstruct and liberate – to lay bare. In pornography the woman frenetically undresses and reveals her sex, and it's not by chance that she – and her sex – remain its principal actor: in our society the naked woman has always been the allegorical representation of Truth (as we know that, for Freud, the will to know is displayed in the child's discovery of the 'mysteries' of sexuality).

However, this does not imply that the (relative) success of pornography occurs essentially, if not exclusively, through cinema, or suggest why it should be that cinema is pornography's privileged mode of expression. It is possible that cinema appears as its best functional response and as the driving force of its representation. If pornography expresses itself, as regards its themes, as a language of truth, its privileged use of cinema makes cinema operate as a vehicle of truth, a vehicle which reveals that it is through the image and its movement (through visual observation) that the enunciation is *verified* (the sound contributing a supplement of information confirming what the image tells us). This presupposes that there exists a profound proximity, indeed an identity, of system between pornography and cinema: that there can be no pornography other than the cinematic. In other words the question – how do the processes of cinema manipulate sex? – rather than leading to an interrogation of what sex gives up to this mode of representation, should lead to a consideration of what is revealed by the cinematic representation of sex and cinema's strategy of operations in general. To examine pornographic cinema does not amount to examining pornography (or, more universally, the status of sex) in cinema, but to examining cinema in itself, and how it allows such a discourse to be inscribed in it.

Mechanical sex

Pornography or the strategy of the close-up

The basic element of pornography is the close-up. Therein lies its truth, and this is why the plots are always poor and the actors mediocre: they are nothing more than accessories, supporting the staging of sex which, at the same time, aims always to be economical. The close-up is the powerful expression of the insignificance of actors and plot because pornography is concerned with closing in on sex as tightly as possible, with giving it the clearest, closest possible image. Through the organization of its framing, angles and focal lengths the camera shows us the sex of the man or woman as no one has seen or will ever see them, as indeed they have never existed.[3]

In the restricting space of its frame the pornographic close-up explores what it represents, what it refers to, making its exhaustive inventory. It aims to be the total (and totalitarian) recording of the field of sex, it aims systematically to saturate and map it out, while enclosing sex in this representational space.

Far from awakening desire in the spectator, the microscopic proximity that characterizes the close-up is conveyed by a distance between the spectator and the spectacle, a *de facto* exclusion that eliminates any fantasy. From the moment that the pornographic close-up blocks the spectator into its single dimension of reality any association of ideas is closed down. More precisely, this is the crazy ambition that gives birth to pornography, the despotic fantasy of *producing* the fantastic that precisely bars the work of the imagination: we know that pleasure planned is its best prevention (just as we know that the madness of this fantasy has given and still gives us the finest moments in fantasy movies, as with *The Island of Dr Moreau* for example, or the Frankenstein films). For the close-up neutralizes sex: the violence of sex is averted by its observation in close-up, in the same way as the microbe's virulence is under the microscope. Here, as there, the same process of objectification is at work, the same exteriority of the subject towards its object, the same distant manipulation where the intensification, in both cases, of ocular perspective by means of optical apparatuses (by object lenses), in bringing the subject up close to its object of observation, both separates it from and protects the subject. What is fundamentally dismissed in such ultra-powerful optical perception is touch, contact. McLuhan defines cinema as a '*hot medium*': 'The "hot" medium excludes us while the "cold" medium includes us,' he writes. 'The "hot" media require only a weak participation, a light involvement on the part of the spectator, while the "cold" media demand intense participation.' Conversely, television is a 'cool' medium which places the spectator in a relationship as much tactile – changing channels, tuning, etc. – as visual; this conjunction in television of two sensory systems finds its consummate expression today in electronic games, and thus any analysis of television must start with such games.

It is this profound characterization of cinema as a medium that restores an understanding of pornography, with and beyond its subject. If this property is particularly evident in pornography, it is certainly because of the subject of its discourse: sex, which is first and foremost inscribed in a body.[4] The excessive 'heat' of the medium, the heightened realism and sterility of its subject, the closing off of imagination and the reduction of sex to a single dimension of reality – all this is as if pornography were telling us that pleasure is impossible, as if, through the representation of the sexual act, it is signalling to us the prohibition of pleasure.[5]

Certainly, sex is neutralized, there is a repressive sublimation. But here, on the other hand, one can read the political and scientific imaginary in its entirety (an imaginary that presides over the conception and realization of pornographic films): the obsession with truth, with knowing all, that nothing should elude knowledge, the exhaustive saturation of reality up to its very limits, the desire for permanent surveillance and total control, a panopticism whose technological consummation is the camera, in its ability to give a perfect reproduction of reality (and it is used as such in a security context, in order to deter and neutralize within its field of observation, in department stores, banks, Underground stations). It is thus that the slogan of pornography – 'everything shown, everything seen' – must be understood. As a liberation, certainly, but one which, as with all liberations, frees the subject only in order to keep it more tightly bound by power, and as a means of reproducing and enlarging this power. Hence the fascination of porn film-makers with the female genitalia. This emptiness, this nothingness on to which the lips of the vulva open, this pledge of death from which the film-makers must free themselves by concealing it with signs, references and details so as to efface its threat, to banish it.[6]

An obscene sex dedicated to collective consumption, connected up to the viewers as individuals and regarded as belonging to them. A neutral sex dispersed into the anonymity of the homosexual viewing crowd. A sex made obscene and neutral through its very objectification. Mirrored here is an entire technocratic ideology; one that controls the material, one that takes hold of and dominates the slightest detail – micro-knowledge and micro-control, the agenda of production. But equally the ideology of design – that of the perfect correspondence of signifier to signified, of the *transparency* of the object's function. Thus pornography can speak of sex only in functional terms and in *assigning* it to the genitals. Sex staged as sign. By totally enclosing sex within the reduction of its frame, the close-up excludes it from what is off-screen, its subject and its irreducible divisibility. This disconnection of sex, far from being the sign of its 'liberation', on the contrary draws up the site of its imprisonment. Dissociated, isolated (autonomized) from the body by the close-up, confined to its genital materiality (objectified), it can thus freely circulate outside the subject, in the way that goods are circulated and exchanged independently of their producers, and the linguistic sign, as a value, circulates independently of its speakers. The free circulation of goods, people and information in capitalism, this is the freedom represented by the close-up, of sex become a pure abstraction.

The close-up isolates, and it is as an isolated shot that it defines the site of sex, locking it into this definition. But the close-up is always and at the same time the fragmentation of a larger space, a disjunction of what is displayed, an abstraction from its context, which enables its content to be combined in all manner of ways with the other elements of the scenic space which it fragments, or even with other scenic spaces (Kuleshov's close-up of Mozhukhin; Eisenstein's 'montage of attractions'). Thus disconnected from what it represents, the close-up is made available to all possible combinations: fondling, sucking, penetration – pornography always repetitively stages the connecting of one organ to another, of a vagina to a penis, of a mouth to a penis, of lips to a tongue, of a penis to an anus, of a hand to a sexual organ, all this gestural repertoire aimed at designating the site of sexual reality and containing sex within it (it is not without cause that sexual relations thus represented immediately evoke the workings of machines). Clearly what lies behind the scenography of porn is the repeated combination of organs (implements), where the penis, vagina, mouth, anus, breast and hand are the positive terms of a combinative whose alternations and exhaustive combinations are regarded as the last word on sex – and here we have it: the presupposition of a combinative is that one term is always exchangeable with another in a relationship of combinations and therefore, from this point of view, *is strictly equivalent to it*. So two sexes are an *a priori* fact of pornography, but all the terms being substitutable one for the other implies, *de facto*, 0 sexes (or zero sex).[7]

Sex neutralized in the staging of its 'own connections': what pornography demonstrates in the energy of its portayal of sexual relations (of all the substitutive terms of this combination) is their self-neutralization through the fact of their *realization as spectacle*. An absurd illustration of Lacan's statement that 'Sexual relations do not exist'. For where do they start and where do they end?

Another effect of the close-up's fragmentation of sex is the absence of the body, its exclusion (which, one might say, is systematized in pornography); but it is always susceptible to being reintroduced, restaged, as a simple difference within the repetition (and it is thus used in pornography, its portrayal remaining at least as an ever-present virtuality). Put another way, the close-up permits not only attachments and separations with partial objects – but also *the attachment of a sex to a body*, a body which is thus produced, in the scenography of porn, as a body minus organs (why is it that the terminology of Deleuze and Guattari is so applicable here?)[8] The desexed body, disincarnated sex, the identification and the circumscription of sex within the positive values assigned to the genital organs, neutralizes not only sex itself but also the body: the more the body is split by sex; the more sex is split by ambivalence. Sex and the body are reciprocally neutralized through their disjunction and conjunction: the death of desire.

Pornography and erotic cinema: an indifferent difference

There is no difference here between pornographic cinema and erotic cinema (and too bad for the aesthetes). If, unlike pornographic cinema which plays essentially with the close-up, erotic cinema (*Emmanuelle, Histoire d'O* etc.) is generally constructed through medium shots (the scale of reference here being the human body and no longer just the sex), the principle at work remains the same. For the pornographic close-up and the erotic medium shot function along the same lines but in reverse: it is always an extreme concentration on the objectified site of sex, on the genitals, that governs both 'genres'; in pornography this is obvious, in erotic cinema inferred. The whole body in erotic cinema is represented only the better to portray, to underscore, the demarcated and closed sexual space. And as the means of overdefining this enclosed space, it serves only to intensify it. As a consequence, the framing of the whole body is intensified immediately – and *strategically* – in its reduction, its recentring in close-up on the sex (which, here also, is always that of the woman). There is, therefore, the same metonymic process at work in erotic cinema as in pornographic cinema, but symmetrically inverted. On the one hand, the close-up of sex susceptible to opening up on to the body; on the other, the medium shot of the body which necessarily closes down on to the sex. The framing extended or contracted, the whole for the part, the part for the whole, it's always a body that is related back to a sex, a sex related back to a body: an indifferent difference.

It is this closing down, this internal reframing around the sex (exclusively that of the woman), which is, in erotic cinema, always blocked off by a piece of lingerie, by a thigh movement, by the angle of the framing, etc.; the presupposition of this set-up being to suggest the female sex, even in its concealment, as the positive object of desire and the definitive site of pleasure. Its aim being, conversely, to ward off the threat of castration, to avoid sending the subject back to his own lack. The piece of lingerie, the thigh movement, the angle of the shot,[9] or any other strategically equivalent element, are to erotic cinema as the penis-dildo is to pornographic cinema. To each his own fetish! It is therefore simply through a superior degree of refinement, of artificiality, that the fetishism of erotic cinema is distinguished from that of pornographic cinema. In *Histoire d'O*,[10] Sir Stephen locks a ring around the lips of O's sex. Far from indicating the openness of O's sex and its deadly gambit, the ring on the contrary, in its very process of truth, locks it up, annuls it in its ambivalence, averts its threat. The ring thus stages (and signifies) the castration the better to deny it, a fetishistic operation *par excellence*. But this locking up of O's sex confines the very wholeness of O's body and, the body complete and unfragmented, erects it as a phallic effigy for the viewer – and it is as such that O is desirable. This returns us at once to the close-up of the penis-dildo so dear to pornographic cinema: the penis-dildo is here the whole body of O the doll. The medium shot of the whole body of O – in its naked singularity – is the erotic close-up of the penis-dildo. Consequently we can see why the medium shot is the reference shot of erotic cinema. If the ring closes O in on herself, it is only as the metaphor of the cinematic frame (which moreover it redoubles), in that it encloses O within the limits of the unity of her body and within the self-sufficiency of her narcissism. O is desirable only inasmuch as she desires only herself. The discarding of the viewer is seen in erotic cinema's medium shot just as it is in the pornographic close-up.

The fragmentation of body and sex which presides over pornography is also found in erotic cinema, at a more subtle but basically identical level, in the regulated play of dressing and undressing, in the alternation, whether in time or in the same shot, of nudity and being clothed, of being made up or not made up. The body thus manufactured – nothing but manufactured – and made completely positive, and that nothing can unmake, is with all its accessories (clothes, jewels, creams, cosmetics, and its very skin) only the repetition, at erotic cinema's interior, of what is going on all around it when the technical cinematic apparatus divides the scene through movement, angles, framings, when it selects the space of representation in playing on focal length, when it diffracts colour and lighting – in short, through the selectivity of its arrangement of scenes and in the secondary selection of rushes at the editing stage: the film-making process, an encoding that is directly and naively restored by pornography in its tendency to obliterate the erotic.

It is the same fetishism, the same scenario – a profound lack of distinction between pornography and eroticism, a simple variation of degrees. In the order of simulacra (Baudrillard), pornography has for its model type, in its technological aspect, the *robot*; erotic cinema, in its semiological aspect, the *mannequin*.[11] Put simply, and to confront erotic cinema with the cynicism of its own discourse, pornography is the poor man's erotic cinema; erotic cinema the rich man's pornography. (Here is revealed the primary meaning of the 'X' category for films and cinemas, which endows them with a mark of shame just as long ago the brand marked the adulteress, and through it society's moral conscience washes its hands, burying its head in the sand only to lift it out again very soon, of its own volition and through its own need – this, one recalls, being the origin of the political controversy surrounding *Emmanuelle 2*.)

Non-existent sex: beyond pornography

The exteriorization, disconnectedness and abstraction of sex which is therefore free to be connected in any way; the isolation and identification of sex with the genital organs; the hidden and the invisible reduced to an exhaustive surfeit of representation – such are the effects of the pornographic close-up, and of the way in which cinema portrays sex. The hyper-realism of pornographic sex whose entire hidden dimension, the depth which gives it meaning, has to be reabsorbed into the distortion of the pellicular surface, the body's as well as the film's. The exhibitionist close-up of sex defines the manner in which sex exists. The designation of sex in the genital organs defines them recurrently as its reality principle. The anatomical difference of man and woman – behind which lies biological difference – defines the sexual field and its practices. The sex *inferred* by the human sexual apparatus is *produced* in the close-up. This codification of sex proffers itself, in the evidence of its demonstration, as the existential truth – it wants to be its proof; in other words, it *verifies* it.

At issue here is the entire realism of the cinematic image (the fact that the perspectival space of cinematic representation offers itself as the duplication of the 'objective' perception of space). And it is in this sense that pornographic film, in its project of showing the reality of sex, turns against itself and fails. Because any close-up is abstract (precisely as the Kuleshov experiment demonstrated); it is the excess of reality in the pornographic close-up itself that puts an end to the object of its portrayal and to its reality – the actuality of sex. More precisely, it restores its idealized abstraction. The physicality of the cinematic representation of sex re-establishes it at the metaphysical level of its origin. Pornography not only neutralizes sex, it also tells us, through its very own distortion, that it doesn't exist, that it is only an *artefact*. Pornographic representation, the objectification inherent in the way it is focused in films on the material space of the genitals, has the opposite effect of demonstrating the objective non-existence of a sexual site, its material lack of place, its referential absence. In multiplying the identificatory terms of sexual exchange in order to avert the lack, by virtue of its own representation and in spite of it, pornography tells us that in the final analysis sex is unrepresentable, unshowable, what the conjunction of the phallus and the castration threat (which is the sole reality of sex) otherwise tells us is that it is a symbolic relationship, the space of an exchange from which neither term can be isolated, distinguished, designated (and particularly not, in this case, in partial objects or the materiality of anatomy) because they are sealed into the ambivalence and reversibility of this exchange. It is precisely what forecloses the cinematic enactment of sex, pornographic or erotic, that at the same time almost always re-emerges, though only in the form of its absence. In pretending to render visible the reality of sex, but by obliterating its symbolic dimension wherein this reality is dissolved, pornography can only simulate it, reconstitute it through the proliferation of representational signs by closing off sex from the risk of not being realised. So pornography is finally only *the model of the simulation* of sexuality (*its code*), and cinema, because of the realism of its images, its privileged medium, the exemplary *means of simulation* – and, its corollary, its *means of verification*.

In prohibiting any expression of imagination, in restricting all fantasies, in reducing the content of the cinematic image to the unique and exclusive dimension of reality, pornography returns us to the cinema as a technique for producing artifice – sham and show – even within the reality of the image's configuration. Through the clarity of its aims in terms of its object, pornography reflects cinema's established position as a means of reproducing reality: as though cinema, aiming to reconstitute reality and to indulge in fetishism (in the etymological sense of the word), is put on trial by pornography.

Cinema, or the art of prostitution

It is here, moreover, that one truly locates the scandalousness of pornography and the violence it does to cinema, disqualifying its artistic attributes and by the same token identifying its current crisis, if such a crisis exists (we will come back to this).

For pornographic cinema is not the cinematic representation of sex, nor is it even simultaneously sex and cinema: *it is cinema itself, as a medium which is pornographic*. This is pornography's ultimate – and perhaps its only – message: the eruption on to the cinema screen of the close-up of sex is not the prostitution of the Art of Cinema (as the *auteurs* of *Emmanuelle 2* were among the first to try to have us believe, along with the enlightened liberal critics who,

211

unanimously awarding the film full marks, were capable – in their traditional servility – only of trotting out the official line: 'at last, sex in the cinema which isn't pornographic!'); it rewrites the basic nature of cinema as an *art of prostitution*. It is not sex that is obscene but, fundamentally and in the literal sense of the word, cinema, the *ob-scene* crystallized by the close-up. It is this founding obscenity, constitutive of the medium, which resurfaces and declares itself in the pornographic close-up of sex (doubtless it needed the arrival of the advertising of sex in the cinema, the detour through sex, in the identification with its pornographic treatment, of a cinematic representation, for the latter to prompt the appearance of hard-core obscenity).

André Bazin:

> One does not die twice. On this point photography does not have film's power, it can portray only death agonies or the corpse itself, but not the imperceptible passage from one to the other. In the spring of 1949, in a newsreel magazine, you could watch a fascinating document on the anti-Communist repression in Shanghai, the 'red spies' executed by revolver shots in a public square. At each screening, these men lived anew, the crack of the same bullets jolting back their necks. There was even the gesture of the policeman, his pistol jammed, having to fire twice. The spectacle was unbearable, not so much because of its objective horror as because of *a kind of ontological obscenity* [my emphasis]. Before cinema we only heard about the profanation of corpses and the desecration of graves. Thanks to film we can today desecrate and expose at will the last of our temporally inalienable human goods. The dead without a requiem, the eternal living dead of cinema!
>
> ('Deaths every afternoon', 1951)

Bazin is extremely lucid in showing here, beyond death as content, the manner of cinema's functioning and the effect it has of short-circuiting its content in the very form of the medium (Bazin goes on to imagine the 'supreme cinematic perversion' of an execution: its projection in reverse).[12]

We must take Bazin at his word – and also despite himself: the obscenity of cinema is based in its technical and scenographic operations, independent of the content submitted to these manipulations. The cinema is obscene because it is an obscenic art. Its entire process of staging consists of bringing to the fore the hidden side of the scene and rendering our relation to it clear and transparent where it had only been confused and opaque. The consistency of the varying framings – combined with the movements, angles and focal lengths of shots – depends on their efficiency in dividing up and fragmenting the here and now of the scene to show, in the sequence of shots on the white surface of the screen, its secret, invisible depth. Secret and invisible because the scenic space, in daily life as in theatre or in a painting, is always seen as part of a whole: the look may well choose to turn and stop at a particular element but the vision of the whole remains no less coextensive and a disruptive factor; above all, the scene cannot be summarized as being simply the sum of its component parts. Furthermore, the point of view is always distant and distinct. Cinema destroys this primary unity of the scene, breaking its façade and its illusory perspective. In decomposing and recomposing the scene, it puts an end to what binds it: its temporal and spatial oneness and the indestructible unity of its wholly containing, in its enclosed figuration, its own evolution, as an effect of its internal regulation and a field protected from the viewer's contact. As regards the sealed unity of this scene, cinema acts like a surgeon, penetrating vigorously into the closed body, opening it up, cutting into the flesh, cataloguing, exteriorizing and reincorporating the texture. Tearing, saturating and suturing this reality, it suppresses the distance between spectator and spectacle wherein not only contemplation but also thought had their root.

The obscenity of the complementary manipulations of shot arrangement and editing does not arise from a loss in the scene or an alienation of its meaning, but in a consecutive transformation of our relationship to it just as it changes the status of the spectator – to the point at which one might ask whether it any longer has anything to do with a spectator.

In fact the cinematic reconstruction of the scene merges it with the medium's own operations of reconstruction; the reality becomes inseparable from its redoubling as spectacle, by removing the separation of the technical operations which reveal it for what it is. More precisely, these operations constitute the new reality of this scene or event which, even though it happens, is only its simulacrum. The obscenity has more to do with the remaking, the reconstitution of the reality, if possible in its original place, of which the film, through the exhaustiveness of its recording, is its secondary fabrication, inseparable from the original (though this exists only as a *support*), but no longer its identical copy – a second but co-present reality, an existence diverted on to what the primary reality, the referential scene, can only fall back on and draw from it its final meaning, which will also be the end of its initial meaning, its difference liquefied and transmuted through its serial reproduction. Obscenity resides not in the *act of representation* – wherein the referent remains perceptible in its specificity – but in the *act of reproduction*, where the only reference is the subject's potential for reproduction (its *reportage*), the subject being no longer distinguishable from the technical operations that reproduce it on the scene as its immediate double. If, in Bazin's example, death is obscene, it is because it has no justification – even at the time of its happening – other than its potential as spectacle: aleatory, any other death, any other event, being substitutable for it. Its entire reality has capsized into the image – even if it is no less true for all this: the event can no longer happen. Thus this obscenity of death comes less from the dispossession of the subject's experience of death than from the fact that, being filmed, it is apprehensible only in the dual form of its mass reproduction, in its incessant repetitions when projected and in the multiplicity of prints of the film. It is not the spectacle of death, the invitation to the public to participate in the capital execution of a man – as in the tortures of earlier times – which is painful, but the denial of a death which is at the basis of its being made a cinematic spectacle. This is in fact no longer a death: too real to be true; it certainly took place, yet it repeats itself endlessly through its screenings. Forever replayed and projected, always liable to recur, this is precisely death without end. Its reality, whatever the tragic dimension, verges on the unreal. The redoubling of the act as spectacle, in its contemporaneity, puts an end to the reality of the act: though dead during the projection, though dying on screen, the victim can no longer die. He is condemned to live his death, eternally, immortalized by technology: death fetishized, without dying, without life, without anything beyond it.

The cinematic reproduction of reality shapes both its mode of production and our mode of perception. Not only is it conceived in a way that has never been that of its direct apperception, which loses all its original value, but we ourselves are placed in this same relationship of operation and observation – of manipulation. Our look becomes localized and selective. Situated on the camera's trajectory, it supervises and directs operations, immediately decoding the information transmitted: it is turned into a controlling reader. The technical defining of the image-object of the look defines the manner of our looking.[13] The image conveys information to us only to the extent that we comply with the technical operations that produce it. And it is these operations that are the first object of our look. Thus they simultaneously produce our look and the object of the look. In performing the operation of registering the image, the eye has less a visual relationship to the reality portrayed than a *tactile relationship* (it is this, moreover, that inversely signifies the immobile exteriority of the body of the audience to the images that unwind on the screen). If the audience suddenly finds itself being manipulated – but just as much manipulating – it is not so much through cinema having turned it into a passive and immobile body and capsized all its activity into the camera and its fashioning of the scene (and even less that it has nothing else to do but watch), but through the fact that the audience can see the film only in the opposed and paradoxical forms of action and the abolition of the distance between the agent and the act, between subject and object, which characterizes it, and that such visual perception can only come about in the form of contact. The camera, as a form of prosthetic extension on to which the spectator's eye grafts itself, is less an autonomous, mobile eye (or, if so, is an eye which touches more than it does not see) than a hand with the gift of sight, a 'hand-eye' (as confirmed by the 'Paluche' manufactured by Jean-Pierre Beauviala[14]). If there is manipulation of the spectator, it is not through the artificiality of the representation or the loss of immediacy in the relationship between man and the world (which anyhow would be true), but because cinema reduces man to a single and exclusive relationship of intervention and production, of calculation and foresight, which confines him to the single status of operator: in cinema there is no relationship other than that of manipulation. The spectator's relationship to the film is one of action and *projection:* he follows the camera in its intrusion into the field of the scene and completes this intrusion. Cinematic images are only a long sequence of *trompe l'oeil* effects masking the work of the camera-robot, fashioning and fabricating the world and – simultaneously and complementarily – the spectator, who has only to complete and predict the successive stages of the operation (all the charm of a film comes precisely from the failure of such predictions). The distance of the spectator from the projected images is removed by the active surveillance of the regularity and sufficiency of the technical and scenographic operations, and in the reconstitution of such operations. This is the paradoxical effect of making everything visible: the spectator occupies a place outside the film only the better to penetrate within it; he only sees to the extent that he undertakes and adequately completes the cinematic manipulations that govern the recording of the scene.

So this is what makes pornography intolerable in cinema, and explains its proscription. For pornography shows us only this: this surgery of bodies, this butchery of sexes which it flaunts across the screen, is to be censored (or marginalized) because of its exteriorization, in all innocence, of the ontological obscenity of cinema which is at work in any film (only the other genres of cinema have known how to conceal this through the secondary artifices of *mise en scène*, through density of plot, decors, actors' performances, etc.). This is the ultimate reason for the censoring of pornographic films, a professional censoring that has little to do with the films' content. If in pornography the framing is rudimentary – though, as we have seen, restricting the field of view suits the book cinematically – the angles of the shots are themselves highly sophisticated and have no equivalent in human perception. The spectator assists (participates) in these operations – separates with the camera the bodies that obstruct the view – but the price of such participation is the body's exclusion.

Pornography, or the return of origins

It has of course been possible to speak of pornographic cinema as a regression, as the negative, reactionary vision of the progressive ideology which only conveys its refusal to see its real mode of production, a permanent effect of the cross-eyed vision which blinds it: the more it sees ahead, the more it is looking behind itself. It is less a case of a return *to* origins than a return *of* origins, and pornography is happy to bring them into being again. For what pornography sums up and re-presents is the entire history of the invention of cinema, the objectives that were then assigned to it, and the subsequent discovery of the particular procedures of cinematic representation.

This is because of pornography's subject, sex, in that it is the metonymy of the body and pornography objectifies and neutralizes it. Pornography of course goes back to Lumière, and further still, to Marey and Muybridge; to Lumière through his invention of the cinematograph and the scientific function he attributed to it on account of movement being shown for its own sake without being re-enacted; and, more profoundly, to Marey, by profession a physiologist, and to Muybridge, when the former, with his chronophotographic gun, and the latter, with his battery of photographic equipment, attempted to catalogue and break down human and animal locomotion. Along with the need and the scientific desire to analyse movement (cf. Marey's *The Physiology of Movement*, and Muybridge's *Animal Locomotion* and *The Human Figure in Motion*), it is the whole problematic of bodily techniques that is at the origin of cinema's invention (Lumière included), this problematic necessarily also involving the search for a process of observation and recording of movement which, in indelibly fixing it, permits its analysis.

It is this scientific foundation of cinema which returns in the sexual technologies of pornography ('Nothing is more technical than sexual positions': Mauss, *Techniques du corps*). It is from the point of view of this scientific ideal that sex is represented cinematically.

Now this body (and its sex) in motion which is reproduced objectively in cinematic images, for its psychological analysis and thus its release from social and psychic determinants, in fact stands in for the inert body, the *corpse* of traditional anatomy lessons to which cinema gives back the vital, vanished element of movement.[15]

If this whole primary configuration of cinema comes back to us with pornography, if this realistic programme (means of stimulation/means of verification) is the real object of pornographic representation – it is undoubtedly because it has never ceased to exist even in films of complete fiction. In reverting to bodily techniques pornography recalls the principle of abstraction which is the basis of their recording. The bodies in movement of Marey and Muybridge (where cinema's first naked bodies appear) are not represented in their corporeal density, in which the body is only the moment of a relationship and does not exist outside this relationship. On the contrary, their representation presupposes a liberation from this relationship, their being made autonomous, which alone allows scientific observation – beneath the protective surface of their skin – of the internal relations of the bone structure and the musculature of the body closed on itself and its movements, through its inscription on the film's celluloid surface (the first cinematic projections were contemporary with Roentgen's presentation of the discovery of the X-ray, the public being invited to experiment with this fabulous invention on their own bodies, i.e. to see their invisible skeletons outside their bodies – a pure coincidence?).

It is in this sense that the bodies of cinema are walking cadavers, consigned to the same process of abstraction, dissection and measuring as the inert bodies of anatomy lessons. Now this abstract, arbitrary body (which in the end has about it the same ideal, universal transcendence as the one from which Le Corbusier conceived his 'Modulor'[16]), this model which contains in itself the principles of the partition and regular and alternate organization of its elements, is precisely the body which governs all cinematic framing and is its measuring principle, the conventional scale of reference. In fact, the scientific desire to capture the body in its mobile materiality, on which cinema was built, could only be fulfilled in its cinematic representation through constituting it as a metaphysical entity.

Lumière, despite his intentions, represents a break with this tradition of the objectifying look, into which he introduces an element of falsity, artificiality, fetishism. *Le Goûter de Bébé*, *La Sortie des ouvriers de l'Usine Lumière* or *L'Arroseur arrosé* are, despite the reality of their referent, already tableaux or theatrical scenes. Méliès was only (though it was a lot) to isolate this illusionist strain, this imaginary dimension (which, from the beginning, facilitated the distribution of Lumière's films), to work at it alone – a theatricality from which came special effects, studio decors and animated films.

Whatever the intentions of the two film-makers and the difference in their understanding of cinema, both of them always played on the two dimensions of reality and the imagination. In one as in the other, reality is representable only in its repercussion at the level of the imagination, even if Lumière accentuates the immediacy of reality (for example, in sending news cameramen throughout the world), and Méliès the immediacy of the imagination. There has never really been any distance between the two film-makers: Lumière may well have sent cameramen around the world, but they would always report the never-before-seen, the extraordinary, the exotic (which, after all, is only the technical capacity of the cinematic apparatus); the realism of his films is no less imbued with dreamlike effects. Méliès may well have invented the cinema actor, special effects and animation, he may well have made films of fantasy, but he also liked to *reconstruct* current events in the studio (*Cortège du Tsar allant à Versailles*).[17]

After Méliès, the preference that was to be given to fiction does not result only from its greater public approval (the makers of newsreels and documentaries would themselves also rely on fiction, if not for content, at least in their methods of representation; and the cinema of fiction would be oriented towards a greater realism of story, character and decor). The strategic predominance of fiction introduces into the representational frame's interior, as a representation, the artificiality and pretence of the medium's processes in their function of representing, thereby blocking out the fetishistic perversion which is cinema's origin. Written within the *trompe l'oeil* of the scene is the mechanical reality of cinema and its nature as a process of simulation, the essential fiction of its reality, its reality as science fiction.

The introduction of fantasy (of imagery) into cinema seems to have been the film-makers' own means of defence against the intensely perverse in cinema, a means of warding off cinema's capacity to (re)produce reality and, at the same time to finish it off through the loss of its territorial identity. Consequently, the realism consubstantial with cinematic grammar has to appear as an artifice of fiction, as a trick of filmic narration.

Epilogue

The wily old foxes of Hollywood liked to say that the musical comedy, and, more widely, the entire production of Hollywood's Golden Age, was much more erotic than erotic or pornographic cinema. It was because it was geared to the Law and its transgression by desire, and from this dialectic between desire and the forbidden came its charm, which even in its obsolescence still holds us today. In these films love might certainly be idealized, the *mise en scène* being legitimized by moral puritanism (and criticism has not hesitated to pick up on these two complementary aspects of American film). But on the one hand Hollywood, in aspiring to be a 'dream factory', produced only what this implies (it is pointless to make more of it than this) – an ever-mobile *imagined* reality, and thus one unrealizable, a fiction conscious of its content, successful in its very negation of reality. On the other hand, the film-making process (the soft-focus close-ups – address unknown, sender even more so – the lighting effects, the dissolves and the cuts), in short all the logistics of the star system (and its ostentatious waste of stars) would recall, within the story's linear clarity, an indistinct surplus, the residual opacity of the love relationship resistant to all representation, a flimsy and shadowy thread whose emergence the cuts, dissolves, lighting and close-ups emphasize even in erasing it. The breaching of this line where the real and imaginary lose their distinguishing marks, confront and overlap each other, was here unthinkable. To cross this boundary (or to condemn it to a permanent mobility, which comes to the same thing, since this mobility signifies the loss of the conventional order which would mark out this boundary as a necessity: floating and arbitrary, it at once becomes useless) was equivalent to making the imaginary real (to realize it) and to pronounce, through the death of the imaginary, the death of the real. Thus merged, they became indistinguishable. It was also to pronounce the death sentence on the Hollywood machine.

Direct Cinema failed to isolate this demarcation line; it could only show the impossibility of fixing it, save for stopping at appearances. Pornography has naively crossed this boundary. Hence its violence: to have shown the artificiality of this limit, and not to have transgressed sexual taboos. Pornography succeeded where Direct Cinema failed and that is why it is subjected to the violent (or silent – it comes to the same thing) reactions of film critics. In fact, it crystallizes the crisis in which cinema is currently caught up as one inherent in the medium, and not as a simple effect of present circumstances. It is because pornography epitomizes the entire crisis of cinema and is its *critical* genre (carrying within itself the death of each and every genre, its own included[18]) that it is necessary to criticize it, proscribe it and shut it away.

Today the musical comedy can only stage the tricks of its own *mise en scène* – and precisely *under realism's critical eye* (*New York, New York*). A large number of current films are remakes (the 1976 version of *King Kong*, *The Island of Dr Moreau*, *Farewell, My Lovely*, and indeed *Cabaret*), and when they are not, they are retro;[19] just as in pornography, they never stop repeating themselves. Cinema never stops feeding off itself, consuming itself, as if it were only capable of restaging itself, of being its own object of representation. It multiplies its production in an intensified proliferation of its signs to ward off its death (cf. 'disaster movies').

In pornography the origins return, but precisely as *ghosts*. At the moment when hardcore was making its mark, resurrecting the spectral origin of cinematic spectacle, this *mise en scène* that it created in all innocence was clearly programmed elsewhere: it has produced, at the same time, a film that comes from the Muybridge photographs – doing Muybridge better than Muybridge: the intervals between each photograph where the movement lay was being filled in on film, its characters now having life on the screen. By sheer chance?

Because it poses all these questions we should not deprive ourselves of the detour that pornography offers us.

Translated by Chris Darke

Notes

1 *La Volonté de savoir*: translated by Robert Hurley as *The History of Sexuality: Volume 1*, London, Allen Lane, 1971.

2 Council of Trent: the council of the Roman Catholic Church which met between 1545 and 1565 at Trento in Italy. Formed to combat the rise of Protestantism, the council reaffirmed Catholic doctrine and launched the Counter-Reformation.

3 All the 'tricks' of realism intervene here: sound effects, noises, colours, maximum depth of field without distortion of a minimal space. It is however, in its own movement, through its excessive need for realism, a moment where pornography absorbs itself; where the over-realism of its images, the excessive materiality of its representation, tips what is portrayed into the purest abstraction, and thus puts an end to its referential object – sex. Certain shots are already brushing against this boundary. This is the extreme moment at which pornography, through its own logic, arrives at its *limit* – precisely that of its *self-destruction*. (Author's note.)

4 That said, the cinema as a hot medium particularly affects contact in the relationship of the body to the exterior, to the images that unwind on-screen; which is to say, the spectator's kinaesthetic dimension is undermined and reduced to its most feeble degree. In this immobilization, in the spectator's forced immobility, the synaesthetic dimension subsists, even becoming dominant. The particular force of McLuhan's argument is that it restates the primary and fundamental dimension in all media of the aesthesic above the aesthetic, and that in cinema this dimension is transferred, one might say in its entirety, to the viewfinder which orients itself within the space recorded, fragmenting and reassembling it, dismantling its unity and recomposing it for the greatest possible fascination of the spectator who, although distant from these operations, remakes them in the form of his or her visual control of the scene. It is this absence of the aesthesic dimension – or its remaining entirely interiorized – that is evidently restored in pornography. The pornographic film, as with the erotic film, is in fact a fine example of the short-circuiting of the aesthesic by the aesthetic, and vice versa. In pornography the neutralization of sex and the body is accompanied by a neutralization of the spectator. In reality, this inert sex is the spectator's: one is a spectator only inasmuch as one is *inert*. And if we have spoken of a loss of contact it is not a loss of contact and

manipulation as such, but rather their complete integration into and appropriation by the camera (in cinema there is no other manipulation – nor is there in television – so there is no *message*, only the *materiality* of the event and of the spectator's body), and the exclusion of the spectator which is signified by this.

Traditionally, the cinema has always known how to reconcile these two moments, the aesthesic and the aesthetic, the cinematic and the spectatorial body, because its realism is always redoubled by an imaginar, the spectator's aesthetic pleasure at the end of a film ('That was a beautiful film') comes from the film's aesthesic power, from its capacity to *incorporate* the spectator, who 'feels' and 'lives' the film. Or, put another way, from its power to produce the imaginary. In reality, the aesthesic is no more present in cinema than the aesthetic, but immediately one and the other, and the conjunction of each of these terms with the real and the imaginary, themselves always linked. (Author's note.)

5 Ultimately, pornography addresses adults about sex as sex education classes address children. In terms of denotation (the first through its anatomical materiality, the second through its biological determinism), a denotation being, as we know, 'only the last of the connotations' (Barthes). More than forbidding pleasure, pornography is a matter of its dissuasion, and doubtless the spectator attends pornographic films in order to confirm the impossibility of pleasure and to comply with this. (Author's note.)

6 Conversely, and in spite of its erect penises, pornography does not induce erectility, because in any erection can be read the weakness, the lack, the irreducible reverse of pornography which, in order to exist, it must deny. The phallus (the term is too emphatic – it is always subject to castration) is unrepresentable. Also in pornography the penis, objectified and made autonomous by the fragmentation of the framing, is always reduced to the status of a dildo (the two often being shown alternately); this is its pornographic existence. If, on the other hand, pornography always revolves around the woman, it is because she does not possess the Mark. But the threat that the female sex constitutes through the absence of the penis, which returns the subject to its own lack and its irreducible divisibility, is itself averted by the penis-dildo – or by the exhaustive description of the female sex and its anatomical details, its folds of skin, its hairs . . . Put another way, pornography is constructed around the *denial of castration* and *its truth process is a fetishistic process* (this is equally the case for other processes of truth). It can operate only at the level of secondary repression; primary sexualization remains inaccessible to it. It is in this sense that one might say pornography *neutralizes* sex. (Author's note.)

7 This is why, logically, there is no limit to pornographic spectacle, and why its norm is that of perversion: fetishism, male or female homosexuality, voyeurism, exhibitionism, sadomasochism, even incest. All these 'perversions', big or small, are here present and designate the norm, the model that 'normal' heterosexuality falls back on. But *perversion as a norm of desire* does not come from any boldness on pornography's part, it does not dispense with any prohibitions. If perversions are presented as normality, it is because they are just as much models of a sexuality that is engendered – logically and sequentially – by the structural partition of the Masculine and the Feminine, and that here they can be alternated one with the other, and with 'normal' sexuality in a rigorous equivalence. Now, the binary opposition Masculine/Feminine is not specific to pornography: it is the same principle by which the body and its sexualization are coded in our society (we know that, in fashion, the two terms combine in the *unisex* style).

Only two big perversions remain, with rare exceptions, excluded from pornographic spectacle: zoophilia and necrophilia. Not simply in the name of the singular horror of such a spectacle (if this was so it would attract rather than repel the public, given this type of logic), but because from zoophilia, from the liaison of Beast and Man (man or woman, it matters little), comes the re-emergence of ambivalence: the humanity of the first being shunted on to the bestiality of the second, which is to abolish the great opposition of Nature/Culture and the implied predominance of Culture over Nature. It is because, as regards necrophilia, the liaison of man and corpse introduces the fundamental ambivalence of eroticism, in its reinscribing the death-drive into the erotic act. If, in pornography, the Beast and Death are unrepresentable it is because (as with the phallus, always coupled with its castration) their ambivalence spells the end of the schema Masculine/Feminine in its bipolarity, the extermination of its two terms and their regulated opposition – on which pornography precisely bases itself. Ultimately, zoophilia and necrophilia may well be present in pornography: it is enough to objectify the Beast in the *animal* (to reduce it to the state of a domesticated being or as the subject of experimentation and scientific knowledge) and Death in the *corpse* (to reduce it to the state of a body submitted to medical knowledge) – in short, to enclose these perversions within their clinical denominations, as pornography now reduces the phallus to the penis-dildo. But the process remains a risky one: the symbolic, thus averted, is always liable to re-emerge and this, once again, is unthinkable in pornography.

Another motif of death's unshowability is in its already being there (as in any film work); sex frozen in its optical recording, sex conserved in its inscription on film, can only be revived as a witness to its disappearance (the film as a process of conservation and memory – cf., among others, ethnographic films, the only problem from this point of view being . . . the conservation of films?). The skin disappears. (Author's note.)

8 In *L'Anti-oedipe: capitalisme et schizophrénie*. See Ch. 8, note 3.

9 Particularly interesting here is the angle of the shot of the woman's back. She is taken from the back only inasmuch as, knowing that she is being looked at, she is liable to turn round and, in particular, to offer herself from behind. Such shots of the back refer to sex as its underside. (Author's note.)

10 *Histoire d'O*, directed by Just Jaeckin in 1975, a version of the classic pornographic novel (1954) by 'Pauline Réage', the *nom de plume* of a distinguished French literary editor whose identity was unrevealed at the time. (She died in 1998.) The film caused a stir in France when, oddly but in tune with the contemporary fashion for lending 'serious' pornography a veneer of respectability, it opened at a cinema in the Champs Elysées.

11 Conversely, Oshima's *Empire of the Senses*, being neither pornographic nor, for that matter, erotic, describes the cyclical figure of a lovers' wager whose finale (the man's death and castration) is inscribed as the film's starting point. The relationship of domination between a man and his servant is seen to be inverted here (the domination of the lover by his *mistress*; reality made to disappear) so as to be abolished. Death and castration – the sacrifice of the master through which the woman, having appropriated the phallus and broken the symbolic exchange, suddenly has dominion over nothing; which demands the return of the real in the dry, harsh guise of a voice-over commentary in order to block out the generality of the process, which always shows through behind the concrete singularity of the events, the realist delimitations of the shots which, themselves, tend to contradict the story. (Author's note.)

12 Conversely, the remarkable contempt of 'political' or 'social' film-makers, fanatics for messages. The finest example of this at the moment is without doubt *L'Amour violé* (Yannick Bellon). The whole process of short-circuiting and perversion that the cinematic representation makes of its drama, and which Bazin lucidly explains

above, is verified quite specifically in this film (and by reason of its very subject matter). Yannick Bellon's film is successful inasmuch as it rests on this reversal of an event's meaning in its retranscription at the reproductive behest of cinema, and not through any conscious motive of its own (but is it not this too that, as a last resort, is secretly desired? The failure of an act being, in essence, its successful consummation). Hence the mirage of militant cinema in which it is swallowed up and lost, the trap where it is caught in its own game. (Author's note.)

13 We have to dispense with the 'voyeurism' so dear to those who hold pornography in contempt (it is, on the contrary, a very good argument for separating off X-rated films and their auditoria – and their public – and avoiding what pornography says about cinema in general). If the scopic drive has a meaning, it is necessary to understand clearly that the audience sees something that is never what they wanted to see; a delusion in which the denigrators of pornography are also caught up in when stigmatizing the 'voyeurism' of the audience, which is doubtless at work elsewhere in cinema just as much as in pornography (for what does one go to see when one goes to see a film?), where it is much more loaded, by virtue of the fetishistic clarity of pornography's subject matter. Because it is, of course, in the characteristic of cinema's *trompe-l'oeil* manner of representation that the pornographic object of the look is elaborated, and in the camouflaging of the technical processes which, *artificially*, reproduce sex for the screen. (Author's note.)

14 'Paluche': a small video camera held in the hand like a microphone or a flashlight. It was developed by Jean-Pierre Beauviala, who founded the Grenoble-based company Aaton. Beauviala had a long-standing involvement with *Cahiers* as its technical adviser and as a partner in the magazine's publishing imprint, Editions de l'Etoile. He also developed a camera for Godard, the Aaton 8/35, which Godard used to film sequences in *Sauve qui peut (la vie)* and *Passion*. See Jean-Pierre Beauviala and Jean-Luc Godard, 'Genesis of a Camera (First Episode)', *Camera Obscura*, nos 13/14, 1985. (Translator's note.)

15 'Cinematography is not, in its essence, a thing of pleasure, an amusement for big children. Being the absolutely faithful reproduction of natural movements, it produces the most astonishing conquest of forgetting man has ever accomplished, it stores and restores what cannot be made *to live again* [my emphasis] by simple memory, and even less by its auxiliaries, the written page, drawing and photography, (B. Matuszewski, *La Photographie animée, ce qu'elle est, ce qu'elle doit être*, Paris, 1898). (Author's note.)

16 The architect Le Corbusier's 'Modulor' was a building system using standard-sized units whose proportions are calculated according to those of the human figure.

17 In *La Chinoise* Godard has one of his characters say, in substance, the following: 'It's always been said that Lumière made documentary films and Méliès fiction films. Wrong. Lumière made impressionist films and Méliès reconstructed current events.' While these words need a little qualifying, they remain basically true. What Lumière shows immediately (cf. *L'Arrivée d'un train en gare*) is the power of fiction in cinema. And it was this that Méliès understood only too well when he turned to cinema, but he also grasped the extent to which cinema's dreamlike dimension rests on the realism of the image and its movement, repeating in reverse the happy accident that opened up the world of special effects to him (even those films in which the frame is internally duplicated by a theatre curtain, or the animation films, share this principle). (Author's note.)

18 Paul Vecchiali, in *Change pas de main*, short-circuits the element of pornography in his film by recoding it in a police film, but one which comes undone through its erotic plot. The two genres retract from one another through the co-presence of their effects and their rules, which really become the spectacle's sole elements. Here

is another of pornography's limitations, its extinction when set within other genres where it loses all its distinguishing criteria. In Vecchiali's case *Change pas de main* was shot at the same time as *Exhibition*, the shooting of *Exhibition* or of sequences of it constituting the plot material of *Change pas de main*: pornography programming its own death? (Author's note.)

19 For 'retro', see Ch. 2 and Ch. 12 in this volume.

Part IV

THIRD CINEMA

18

OUR CINEMA

('Notre cinéma', *Cahiers du Cinéma* 285,
February 1978)

Sidney Sokhona

If you want to talk about African cinema today, you're obliged – even if this seems an over-deliberate way of doing it – to go step by step through the different stages involved in the making of a film and the distribution of that film in the world and in Africa itself.

At any time and in any country, to talk about films is to talk about money. And for a film, once it is made, to earn money so that its director can make another film, it has to be distributed. Now the fact is that Africa – which we can no longer refer to as a colony but as a 'neo-colony' – has neither of these two elements: production and distribution.

Yet people still talk about 'African cinema'. For us, this term is valid only if it means – as elsewhere, with American cinema and European cinema for instance – a cinema made by individuals who live in a given continent. In reality, however, in Africa as elsewhere, different people make different kinds of cinema. People who share neither the same ideology, nor the same social background, nor the same class.

If there is one thing perhaps that all African film-makers have in common (except for government film-makers, or more precisely the *griots* of the ruling authorities), it is that because there is a lack of cinematic structures and they are denied access to established institutions, they are all simultaneously directors, distributors, sometimes even actors – in a word, jacks of all trades.

Film-makers in Africa today

At all the festivals in which African films are shown, and particularly at the Pan-African festivals like Ouagadougou in Upper Volta [Burkina Faso] or Carthage in Tunisia, the films shown reveal different strands of ideas and different classes. In black Africa, therefore, it is possible to 'distinguish' between different categories.

227

First, the theme which recurs most frequently is the one that makes allusions to ancestral traditions. A danger crops up here, and it is one that applies not just to the area of cinema. In general, dual marriage, the problems of caste and tribal rivalries are referred to with some authenticity; they are subjects which can be treated in different ways, and that includes having a progressive or oppositional character. But at the moment more than 80 per cent of the film-makers who make use of this theme are either tied to the authorities, or anti-progressive, or else, in the majority of cases, want to be seen as film-makers pure and simple. So there is no question of them including in a film subject matter which risks displeasing the government or the sole party in power.

Second, immediately following, there is another category of film-makers whom one might describe as the 'undecided'. They subscribe to neither the reactionary nor the progressive ticket. They are the 'don't knows' you can find anywhere.

With regard to the West, they too play the authenticity card. This extends from negritude to local customs, from the nice black to the very small rebellion or the melancholy of this black. Their sole aim is to pick up the Western humanist vote (those who, remembering colonization, believe they still have a debt to pay to Africa), and at the same time to set themselves before the mass of politically unaware Africans who, having been bombarded by Western films for fifty years, are hungry to see blacks on the screen, while not asking for political content or cinematic form.

Next comes a third category, a more interesting one for African society and for outsiders who want to inform themselves about our reality. This ranges from films dealing with national liberation struggles, or struggles in the colonial and neo-colonial periods, to films showing the problems of rural society or of the town. These films are handled in a very calculated fashion, cinematically as well as in their dialogue and commentary, with – always as a secondary motive – whatever concessions may be necessary. In short, they are films with a double edge. These film-makers say things that the film-makers referred to above would not dare to say, but at the same time they don't make the effort to follow their ideas through to their conclusion.

Fourth, a final category, which closes the circle, comprises those who are 'film-makers' more in theory than in practice. All of them may be defined in terms of a political ideology: Marxism-Leninism, Trotskyism, progressivism, etc. But more than half the film-makers in this category have yet to make their first film – they have only projects. It is in this category, however, that we find those few film-makers who take up a political position about what is happening in the African continent as well as in the world at large; or who can articulate a political critique of all those categories of film mentioned above, which currently range from porno films through to authenticity via adventure films, morality tales and tedious stodge. Also included in this category are a few film-makers from our continent who are exiled abroad and whose films, conceived and made outside Africa, reflect a progressive character. In any event, we would certainly like to be in the crowd that flocks to the cinema when their first film made and shot in Africa is shown!

African cinema and production

To simplify, we can divide production into three categories.

First, government-backed production. This type of production involves only those film-makers described above as 'government *griots*'. For these film-makers, finance is automatically made available from the budget of the Ministry of Information or the Ministry of Culture, or from the only existing party. The films made are intended for the local population or, through embassies, for the outside world. They are documentaries, tourist films or portraits of presidents or prominent ministers, industrial films, etc. Distribution is guaranteed for this category of films, and there is never any question of financial difficulties. Most African film-makers in this category enjoy a standard of living and technical facilities on a luxurious scale.

Second, foreign, especially Western, productions whose locations need an exotic African landscape. These productions, ranging from large-screen fiction to television series, enjoy almost automatic aid (despite being foreign); or, when aid is sought, in 98 per cent of cases they are supported by the government in power. One example: the French television series *Fachoda ou la mission Marchand*, which was filmed in Senegal and which had the benefit of some tens of millions of French African francs, on-the-spot shooting facilities and local labour and extras, in return for a 16 mm optical print of the finished film!

Some years ago just a few countries adopted a film production policy. In North Africa this happened in Algeria, where the policy is still in force; and in black Africa, until 1975, in Senegal. These countries managed to produce films that were different from those in the categories mentioned above. In all the other francophone countries of black Africa (including Senegal, following the demise of the state production company, the SNC), every film-maker who has managed to make a film has done so outside the national structures. Other film-makers have not been able to make a film; or, like Ousmane Sembene in Senegal, have made films by arranging a bank loan through the mortgage of their properties.

Third, another production opportunity exists for young film-makers in black Africa. (I say black Africa, because it is not available to film-makers in North Africa.) This was set in motion by the French Ministry of Cooperation, which helps young African film-makers to complete their film in return for twenty-five prints for showing to cultural centres in Africa. You can imagine what kinds of film are helped in this way: films with no political character, co-operation with 'normal African films'.

The film-makers thus sponsored belong to the first two categories outlined above; and even if it occasionally happens that by accident a film-maker from another category is supported, the process is not repeated. It is important to emphasize that all the films made under these conditions are virtually doomed commercially in black Africa because of their non-commercial distribution, in advance of a potential commercial distribution which in fact rarely happens.

Making African films in Africa

An African film-maker who, after overcoming a thousand difficulties, is ready to shoot a 16 mm film, whether in black and white or in colour, finds himself in a country where there is no film stock, no film equipment, no laboratory, dubbing studio or competent technicians. In short, he has to shoot his film when he has no control over the technical variables; he has to shoot thousands of feet of film without seeing a single foot of rushes.

These are the conditions in which most African films are made today. After several months of shooting, the director goes to Paris to reassemble the thousands of feet of film which have been sent to the laboratory. Often, he is unable to view the rushes because he hasn't the money to pay the laboratory and he can't get credit because he has no production company behind him. If, after seeing his rushes, he notices a technical fault, caused for example by a defective lens or a bad sound cable, he does not have the resources to reshoot the scene, which is therefore automatically cut from the film. This is what, in the majority of cases, produces a more than disappointing result. Add to that everything caused by a poverty of resources: direction that is sometimes rudimentary, mediocre actors . . .

All these circumstances put us on the bottom rung of world cinema.

This is why – and it happens very often at festivals – Westerners almost automatically excuse the poor technical quality of African films by saying simply: 'That's African cinema.' For us, these words are more than a stab in the back! Not only because our African film-maker colleagues have proved that they can make films in the same class as any film-maker in the world, but particularly because – I remind all my colleagues – it is for us African film-makers, who have to carve out a place for ourselves, to make films politically better than anyone else, given the economic and political situation of our countries; films that are also technically better made than others!

African cinema and distribution

As regards distribution, there are two important points to be made about distribution within the African countries and distribution of African films abroad.

In all of Francophone black Africa, with the exception of three or four countries who have recently nationalized their distribution circuit, every resident African film-maker who manages to make a film is obliged – if he wants it distributed in his own country – to take the plane to Paris and approach Sopacia, a subsidiary of the UGC [Union Générale Cinématographique]. Sopacia is simply the old Comacico Secma, which was bought out and recapitalized. It has the same standards as the Ministry of Co-operation: a political nonentity.[1]

As for those countries which have nationalized their cinemas, they have poor resources and are still supplied by Sopacia. Indeed in Senegal, which has nationalized the cinema, the state has an 80 per cent holding and Sopacia owns the remaining 20 per cent, yet this 20 per cent actually has more control than the 80 per cent since Sopacia is particularly concerned not to allow any threat to itself or for there to be competition in Africa between Western films and African films. Its additional power lies in the fact that it owns the cinemas, the seats and all the technical equipment in a great many African countries (including the colonial territories).

As far as African cinema abroad is concerned, everyone has noticed the increasing African presence at international film festivals. Surprising perhaps, though there's nothing extraordinary about it. There could well be a comparison to be made between the African presence at film festivals and what is happening in the United States, where every serial now has to have a black actor. Just to make a contrast! It is the same for us Africans at international festivals – just a matter of seeing long dresses and caftans at gala receptions.

Outside of a few progressive festivals and a few journalists who are endeavouring to do something about it, it's simply a clearing house operation. African films exist, so why not make an occasional gesture? Take the last [1977] Cannes Festival. It would have been absurd not to have a single black film, so there in the official programme was *Black Joy* or *Car Wash*, but especially not a certain Ousmane Sembene's *Ceddo*, which was programmed in the Director's Fortnight.

Nevertheless, at the moment the survival of an African film partly depends on the West. An article in a Western newspaper about an African film threatened with a ban in its own country may help to have the ban lifted. Yet in the West, except for German, Swedish or French Canadian television and some small distributors, African cinema does not exist because no one sees it. This at a time when, despite the thousand problems film-makers face, there are dozens of feature films.

Africa and cinema in general

In Africa today it is almost true to say that everyone who has a cinema in their village or town goes to a film every other day: not because the film has been publicized or praised by the critics, but simply because the cinema is one of the few leisure activities there are. Africa was colonized, and so is its cinema. So for fifty years African cinemas have shown the same films, films that have been little seen in the West, the worst kind of rubbish like *Django*, *Ringo*, Hindi films, karate films, not forgetting the unforgettable Tarzan.

Of the few African films which have been seen on African screens, it must be said that they could be profitable. In 1975 Ousmane Sembene's *Xala* broke the box-office record in Senegal,[2] followed by *Operation Dragon* (with Bruce Lee). This confirms our view that, even if our people are accustomed to seeing escapist entertainment films, they are also interested in our own films, and that it is purely and simply a deliberate and concerted policy which dooms us on our own territory.

Without this policy, the problems of African cinema would not exist, and every film which had normal distribution in Africa would be enabled not only to recover its costs, but also to allow another film to be made.

Finally, it should be said that all the African film-makers caught up in this situation are beginning to organize themselves and to draw up battle plans for this cinematic independence. But we are aware that this independence is bound up with the independence of the African continent itself, politically as well as economically. We are seeking to create a coming together, a solidarity in the struggle, with a number of countries in other parts of the world who are caught up in the same situation, and also with Western film-makers whose own films are denied a place in the Western system. I am in favour of the free circulation of films from one continent to another, provided that this is seen as a reciprocal agreement between two individuals or two independent systems. Because in my view the cinema, used properly, can be a messenger between peoples.

Translated by David Wilson

Notes

1 For an account of the problems of film distribution in Africa, see Emmanuel Sama, 'African Films are Foreigners in Their Own Countries', in Imruh Bakari and Mbye Cham (eds), *African Experiences of Cinema* (London, BFI Publishing, 1996), originally published in *Ecrans d'Afrique*, no. 4, 1993.
2 *Xala*: see Ch. 23.

19

INTERVIEW WITH ABDELAZIZ TOLBI

('Entretien avec Abdelaziz Tolbi', *Cahiers du Cinéma*
266–7, May 1976)

Thérèse Giraud, Mohand Ben Salama

First, why this film and how do you place it in the context of Algerian cinema?

The script of *Noua* was written in 1968 and it was filmed in 1972. The film is about life in a *douar* [village] exactly two months before and after the start of the war of national liberation. For me, starting the film, it was a case of bring-ing out the historical reality of independent Algeria: in 1968, as in 1962 and also during the making of the film, the situation of the Algerian peasantry – the core (the fire) of the war of liberation – was exactly the same as before 1954. And I wanted to record this fact with reference to the Algerian people, but also with reference to the French people and all people who fight for their freedom. You don't wage a war of liberation to change the faces of the bosses, you wage it to make a revolution, a universal revolution, radical reforms of the old systems of the exploitation of man by man, like 'Either you kill me or I kill you, I work for you or you work for me, you're the slave and I'm the master.'

In the context of Algerian cinema? Algerian cinema is part of the general culture, and in Algeria we're still finding our way, as in every other country, of course. We're trying to discover what culture is: the old, the new, etc. But as I see it, there *are* Algerian films, although that's quite a different thing, because the films depend on the personalities of their directors, their makers. There is no official ideology, no particular orientation as there is in socialist countries.

Can you say something about the different trends in the area of culture? Or more pre-cisely, since you don't accept the term 'culture' in Algerian films, is there a dominant trend, what differences of approach are there, and on what level?

The problem with culture generally over there is tied up with the fact that it's only ten years since Algeria became an independent country. Before colonialism,

233

there was an Algerian culture bound up with Islam, the ancient culture. During colonialism there was no culture, and the result was 80 per cent illiteracy, because French colonialism – particularly in Algeria – barred Algerian culture. It was forbidden to read Arab books, to be taught Arab culture. The only things that survived – though very, very discreetly – were certain traditions within the family, relationships between people, which were very closely bound up with Islam . . . So now we are trying to find a way out of this vacuum, we're trying to find a direction for our culture. We certainly have ties with an Arab-Islamic civilization, but at the present moment, in terms of the real situation of our people and the socialist road that Algeria has chosen to liberate the Algerian masses from all their former oppression, that's a very distant thing, the more so because for five or six centuries it didn't really exist, it was dead: first during the Turkish colonial rule, which lasted for four centuries, and then during the English and French periods of colonialism for a century and a half. In other words, nearly six centuries of cultural death. Nothing, except for what came out of Egypt, which in any case was more in the area of theoretical research, palace scholarship, with no connecting roots to the everyday problems of the people. It was theory tied to ancient history, which had nothing to do with the realities of our own century. The result is that we are looking around, feeling our way, on every level – in the schools as well as in the cinema.

You must understand that during colonialism an Algerian could have no individuality. If people were educated it had to be within the culture, in the French language. Otherwise, there was nothing at all, and that's a question of class: French culture or nothing. One example is those Algerians who were in the French universities: for a long time they wrote and produced nothing about the Algerian nation, because for them it was a totally external civilization which had no internal echoes for them. Except for a few people like Kateb Yacine[1] – and they were a minority – who did not come out of the university, and who expressed their experience of the Algerian people in the French language. But this was not an Algerian culture interiorized and transformed by contact with a new reality. So for a hundred and thirty years there was nothing coming from educated people, nothing that dealt with or touched on the problems of the Algerian people; because they were completely uprooted from their own individuality, and everything they learned was from the outset totally foreign to them, which is another reason that for so long there has been nothing new.

From that perspective, can you say something about how these problems affect cinema?

First of all, it ought to be said that representational art has no place at all in the Arab-Islamic culture I'm talking about, and it's only very recently that cinema has come to be recognized as a vehicle for artistic expression. And since art is part of culture and we are trying to find a direction for our culture, we're also trying to find a way of expressing ourselves cinematically. That's why Algerian cinema is very varied. You find every kind of trend – Hollywood cinema as well as Italian neo-realism and Soviet cinema – and there is also a genuinely national cinema which comes out of ourselves, out of our own realities. Unfortunately, the colonial period established a very strong bond with Western bourgeois culture which we badly needed to loosen, and that's something you find particularly in the cinema because it has no roots in the national culture. Another factor that very much comes into play is that most of the film-makers were formed by and are still imbued with this Western civilization. This is something well understood by the colonel at the end of the film when he is talking about intellectuals. So this is why, although it deals with the realities of our people (and that's true of all the films), because its idiom is still tied to the West the cinema presents an image of this reality which for most of the time remains foreign to those who live that reality, without really touching them or unsettling them in their everyday sensibilities.

And there's something else that should be said here, since we are at a festival [Toulon]. Which is that this Western influence continues to work in an active way, through the agency of the critics, who on the one hand are largely controlled by international cultural imperialism with a view to killing off any different kind of voice, particularly in the so-called 'Third World' countries; and who on the other hand organize these kinds of strategic bases like festivals so as to turn all this film production into a meaningless miscellany and hand out prizes, set up reputations, from their own perspective on it. I've never been to Cannes myself, but at Leipzig I met a Bolivian journalist and when I asked him what the Cannes festival was, he told me that it was the 'Watergate of cinema'. So here I am for the first time at the Toulon festival, and it's incredible.[2] I don't know what you think of it, but one could describe Toulon as the 'tomb of the unknown cinema'!

Your film starts with a precise date and it takes place within two precise dates, four months during 1954, in other words the past, the colonial past. However, it extends beyond this moment of history and works also as a witness to the present situation. Can you explain a little more precisely what you were trying to do here?

What's important here is that throughout the film you find the Algerian people as they are, tied to their roots, in other words isolated from colonialism. This starts with the Koranic school, then the *taleb*, the marabout,[3] all personal relationships, the whole social process: the Algerian character as it remained during colonialism. It's only with the police and the army that you see colonialism for what it was – an outside phenomenon.

We see it for the first time in the village souk, more or less in the film's third part, after we've been watching life in the douar, *but it's also there immediately in the Algerian intermediaries, the country policeman for example.*

In reality, French colonialism was there in the towns and the villages, but not among the Algerian peasantry. With the peasants it was Algerians themselves, those who were with the French, who represented it – the village chiefs, the *bachagas*, the country policemen. In the mountains, it was all the Algerians themselves. Except when there were settlers owning the land; but the majority of the peasants had no direct contact with them.

Yes, apart from a moment when you show a French couple (but only as witnesses to a sit-uation involving Algerians), the French presence is only a military one. And through-out the film the police are shown as a repressive force in the service of Algerian exploiters. It's only in the final shot – the French army officer – that this is turned round and we see that it is these same Algerians who are serving French colonialism.

Yes indeed, because at the social relations level – and that's what is important – the Algerian people and French colonialism were, culturally and socially, completely and absolutely separate from one another. The only contact was on the administrative level, with the authorities, but as for questions of intercom-munal living, working, eating or marrying, there was no contact at all. Except for certain ranks of the aristocracy and some functionaries, and even then these were principally business contacts. So, very little direct social contact, as you see in the film, in every scene; you see what the Algerian character is, and the position and role of colonialism in relation to it. Man's exploitation of man is of course a colonial fact, but it's also and above all an Algerian fact, in Algeria. And I think this is the main difference between this film and other films which have dealt with colonialism, making colonialism the *sole* cause of all the prob-lems that exist today.

One senses in the film this wish to put back, redistribute certain elements of history, a wish to jump beyond the 'drama' of the moment (colonialism) and photograph what has remained unchanged, rediscover a certain timelessness. Certainly your film is a bit like a series of photographs, photographs of social structures caught in their everyday function-ing. In this sense, I'm reminded a little of another Arab film, Kafr Kassem, *which also works as a testimony, as a return to historical sources in order to throw light on the present.*[4]

Well, I've not yet seen *Kafr Kassem* myself, but my approach was quite simple. I was a child when the war started, and then I was wounded; so I went abroad and I didn't return until after independence, in 1967. First I finished my edu-cation abroad, in Germany, and then I went back. And when I got back, I found that the situation was the same as when I had left. By which I mean that after a war that left a million and a half dead, sacrificed, after an international movement which shook up the whole of Africa, the situation of the Algerian peasant was precisely the same. So I became actively aware of the fact that something was really not working in Algeria. Well then, one had to record that fact photographically, as I saw it with my own eyes. The film is supposed to happen in 1954, but the basis of the script was the life of these people, their everyday reality as I saw it around me. It's these people who are the actors in the film; all the people in it, the main roles as well as the minor ones, are played by people who come straight out of that situation. So they recognize themselves. And in any case there is a short text at the start of the film which says that the film was made in 1972, with no sets or make-up. 1954 and 1972, they're the same!

Can you elaborate on that a little?

I can tell you a story. After the screening of *Noua*, I was involved in a small discussion and I was taken to task by a member of the jury, who told me that before 1954 the French army had never executed anyone! And the audience more or less agreed with that. When I replied simply from what I lived through myself – I mean, in 1945 there were 45,000 people killed in three days – no one believed me. And that's the whole point: for the duration of the festival, audiences have been learning a great deal! That's to say, in the name of the new young cinema, behind all this, there are all these little notions trying to stop a historical movement from heading in its own direction. An attitude that exists even among certain Arab critics in our festivals at home.

Yes, but in the context of all this how do you yourself situate your work? What route should a new culture follow?

In Algeria, people say that so-and-so is either Arab-inclined or French-inclined. That's to say, there are those who stick with the Western cinema and prick away at bits and pieces of the Algerian reality. And then there are the others, the Arab-inclined, who are caught up in the whole character of our peasant civilization; not the written culture – there is none – but the culture that connects with the roots of the people. And that's what you have to start from: for instance, the *you-you*[5] of the women, the folk poetry and folk sayings, all the customs, habits of speech . . . like the lullaby that the sister sings to her little brother to send him asleep although he's hungry; or the mother who tells her children to eat slowly so that they won't forget that they've eaten. Moreover, all these things are untranslatable into another language, another culture. For example, when Noua says to Djebbar that he is going to leave school when he is ready to 'throw away the slate', in the film that's translated as 'ready to succeed', which is pretty disturbing, but in fact what it means is something like 'to be fully himself'. Or when old Amar, during the wedding, asks the man with the flute, not to 'play us a tune', as it's translated, but something like 'give us a bit of oxygen'.

Yes, that's certainly an aspect of the film, and all these details about the everyday life of the people are very much in evidence. That's doubtless because the camera always stays at

THÉRÈSE GIRAUD, MOHAND BEN SALAMA

its own level, within the framework of the life of the douar. But at the same time there is a historical dimension to this, and it's this approach which strikes me as interesting. I mean, this is in no sense an ethnographic film . . .

But that has to be the point you start from. It's only from that point that you can intervene in our reality, and at the same time share in the universal riches, be part of the movement of history and understand the universal laws that govern the world. What seemed very important to me at this particular time, in Algeria, was not to focus everything on the colonial period, as we have tended to do – and still do – but to make a leap into history, to take account of the social process of the whole Algerian people beyond colonialism, which was only a period and a fairly short period at that. Before colonialism, during colonialism and after colonialism – these are the three periods in *Noua.* Our society was founded on a social and ideological system which is one of the exploitation of man by man. Colonialism only grafted itself on to this and reinforced it. And this is why I show the close connection between the big landowners in Algeria and the French military, who exploited the Algerian people in the same way, in the same language. Before colonialism, this class and this situation already existed, and we must not forget that. And they went on existing afterwards, at least until 1972 and the start of the agrarian revolution. Even now, there are still enormous difficulties.

One important thing, it seems to me, is that in most of the relationships that the characters have you show the relationship between their actions and the material things around them. The shot of the woman who is killed for a handful of corn is a good example of this: you start with the corn, and then you go down to the hand before you go to her face and we see the blood on it. Human beings are always placed within a wider, material context.

That's because I felt I had to do it that way to show what the situation was, give a clear picture of it. For instance, with the shot you're talking about, as I saw it I didn't need to stress the woman's death, or dramatize it. What I wanted to show was the contrast between this mountain of corn on the one side and the dead body on the other – dead because, although she'd worked all her life, she had been reduced to stealing a handful of corn to feed her children.

The final shot, with the colonel, is quite unexpected. It completely changes the ambience – it could be a television shot . . .

Ah yes, that was thanks to the cameraman. I wanted to give an official dimension to the image here. And he said to me that to do that we didn't have to film him in close-up, like a film star for instance, and so we should follow the conventions and use a medium shot for him. He would have been ridiculous in close-up, and since he is reading an official text we should stress this official

238

side through the image – and the official image is the television one. At the time I agreed, though I wasn't too sure about it. Now I think he was right. Don't you think so?

My first reaction while watching the film was that I was surprised that it stopped there. And afterwards I thought that actually it was television that had just spoken, the official voice: a representative of colonialism, of the bourgeoisie, who was speaking politically, in the terminology of class struggle, via an apparatus of the State . . .

Yes, as a summing up of everything you have seen in the film.

When you got to the village with your script, how did you proceed? How did the people in the village respond to the film, how did they react, and how did you work with them?

When we got there, it was with a very limited crew – six people. At first, we didn't shoot anything. We set up the camera on its tripod and we left it like that in the village, with just the cameraman standing some distance away to keep an eye on it, in case an animal came and knocked it over. Everyone could come and see it, touch it, look inside it to see how it was made: ah, so that's a camera. And this went on for two weeks, two weeks in which we lived the life of the village, wore the *gandoura*[6] like them, ate with them, until we and the camera became part of the village. There was no one in charge, no direction, we were simply there, part of the *douar*.

Even so, they knew you had come to make a film.

Oh yes, they knew. The first and second day it was a bit disturbing, but in time we became members of the *douar*, and in the village the camera was just like any other object, a bottle or whatever. It was only then that we started to work. It wasn't the first time I had worked in this way. This was my third feature. The first time it was very difficult, the second time a little less so, and so for *Noua* I had some experience of working directly with the people. When I say we started to work, I mean we started to talk about some of the scenes, but these conversations took place within the daily social round, during meals for instance. They learned the dialogue like this, in conversation, indirectly. Because, you know, they were all illiterate, they couldn't learn dialogue by heart.

But how did you cast the parts? Did you take their social situation into account? For instance, what position did the man who played the sheikh have in the village? Was he a man of influence?

No, not exactly. Previously, he had a job as a country policeman. But in this respect, some really extraordinary things happened while we were filming, moments when people played it for real. For instance, during the scene with the tractor at the beginning of the film. There were a lot of people watching during the rehearsals, peasants and children. And when the sheikh started insulting the young peasant, all those who were standing around began pelting him with stones. Or when the sheikh takes his horse and goes back to being what he was before, the peasants who were there felt it and started to attack him. Another example: when the two sons attacked a girl because one of them had been attacked by the girl's father, the police came. When the sheikh said to the peasant, 'So *you* dare to abuse my son, who's of noble birth by the way', he was attacked by the spectators – 'It's you who's the dirty bastard, you!' So you see for the people of the village all this was still very close to them, and they weren't play-acting, they were living out their lives.

Something you have been much criticized for here is using European music to stress the big moments in the film, alongside passages of Arab music, and for playing up the melodrama a little.

I should make that clear. As far as we are concerned, it's really not so unusual. I prepared two versions of the film. One version for the Middle East, the Maghreb, with this music, which isn't European because for us it's a universal music. And another version without music, which has already been shown at the Cinémathèque in Paris (and it's hard going, to the extent that half-way through the film people have to go out for a breather before they go back in). Well, maybe you're right and the music is a bit melodramatic, but over there we like that, and the funny thing is that the critics there – in the Middle East, Lebanon, Syria – liked it, whereas here in Europe they're troubled by it, because they know it by heart, it already means something to them, whereas we don't know it. So I took it out for them.

Yes, but it's not just that, because there are two kinds of music in the film and they don't come at the same time, they're not interchangeable. It seems to me that the Western music underlines the big moments in the film and in the lives of the people – for instance, that long walk as the peasants are returning from the village on foot and they're covered in dust from the cars racing past. And on the other hand the Arab music reflects the most intimate moments in the peasants' lives, in terms of what you called just now the Algerian character.

Yes, for all those situations that closely involve Algerian – typically Algerian – social problems, there isn't any Western music. The death, for instance: that's a typical event and we can't have Western music there. The marriage – this little insignificant marriage which comes just after the scene where the people return from the village – there we immediately have Algerian flute music. And also when the animals come back to the farm. Because all of this – this ambience – is typically part of the lives of the Algerian people, their actual everyday reality. When there are action shots, particularly when the Algerian people begin to organize themselves for the revolution, I put in music from the October revolution, to intensify the action and give it an extra historical dimension. For me, this is a universal music, because we don't have music like that at home – we don't have an orchestra to play music like that.

For the resistance, the music plays in counterpoint to the image. That's something fairly new in terms of the image the cinema generally presents of a historical movement, an event like this. It doesn't seem at all like something given a date in the usual way: 'And so the resistance began . . .' When you recognize it as a moment of history, a great many things have already happened as far as life in the village is concerned: to some extent we've been put in the position of the people of the village, we have their view of history being made (being made in the shadows). First, there is the tree cut down, then the dogs slaughtered and also the reconciliation of the two clans . . .

Yes, it's very important to de-dramatize this moment of history, to give it back its everyday quality. To de-dramatize it so as to bring it closer. And that's in fact how it happened: the armed struggle didn't fall from the sky or spring from the ground at a stroke, just like that; it was the fruit of extensive work on the inside, and it was only after this that the armed struggle and the war of liberation took place.

This is a film made for television. Does that change anything in relation to a film made for the cinema?

The fact is that the Algerian system is not at all the same as the system in France. First and foremost, it's the state who pays: there is only one company, the ONCIC, and Algerian Radio-Television. Next, all features made for television get into the cinemas, and all features made for the cinema get shown on television. But the important point is that very few people in Algeria go to the cinema. Only a small minority of women go, so already almost 50 per cent of the population don't go. Then there are the old people and the religious people, and also all the senior officials and authorities who don't go to the cinema. In contrast, television has reached every household and it plays a big part in them; which is why all films also get on to television. Even *L'Héritage*, the most recent ONCIC film, has just been shown on television.

As for *Noua*, it has been shown three times on television, and the first time it was quite extraordinary. In Algiers and the other towns in Algeria, there is usually no one on the streets after nine o'clock in the evening. That night, at midnight, after the film, a great many people went out into the streets for a breath of air before they went to bed. Some journalists recorded this because it was such an extraordinary thing, and they showed it two days later on television. Subsequently, this happened twice more. Now the film is going to show in cinemas, and it's also going round the country districts, with the 'cinebus' operation which tours the country because there still isn't much television in rural areas.

How do you account for these reactions, the impact the film had on people in the towns?

Well, first of all 80 per cent of the Algerian people were peasants. And after independence, a great many of these Algerian peasants came to the towns, where they now live more or less affluently. So gradually they have forgotten their past. With the new alignment of the present administration, the new state, the turning towards Europe, international relations, diplomacy, etc. – modern life in the big state, in other words – they have forgotten everything; and they have forgotten what's happening behind them, in the interior of the country, among the peasantry. Suddenly, with their new house, their new comforts, their television, they've rediscovered a whole set of circumstances which most of them used to know and which haven't changed. But despite all that, they have all been changed in their own lives. One man may have been 'saved', but maybe all his friends, his neighbours, all those he left behind are still in a mess. And then there's another thing: in the film there is also an analysis of social relationships, if only the one made by the colonel, which is one that you still find in the towns as well.

After this film, there were also four or five others made about the relations between the peasantry and the Algerian towns. This created a network of forces that contributed to the starting up of the agrarian revolution. It was as a result of this gathering force that the authorities took the decision to return the land to those who work it. And much has already been achieved: today the peasants have social benefits, free medicine, free education, social security, and a national wage. Among the whole new generation now there is a big movement to ensure that this new social process is secure, and that there is a radical change in our social relations. There is an enormous struggle going on at every level. Maybe it will succeed, or maybe we could have what has happened in Chile.[7] Because this problem of the agrarian revolution is the fundamental problem in Algeria today.

Translated by David Wilson

Notes

1 Kateb Yacine (1929–89), a leading Algerian writer who was involved in the movement which led to independence in 1962. His best-known book is *Nedjma*, written (in French) in 1956; it was translated into English by Richard Howard (University of Virginia Press, 1991). In 1970, Yacine abandoned French for Arabic.

2 The Toulon festival, inaugurated in 1964, was dedicated to 'Young Cinema' and showed a number of films from 'developing' and post-colonial countries.

3 *Taleb*: religious student or scholar; 'marabout': Muslim holy man.

4 For *Kafr Kassem* see Ch. 22 in this volume.

5 *You-you*: ululation, the high-pitched yodelling chant used by grieving women in North Africa.
6 *Gandoura*: long cape or coat.
7 I.e. the overthrow of the Allende government in 1973 and the dismantling of its agrarian reform programme.

20

THE PROMISED LAND

('La Terre promise', *Cahiers du Cinéma* 253,
October–November 1974)

Serge Toubiana, Pascal Bonitzer

These two texts (which will be followed by others) show the importance we attach to the fact that Miguel Littin's *The Promised Land* [*Tierra prometida*] has opened in France. It would be totally wrong to believe that the position he defends has already been accepted, that the film is easy to read and like, and that its lesson can be assimilated without difficulty. It is precisely because the film has been seen as easy that people have not understood that our support for it derives neither from aesthetic attraction nor from political charity. Conversely, among petit-bourgeois, politically active cinephiles it is precisely those two things (the cinephile's aesthetic pleasure among those on the right, activist charity among those on the left) that worked for the potential audience of the film. And this is exactly why our fellow journalist Delfeil de Ton was led to condemn it out of hand. Our view is that far from having settled the questions which *The Promised Land* poses, we are only beginning to address them.

The power of speech

The Promised Land comes to us Europeans, for whom it was certainly not intended in the first instance, as an echo of Chile before the descent of the barbarians. It is a film of exile, which has been uprooted from the countryside and the *poblaciones* where it would have had a quite different impact from the one it has had here. We have the same affection for this film as we have for all exiles, and it inspires tremendous modesty in us. It is a film which is in every way exemplary and, provided we treat it neither as an exotic product nor as a universal model, it can help us to work towards the creation of a popular, militant cinema in this country.

First, the film *The Promised Land* was produced in 1972 in the very particular context of the Allende regime, about which the film-maker has a certain number of reservations and doubts (concerning the legalistic policy being pursued). The film appears to have been made for a specific stratum of the Chilean social formation, namely the peasantry, whose support for the processes of revolution or reaction was to be decisive for the future of the country. Revolutionary elements are fairly well established among the poor peasants. The occupation of the land, the arming of peasant militias, hunting out particularly reactionary landowners, and the beginnings of agrarian reform, make up the elements of a revolutionary policy which in this particular area runs counter to the legalistic and gradualist policy of the Left in power. The question of agrarian reform gave rise to a truly mass debate which split the Left into two camps. *The Promised Land* contributes to this debate by basing its position on the reconstitution of another moment in history, and on events which took place forty years earlier in the same place and in conditions which were in many respects similar.

And what does the film say? How can it be ideologically summarized? Its idea is very simple. It consists in saying to the peasants of 1972: your forefathers did the same thing, forty years ago, when they occupied the Palmilla lands under the guidance of José Duran, and the rich men's army came and massacred them. Let this memory serve to avoid the errors of the past.

Second, the rich ideological relationship between the historical setting of the film (Chile in the 1930s) and the time it was made (Chile in 1972) is disrupted by another historical moment, that of the time when the film was premiered and publicly shown in 1974, a time when Chile was of course no longer what it had been. It would be a great mistake to read the film teleologically, only in the light of September 1973, which would suppress its original conditions of production. The approach of a film-maker such as Littin becomes all the more interesting in the light of the ease with which some on the Left in Europe find pretexts for lamenting the defeat of the revolutionary movement. It may well be that his project was inspired by enthusiasm and that, at bottom, it was the desire for revolution, and the transmission of this desire from the peasants of Palmilla to the Mapuchos peasants in 1972, the work of popular memory in its influence on present-day consciousness, which constituted what was essential in the film.

If we were to set one period against another in the same way as Littin, *in an entirely non-defeatist manner*, sets the period in which the film is located in relation to the period in which it was made, we would also say that it is the defeatist reading of the film that must be eliminated when the period of the setting (Chile during the revolutionary period) is contrasted with the moment (under Pinochet) when this critique is being written. Indeed, it is undeniable that the criss-crossing between two periods in time and these overlapping readings are part of the text of the film so that it invites us to speak of the 1970s today, despite Pinochet, in the same way as it speaks of the experience of José Duran in 1932 with an optimism that runs through the whole narrative, although Duran was defeated. What is at stake in *The Promised Land* is an

245

ideological discourse on History, a discourse which brings with it many questions such as *how, for whom, and against whom must we make History speak today?* These are followed by another question which must be posed if we wish to understand what happened in Chile before the coup d'état. This question concerns the precise conditions under which the discourse on History, the discourse on filmic representation as contained in *The Promised Land,* can reach out towards the revolutionary movement, how it is placed in relation to the existing government and how it is articulated with, or runs up against, ideological practices which have survived from the old superstructure. In other words a film such as *The Promised Land* allows us to see how an artistic product which grows out of a mass political debate can return to this debate, using its own specific language, and participate in the *ideological struggle in which the dominated ideologies attempt to assert their hegemony.*

Third, film-makers do not very often show sensitivity to the prevailing ideological and political reality, nor do they frequently attempt to inscribe their practice within such reality or to support the ideas put forward by the Left. Such attempts are too rare for us not to wish to comment on them. But in addition, it is virtually unheard of for a film-maker to try to contribute to the debate by producing a particular object called a 'film', without this object being shown to the audience in the traditional, dominant form of film-object in which it is normally shown in capitalist countries, and in countries dominated by imperialism – an object which is wrapped up in the discourse of the ideological apparatus of cinema, and is crushed or absorbed by it.

It should be noted immediately that a certain number of concrete conditions, which are external to the contradiction we have just described (the contradiction between making a film and making use of a film), render such a problematic possible. These conditions have to do with the specific situation both of Chilean cinema and of the cinema in a certain number of dominated countries (such as Bolivia) in which the ideological apparatus of cinema has not existed for very long, is not powerful and has not yet succeeded in establishing a permanent routine of *dominant genres* and sub-Hollywood systems of representation dependent on foreign figurative patterns. This apparatus produces relatively few 'national' films and its formal and aesthetic codes are not yet thoroughly hegemonic.

When the class struggle and the ideological class struggle become more acute, as they did in Chile between 1970 and 1973, such an apparatus is not well equipped to resist ideological movements and radical changes. It may well become incapable of producing or reproducing on behalf of the dominant ideologies (the class struggle is much more intense in other ideological apparatuses such as television, publishing or the press) and this may allow films such as *The Promised Land* to be made.

This may help to explain the conditions under which such a film can be produced, even though we know little about the economic and administrative difficulties Littin may have encountered in his work. But we can still see that the most important thing is to discover the elements of the film, particularly its narrative principles, which allow us to say that it is an integral part of the process of the constitution of an ideology which is dominated in terms of material strength but which intervened in the debate about ideas that animated the political scene in 1972.

Fourth, *The Promised Land* works through the articulation and simultaneous mobilization of different forms of knowledge within the film – discovered through research and links with the peasants before shooting began – and the relation of these to the knowledge which the spectator is assumed to have.

The different forms of knowledge which circulate in the film are attached to particular characters who have a part in the story as well as to the narrator who intervenes in two ways, both as a young person depicted within the narrative and in the form of the hoarse, cracked voice of the same character forty years later (the voice-off). The work of this voice and its relation with the images and with the other sounds with which it is juxtaposed is certainly the crux of the film, since it brings into practical and material contact the period in which the film is set and the period in which it was made, through a recourse to memory, and so makes concrete use of past knowledge for the benefit of the present or future knowledge of the Chilean viewer.

Power and *knowledge* are articulated by means of the relationship between José Duran and 'Double-breasted Suit'. This is a relationship between a leader of the people and a revolutionary intellectual, a relationship between rebellion and knowledge which creates a power struggle. The articulation mirrors that of a geographical space – the Palmilla plain – which becomes the theatre where the performance takes place, a so to speak 'liberated' arena in which a new local power is established. It is because this arena is for a time economically and politically 'liberated' that the ideological theatre of these new social relations, these new relations between knowledge, rebellion and power, becomes visible, overdetermining and active. The ideological and political signifiers expressed by the different carriers of discourse are taken up, mediated and reflected by the discourse of the narrator, but there is no elimination of the characters' different levels of knowledge.

Fifth, democracy in speech and speaking about democracy. From the theatre of these multiple discourses, this polyphonic theatre in which different voices peacefully vie for the precarious power of speech and the position from which to speak, it is essential that a leading point of view should emerge, a voice which becomes privileged in the last instance, which dictates its rhythm, its tone and the moment at which it speaks. The surprising thing is that this is neither the voice of José Duran nor that of 'Double-breasted Suit'. It is not the voice of total knowledge which no one in the film can have, but an average voice belonging to a character who is not central in the film – who is neither the unhappy hero, nor the primitive and stupid character whom History exploits (or film exploits History, as is the case with Lacombe Lucien in the film of that name).

This hesitant and approximate voice is that of experience and wisdom. Its role is to act as a translator — to present other voices, conversations and snatches of song in the film and to make them heard, and, to the extent that different voices say different things, to give them credibility. A typical example is the scene where the red aeroplane of socialism descends from the sky. What is shown in this scene? The peasants of Palmilla holding meetings day and night on the hill with the pilot. That is all. We know nothing of the discussions between José Duran, 'Double-breasted Suit' and the pilot (in the sense that we *hear* nothing and the signifiers escape us just as they have escaped the narrator at that particular moment). But the meaning is there. In the distance we see people asking questions about the Palmilla experience or about Marmaduke Grove's socialism. The content of what is said is not so important. What counts is that the discussions lasted two whole days and nights, that everyone participated, even if not everyone understood everything, that there was an enthusiastic meeting of two revolutionary experiences, both of which, at this particular moment, had to be talked about.

Sixth, what ideological preoccupations does such a narrative economy depend on? Why give the power (the role of *decoder*) to an ordinary person, who in this way recasts the inscription of the other characters and their role in the fiction? Here we need to take account of Littin's work on the relationship between stereotypes and History. He makes an average person talk about a historical process which he does not completely control and which sometimes even mystifies him, and places this person who is transformed by the struggle in contact with the stereotypes and the signifiers that are contained in this struggle, without, however, allowing absolute knowledge to take over the process, to pin it down and codify it. In this way he achieves two things at once. He shows both the objective, historical signifiers, within his *mise en scène*, and at the same time the way they are grasped, understood and appropriated through the narrator by the broad masses. The inscription of History is to some extent a 'dehistoricization', a deconsecration, a process of making it as 'relevant' as possible to concrete conditions and to the life of the subject living in those conditions from day to day. The Chilean viewer in 1972 surely recognized himself in these situations and derived from them a greater commitment to struggle.

To this extent it is surely of no consequence that the narrator does not control History and is not master of the signifiers. As well as learning how to read and how to use a rifle, he also learns to read images; he has the power to show them to the viewer in a meaningful order. Through him the masses learn that before seizing power they must speak about it, animate it, give it life wherever possible. Surely this is a sign that the ideological preparations for seizing power are well under way.

Serge Toubiana

The voice keeps watch

Let us formulate a principle. No political film of revolutionary inspiration can have a really deep and lasting impact on the masses unless the form and content of its fiction are rooted in a cultural space which is both *popular* and *universal*, unless it is a crucible given life by a materialist conception of history which embraces all aspects of life.

In this respect progressive or revolutionary political films can be divided into two categories: those which depend on a very narrow realism that reflects in a univocal and dogmatic way an abstract analysis which transcends the 'form of expression'; and those with a deeper realism that can include fantastic forms and the many representations that make up the 'rich, living language of the masses', films which subvert the language, representations and codes of the dominant classes by means of crude parody. There is a popular culture which is profoundly subversive, which has a history (all the manifestations of which were savagely repressed and stamped on during the classical period and even more thoroughly by modern capitalism), and which is now re-emerging in different forms, including the cinema. This is the ideological space which Mikhail Bakhtin calls 'carnivalesque' and which in the arts is reflected in 'grotesque realism' (Rabelais, Cervantes).[2]

Revolutionary artists today must try to follow the example of this kind of realism; otherwise their efforts will become sterile, frozen into dogma. This is a lesson which is well taken by Dario Fo, for example. One of the most fascinating – and of course the least well understood – aspects of *The Promised Land* is precisely the carnivalesque structure of its fictional narrative.

This structure can be discerned on at least three levels. First in the subject matter, since it concerns the land, the promised land which has been won and lost, the land which is both graveyard and fertile womb. Carnival, of course, celebrates this land in its twin roles as the grave of the old powers and the womb which gives birth to the new. Second in the theme of the 'two virgins' which runs through the film, the virgin who represents the bourgeoisie, the landowners, and the virgin who represents the people, a parodic travesty of the first (who is solemn, official, devout and ethereal) whom she 'pulls down to her level' and carries off to the brothel. Finally in the structure of the narrative which is directed by the voice-off of an old man who is the spokesman of the masses but who is represented as a young man (since the story is narrated thirty or forty years after the events took place).

The voice-off in *The Promised Land* has a complex and various function. Historically, it distances events, so that the process of narrating them invites the spectators to reflect on these events (this is the 'epic' side of the film). Similarly, by means of the slightly mocking distance it maintains with respect to the activities of those in charge ('Double-breasted Suit' and José Duran) it shows the critical point of view of the masses and so reinforces the critical reflection of the viewers. But, in addition, from a broader perspective, it introduces the carnivalesque element in the old giving birth to the new, the older in paradoxical association with the younger. The old man's broken voice describes (in the very corpus of what he says, in what one might call the grain of his voice) the death of old heroes, the failure of old struggles and their rebirth in new forms. This voice finds its echo in the last image of the film, which is slightly parodic, when the old officer holds the sword out to the young peasant (the narrator who is thus both the old man and the young man in a communication between the old and the new), the sword of armed struggle against the oppressor, and José Duran gives him the gun. This is the popular memory from which struggle is reborn.

Bakhtin sees in the Kertch terracotta figurines which represent *pregnant old women* an exemplary instance of the carnivalesque (or grotesque) mind.

> Old women whose hideous age and pregnancy are grotesquely empha-
> sized [. . .] What's more, these pregnant old women are laughing.
> This is a very characteristic and expressive form of the grotesque. It is
> ambivalent: it is pregnant death, death which gives birth. There is
> nothing completed, stable or peaceful in the bodies of these old
> women. The form associates the body which is decomposed and
> deformed by old age with the still embryonic body of new life. Life is
> revealed in its ambivalent and internally contradictory processes.

> (*Rabelais and His World*)

This reminds us of the 'old woman' in the film who 'enjoys' being raped by eight men, one of whom is the narrator, the woman who personifies the women's revolt and who dies with a pitchfork in her hand; she makes the contrast between the ambivalence of death among the people and the terrifying, emaciated figures, the purely negative representations of death among the dominant classes, those phantom death's heads which follow José Duran and his companions on horseback as they flee from Los Huiques.[3]

The death of the people of Palmilla is quite the opposite of tragic, that is to say the individualistic and nostalgic attitude of the dominant classes towards death. The vibrant formal opposition to tragedy and ruin is not comedy (which is no more than its servile bourgeois imitation) but parody in the full meaning of the term, which does not reject death but proclaims its ambiguity as the fall of the old powers and the birth of the new.

Pascal Bonitzer
Translated by Jill Forbes

Notes

1 Marmaduke Grove, commander of the air force, initiated a short-lived coup which led to the proclamation of a socialist republic in Chile. The coup was overthrown by

another military revolt, one of several during the period of unrest after the collapse of the Ibañez government in 1931.

2 Cf. Mikhail Bakhtin, *Rabelais and His World* and *Dostoevsky's Poetics*. (Author's note.)

3 Some critics have been foolish enough to accuse Littin of using 'Hollywood' or 'Western-inspired' forms in his film. The Western is essentially an ultra-individualistic glorification of primitive forms of free enterprise and its spirit of adventure. Its aesthetic is quite the opposite of that of *The Promised Land*. Clearly the odd scene of men on horseback is enough to satisfy the urge for classification behind which there always lurks a lack of thought. (Author's note.)

21

THE FEMININE EYE OF THE TOWN (*EL CHERGUI*)

('L'oeil féminin de la ville (*Chergui*)',
Cahiers du Cinéma 262–3, January 1976)

Abdelwahab Meddeb

Here at last is an Arab film which will have popular appeal without being stripped of its central ideology by means of the kind of critical voluntarism which tends to gloss over the paradoxes of reality in order to recast reality in a predetermined mould. *El Chergui* is the work we have all been waiting for, a work which is important for the way it makes popular action supreme by allowing it to be shown as it is, rather than in the way people choose to fossilize it. The latter takes the form either of epic abstraction or of a predominating view that renders the people's actions void of meaning in order to turn the people into an idea on to which a conventional notion of intervention is foisted. Here the people's ideology is a global order which lends the film a documentary tone that borders on the ethnographic.

What distances Moumen Smihi's film from an exercise in passive observation is the way in which fiction penetrates the complicated networks that make up the city, whose opacity tends to elude the gaze of the protagonists and to take on its own life, reinforcing the narrative discontinuity by adding independent segments that make it even more discontinuous, creating a series of minor key dead ends which temper the final outcome, the death towards which all the dramatic elements have been leading.

El Chergui tells the story of the imminent arrival of a second wife in a family. This is a classic – even commonplace – theme in Arab societies which are still ruled by Muslim law. From the first images of the film Aïcha seems frozen by the mute violence of her refusal to be imprisoned in the role of victim into which the male decision has thrown her, a decision which sees happiness in the rediscovery of sexual excitement given value by an initial transformation of defloration into fable.

Aïcha goes to see a marabout so as to help make the forthcoming event fail. But she does not do so with blind faith. In some part of her she knows that the rituals to which she is about to submit herself do not always work without fail. She know that what is at stake is her body. Conscious of the limits of the knowledge in which she is putting her trust, she throws herself proudly into the struggle, more in order to affirm her refusal – which immediately leads her vertiginously close to death – than to change the mind of a husband who appears to be both determined and inaccessible. A disdainful attitude which she develops in order to make her despair positive.

Though it is not an integral part of the plot, the ground covered by Aïcha is enclosed by female solidarity. Men have no power in it; they are seen as a coveted prey but one that is difficult to trap. This field of struggle – the only one to which a woman has access socially – is of course organized round the complex web of maraboutism. This tactical choice does not so much guarantee a sacred memory as erect a protective wall, creating a refuge which shelters female action by protecting it from a politics based on action which works only if there is a certain right to speak. But here, everything is done wordlessly, in heavy silence. No one speaks in the married quarters. The domestic space only receives the mechanical repetition of a sacred discourse: the mother-in-law endlessly recites prophylactic formulas and phrases of lamentation or consolation; the husband can recite verses from the Koran only in an intimate whisper. The only place where men and women speak to each other is the socially marginal space of the brothel where, as a small Oriental luxury, the prostitute can be listened to by the man who is out of work, and her story, her floating memory, finds a willing ear in the man who wanders across the town looking for a burden to bear. As soon as speech is heard in the centre of the urban space it loses its meaning. If two women meet in the street their endless greetings are mechanically repetitive. Even if a piece of information is imparted, it can reach its destination only through the familiar and necessary veil of many neutral words. And when the words spoken go beyond the function imposed on them by the place where they are spoken, communication breaks down. This is what happens when the young girl interrupts the animated conversation of the cobbler, who just for an instant conjures up the delights of the alcove at the back of his dark and narrow shop.

The way in which words are rationed means that *El Chergui* is difficult to read for anyone who does not understand all the minute detail of the allusions. Every one of these slow, separate steps marks a precise point in the route assiduously taken by female action. But the coherence of the work is provided by the general structure of the movement, which is always downwards. It is no accident that the film begins in a topographically high place, in the mausoleum of Sidi Charf high on a hill above the town, a place which, in the past, was visited only by women who built up their own power thanks to the great magical qualities of the place. This amounted to the female eye of the town which looked down into its lowest part, to the place where the course of Aïcha's struggle was to come to a halt as she let herself be swallowed up in the raging sea, where the jumble of rocks, famous elsewhere under the name of the

Grottoes of Hercules, are called Hjar da-Shaqqar and are associated with a ritual to encourage miraculous fertility because this woman committed suicide there.

However, the heights of the city and the sea are not present just at these moments. But every time they appear they become richer centres of meaning. The mystic seance[1] of the men takes place on a hill behind the town and follows the *agape* which brought them together to eat a magic couscous and which is rapidly related to the sea, that unknown space which they merrily proceed to populate with monsters. Thus both the male sacred practices and the separate female symbolism are made active on the heights. The sea, however, seems as mysterious as a warning of danger, and we see it lapping against two different shores. It beats against the heavily indented rocks when Aïcha brings money and food to the people 'down below' in Sidi Bouqnâdil and which adolescents playing at being non-believers rapidly steal; elsewhere the rage of the sea, which turns into a murmur as it wets the sand, masks the transparent song of the Gnawa, a slave abandoning himself to some providential hand just at the point when the funeral procession conducting the black-shrouded Aïcha to her last resting place goes by. The sand is also the location of another particular scene which lends ambiguity to the homosexual threat that hangs over the street urchin, a scene which begins realistically and quickly turns into a nightmare. These beaches and coastlines constitute a point beyond which it is impossible to sink (represented by the abysses into which Aïcha will fall) and act as a backdrop to a chain of events each more violent than the last (rape, slavery, suicide and what leads up to it).

Caught between these two extremities, stretched out between the heights and the depths, the city itself becomes a subject to be filmed, oscillating between its autonomous motifs and the dramatic necessities of the plot. Adventure films have accustomed us to Tangier as a criminal city used as a backdrop for stories of drug trafficking or spying. Here it is filmed from within, and shots of the architecture establish its component parts: Arab mazes and pompous provincial neo-classical cornices. The economic functions of the town are shown in this hotchpotch, in which different modes of production cohabit, from the early morning labour of the baker to the shepherd who goes by with his flock of goats and who turns into a milkman when required, to the regional grocer – all components of the traditional economic sector of the medina, which are contrasted with the bustle of the city's main market, frequented by foreigners and represented as a place of urban modern/colonial exchange. However, following Aïcha's gaze, we discover two closed spaces in the city: when during a walk she stops close to the prison, a very sinister building, just as three women, visiting relations who have been condemned to death, open their baskets to be searched by the guard in front of the gate at the entrance, and we are offered the image of a repressive power which does not leave Aïcha unmoved since she is a potential victim; and when Aïcha similarly slows down as she walks past a villa on the heights of the city in whose garden there is an evening reception for foreigners, diplomats and very rich inhabitants of this other Tangier, analogous to the 'white' and hermetic Calcutta in *India Song*.

As she wanders, Aïcha is led to discover unfamiliar places and enlarge her experience, and this precedes the process by which she is gradually stripped bare, in which she will be lost in her irretrievable movement towards death. This is a process which serves as a counterpart to the accumulation of magic practices or signs which weigh down on her body and the domestic space. The classic equation between being stripped naked and being put to death is judiciously used here for dramatic effect.[2] Continuing her secretly vindictive walk through the town, completely muffled up in the grey *djellaba*, whose hood covers her hair, she begins by tearing off the *iltam*, the white cloth which has masked her face, leaving only her eyes uncovered. Just at that point she comes across a beggar with wild hair, laughing crazily at the unbearable squeaking noise of the door on which his young benefactress keeps swinging. Why should she replace her veil since male treachery is imperceptibly following her? After the visit to the Sidi Kacem *moussem* where she walks through the camp of musicians and merchants, and where she makes a propitiatory offering of the blood of a black cock, we find her buffeted by the *chergui*, the east wind which always has a strange effect on people and which, whenever it blows, creates havoc in the town and drives its inhabitants mad, as they admit, making them irritable or exhilarated. So there she is without a hood, her hair only half covered by the *iltam* which has been transformed into a scarf, half blown about by the wind, clinging to a stunted eucalyptus tree, sobbing and sniffling, in indication of her uncontrollable breakdown. Half crazy, having lost her way, her body buffeted, her hair blown everywhere, her weary, unresisting steps now take her towards the grotto which is threatened by raging waters. In a strange way her gestures, her white tunic, already suggest a corpse to be washed and ready to be buried. And all it needed was the ambiguity of her losing her footing for her body to be swallowed up by an insatiable sea. She has succeeded in saving her body right to the end and has refused to deliver a corpse to be exhibited for the emotional excitement of a funeral, justifying a desire for expense. Her tomb will contain only a memory which rings hollow in the minds of those who weep, her sisters.

In this struggle for survival which, in accordance with its ultimate requirements, leads to a decision to die, the woman is not, therefore, assimilated to the silence in which the city sleeps peacefully. Thanks to this strictly female network the apparently unchallengeable authority of the man is violently excluded. But the man continues naively to carry the illusion of his imposing status, even though this would mean nothing were it not supported by the patriarchal consensus. In the face of aggression and negligence the woman's struggle is so total that it has to turn into madness or death. She has to go over to the other side.

But the woman's gesture is not simply inscribed in this instance of survival.

Women can take mass action; they can participate in history even with their degree of religious belief and with the limited means at their disposal. After all, it was they who invented the image of the exiled king to be seen on the silver disc of the moon at the time of the greatest resistance against the occupier, whether French or Spanish. And was it not also women who countered the helmets, rifle butts and gunfire with their strident cries and wailing, horrible to the foreign ear which is ignorant of Arab women?

Two worlds, two instances of power, feminine/masculine:[3] the woman makes an autonomous social space fertile even when she appears to be most oppressed, and, though she aims at neither preservation nor compensation, she affirms her identity in the pain or joy of a fertile despair, constantly confronting power with a strategy that pushes against the limits. From this point of view the practice of maraboutism which belongs to the women cannot sustain the positivist criticism which blindly associates maraboutism with obscurantism. In neighbouring Algeria, where the adoption of such a position gives rise to constant criticism[4] and maraboutism is driven out, it becomes a nocturnal practice and its centre of power is displaced, but it does not disappear so easily (especially in rural areas). Not that one should underwrite the cult of the saints in this form, nor join in any nostalgia for such practices. But we should be able to safeguard this space in which the female gesture has been developed – as proof of the hierological experience which allows the sacred to be dissociated from the religious.

Is it possible for us to retain this archaic practice, at the same time as stripping it of the fiction with which it is surrounded? First, it should be said that the theological position has always – in Sunni (orthodox) Islam – rejected maraboutism as a pantheistic and uncivilized relic which violates by its tears, its dancing and its songs the reasoned wisdom that produces legal thinking as a weapon in the hands of the merchant aristocracy which dominated urban society. Curiously, however, contemporary Arab critics of such popular practices are at one with the great theological tradition of the Muslim world, though they perceive this tradition through the veil of a latter-day colonialism and by participating in a universal reductiveness which is a limitation of a certain kind of left-wing thinking that airily covers up all questions relating to religion.

For in the end, it is in this place, and in no other, that the unchanging specificity of our people is to be found, our people who have been able to continue with their vernacular practices. Of course, the recuperation that we are recommending is not immune from the risk of barbaric tendencies. We must become orphans in this specific area, through the use of a knowledge destructive of illusions and regressions. We must lead our way of life towards corporeal practices which can determine their own ends without subscribing to the ideology of suicide: the flames of knowledge consume, and their light blinds, but the sands of barbarity swallow up everything.[5]

In two scenes, the epilogue of *El Chergui* places the historic destiny of this reactivation within a specific evolution:

- It is midday. The wailing of the sirens hangs heavily in the air; the dockers and the workers are coming out of the yards. The eye sees workers' bodies walking, filing past in a predetermined sculpted mass. They resemble in every way those who preceded them on the screen. They belong to the people. However, they signal also that they will certainly take part in the event which will transform reality; these men will be able to change their knowledge and perish in jubilation and triumph as a people ready to sacrifice their illusions and to continue to profit from old forms of pleasure.

- To end with, there is the school (where among the pupils we see Aïcha's child[6]), this other institution which acts on reality by producing people who are destined to suffer the crisis of heterogeneity produced by the confrontation between their daily lives and the assimilation of an alien knowledge. A crisis whose artificial repression or resolution will be the job of the watchdogs who will denounce barbarism and condemn scandalous popular practices in the name of a modernity capable of reconciling these things by turning away from egalitarian necessity towards a deadly uniformity.

The infrastructure of what is at stake here makes the entry of these various forces into history a matter of vital significance. Even today (*El Chergui* ends in 1956), this has not ceased to exacerbate the situation in which a besieged Arab identity finds itself.

Translated by Jill Forbes

Notes

1 This is the *dhikr*, a rhythmic chant consisting of the repetition of the names of Allah so as to achieve the annihilation of the self and experience ecstasy as the faithful follower and lover of God. (Author's note.) An *agape* is a 'love feast', or reunion of friends.
2 Aïcha's silence, right from the beginning of the film, already prefigures her being stripped naked. The lack of speech implies the lack of clothes, a refusal to seduce, a decision not to be reconciled. Moreover, the wise *dogon* Ogotemmêli reveals this to the person who transcribes his thoughts, Marcel Griaule: 'To be naked is to be without speech', *Dieu d'eau* (1966), p. 77. (Author's note.)
    Marcel Griaule (1898–1965) was an ethnographer who worked in Africa from 1928 to 1956. His *Dieu d'eau* (1948; translated as *Conversations with Ogotemmêli*, London, London University Press, 1965), drawing on his extensive conversations with a Dogon elder, was a landmark in ethnographic literature.
3 This is a separation which disguises a form of castration. Is it nothing except a sign of modesty which graces bodies that, as a result, are well developed and beautiful but do not burn like wildfire in the desperate search for pleasure to beguile them? Here everything is sexual but is never revealed in the sexual act. Not that a fig leaf has to be worn to exaggerate the effect by paraleipsis. The absence of cries, the contained ferocity, the half colours, the slowness, the repetitious montage, the strangled energy, the guards which are never lowered, are not so many signs of repression.

They are simply a form of melancholy which knows that a vagina can steal and a phallus charm. But one can be very close and still fail to get what one wants. (Author's note.)

4 'The factory sweeps away the marabout', as Kateb Yacine would say, somewhat naively. (Author's note.)

5 See Nietzsche, *Dawn of Day*, Fragment 429. (Author's note.)

6 A boy who enters the world of adults only through his mother. In Arab circles childhood is socially spent among women. See *La Sexualité en Islam* (1975) by Abdelwahab Bouhdiba, a book which, despite its university-style vulgarity, contains illuminating details about sexual representation in certain Arab milieux. (Author's note.)

22

BLOOD INTO SIGN

('Le sang changé en signe', *Cahiers du Cinéma* 256,
February–March 1975)

Jean Narboni

What purpose does a massacre serve? How can it be made *useful* to those who experienced it, directly or indirectly, and to their successors? *The Massacre of Kafr Kassem* does not fight shy of such iconoclastic questions. Militant thinking of whatever kind – specialist, non-specialist, reverent or critical – generally avoids them altogether. It's a big mistake, according to some, to recall the failures of the people, the defeats of the working class, it's discouraging, depressing, doesn't open up 'perspectives' – unless of course it allows the experts, blind to their own limitations, to pontificate on how similar disasters can be avoided in the future. Such and such a film, *The Courage of the People*[1] for instance, is dangerous, positively harmful, because it doesn't 'arm' people against a possible repetition of what happened in the past: thus the omniscient Parisian political avant-garde. Elsewhere, on the other hand, people are content with simple reconstruction, the respectful exchange of memories, the roll call of the martyrs: it is enough for the violent glow of the catastrophe to be repeated and periodically rekindled in people's memories for their anger to explode and for their longing to take up the struggle to be translated into action. But there are commemorations and funeral chants which kill just as surely as a real massacre, which kill for a second time, taking up where the massacre left off. The whole empty business of canonization – and you cannot get away from it by adding the obligatory magic formulae (military defeats will 'inevitably be transformed into political victories'), by ritual exorcism, or apologetic dogma: 'losing a battle doesn't mean losing a war'; 'the working class will win through, despite all the obstacles . . .'; 'the people will surely be victorious in the long run, despite all the difficulties . . .'

On the one hand, then, denials and censorship; on the other, the belief that one thing will inevitably be transformed into its opposite, that something bad will become something good . . . some day. An opposition that is complicit with silence or an apology for revelation: either you musn't remember anything, you mustn't say anything about those past events: or else it is enough simply to recount them. The difficulty begins when you begin to realize that the forces of oppression do not always disguise their exactions, even if they usually do. They may even brag about them and put them on display, and they too may reflect on how such an 'open' approach can help them to maintain their dominance. Public executions, the exhibiting of tortured bodies in public squares, villagers forced to file past the bodies of murdered 'terrorists' to create more terror, to make people even more terrified by tales of the massacre and the spectacle of it that is offered than by the massacre itself. After the slaughter of Deir Yassin in April 1948, photographs of dead Arabs are exhibited and leaflets dropped on the villages. 'If you don't leave, this is what will happen to you . . .'[2] The survivors, the wounded, are paraded in the other villages to intimidate people and in a way, here also, to refresh their memories, to keep the memory of the atrocity alive.

And so we find ourselves facing a different question: we cannot merely repeat, putting our trust in the intrinsic power of repetition, nor is it our task merely to inform, although of course this is important; it is rather to understand the process whereby repetition becomes a powerful force, to acknowledge that this occurs only when *something new is produced* and not when the same things are endlessly repeated. A murder scene replayed *ad infinitum* can only produce a determination to fight, a positive and active anger, if people are willing always to reflect on the circumstances in which it is inscribed, and the power relations that obtain, if the event is reinvented bit by bit in the retelling, so that it cannot be appropriated by the opposition. Failing this, all kinds of nasty surprises are possible: in 1940, the Nazis filmed the Warsaw ghetto to demonstrate beyond all doubt the subhuman status of the Jews; a few years later, these same films are used as damning evidence against the torturers . . . Nico Naldini, in *Fascista*, faithfully recreates propaganda documents from the Mussolini era, imagining, irresponsibly, that the masses who fell under their spell couldn't possibly exist today, because all he is doing is to hold up a mirror to the past.

It follows paradoxically that what is new is faithful to the past, and what merely repeats the past betrays it. What elements have to intervene to transform the terror caused by the spectacle of death into revolutionary violence? At what precise moment and why does a crime intended to intimidate and dissuade alter its meaning and encourage people to fight?[3] A problem which is not simply that of understanding things better, but of translating theory into practice, knowledge into force. 'The important thing is not what someone is convinced of but, rather, what his convictions lead him to become' (Lichtenberg).

By the time that Borhan Alaouie and his crew are making *Kafr Kassem* in 1973, what is left of the massacre of 1956? How could it be taken into account and made useful to the Arab people – and first of all the Palestinian people – in their struggle against oppression? What is the nature of this event defined as a massacre, registered as a trauma in the collective memory of the Arab people, condensed in the muffled double explosion of a name – Kafr Kassem – a name that has transformed itself into legend, poetry or myth? How have the layers of narrative that have accumulated over the years, the memory traces, the innumerable accounts of the massacre ended up – by the very fact of describing it, replaying it and repeating it – becoming a part of it? A layering and an intertangling of words and facts, from which the first level, the founding one, stands out nevertheless.

On 29 October 1956, on the eve of the invasion of Egypt by Israel, France and Great Britain, the Israeli authorities, anxious to preserve absolute calm on the Jordanian frontier, decide to establish a curfew in certain Arab villages in the area. Frontier guards are ordered to do whatever is necessary to ensure that it is strictly observed. At 4.30 p.m., half an hour before the curfew comes into effect, a frontier guard informs the mayor of Kafr Kassem of this decision. The mayor makes the point that many villagers, some of whom work a long way away, will not have returned and that there will be no chance of warning them. He is given to understand that they will be allowed to make their way home. From five o'clock onwards, in the space of a few hours, forty-nine men, women and children are systematically shot down, in cold blood.

In the interests of producing an accurate account of the slaughter, Borhan Alaouie and his crew based their work on articles published in the Israeli press, and above all on the record of the court case which the government was unable to avoid – despite strenuous attempts to hush up the episode or play down its importance – when those responsible were brought to trial. The sentences were light, even by the standards of the Israeli legal system, and were subsequently reduced several times. The most senior figure in the chain of responsibility was tried separately and found guilty of a simple 'technical error'. He was reprimanded and sentenced to the symbolic punishment of having to pay the sum of one Israeli piastre.

The space occupied by this event in the popular memory of the Arab people is immense. From 1956, the Kafr Kassem slaughter has been commemorated annually in meetings, gatherings and demonstrations more often than not suppressed by the authorities. It is here, where the trauma is repeated and *reactivated* (made active again), that legend is not content to celebrate the event but becomes a part of it, transforming it in the process. How can you distinguish between what really happened on each of these occasions and what gets passed on by word of mouth? In any case, everyone in Galilee and the so-called Triangle area *remembers* the ninth anniversary of Kafr Kassem in 1965 when the police stopped the demonstrators as they arrived and the Palestinian poet Samih Al Qassim recited his poem which was then taken up, chanted, and repeated by the crowds of villagers held back behind a barricade of barbed wire . . . In militant Palestinian poetry, Kafr Kassem is preserved and transformed in narratives which blow it to pieces, turn it upside down, twist it around: here it becomes an arm which stretches out and produces light, elsewhere it takes the form of fifty bleeding stumps. Mahmoud Darwish, another Palestinian poet, writes: 'Teach our sombre history/To your children/So that our blood/Remains on the criminals' flag/As a sign of the catastrophe.'

'It was not our aim to create a bloody spectacle, of the sort favoured by bourgeois artists, our aim was to make this massacre meaningful', wrote Borhan Alaouie in the last issue.[4] The question he asked, then, was this: *how can blood be transformed into a sign, thereby acquiring force?* But to begin with, what is it a sign of? And for the others, for the enemy, what was Kafr Kassem a sign of before it came to mean blood?

To answer that, he had to go back to the idea of both the village and the massacre as a crossroads, a junction or point of intersection. He had to disrupt certain chronological sequences and establish other temporal connections: reorganize the facts and the places along different lines. Time, first of all: the film opens on 23 July 1956, the date when Nasser announced his decision to nationalize the Suez canal, a decision which led directly to the tripartite invasion of Egypt, on the very day after the massacre. Then space: the village of Kafr Kassem, officially included within the borders of the Zionist entity, and its Arab inhabitants, 'Israeli citizens', had to be given back their Palestinian identity, as well as their broader identity as a specific component of the Arab world. The bloodshed too had to be presented as having a logical necessity, as being simply one moment – explosive, certainly, but inevitable, not extraordinary – in the experience of death practised in other forms and on a daily basis by an oppressive regime. It was important that the massacre should not be perceived, as many people wanted it to be perceived at the time, as a 'regrettable blunder', an 'unfortunate accident' or a 'technical error'. It had to be *out of the ordinary* in the double sense of emerging out of and going beyond the ordinary. But this is doubly difficult for a film-maker for whom it isn't easy to inscribe logical necessity *and* logical rupture, use *and* abuse, the exception that proves the rule.

It was by working as closely as possible on the two-way relation between the particular and the general, by emphasizing the remarkable character – both unique and exemplary – of daily life in the village of Kafr Kassem that Borhan Alaouie was able to avoid the trap of making this either a marginal case of no general interest or a tedious small-scale illustration. It was by refocusing the narrative as closely as possible on the villagers themselves, by going into details, by investigating every peculiarity, and only in this way – by letting the absolute emerge from the relative minutely examined – that he was able to account for the experience of a dispersed but single and united people. It was by keeping the camera firmly within the village boundaries that he was able to show how this small place opened on to everything else, how in a thousand ways it was linked to the rest of the Arab nation. And as for the problem of Palestinians living outside Palestine, this was compounded in the case of

Palestinians living within the Zionist entity and regarding themselves, in Mahmoud Darwish's words, as 'Palestinian refugees in Palestine'. Exiles in their own homeland. *Kafr Kassem* raises an important, urgent and disturbing question: that of the national identity of those regarded by Zionist propaganda as Israeli citizens like any other, separated from the rest only by a few 'cultural inequalities' or inconvenient security measures. A confusion which has long troubled both these 'citizens' and Palestinians experiencing the situation 'from without'. What if they were really assimilated, integrated, lost their Arab identity? A concern to which the poet Emile Habibi attests, from within: 'I once thought . . . that they had cut us off from their tree of life . . .' That was until militant Palestinian poetry, the people's defence against loss of identity and cultural amnesia, produced from 'within', repressed by the Israeli authorities, ignored and then censored by the Arab regimes, was smuggled into the entire region after the Six Day War of June 1967, reached the broad mass of Palestinian and Arab workers and fired them with enthusiasm, was recognized and accepted by them as a weapon and an emblem, and finally assumed its rightful place among resistance texts. 'I once thought that they had cut us off from their tree of life . . .' But, adds Emile Habibi: 'Now we are a branch that is alive and in blossom.'

The film shows in a concrete way this belonging to the same 'tree of life'. Of political life in the first instance: coinciding with the violent response to the (anti-imperialist) nationalization of the Suez canal, the massacre – a qualitative leap in the daily experience of death – made so-called 'Israeli citizens' aware, bloodily, of their Arab identity. Another division, another split in the artificial unity, can be seen in the fact that people are beginning to be critical of the strategy of the Communist parties in the Middle East. They are shedding illusions and preparing to struggle for national liberation: in the scene that shows the Communist cell in the village, scepticism is expressed about Arab and Israeli workers burying their differences and fighting side by side against their oppressors. People are beginning to realize that an oppressed people *does not have to wait* for unity with the proletariat of the colonial power before the struggle can begin, that the oppression and exploitation which affect the two groups of workers are qualitatively different, that the revolt of the dominated people must begin independently and without delay, and that when Jewish workers make up their minds, they will do so *in relation to this struggle*. The choice is between a logical strategy for national liberation and the pious invocation of a socialist Middle East, achieved immediately, here and now, without a struggle and without the complication of transitional phases.[5]

Debates, polemics, which the film includes in a living, concrete way, not by working around well-established political positions but by reflecting daily events in the lives of the villagers.

But also, on a deeper level and cutting across these directly political concerns, the whole network of links, affinities, reciprocations which expose the sham of artificially created territorial entities and make the village part of the

Arab world: the daily departures and homecomings of the workers which give the narrative a rhythm, this displacement of human goods which duplicates, in miniature and in a single location, the rootlessness and dispersion experienced outside, on a much larger scale, by a whole people. Borders which have to be crossed *inside* a country, criss-crossing/cross-checking, internal passes.

And even more subtly, running parallel with this displacement of humanity: the dispersion, explosion, migration of voices coming from everywhere and proliferating everywhere. Arab radio, precious voices from 'down there', listened to clandestinely, announcing that the canal is 'ours'. The radio, almost a shrine, which brings all the villagers together in the café. A voice that helps them make up their minds: the enthusiastic supporters of Nasser ('He will be our liberator'), the cautious Communists and those in the 'middle', worried about the consequences ('This won't be good for us'). A voice that is first heard, then quite literally filmed, one that becomes *visible*, determining successive shots, slipping into houses whose occupants are anxiously waiting, resonating in the deserted village square, enveloping everything. Solidarity with the people 'down there': 'Cairo must be going wild with joy tonight!' But also voices of despair, unleashed in all directions: the arrival in the village of Radio Israel, the pathetic sight of people taking their turn at the microphone to say a word to their lost friends and relatives, voices punctuated by the ritual and obligatory 'We are well.' 'I heard on the radio/The message of the exiles . . . to the exiles/They all said: we are well/No one is sad/How is my father?' (M. Darwish, *Lettre d'exil*).[6]

The film-maker faced another problem: with the massacre known about in advance, how could he avoid it hanging over the entire film like a threat, making it into a metaphysical discourse about imminent death and waiting for death? How could he avoid death appearing as an abstract, transcendent force? A certain idealism has, after all, regarded the cinema as a privileged vehicle for its phantasies: from Cocteau, for whom the cinema was the only art capable of showing 'death at work', to Bergman, whose characters are all fatally doomed. Borhan Alaouie was very aware of the risk of making his characters appear as being under sentence of death, as destined to die; he knew that playing down the element of suspense was not enough to disguise the aura of death. This brings us back to the question raised earlier: given that the film is a retelling of an event which actually took place, and a well-known one about which so much has been said, sung and written, how is it possible, by repeating it, to produce something new, and what sort of novelty might this involve? The reply that is offered is this: 'Precisely because we know that they are going to die, we had to be interested in their lives.' There is something in this that touches the depths of the Palestinian people's relation to death, a constant, obsessive theme, so poorly understood in the West, so often caricatured (suicide bombings, people sacrificed in the cause, people to whom death doesn't matter). On the contrary, it does matter, and it matters a great deal: when

264

people suffer the most basic kind of loss of self, when they are robbed not only of their possessions but of themselves, when day after day their identity is denied, *life itself is counted in hours of death.*[7] The precariousness of people's existence, lives lived moment by moment, death ever present for everyone – all this means that life and death co-exist easily, are in constant touch with each other. And life is built on this edifice of familiarity with death. This contradiction, this duality (close in a way – though there are differences – to the carnivalesque culture recently described by Bonitzer[8]) can be found in all Palestinian poetry. It has little to do (except occasionally in a loose sense) with the religious and metaphysical vision of death and resurrection, demonstrating rather the logical simultaneity of life and death, the holding together of the two contradictory terms, the tension involved in this union that is not a synthesis. A dialectic admirably expressed in the Arab proverb (included in the film): 'You can't clap with one hand.' A proverb where the coming together (of the two hands) does not claim to *overcome* the division, to make the two into one, but amounts to a dual, moving, syncopated unity. 'Birth and death are twin gods in my country where everything is deified', writes Darwish. Life and death are paired, inseparable; they are experienced together in their contradiction.[9] The greatest quality of a film like *Kafr Kassem* seems to me to be that it does not contaminate the lives of the villagers of Kafr Kassem with the spectre of death, but shows, against a background of routine violence, the richness and prodigality of the lives they manage to lead. A wrenched out existence that still bursts with life, a discreet distance (or irony) in relation to misfortune, concern for others, secret joys, a subtle reticence. You really feel that no force, however strong, will withstand this oblique mockery, this popular wisdom expressed in proverbs, sayings, jokes and stories which miss not a thing: neither the inflexibility of the oppressors, nor the cowardice of the intermediaries, nor the endlessly repetitive liturgy of those resigned to the situation, whose vocabulary, whose mumblings, whose pathetic chants are actually borrowed only to be caricatured and used against them. What then takes shape and gathers strength, in a struggle that is continuous, is a fraternity all the more poignant for the poverty, all the more alive for focusing not just on possessions but on the human being, all the more dangerous for the fact that whoever becomes aware of the situation knows that he or she belongs with the poor, which is to say the majority.

'So that our *blood* remains . . . as the *sign* of the catastrophe'. When the catastrophe finally happens, should the artist be concerned with the *sign* or the *blood*? A false alternative, and a very old one, which fuels the thinnest of debates. The would-be Brechtians ('Distance, detachment, a calculated approach – let's not get carried away!') versus the proponents of raw emotion ('Let it be spectacular, moving, gripping!'). In the case of a massacre carried out in cold blood, the 'cool' approach is generally considered to be the more appropriate. 'Detachment', for instance, or 'the clinical analysis of relentless oppression' are found to be in good taste, while critics indulgent of their own interpretative abilities will adore the film's 'sense of propriety' and 'lack of indulgence'. Here again the problem has to be redefined: every important film, when faced with this choice, has conveyed bloodshed *and* meaning, or, rather, bloodshed transformed into sign, *transforming* into sign, the process whereby meaning *rises out of* a writing traced in blood. This was a problem that constantly haunted Eisenstein, for example: how was it possible, without missing the moment of revolutionary lucidity, of conscious adhesion to progressive values, to make the spectator 'lose himself' in the spectacle, how could you make him 'leap up from his seat', how could you lead him – yes – to 'ecstasy'? Ecstasy, *ek-stasis*, means literally to 'come out of one's normal state' or to 'come out of oneself'. What did it mean, what was involved in this idea? Was it a case of producing dubious outpourings of emotion, of bringing about a kind of emotional purge in the spectator? Not at all; it was a case, rather, of maintaining the internal tension between blood and sign, of producing a dynamism whereby each would be implied and negated by the other, of setting in motion *both* the emotional charge *and* the signifying mechanism. All Eisenstein's research (on pre-logical thought in particular) was concerned with describing this double mechanism, and then producing it in the spectator: discharge, shock, emotional extremes experienced over and over again in the terrible injuries inflicted on the bodies, and simultaneously the production of ideas, arguments, concepts. Political meaning and physical action brought into play one after the other and at the same time, cancelled out then re-established continuously.

It may seem odd to be evoking Eisenstein in connection with a film like *Kafr Kassem*: there's a big difference between Eisenstein's baroque presentation of the massacred people as a single dismembered body (*Strike, Battleship Potemkin*) and the dry enumeration of victims produced by Borhan Alaouie. But it seems to me that they are both attempting, in very different ways, to maintain this tension between mind and body, meaning and massacre. *Kafr Kassem* rejects the cold, clinical approach with its detached indifference to horror. Running through and beyond the conscious revolt, it is impossible not to be aware, in an almost physical way, of a kind of line or tightrope which the film-maker must walk, in space and time: after the initial scattering and splintering of voices and bodies, the slow refocusing on the slaughter which seems to go on for ever, on the strip of road where the workers gradually appear in groups, as daylight fades and the shots become darker. Out of the death coldly and methodically delivered by the soldiers there emerges neither the feeling of bodily disintegration, as in Eisenstein, nor the indifference of scientific observation, but a kind of heavy fullness that the body as well as the mind must suffer, that the body and the mind have to face: a progressive numbing, an aching, *death in slow motion*, the surfacing of a deeply buried violence and grief, its now persistent *throbbing*. Images a touch remote and strangely calm, that hardly live up to their legend but build on it instead, setting off howls of protest. While the names of the forty-nine dead spell out the unique name – a name made flesh, already meaningful, massacre and meaning in perpetual interaction – that Kafr Kassem has become in people's memories and in their struggle.

Translated by Annwyl Williams

Notes

1 *El coraje del pueblo*, directed by Jorge Sanjines, a 1971 Bolivian film about the massacre of a tin-mining community by the army in 1967. Alternative English title: *The Night of San Juan*.

2 Deir Yassin, a Palestinian village, scene of a massacre by Jewish Irgun terrorists shortly before the British mandate in Palestine ended and the state of Israel was proclaimed.

3 A question illustrated in popular history by the shining example of the Paris Commune, and one addressed by Marx and Lenin: *at a certain point* it is better, for the sake of the example it sets, to be crushed in the struggle than to give up without a fight. *At a certain point*: it all hangs on that . . . It is not surprising to find that there is collusion here also between the Party dogmatists ('If only they had understood that they had to construct a Party of the proletariat') and the macabre connoisseurs of failed revolutions ('They are exemplary for having *refused to seize power* and preferred celebration to unprovoked violence'). (Author's note.)

4 In an interview with Jean Narboni and Dominique Villain, *Cahiers* 254–5.

5 The history of the betrayals and capitulations plotted – following Lenin – in the name of 'internationalism' remains to be written. Didn't Guy Mollet use internationalist 'Marxist' arguments to justify the total engagement of the French army in the Algerian war, against the nationalism of the FLN? And while we're on the topic, wasn't it in close collaboration with his socialist colleague Golda Meir that he perpetrated the Suez intervention, against the 'chauvinism' of Nasser. (Author's note.)

6 Against the silenced voices of the people we can also set all the *written* documents of local government and imperialism: the poor peasant, Abou Morai, is forbidden to work his plot of land for reasons of military security, and a few months later has it taken away from him 'for having let it lie fallow'. Documents from those in authority which have to be translated by the local letter-writer or teacher: 'Under the Turkish occupation we had to learn Turkish, under the British mandate it was English, and now it is Hebrew.' Later the body of this same Abou Morai can be identified from his shorts, made out of a sack stamped with the identification mark of imported American goods . . . (Author's note.)

7 In *Appel de la tombe*, devoted to the 'charnel house of Kafr Kassem', Darwish writes: 'Our age is counted in years of death.' (Author's note.)

8 See Ch. 20 in this volume, p. 249.

9 If this theme of life and death lived together is, as we have said, quite the opposite of life after death, it is also very different from the figure of the *martyr* (which features prominently in the Palestinian ideology of resistance): a life given as a ransom to death in the general movement of national rebirth, a death that is no longer individual but emblematic, in which the individual is abolished as such in the impersonality and collectivity of the revolutionary movement. (Author's note.)

23

XALA

(*Cahiers du Cinéma* 266–7, May 1976)

Danièle Dubroux

The 'xala' is something you catch, also something like a foreign body that has attached itself to your own body. Some people – women, marabouts, beggar-magicians – have the power of making it stick to you or releasing you from it.

In French, this is called impotence, in other words a mask that covers two areas – sexual and psychic. We have known since the beginning of the century that these two areas overlap more than used to be thought, but there are various ways of saying this to people, there is even a certain way of 'telling' it, for example by taking literally (to the letter) the foreign body that has just grafted itself on and is simply the foreign body that someone has stuck on to his body (a supplementary John Smith), something like 'You're neither fur nor feather', something like a disguise, a denaturing (or denaturalizing).

But *Xala* is also a title, hanging there like a theatre illumination,[1] a light on a double stage, a double body, a light that reveals as it casts its full flood on a recent fixed image: a denuding.

It is thus the first stage on which the 'tale' will be enacted. Like every marvellous tale, it opens in a setting of radiant, unrestrained happiness which, however, cannot last (the glamorous wedding of Hadji Abdou Kader Bèye). The happiness is always going to be lost and the telling of a tale is no more than the proofs of a quest.

Marvellous, we might say, in that the magic (a character endowed with supernatural powers, taking away/getting back a magic object) causes no surprise for either characters or audience; it is part of the 'natural' (in the telling of the tale), with the distinction that this 'natural' is in reality outside of the book.[2] We have to consider magic as being part of ordinary, everyday life in African society (as opposed to being extraordinary, paranormal here), so that the marvellous, as a formal genre, sticks closely to actual experience without the mediation (necessary for us, however) of a prior reading of the story book.

On the other stage there unfolds what one might call a bourgeois drama: the power and fall of an African businessman after the failure of his third marriage (because unconsummated). It is here that we see presented (theatrically staged) the new Senegalese bourgeoisie, flashily and expensively decked out (the largess they dispense to the beggars at the gates of the villa) in the luxurious trappings which the bourgeoisie likes to show off.

Whereas the story is played on two notes (the beggar's flute), the drama itself is played with the dissonance of a fanfare, the swagger of the brass; it's the heavy machinery (the wedding party), in fact it's all the dissonance of a threefold representation, a harmonic and visual disjointedness that is unnerving. The actors chosen by Ousmane Sembene play the part of the Senegalese new bourgeoisie, which in the real world itself mimics the representation (in the cinema, in the theatre, or elsewhere) it is given of the Western bourgeoisie. It is a third generation mime play, just as the last prints made of a film, destined for suburban cinemas,[3] take on extravagant colours disconnected from reality (denatured).

On this point, some critics have seen Ousmane Sembene's film as a vulgar, simplistic portrait. The caricature is indeed an exaggeration of particular features, but it is productive of meaning, it signifies at the point where there is only an image, it shows up the specular relation to the 'other' (to the foreign body, for example), it registers its dangers; the exaggeration should be heightened even when 'reality itself is caricature' (Sembene).

Within these two spaces of the fiction we witness the disappearance/reappearance, appearance/disappearance of a magic object, through the 'potency' which it 'instils' in whoever is carrying it; it's a matter of virility and the attaché-case. In both cases, others have the power to give or to take away ('what a hand has taken away it can return'): the one, a good object, is a requisite of unselfconsciousness (it is in the hands of the people, the beggar-magician); the other, a bad object, is artificial, imported by the foreign body (the representatives of colonial France handing out attaché-cases).

This fetish object – the attaché-case – as its name implies, has the power of 'attaching' (making attachments with France, for example) whoever is carrying it, but it also identifies him, denotes him as a power: monetary (it has the form and content of French African francs), technical (designed to hold documents of the huge investment project type). It establishes a sign value in this sudden proliferation of signs by which the new Senegalese bourgeoisie is designated. Here we see the camera's authority, to dwell on these signs, to fix them for an instant (as a photographic print) in their manipulatory circularity: a lounge suit, a chauffeur, sunglasses, an air conditioner, Evian water, Coca-Cola, champagne, a white bride and groom on a wedding cake. Also posters: Cabral in Rama's room, the third wife in a photograph, television set style.[4] Overcoding: the still photograph in the rapid stream of cinema's moving image; and it is the film-maker who is characterized, authenticated (a poster of Sembene's *La Noire de* in Rama's room) by this forest of signs, since there is constant signifying in a feudal society and these are the same rigorous codes of the working of the sign ('at the point where the assigning is complete, confined, it refers to a status, a caste') that are reinvested in neo-colonial society.

Small wonder that the attaché-case is here the sign of belonging to the power caste.

So the film-maker's role will be this: to show his people the theatre of counterfeit, the game of mimicry which surrounds them without their realizing it, since for them these signs still have an absolutely clear meaning – the rags on the beggars (the caste of the untouchables), the *djellaba*, the dialect spoken by the man from the village etc.

The moral – and there is one in this story, at the point where the two stages converge – is that the object cannot be replaced by the sign (power, virility, cannot be replaced by the sign of power: the attaché-case). And the latter has to be got rid of in order to rediscover the former by way of the law of the people: the final scene.

Translated by David Wilson

Notes

1 Ousmane Sembene's didactic aim – 'to enlighten the masses' – is illustrated in serial metaphors of sham/exposure: masquerades of dress, false cheques, false luxury, false identity, exposed – that is, brought out (to light) – little by little until the final, total exposure of the body, the lifting of the mask of theatre, the trappings of the stage. (Author's note.)

2 Sembene states in an interview: 'For me, the cinema begins with literature, but when I write I want the end result to be cinematic. I try to make the words become images and the images become words so that a film can be read and a book can be seen.' (Author's note.)

3 Samir Amin talks of the 'suburban bourgeoisie' to describe the new bourgeoisies of the Third World. (Author's note.)

4 'A television set can also be beautiful.' (Author's note.) Amilcar Cabral, independence movement leader and revolutionary theoretician in Lusophone Africa.

Part V

REVIEWS

24

ON *AVANTI*

('Sur *Avanti*', *Cahiers du Cinéma* 248, September
1973–January 1974)

Pascal Kané

How, today, can one not talk about politics? What subjects are grandiose enough to dispense with politics (wish to place themselves beyond it)? The most recent of these screen subjects, sex, is, as we know, having a difficult time of it. New sexual practices are also socialized, rendered ideological; and even from this perspective a large number of Reichian themes linking repressed sexuality to capitalism have been taken up by the bourgeoisie which has, after its own fashion, made progress, as everyone can confirm.

In truth, there is little left but that last great metaphysical theme, perhaps the last card that the bourgeoisie can play to turn the spectator away from History – and that is death. Several films of the moment serve to illustrate this thematic slippage which invests death with an overvalued, over-mystified role. For example, Preminger's *Such Good Friends* (1971), in the coffee house conversation style ('Well, here we are, with this going on, he's in a coma, and we're having mean little private quarrels');[1] or, more ambitiously, *Cries and Whispers*. But even in Bergman's film we are not entirely free of a mystificatory vision of death. Of course, sooner or later everyone must die. But there are various ways of reflecting this: death can serve to address social injustice or, conversely, can be addressed as a social ritual.[2] You can stress either the passing away (in cinematic terms, the offscreen space) or what remains (the corpse). The first theme is idealist, metaphysical; is the second therefore materialist? Certainly the corpse makes death material and so in a sense it is its dedramatization, its despiritualization, in that it invests death with its specific social existence. But is it enough simply to return to the material – in this case, the corpse – in order to be materialist?

Let's not confuse things; the body and the corpse are supports like any other that can be valorized for a variety of reasons (fetishistic included) just as idealist (as with film-makers like Bertolucci, Ferreri or Warhol, who focus on the concrete metamorphosis of the body). Equally, in *Cries and Whispers* there is a corpse between the two sisters, but it is there in order to add greater weight to their internal agonies and not to annul the metaphysical theme. In this it is the opposite of *Avanti*. Wilder's film centres on the material presence of the corpse and on the refusal to consider it as not having always been a corpse, a useless, impractical and unproductive body, involving an endless struggle to dispose of it. In Bergman's film the corpse is caught in a movement that goes from agony to burial – two means of sublimating it, of making it say something else. The corpse in Wilder's film, which picks up a little from where Bergman's leaves off, goes from its identification in the morgue to its registration for burial. Whilst its metaphysical sense produces the corpse with a view to death (the former being the figure bought down by the latter), in *Avanti* one thinks of death only with a view to the corpse that it leaves behind: the positive aspect of the film being that it does not evade any of the socialized forms of death (starting with the fact that a corpse is something entirely ruled by the law, and that it does not have the same value for those who bury it). The corpse in question, that of the president of an American company who has led a double life, which his son has come to look for in Ischia, takes on, as a piece of merchandise, a triple exchange value: economic, political and ideological.

The economic value, first. The body of a rich American in a poor country is worth money – hence the episode of its kidnapping by the Trotta brothers (an echo here of other practices now obviously associated with the Third World, but ones that are directed towards the same goal – taking back from the colonizers a part of what they have acquired).

The political value: the need to bring the corpse back and the recourse – in order to obtain both coffin and permits – to multiple backhanders, schemes and all manner of corrupt practices, culminating in the intervention of the State Department. So the revelation of the United States' real interference in a country of which it has economic control and where is reproduced a similar institutional corruption (southern Italy, a land of emigrants, living principally off tourism, to a degree stands metonymically for the Third World).

The ideological value: this resides in the manner in which the corpse is made to signify and in the re-use, renaming and manipulation it is subject to. Two strategies, two discourses confront one another: those of Ambruster and his paean to great ancestors, men of morality, workers and capitalists; and that of the hotel manager, Carlucci, more subtly mystificatory and nationalistic, who aims to conceal the truth for his own benefit (that of the national bourgeoisie).

This is the film's main point of view, but also the reason for its ambiguity, since two constraints are superimposed:

First, annulling, silencing, masking and obscuring the ideological signification of the corpse: narratively, this is the strategy of the characters; structurally, it is the way the fiction plays.

Second, revealing, across this uncertain invalidation, a real ideological opposition. What sets Ambruster and Carlucci against each other takes on a meaning and a value beyond the Hollywood system of references. These are not simple imponderables conveniently found for the occasion; they reflect the reality of a struggle which goes far beyond the way Hollywood would like to go on seeing it. To show the State Department's actions in a 'colonized' country, the way capitalism sees and uses women, is to portray a social reality which – even when the story loses interest in it – is not too easily shrugged off.

And Wilder knows it. However, his anti-Americanism – as incisive and deep-rooted as we know it is – can come into play only within the fixed limits of the Hollywood system itself. The film's fictional system duplicates the Ambruster/Carlucci strategy: here too it is a matter of annulling, balancing, making out as if the whole film was there only for its incidental bits and pieces, was concerned to be only an 'entertainment'.

Herein lies the ambiguity of the *auteur*'s position and the problematic site of his enunciation. The *auteur* has always been thought of as the 'deus ex machina', the absolute master of a mechanism that he has to make work as perfectly as possible. That he should situate himself elsewhere, in the mechanism's flaws, in the grinding of its gears, does not in any way modify the kind of rapport established with the public. It is clear that this type of rapport determines what the spectator will take away from a film today. *Imperialism, the proletarianizing of women, are perhaps inscribed as statements in* Avanti*, but are they readable if they are thrown out beyond the enunciation?* More precisely, why should the spectator believe in the ideological theses proposed to him, when the film's system endlessly devalues and cancels out their impact on every scene that is not directly spectacle?

What is Wilder showing us here? A fiction that *replays* itself. Ambruster Jr and Pamela repeat their parents' adventures: every year they will meet again in Italy. But with a slight difference. This time round, Ambruster knows everything – that Pamela is a proletarian, that his desire for her has a slightly perverse edge, that the Italians want him only for his money and that they have a score to settle with America. This is undoubtedly the maximum freedom for manoeuvre allowed within the Hollywood machine: to demystify the syrupy, comfortable stories of yesteryear, and, for the present moment, to admit that there is no possibility of being given the real means of talking about something else.

Thus what is involved in criticism of the film is neither yet another re-reading of Hollywood cinema nor one more act of deconstruction, but the bringing to light, in a narrative system that remains highly coherent, of a profound contradiction between the emergence of increasingly insistent ideological themes – and their increasing prevalence – and the way in which a filmic discourse (the overall narrative constraints that are involved in a certain kind of relationship to the spectator) appropriates them to itself.

At the moment, it is the insistence of the referent that disturbs these systems and, in a case like *Avanti*, breaks up the discourse of the *auteur*. These questions, moreover, concern not only a cinema that is already old – Hollywood – but also, and in other ways, a large part of commercial cinema. In short, we have only set out the problem, and in a way that is still too negative. It could well be time to think of the referent as no longer being a grain of sand in these archaic mechanisms but, from now on, as the necessary vector of positivity.

Notes

1 Preminger's *Such Good Friends* is about a man who goes to hospital for a minor operation which goes terribly wrong. His friends quarrel over him as he lies comatose. Kané's point is that the presence of a body in a drama offers a pretext for a thematic debate about the meaning of death, not for the dead, but for those who are confronted by the dead body – a dramatic theme which in fact goes back as far as Sophocles' *Antigone*.
2 The high bourgeoisie expires in agony amid sumptuous decor and the bourgeois critical fraternity will talk about 'Meditations on Death'. But when the working class die in shanty towns, we hear talk of social injustice and human misery. The theme of death is not as unifying a factor as that; it is a luxury. (Author's note.)

25

AN INDIA AND ITS OTHER
(*INDIA SONG*)

('D'une Inde l'autre', *Cahiers du Cinéma* 258–9,
July–August 1975)

Pascal Bonitzer

> She, deceased, naked in the mirror, even though, in the oblivion
> enclosed in the frame . . .
>
> Mallarmé

Anne-Marie Stretter . . . Michael Richardson . . . The beggar woman of
Savannakhet . . . The French vice-consul of Lahore . . . The lepers of Shalimar
. . . Who could resist the charm, the sensuality, the musicality of the words and
of the imaginary space that Marguerite Duras constructs with her usual amazing economy of means? The sounds, the scents, the dreams conveyed by these
names, and the date, 1937. But what kind of charm is this? Colonial India,
1937. Not just the music and poetry of the names, but Bruno Nuytten's fine
photography, the costumes of Claude Mann, Mathieu Carrière, etc. (Cerruti
1881[1]), those slender white silhouettes, those phantoms in linen suits or white
dinner jackets or evening dress, standing still or moving slowly around, unable
to give much definition to a narrative as vaporous as incense, as vague as twilight on the Ganges delta, as hazy as the air in the tropical heat. Yes of course,
here it is again, and with a vengeance: the 'retro style'.

Let us return for a moment to the 'retro style'. Retro means nostalgic, hence,
to a greater or lesser degree, reactionary. Is Marguerite Duras's film therefore
reactionary? Is its main effect to give purchase, or substance, to the kind of
nostalgia usually designated by the term 'retro'? And what is this nostalgia
about in the first place?

It is about *pleasure*: the pleasure of the masters, which is to say heightened
pleasure, absolute pleasure. They were good-looking, they were racist, etc. –
but they knew how to live. And what does it mean to say this except that we
who are not what they were – racist, good-looking – or who are the same as

them but with a bad conscience, so that our pleasure is diminished, have lost a certain innocence, a certain sensuality, a certain 'art of living' that is gone for ever, except for 'what we still have from them', that derisory ersatz, Gold Tea. In its amber colour and cool, smoky taste you will experience something of the lost object it evokes.

India Song does undeniably mimic this discourse, this seductive idea of greater enjoyment in the colonial era – an idea whose historical reference point, as Jean-Pierre Oudart tells us, is feudalism.

Let us for our part add a Hegelian emphasis: those good-looking racists (the Southerners, the SS, etc.) *had* to disappear, historically speaking. And in this sense the 'retro style' designates its public as servile (or, more simply, petit-bourgeois) in that it never shows master-pleasure, the pleasure of the master, without also showing its death: consider *Lacombe Lucien*. *The Night Porter*, or, give or take a few differences, *Chinatown*. *They* are dead, *you* are alive, and between you and them all that remains, O Seduction, Goddess of Marketing, is this image of an earthly paradise, this bloodstained finery or, more exchange-ably, a small bottle of the tea-flavoured drink called Gold Tea: if retro films are always tragic, they also always have – the merit of the Gold Tea advertisement is to show it – a hidden comic potential.

In some ways, *India Song* follows this pattern very closely, even a little too closely, to the point of caricature and parody. This forced quality clearly derives from the techniques of the *mise en scène*: the long shots, the hieratic play, and especially the disjunction of image and sound, of what is in and out of shot.

I have spoken elsewhere of the strangeness that the voice-off always intro-duces into a fictional system. In this case, the strangeness is of at least two kinds: on the one hand, the many voices which fill the off-screen space and bring it alive (describing, suggesting, in effective little touches, the deathly smell of incense, the purple mist of the Ganges delta . . .), these voices which can never be pinned to a face on the screen and which belong sometimes to the figures we observe, sometimes to invisible characters we cannot identify and sometimes to no one at all ('voices out of time'), these intermingling voices make up a loose and disconnected network of words and phrases, words and more words which billow like smoke or incense fumes around the slow-mov-ing silhouettes held in the frame. The impression of life in slow motion, of tropical torpor, of colonial idleness, is thereby reinforced. On the other hand – or rather at the same time – the soundless, voiceless image and the sounds, the music and the voices floating around out of shot combine to 'split' the narra-tive, introducing between it and the spectator as it were an extra screen, the screen of the past, since these bodies, these faces never say anything *live*. (In the cinema, the live voice is always *in*, never *off*.) One thinks of *Céline et Julie*, but even more of *L'invenzione di Morel*:[2] these people sliding by in front of us are dead, ghosts, traces, as insubstantial as fireflies.

And so this would seem to have the makings of a Hegelian retro-style drama, the pleasure and death of the masters (in this case, of a colonial upper-bourgeois caste). But an essential dimension is lacking: historical *seriousness*, that Hegelian seriousness that is reflected in retro films in the realism of the *mise en scène*. And there is, above all, something else in the narrative which changes the picture completely. This something else has to do with a residue, but not the residue of a heightened pleasure that has an exchange value and can be represented, as in 'what we still have from them, Gold Tea'.

It is the residue of representation, what cannot be represented. That is also what off-screen space is used for in *India Song*: to inscribe the obsessive fear of something which cannot be handled by representation, by a historical discourse, by the tragic. And so there is something in *India Song* which, it seems, has no narrative function in the quasi- or pseudo-narration of the loves and suicide of Anne-Marie Stretter, but cuts across it to haunt and secretly modify the narrative. This something is for example the song of the beggar woman from Savannakhet or the evocation of the lepers of Shalimar by the French vice-consul from Lahore, and it is also perhaps the shout, the passion, the madness of the man from Lahore.

The beggar woman and the lepers are most definitely not servants or workers waiting for the death of the masters. No doubt they evoke the Other, but not the dialectical Other, linked via contradiction to the One (the Master) and historically destined to occupy his place. Completely out of shot, they are completely foreign, completely strange. The beggar woman and the lepers do not work. Social parasites and rejects in real life, they are here literally the parasites and rejects of the narrative.

They do not work, they do not have the status of legal subordinates; if they did, we wouldn't be far from a classical political fiction and a classical representation of class contradictions. But what can you do with the lepers of Shalimar and the beggar woman of Savannakhet? (Of course, the Marxist-Leninist grid operates for them also: *lumpen* – but everyone knows that this is one of the vexed categories of Marxism-Leninism.) What do you do with the Other's unintelligible song? In *Nathalie Granger*, the book, there is a small footnote in which Marguerite Duras opposes to the classic notion of class violence another which is unthinkable, impossible: that of a *class of violence*.

Class violence belongs to the possible and the thinkable since it is the *means* whereby History advances: it exists historically, as Hegel argued, to be incorporated, channelled, controlled and 'overtaken' (by the Party, by the state, on behalf of 'the whole people'). It is a devious figure of reason. But a class of violence? What sort of class is this and how can it be classified? Violence, in this sense, is precisely what negates any notion of class, as well as the very attempt to classify, to conceptualize. A 'class of violence' is a travesty of a class; a 'class' of pure intensity where the beggar woman and the vice-consul, and the lepers he shoots at (not to mention the silence of Anne-Marie Stretter: there is always a place for silence in Marguerite Duras's fictions) communicate sideways, musically, on the wavelength of the song and the shout, of the musical shout, of the non-musical song. One is bound to laugh at these couplings (if one is serious);

and indeed a class that includes lepers, beggars and vice-consuls can't be taken seriously.

From a serious, tragic or historical-scientific viewpoint, one ought to stop there and accuse Marguerite Duras of being a Vicki Baum,[3] at once retro and modernist. But I would prefer to see in her evocation of the lepers of Shalimar something other than exotic charm. The question of lepers and leper colonies has indeed been a burning question in the West, and one which has been systematically repressed, ever since the classical era (Michel Foucault reminds us of this at the beginning of *Madness and Civilization*: 'What doubtless remained longer than leprosy, and would persist when the leper colonies had been empty for years, were the values and images attached to the figure of the leper [. . .] Often, in these same places, the formulas of exclusion would be repeated, strangely similar two or three centuries later. The poor, vagabonds, criminals, and "deranged minds" would take the part played by the leper.') Leprosy is the architectural model of our world. The fiction of *India Song*: a mobile leper colony whose ever-shifting boundaries are traced by society in the gesture of exclusion through which it is established.

Translated by Annwyl Williams

Notes

1 Cerruti 1881 is a men's perfume, promoted in advertisements as being used by men of elegance. For 'retro style' (*mode rétro*), see Ch. 12 in this volume.
2 *Céline et Julie vont en bateau* (Jacques Rivette, 1974); *L'invenzione di Morel* (Emidio Greco, Italy, 1973).
3 Vicki Baum: Austrian-born American writer whose novels include *Grand Hotel* and *The Mustard Seed*.

26

AN UNCANNY FAMILIARITY
(*JEANNE DIELMAN*)

('Le familier inquiétant',[1] *Cahiers du Cinéma* 265,
March–April 1976)

Danièle Dubroux

Talk of woman's confinement, social, spatial and temporal (a time that is measured, calculated, always the same), is bound to touch on 'the big confinement',[2] the confinement which leads to prison or a lunatic asylum, those safe
places where others will (finally) be responsible for confining (interning) her.

This ending, which, though it is not shown, is the logical conclusion of
Chantal Akerman's film,[3] is a tragic, pathetic, classic ending (the murder
and/or the onset of madness in classical tragedy). But wait a moment: the heroine of this film, Jeanne Dielman, simply doesn't correspond to those sorrowful
archetypes of human suffering, those tragic figures as old as ancient drama
itself. She is just a housewife, a house-bound mother, one of those ordinary,
inconspicuous people you meet in the grocer's or at the school gates. She has
never occupied centre-stage; she is elsewhere, she is in us, she is our mother,
everybody's mother, strangely transformed into spectacle, transported to the
screen in her daily gestures, endlessly repeated, those gestures that we finally
look at and stop to question.

Jeanne Dielman is like thousands of other women, immersed in only one
social (or rather asocial) practice, that of the family, in the closed space of the
family apartment.[4]

Every woman discovers this 'compulsion to repeat' in the routine tasks of
housework. The behaviour pattern has been drilled into us more or less suc-
cessfully, but isn't easy to shake off since at some level it functions as a defence,
a protective wall for the territory (the kitchen!) we have won.

In this kitchen territory we know so well, every object has its place, there's
a strict order – reflecting a social order – according to which *everything must
remain in its place*: the washing-up brush on the hook above the sink, the shoe
polish in the cupboard under the sink, the teacloths to the right of the sink,

the soup tureen on the dining-room table, the knick-knacks in the cabinet, the towel on the bed ... just as the son must remain the son whose buttons are sewn on, whose bed is made, whose shoes are polished, who is well fed (more so than his mother) but with whom one cannot talk about certain things (sex, for example, when on the second evening he tries to broach the subject), and the mother must remain the mother, all servitude and duty, always there, always ready, always clean, a model of cleanliness.

She reigns over a world of objects, of obedient things which are the only witnesses of her life, the only signs of her dominance. Indeed, it's when this dominance can no longer be taken for granted that her downward slide begins, for this is her only link with the world outside herself, with anything really tangible.

Her daily round is made up of shadow and light. As she leaves each room, Jeanne switches off the light (a candle-end economy), she makes everything around her dark (the outside world dark); the only thing that can be illuminated is the *ritual*, the ritual of household chores, of cooking which she does with the care, the fascinating precision of a magician, 'the fairy fingers of the housewife' or 'the house fairy', expressions which here assume their literal, supernatural meaning, such is the perfection.

Until this point everything is *'heimlich'*: 'recalling the familiarity of the home, arousing a sense of agreeable restfulness and security as in one within the four walls of his house'.[5]

And yet, in the afternoon, Jeanne Dielman engages in prostitution (which sets her apart, so it seems, from the common run of housewives!). She reconciles two roles that are seen as contradictory in our society, which is for ever emphasizing the difference: the mother in the home/the prostitute, the reassuring paradigm.

The afternoon client is received in the bedroom she once shared with her husband; she lets it happen, you could say, like many married women 'doing their duty', without pleasure or involvement; she simply exchanges her body for money that will pay for her teenage son's studies, a situation similar to that of the non-working wife, whose husband/money relationship is the same as Jeanne Dielman's with her clients; everything happens in the house, with the maximum dignity and cleanliness (the towel on the bed); the woman is rewarded for her services (the money is put into the familiar receptacle: the soup tureen).

That is where the second sense of *heimlich* begins to intrude on the first: 'a secret concealed, kept from sight, so that others do not get to know of or about it, withheld from others'; *'heimlich* (clandestine) meetings'.[6] The mother hides this other life, her sexual life, from her son; propriety demands that the sexuality of parents (it's dirty, or it's dangerous!) should be hidden from children.

It's on the eve of the third day that things start going wrong: the potatoes burn, she has no time to wash, there's a delay between courses, things aren't running smoothly any more, something *'unheimlich'* (unsettling, abnormal) has worked its way into the machine and is interfering with its automatic functioning. There is worse to come: on the following day, the third (the decoding becomes more precise), she is early, which is to say that there is *time to kill*, time that cannot be filled by the obsessional prescriptions.[7] Her defences crumble (a long shot of Jeanne slumped in the armchair, with a duster in her hand).

The general direction of events is indicated, in the film, by tiny details which become signs, clues: the coffee isn't right (she throws it away three times); she drops a piece of cutlery; she forgets to do up all her buttons (which means forgetting to close herself up, to keep herself safe, leaving herself open to penetration by the foreign body, the alter ego, the Other, that is to say also the other, the client on the third day through whom pleasure is introduced, an invasion of pleasure incompatible with repressed desire). The barrier of the 'two Egos' is breached (the destructive instinct of the repressed resurfaces with all the violence of an appeal to murder), and Jeanne kills her client. We cannot think of her as a criminal, she is too 'familiar' for that; what has taken place is, rather, the ultimate, unreasonable transgression of an order of her order (in the sense of moral order and of someone who is orderly, meticulous).

And so all familiar things, the house, the home, become instances of the '*unheimlich*' (bloodstained hands, darkness, silence), the kind of horror that is attached to things we have known for a long time, that we have under control: the privacy of the (woman's) house which, having been repressed, one day returns. For the duration of the murder (one second in a film three hours and twenty minutes long) we are taken into the abnormality that is contained within, that is always potentially there, in the normal (the norm).

'In telling a story, one of the most successful devices for easily creating uncanny effects is to leave the reader [or spectator] in uncertainty whether a particular figure in the story is a human being or an automaton' (Jentsch/Freud).[8]

Translated by Annwyl Williams

Notes

1 In his study of *Das Unheimliche,* translated into French as *L'inquiétante étrangeté* and into English as *The 'Uncanny'* in *The Standard Edition of the Complete Psychological Works of Sigmund Freud*, trans. J. Strachey, vol. 17, London, Hogarth Press, 1955, pp. 217–56, Freud lists the different meanings of the word *heimlich* and of its opposite *unheimlich* as given in German dictionaries. What emerges from this list is that the term *heimlich* evolves through a series of nuances towards a meaning which coincides with its opposite, *unheimlich*: familiar, comfortable, tame, likeable, but also hidden, secretive, dangerous (this second meaning being the one that is usually attached to *unheimlich*).

In Schelling's more recent interpretation, ' "*unheimlich*" is the name for everything that ought to have remained . . . secret and hidden but has come to light' (Freud, *Standard Edition*, vol. 17, p. 224).

'We call it "*unheimlich*"; you call it "*heimlich*". Well, what makes you think that there is something secret and untrustworthy about this family?' (Gutzkow, quoted by Freud, *Standard Edition*, vol. 17, p. 223). (Author's note.)

2 A reference to M. Foucault, *Histoire de la Folie* (1961), Chapter 2 ('Le grand renfermement').

3 The full title of the film is *Jeanne Dielman, 23 Quai du Commerce 1080 Bruxelles.*

4 The apartment appears, in the film, as a prison-like universe, as a place in the unseen grip of some superior (and occult) force which has worked out Jeanne's timetable, programmed her activities and limited her movements (inside and outside) to the strict minimum (a walk round the block in the evening, a trip to the shops in the morning, all within a radius of some 300 metres, with permission to go out on the third day to look for a button). (Author's note.)

5 Daniel Sanders, *Wörterbuch der Deutschen Sprache,* quoted by Freud, *Standard Edition*, vol. 17, p. 222.

6 Ibid.

7 As for obsessional ritual, there are some obvious signs of it in the film: the obsession with the washing of hands, with folding (Jeanne folds everything: clothes, paper, newspapers), and the expedition in search of a button which must be absolutely identical to the other buttons.

8 Jentsch, quoted by Freud, *Standard Edition*, vol. 17, p. 227.

27

THE SIGN AND THE APE
(*KING KONG*)

('Le signe et le singe',[1] *Cahiers du Cinéma* 273, January–February 1977)

Serge Toubiana

King Kong is first of all a remake, a new way for Hollywood to prove something, to put itself on display. *King Kong* is a re-production – which gives the film that came first the value of an original. John Guillermin's *King Kong* is an exact copy of the *King Kong* of the 1930s. 'It's the reproduction of the sign that really destroys what it designates', as Baudrillard says. In other words, this is a film that refers above all else to the cinema. Any differences from or similarities with the original should allow us to read, to see and to note with some precision how things have got bigger in Hollywood, how they have multiplied in the USA. The film provides first the measure of all that has changed, of all that has transformed the economic and indeed the fictional conditions that apply to work in Hollywood. The measure, in a way, of the growth in productivity of American capitalism, of the heightening that has tended to characterize the Hollywood imagination. Everything is bigger and more expensive, beginning with the beast itself – which also has to appear more often. Because of what it costs to make, and especially because it is a copy, the film carries within the conditions of its production the sign, the trace of capitalism's self-destructive urge: the imaginary is the product not of the finished work but of the conditions that attach to it; in other words, the neurosis and megalomania of Hollywood. Which is how all disaster movies operate nowadays: through large-scale machinery they produce the image of their own destruction, and for this to be achieved, for this *simulacrum* to be created, every possible productive resource must be brought into play.

To be less abstract, the De Laurentiis–Guillermin *King Kong* undergoes, at the most basic, fictional level, a process which consists in distilling social effects – universally recognizable, historically situated effects/signs, accessible to any audience – in such a way as to facilitate the reading of the film. Like the 'disaster' films it competes with, the film, before it is actually made, is first something to be marketed, something whose every selling point must be exploited in the interests of commercial success. This approach – part and parcel of Hollywood film production – is bound to detract from the strangeness which characterizes the film's very theme. At the same time, it becomes difficult to compare the two films.[2] The first was produced during a period of economic crisis, at the time of the Depression in America. It was automatically invested with a reading whereby the monster symbolized the crisis, the imminent catastrophe; also present, however, was the need to avert disaster through a condensing and a reaffirmation of the consensus. The monster's function was therefore to take the crisis into the realm of the supernatural, to give it an unreal status, and, while accentuating the disaster and its consequences in terms of wasted energy and sheer panic, and the tendency to eroticize financial prices gone crazy, it also pointed to the need for a radical solution to eliminate the evil. Let us say that the first *King Kong* was immediately invested with a symbolic, primary reading, directly linked to the social conditions in which it was produced.

The second version – or the third, if you take into account the famous advertisement for La Samaritaine which was important, crucially important, since it made King Kong a commercial commodity[3] – is made in circumstances where the producers' only motive is to challenge the success of other disaster movies, like Irwin Allen's *The Towering Inferno* and, of course, Jaws. This difference profoundly alters the second film, diminishing its strangeness and its imaginary effects. The film's international dimension, its commercial opening in 2,200 cinemas worldwide on the same day, prevents it both from working on the power of strangeness and from basing itself on a social imaginary in crisis. *King Kong* is above all a challenge to the cinema, a film made to mobilize all the productive capacities of the American cinema, a film charged with reactivating the great fictional machine. It is one of a number of films of this type, except that it has some particular qualities that the others appear to lack.

For instance, in *King Kong* a whole metaphor of the cinema is woven around the female character, a survivor of a pornographic film in which she was to have acted had she not met the crew going off to look for oil. Let's take this metaphor literally: in Hollywood today if you want to speak of sexuality, desire, you have in a way to *measure yourself* against the pornographic movie, remove the privilege it enjoys of bringing sexual intercourse, the image of desire, to life on the screen. The film, through this metaphor, attempts to engulf pornography, to drown it (the crew of the pornographic film is shipwrecked). The only survivor is the Jessica Lange character, whose knowledge of the cinema stops at *Deep Throat* and who is only too happy to be recycled on the screen in the love scene between beauty, the sexy actress and the beast.

As for doing what is done in some Scandinavian pornographic films, and showing sexual intercourse between human beings and animals, this is simply not possible for *King Kong* or Hollywood. The motivating force in this film is not so much sex – the beast has patently been built without an organ – as desire, hence language. And *King Kong* is one of those Hollywood films where it is plainly a question of desire.

Perhaps it is because Jessica Lange is a star such as Hollywood doesn't make any more; perhaps also because the monster does not exist, it's just an imaginative construction of the Hollywood machine. The monster is not really a monster at all but a pretend monster. This means that *King Kong* is completely different from *Jaws*, a film based on a paranoiac construction. Nothing about the Other is aggressive or dangerous. On the contrary. It's only because Capital is always and for ever seeking to reproduce itself (a double metaphor pointing to disaster movies once again) that the Other is forced to intervene in the human world. In Guillermin's version, the adventurers go looking for oil, a primary resource, only to find the ape, the primate: a pure permutation of signs on the basis of the same: black gold/black beast.

It's possible, in *King Kong*, to *read* the scene where the crew arrives on the island – bearing in mind, however, that no reading of *King Kong* can be sound given that the production of signs is confused with the production of facts, that signs are for ever changing places and cancelling each other out – as a symbolic scene recalling the primitive scene of Capital in the phase of its accumulation: incursions into primitive, traditional societies, the destruction of myths, beliefs, ways of life for purely economic motives. The symbolic scene where the monster is worshipped by the natives is destroyed in favour of an exchange scenario, where the symbol is immediately reinscribed, reinvested in a profit-oriented economy, having already gone through the process of acquiring its signifying emblem: the badge on the monster's head advertising the brand of oil which his tour of the American leisure circuit is intended to promote.

Similarly, the scene at the end of the film when the monster makes his way towards New York's two highest towers. How could you guess that he will go this way? What draws him towards these two skyscrapers? How is this route, across the city to the highest point, being worked out? A reply is offered by the specialist, the palaeontologist. For him, the ape is making for these two high points because they remind him (via connotation) of the two peaks near his hut on the island of savages. This is indeed a reading, an explicit one, and one addressed to the spectator, a decoding of the monster's traces and of his guiding desire. The specialist draws on his precise knowledge of monsters to guess what it is that the beast desires and to attribute a language to him. He deciphers, decodes the beast's progress in the light of what he knows about primitive societies.

But what he doesn't see is that the ape operates on two levels at once: there is the mad love for Jessica which causes his final destruction, but there is also his confrontation with the symbol. He makes his way towards the towers of the World Trade Center to see just how he measures up to them. The palaeontologist brings the ape's language down to simple binary recognition, where only connotation would come into play. But another reading is possible whereby, through his desire to take the towers by storm and rival their symbolism, the monster would designate the capitalist jungle/pyramid. A symbolic, literally savage process would then be taking place, a liberation of the codes that regulate capitalist society. With equal savagery, capitalist society destroys the ape for what he represents: a real and highly eroticized danger, a hypernatural, zero sign endowed with the capacity to designate other signs in the delirium of their orchestrated disorganization. According to this reading, the ape represents the degree zero of the sign, he is the reader, the decipherer of the semiotic networks through which the real is constituted. But not a passive reader. He is also capable of producing change, as we can see from the fact that he is attracted to the beautiful Jessica; he is the bearer of erotic transformations who escapes the commands of the sign.

The strength and the intelligence of *King Kong* derive also from the fact that it does not resort to the classic black-and-white happy ending in which the unclean beast is destroyed by power. He is destroyed as much by the forces of order as by the crowd to whom he is thrown, in a final performance. The final image is of the ape lying on the tarmac, and that other monster, the crowd, consuming this last performance of the death of a sign.[4]

Translated by Annwyl Williams

Notes

1 The French title of this review of course involves a play on words which cannot be rendered in English.

2 *King Kong*, like all monsters, has its weak point, its Achilles' heel, the point where, in a way, it reaches into the imaginary, where the real is engulfed and the great fictional machine can be brought down. For everything rests on a precise fact, which is that the characters are not *cinephiles* (leaving aside Jessica Lange's appeal to pornography) and none of them has seen or heard of the Schoedsack–Cooper *King Kong*. The remake can only be made on condition that the characters are 'pure', uncontaminated by any fiction already seen.

Through this gap we can just see how the place of the spectacle is arranged: it sees and knows what the characters neither see nor know as the adventure unfolds. On the other hand, the film actor (whether the woman, the ecologist/paleontologist or the oil prospector) might be the ideal, but non-existent, spectator: one who is willing to *pay* to see a piece of fiction (all over again). This spectator is non-existent because the film tends to be rejected by cinephiles, who react by saying (and questions arise here): do you have the right to imitate a masterpiece? In asking this question, the cinephile is effectively closing his eyes and saying he doesn't want to find out more about the cinema as an *industry*. (Author's note.)

3 La Samaritaine, a large Paris department store, featured an advertisement showing King Kong finding a Fay Wray lookalike in the store.

4 This final sentence also involves a wordplay between *singe* (ape) and *signe* (sign) which is inevitably lost in English translation.

28

ONE MORE BEAR (*DERSU UZALA*)

('Un ours en plus', *Cahiers du Cinéma* 272, December 1976)

Serge Daney

> Did I advise you to love your neighbour? I will advise you rather
> to flee from your neighbour and love the distant stranger.
> Nietzsche, *The Gay Science*

In the shanty town of *Dodes'ka-den*, we observe a furtive encounter between two characters ('bodies' would be more accurate). The child from Dodes'ka-den and his imaginary train almost run over an amateur painter who has placed his easel too close to the invisible rails. This gag is the best introduction to Kurosawa's cinema, which (paradoxically) brings together spaces that are separate – the spectator has to give up trying to decide which one is the madder of the two, the child in his fantasy world or the painter of the destitute. For one of them doesn't see this destitution any more (he sees only the train, the invisible rails – he looks inwards) and the other examines it too closely (the shanty town becomes an aesthetic object). Kurosawa's approach, his 'humanism' if one must use this term (it would be better to speak of his 'viewpoint', moral and spatial), was about finding the place where the two spaces (that of the psychotic child and that of the neurotic painter) might *seem* to converge, thus creating a homogeneous space. But not exactly, hence the gag.

Dersu Uzala is no doubt a less powerful film than *Dodes'ka-den*, which it does nevertheless illuminate retrospectively. The friendship between the Russian surveyor and the hunter, despite its right-thinking overtones (we shall see what to make of them in a moment), can indeed be related back to the meeting of the non-existent train and the misplaced easel – the fictional space, carved up by the camera, serving as a dissection table.

The surveyor's eye sees big while the hunter's eye sees just right (in the sense that a garment can be big or just right). As soon as he meets Dersu, Arseniev – whose task is to reconnoitre the banks of the Ussuri – decides that he needs a guide. On his own, indeed, he doesn't see very much at all. The surveyor's pleasure (which is also to some extent the spectator's) comes from the fact that for him the territory (where he gets lost) and the map (where he knows his way around) are for ever running into each other, becoming superimposed, as in those Walsh-style Westerns where the map on the wall fades into the territory it represents. When Arseniev gets lost in the forest, he is quite happy: doesn't he have what he needs (writing, sketching, photography) to make good the delay, to compensate for it? As the writer, the one whose book has reached us and made the film possible, and because he has the last word (the voice-over of the commentary), he can lose himself in a risky aesthetic contemplation of what for him is just a landscape. His look is protected, 'covered' by writing. The possibility of writing is what allows him to see things *badly*, and to make mistakes.

Arseniev's mistake, his professional distortion, is that for him there is only one space, *geometric* space. He can think only in *straight lines*. His job, it appears, is to explore the area between Khabarovsk and Vladivostok, two towns linked by a railway line, for there is one of these in the film, a real one this time: the Trans-Siberian railway, completed, as we know, in 1898.

One of the finest moments in the film (a fairly puzzling one if you don't make the link with Kurosawa's earlier films) is the meeting with the old, solitary Chinese whom Dersu has long since identified from tiny clues. The camera gives us, simultaneously, the shack half-buried in snow to the right of the screen, and to the left the column of explorers laboriously trudging to their destination. As soon as he sees the old Chinese sitting at the entrance to the shack, Arseniev makes his way towards him; he goes *in a straight line* across an open space. He offers a mug of (one assumes) hot tea to the terrified old man, who recoils, then thanks him profusely, bows and clumsily spills the tea, while Arseniev tries to help him up. The same action is suddenly seen from a distance, from where the soldiers are. The effect is at once comical and embarrassing, in exactly the same way in which, in *Dodes 'ka-den*, characters trying to be nice to each other end up terrifying each other. Arseniev withdraws, night falls, the column camps well away from the shack where the old Chinese continues to sit, motionless. Dersu, who knows him, explains: 'Him thinking, much thinking. Sees house. Sees garden. Garden all flowers.' Then to Arseniev: 'Not to disturb him.' In the morning it is the surveyor who is disturbed. The old man is there at the entrance of the tent: he is ready to leave and has come to say goodbye.

The film will say nothing more (but never perhaps does it make the point so clearly): *the straight line is the longest route from one person to the next, the direct encounter is a risk, closeness a trap, love a tyranny*. The garden all in blossom that the old man imagines he is seeing is as real as the train for the Dodes'ka-den child. *The real is not what is represented*. And vice versa. We remember, in *Dodes 'ka-den*, the man with a deathly (in fact ghostly) expression who silently haunts an abandoned house, or the father and young son who, from their caravan, pretend that they can see the house of their dreams.

Between people there is a space — a no-man's land — which keeps them together but apart, separate but not cut off. Arseniev's fundamental mistake consists in wanting to fill this space which he thinks is empty. During the exploration of the Khanka lake (a bravura passage, rightly admired) he takes no notice of Dersu's apprehension and walks blithely on into the heart of the icy expanse, relying on his compass which always points him in the right direction, the straight line. What he hasn't realized is that this flat surface of the frozen lake is not really flat at all, but a living thing, changing all the time. The route he has taken becomes impassable when he tries to go back. It's not the same any more. It forces the two men to make a detour: the straight line is never the solution.

The Khanka lake episode isn't only a bravura passage, it is also the moment when the spectator can most fully identify with Arseniev. The discovery of the frozen lake, its sheer immensity, gives rise in Arseniev's commentary, as in the spectators' sighs of satisfaction, to the same general idea: 'How small, petty, ridiculous Man is when set against the greatness, the beauty, the severity of Nature.' An emotional moment that recalls an earlier picture-postcard scene: on the left the moon (already), on the right the sun (still),[1] in the middle and seen from behind, Arseniev and Dersu; between Arseniev and the moon, on the left, in that vast expanse, the tripod of the surveying instrument. Is there any real difference between this noble scene and the trivial one already referred to, that of the amateur painter in the shanty town? I think not. Once again, contemplation is a question of what is invisible. And of what, in the invisible, is blindingly obvious precisely because it cannot be seen.

Dersu knows that this romantic outing will all too soon turn into a struggle for survival, and that from this struggle he will emerge victorious (at the same time saving the life of the other man, the aesthete, the one who 'communes' with Nature) because he is able to transform the instruments of observation into something more useful. Another kind of diversion. The grass which the spectator and Arseniev have seen without really seeing will become the walls of a shelter, and the tripod, opened out, will serve as its framework. What does Dersu do with this equipment? He inverts its function, he turns it inwards, he makes it the *camera obscura* of another space, a place of survival and of a rebirth of sorts.

Once again, as the reader will have gathered, our discussion concerns the eye. When this belongs to a Western intellectual, Arseniev, a sensitive and cultured man mapping the unknown in the interests of Tsarist expansion, he is condemned to the geometric, to a certain blindness. His eye is mobile but doesn't engage with anything – anything precise, at least. Lacan reminds us usefully that the geometric is not the visual.[2] As proof of this he says that if light does indeed travel in straight lines, there is nothing to say that these lines are lines of light; they could very well be sewing thread which a blind man might follow by touch to grasp something that is being described to him which he cannot see. Arseniev is incapable of seeing *as if his life depended on it*. And this being so, he is free to enjoy the spectacle.

Dersu's eye is different. It's a kind of 'reading' eye. It doesn't hand over to writing or photography. It doesn't connect with an empty, infinite and homogeneous space; it starts by describing a circle around Dersu that marks the limits of his visual acuity. When the latter declines, Dersu's space becomes correspondingly smaller. Being a hunter, Dersu is forced to take the long way round and to deal in a space that is broken up and full of curves (notice how in the raft episode Dersu takes the current into account). He and the surveyor have two different conceptions of the world and of optics, and hence of the cinema. Arseniev represents the appeal of what lies outside the field of vision ('appeal' as in 'appeal for help') and Dersu Uzala the patient digging of the field (as you might dig for treasure). Arseniev represents the well-worn and woolly minded (imaginary) communion with Nature (with a capital N); Dersu the constant symbolic exchange with the environment (with a small e). The environment is not Nature. It has nothing to do with it.

The notion of space off [*hors-champ*] is frequently invoked in *Cahiers*. And rightly so. But the in/off problematic can function fully, dramatically, acutely, only if the characters share a similar conception of space, and use it in the same way. They have to see eye to eye, so to speak, in this respect before the in/off paradigm can affect them. It so happens that Kurosawa is the film-maker who has managed, from the start, to film characters who differ radically in their understanding of space. I have already mentioned the encounter of the imaginary train and the ridiculous easel in *Dodes 'ka-den*.

But it is just as true of the more serious films – in *Ikiru* (*Living*, 1952), the elderly Watanabe, before dying, situates the playing field, 'a liberated zone of sorts' in the very heart of the megalopolis – as it is of the lighter ones like *Sanjuro* where the choreography of the fights (Mifune, alone against a hundred) evokes what Lacan (again) says about the Peking Opera: 'In these ballets, no two people ever touch one another, they *move in different spaces* in which are spread out whole series of *gestures*, which, in traditional combat, nevertheless have the value of weapons, in the sense that they may well be effective as instruments of intimidation.'[3]

For Dersu too there is something that functions as 'out of field'. It's not a question of the part of the field he cannot see because it is too far away or momentarily hidden. It is rather what in the field hasn't been seen (but could be). Dersu is for ever digging away at his own out-of-field, one that is inside him, always-already-there, unsuspected: the shack, or again the snares, the black trap under the branches that only he can see and from which the animals escape. This is the theme, dear to Kurosawa, of the *hidden fortress*. The eye as an instrument of discovery. We are haunted by what is out of sight (along with the lost look, contemplation, everything which postulates a beyond) only because we no longer know how to see (we read too much, Godard would say). 'You're like children. Can't see a thing,' says Dersu to the soldiers who are making fun of him.

Such a position has ethical, indeed political implications. The 'progressive' side of Dersu's character is a little like this idea of drawing on your own resources, not looking elsewhere for what you haven't been able to find here. The answer to the enigma is always there, staring us in the face. One is reminded – because it's both the same thing and quite the opposite – of that most geometric of film-makers, Lang, as for instance in *The Testament of Dr Mabuse*. For Lang too, the answer is always there, on the (image or sound) track, but it is given before the question, before the enigma is formulated. So it is never functional (the truth is always probable). Lang isn't willing to film, or to mention, anything for which he cannot immediately provide concrete evidence, visible proof in the form of an insert (this may well be Lang's most characteristic shot, the inserted proof). Inversely, this question of proof, of offering visible proof, is of no interest at all to Kurosawa.

To sum up: Arseniev looks for what is beyond the field and Dersu delves into the field itself. So far so good. But it would be a mistake to think that Kurosawa can be identified with either. There is a third position – his own – which consists in failing to satisfy or, worse, ignoring his character's desire to find something else (beyond the field or inside it). You would look in vain, in *Dersu Uzala*, for what is called the 'subjective shot' (with one exception, and a significant one, that of the tiger). When Dersu interprets a broken branch, the cry of a bird or a footprint, the close-ups which might confirm what he is saying and fulfil our expectations are nowhere to be found. You have to take him at his word. And there we touch on one of the film's major prohibitions: *never separate the characters from what they see*. The shot–reverse shot is absent from a film which people are a little too quick to call classical and traditional. In other words: no direct encounters.

With three exceptions, however (and this is Dersu's whole tragedy). First, Arseniev takes a photo of Dersu. The camera, the very one whose tripod had been turned to other uses, takes a kind of revenge. The revenge of the straight line and the pose. From then on, Dersu's vision will begin to fail. Second, the encounter with the tiger. In this scene, which Bazin would have liked, Dersu shoots and the tiger runs away. From then on, Dersu loses all confidence in himself. Third, the glove shooting. There again, everything has changed. Dersu misses the target, that is straight in front of him, even though he had amazed the soldiers by hitting a smaller, moving target (a rope) right in the middle at the first attempt (but it was a moving target, a swinging one). Direct encounters are fatal for Dersu.

The time has come, perhaps, to bring in ideology. I am not sure that people have really understood to what extent *Dersu Uzala* — which you could so easily mistake for yet another well-meaning portrayal of our common humanity — refuses to base itself on what underpins this type of film: the two-way relationship of man to his other (friend or enemy, man or beast), their identification. Films which bring the savage and civilized man face to face can choose between two resolutions: either the savage can be sacrificed to the requirements of a technological progress which is wholly associated with human progress, or civilized man can be disapprovingly contrasted with the angelic figure of the noble savage. In either case, the law of love is what regulates this head-on encounter in which the one devours the other for the common good. The shot–reverse shot is the privileged figure of this devouring process because it seems to allow people to *change places*. But this is an illusion. Lacan (again): 'When, in love, I solicit a look, what is profoundly unsatisfying and always missing is that — *You never look at me from the place from which I see you*.'[4]

This dissatisfaction is written into Kurosawa's latest film. Arseniev's idea of solidarity (his 'if all the guys in the world . . .')[5] is inseparable from a kind of visual cannibalism. It is under the aegis of the geometric, of the straight line again, that Dersu — once at Khabarovsk — must be transformed into a sort of household pet. Dersu's idea of solidarity is completely different: it involves leaving clues that will be useful to the next man or animal to come along. Immediately after him, in the next shot. And he doesn't have to *see* who it is in order to help him.

At the very beginning of the film, Dersu is mistaken by the soldiers for a bear. Still out of sight he shouts, 'Man! Don't shoot', and goes to sit at the fire. At Khabarovsk, he becomes in effect a teddy bear for Arseniev's son, and the fire he watches, in the stove, is a prisoner like him. Western humanism always ends up by stating its truth, which is that of *police custody,* the reserve, the zoo, the gulag, etc.

This perhaps explains why the Soviets, who produced the film, showed a shortened version at the Paris festival — several of the Khabarovsk scenes had been expurgated. On the one hand, their explicit, official ideology (a wishy-washy humanism, alas all too present in the film's music) is quietly mocked in these scenes. On the other, their political motive (to celebrate the identification and reconciliation of the good Russian and good non-Russian — i.e. Chinese — on both sides of the Ussuri and far away from the Peking government) is well and truly undermined.

With a touch of humour, Kurosawa, who has simply told his story, sends his two heroes off back to back (the last shot: Dersu's *two-pronged* stick planted on his grave). I spoke earlier of Kurosawa paradoxically bringing together spaces that are separate. For him, there is one point — and one only — from which the other can be seen *as he really is*. The cinema must keep contradictions alive and not try to win us over with the spectacle of their disappearance. The minimum requirement for a materialist art.

Translated by Annwyl Williams

Notes

1 Daney's text has the moon on the right and the sun on the left, but this is clearly just a slip of memory. He also implies that this scene is part of the Khanka lake episode, whereas in fact it occurs earlier in the film.

2 J. Lacan, *The Four Fundamental Concepts of Psycho-analysis*, trans. A. Sheridan (Harmondsworth, Penguin, 1977), p. 93.

3 Ibid., p. 117.

4 Ibid., p. 103.

5 '*Si tous les gars du monde . . .*', a popular song and poem by Prévert.

29

CURDLED MILK (*PADRE PADRONE*)

('Lait caillé', *Cahiers du Cinéma* 282, November 1977)

Danièle Dubroux

When I was little, I could imagine myself only, in the future, as a shepherdess or a writer, but with a diploma in applied semiotics in either event. I was highly irritated, I must admit – others would say jealous – to discover, on seeing *Padre padrone*, that the Taviani brothers had basically pinched my subject, for I was indeed nurturing the idea of making a film about my twin ambitions and their disruptive effect on my early adolescence. But as this film is a masterpiece (the critics are agreed on that), I couldn't let my anger rip, I couldn't declare my feelings to all and sundry there and then in the cinema (as I ought to have done if I wasn't so cowardly!), though I did dare to say 'Shit, shit, shit!', playing on the ambiguity of a foreign language imperfectly mastered, just in case someone should object to my vulgarity.

I looked round for potential allies in a cinema that was struck dumb by the thunderbolts of the soundtrack. Perhaps that critic on the right would agree with me . . . The response was curt, decisive: 'Shh!' Next time I'll bring my shawl and my stick (a real bull's pizzle) and then we'll see!

Since then, a steady stream of compliments. The film wins awards at Cannes, and is then showered with praise by Mme Giroud, who must know a thing or two about culture since she was minister of it. *Padre padrone* was like *1900* last year, *the* cultural-aesthetic-left event to see (and moreover to like); if you missed it, you simply didn't belong . . .

Faced with the din, what could I do? I could take no notice, like the film itself which plays it straight. But it would more useful to return to the flock – I had to think of my pastoral career, very much at risk if I was naive enough to show signs of straying.

What could I do? The only thing left was an appeal to heaven! O God, help me, poor lost sheep of your flock, to recover my faith (I even wore a sheepskin as a sign of abnegation). I am trying my best but it doesn't work, I can't bring myself to believe in your saviour, the saint Gavino, the 'filthy' and virtually dumb shepherd who becomes a revered specialist in Sardinian philology.[1]

I can't bring myself to believe it, because for one thing I have never tried to learn your sacred language: Latin. I have only ever read a few bits of the *Aeneid* in translation to remedy my ignorance (whereas Gavino laps up the whole thing). As for learning the dictionary by heart? I confess, to my shame, that what I learnt by heart was the telephone directory, to play jokes on people.

But let's stop there; what do you actually know about this Gavino Ledda? Apart from his red jacket at the beginning and end of the film – a jacket that's a little too red – do you know anything about him at all, have you even bothered to read what he has written?

In the film you only see the real Gavino saying a few words and handing over a stick to the actor who will play the part of his father.

This little didactic sketch is a real find, the handing over of the stick no doubt symbolizing the transition from reality to fiction. A daring distancing device to keep the spectator awake and prevent him or her from sinking into the magic of fiction. One recognizes the Brechtian pedagogical approach; and the stick might well strike the head of the spectator already starting to wobble into the mirror that is held out by the interpretive screen.[2] Beware of identification!

Let us therefore recall the glorious itinerary of this simple-hearted fellow, whose devoted swallowing of 'cultcha'[3] has propelled him centre-stage.

Where does this thirst for '*cultcha*' come from?

Like faith, it's something you don't talk about.

As a small boy, he wet his pants at the thought of having to leave his nice school, his teacher with the face of an angel and his dear friends.

Dragged away by the impiety of a cruel father and sent up the mountain to guard the sheep, his thirst will lie dormant, in the famous latency period which precedes adolescence.[4]

Then one fine day this thirst will be miraculously reawakened, for our shepherd (up on the mountain) recognizes a Strauss waltz which happens to be passing by; stunned, he follows the accordionists who are playing his favourite tune, ready to sell everything he owns to hear it again.

This is what are called 'voices': words that young shepherds, or preferably shepherdesses, hear in the solitude of their retreats and attribute to God, the Virgin Mary or various local saints.

Naturally wishing, as the good Marxist he already is, to appropriate the means of production of that fabulous musical force, the accordion, he exchanges it (symbolically?) for two lambs which he kills in a ritual and bludgeoning close-up throat-slitting.

Trading 'cultcha' and its productive force: art for gross national product.

From that day on, his vocation is clear: he will do his national service, passing his entrance examination in physics (he did revise in the lavatories, after all). And it is at the point when he begins his military service that we discover, three-quarters of the way through the film, that he does not speak Italian. How very puzzling! Italian specialists had all thought it was Italian they were listening to, just as I was bragging to the person sitting next to me that I could follow without reading the subtitles.[5]

The rest follows. He learns so much, listening to Mozart, that he can finally stand up to his father, who is now defeated by this 'cultcha' which he had tried so hard to keep his offspring away from. And in the end, not content with his success in Sardinian philology, he returns to his village with all his diplomas, under the nose of his father who, it has to be said, is left with no option but to concede defeat. For Gavino feels himself entrusted with an exemplary, social role, just as the Taviani brothers feel entrusted with the burdensome historical mission of giving concrete form in images (which is their job) to the hopes of the United Left (or indeed of any other Left, for this programme applies to any period, with an exemplary permanence).

They made some very fine films before this one: 'hopeless, pessimistic', they say now. They have moved into an optimistic phase – so much the better for them. But as Carmelo Bene[6] said recently: 'You have to admit that optimism never did any good.' You don't need to belong to the new school of philosophy to see that the Tavianis' brand of optimism would be just a little ridiculous if there wasn't a chance that one day (if not already) we may have to take it seriously.

Translated by Annwyl Williams

Notes

1 The goat droppings play an important part in the film; they crystallize (are a catalyst of?) the son's desire to rebel against his father. In an interview with the Taviani brothers, the interviewer suggests that an Oedipal relationship may be involved. Without going so far, and while I wouldn't want to deny the pertinence of such a suggestion, I would myself see the goat droppings as the concrete equivalent of Gavino's resistance to the inflexible law of the father. The dialogue between the goat and Gavino adds weight to this hypothesis:

GAVINO: You filthy animal . . . I know you want to do it again, but I'll plug your arse. I'll milk you first, then plug your mouth with your own shit . . .
GOAT: I'll fix you when you turn. You whack me and I crap in the milk . . . then your father whacks you.

And so the milk will curdle and the film too, from then on, begins to thicken and coagulate, with no hope of reversal.

The immediate consequence of the goat droppings as catalyst seems to me to be the *constipation* which characterizes the film from beginning to end (the retention of all humour – though, when you look at it objectively, the 'extreme specialization' of Gavino's eventual position has something comic about it). The subject actually has you cornered, the referent is beyond criticism; how could you not admire this real story of a poor shepherd, oppressed by his father, who through sheer will-power becomes a teacher? The Taviani brothers have been clever enough to intertwine the referent with the film, to lend the power of the one to the modernist assumptions of the other: you *have* to like it, and this is off-putting, to say the least. (Author's note.)

2 All the ingredients of avant-garde production come together in this film; in particular, the sin of narration is markedly and conscientiously refused. After all, this story
could just as easily have taken the form of romantic fiction. It is abundantly clear
that this didn't happen; and the film spends its time telling us as much (by denying
it). The frequent slowing down of the action, the collapsing of successive stages and
the many devices (sound effects, music, etc.) that help break up the film have the
function of bringing the spectator to order, to the order of reason. (Author's note.)

3 The French is *'coultoure'*, i.e. how a Sardinian peasant might pronounce *culture*.

4 This latency period is a period of incubation – of culture simmering away inside. It
has nothing to do with the famous period of sexual latency (for children from five to
ten years of age) of which Dr Freud speaks since, on the contrary, Gavino and his little friends are pretty experienced in that department, the soundtrack discreetly
telling us as much in a drawn-out cacophony of amorous sighs and groans (as in a
dubbed pornographic film). We might be listening to a baroque opera. (Author's
note.)

5 The evocation of the Sardinian language allows the film discreetly to valorize
minorities through its apparent approval of regional speech. But the Tavianis' vision
is of a national language enriched here and there by the dialects which would gradually merge into this one language; those who see it as an affirmation of minority
cultures against a centralizing culture are simply wrong; just look, moreover, at how
military service, a notoriously centralizing force, is handled here, with no distance
this time, as being obviously and unquestionably progressive. (Author's note.)

6 Carmelo Bene: Italian actor (notably in Pasolini's *Oedipus Rex*), film and theatre
director, twice interviewed in *Cahiers* in the late 1960s. His baroque, experimental
films include *Nostra Signora dei Turchi* (1968) and *Un Amleto di meno* (1973).

30

AMERICA WITHOUT FEAR OR FAVOUR (*STAR WARS*)

('L'Amérique sans peur et sans reproche: *Star Wars*',
Cahiers du Cinéma 283, December 1977)

Serge Le Péron

In pursuing the implications of the exceptional success of *Star Wars* and its huge appeal to filmgoers of all kinds, one ought not to lay too much stress on the film's status as 'science fiction'. For a long time science fiction has been the generic repository of fear, madness, disaster, paranoia, of the speedfreaks and depressives. All are absent from *Star Wars*, in the genre's finest authors (Dick, Ballard), the future is only secondarily the place of adventure and escape, distraction and entertainment; the genre's best films (*2001* for example, but also Lucas's very interesting *THX 1138*) do not particularly offer themselves as 'modern fairy tales'. It's pointless to labour this.

Star Wars would rather be 'a romantic, confident, positive vision', atemporal, universal and of course unanimist – but a new kind of unanimism,[1] one no longer concerned with some or other strategy of tension, no longer that of a necessary common front against an enemy within and/or without (disaster films like *Jaws*), but one which derives from a freely felt consensus, being dictated neither by the law of necessity, nor by a pronounced imperative or any kind of reason, without shock, jolts, fear or surprise but with pleasure and confidence. The encounter with science fiction in *Star Wars*, the fact that the action takes place in a science-fiction universe, doubtless permits such confidence to be retrieved and projected towards the future, a future offering immediate ideological benefit. But above all, the reference to science fiction has the immense advantage of allowing the creation of a fluid fictional space, without apparent anchorage, one that enfolds and solicits: something like the pacific and pacifying American Mother who gathers to her bosom, with all the soft technological refinements that are hers, all that the bellicose uncle (a certain Uncle Sam), because of the brutalities of his war machinery, had excluded. Young people, the hippies, counter-cultural figures were basically rejecting this childish make-believe. Now we are witnessing the full-scale return to the territorial

waters of former years, to a floating mass with fluid contours, without frontiers; it's no longer 'to hell with frontiers'. Everyone is invited to play as before
with what Welles called 'the biggest electric train set in the world' – the cinema, Hollywood – as a family (like on television), under the calm, honest eye
of a mother ever-vigilant over morality (the moral). The America of President
Carter? But in such a film it is also capital that talks.

Lucas comes from the ranks of those we used, some time ago, to call nostal-
gics, pessimists, depressives, and we now know that they were right to be so.
It is also men like him who find themselves now entrusted with gigantic projects (like *Star Wars*) in the general fight against depression, and they certainly
do this with the same eagerness with which they struggled against repression
in the previous decade. There has been a sea-change (if not a change of base) in
America. This is a period less of rebellion against the symbols of repression,
more of a determined recharging of flat batteries – through the artificial injec-
tion of a lost imagination. The question is: what imagination? It is no easy
matter to rediscover it. For a film-maker like Lucas, barely thirty years old and
finding himself of the post-Westerns generation, the solution resides in a
return to childhood; more precisely, in a return to the conditions of his childhood and the cinema of easy-going adventure movies in which he was cradled.
Because of the lack of the 'positive'[2] in the available contemporary imagination
(above all in science fiction), the solution is seen to lie in a synthesis of old
forms. The problem, therefore, is technical; it is enough to return to the terms
and themes of this cinema (those in fact brought out by film studies) and make
them more sophisticated, dress them up in special effects, present them as
signs to be recognized, *decoded*. 'Heroes as independent as they are enterprising,
irredeemably evil bad guys', 'the triumph of good over evil', etc.

From this point it is a matter of making the screenplay scientifically *conform*
to this programme, following the computer logic which translates its ques-
tion-signs into response-signs. Equally, story, characters, actors don't in themselves have great importance: they are there simply to attest to the intentions
of the screenplay, they are the supports of these intentions. This is what gives
the film its coldness (not an aggressively dry coldness; the film is more cool
than cold) and the feeling that everything is already played out in advance (in
contrast to the adventure films already referred to) and that the events are only
detours in a standardized plot. You very quickly get the impression of a constant interchangeability (as with those standard parts of a machine which can
be replaced by an identical part), and it is soon impossible to see Princess Leia
Organa as anything other than 'the impeccably brave heroine' of the advance
publicity, or to nod knowingly when the clichés of the Western crop up in the
scene in the city of Mos Eisley, or to do more then see Peter Cushing as the
sign of absolute evil because of his numerous shady dealings with Dracula and
Frankenstein.[3] A reading without risks that rapidly becomes monotonous (one
could also see the wheels turning in *Jaws*, but there were nevertheless a few
moments when the film carried the audience with it, a few troubling passages).

And the whole thing (the vast apparatus of Production-Direction-Distribution), whilst functioning admirably (in the packed cinemas at the end of the film we applaud the heroes when they enter the royal hall on the planet Yavin, at the same time as the enthusiastic crowd on the screen), leaves the lover of fiction hungry for more; but logically so, for the fiction of *Star Wars* functions like nothing so much as a user-friendly computer in perfect working order.[4]

One way or another, fiction requires passion; there is no great fiction without great passion and no great film without there being a great love story behind it. This is what differentiates the cinema from other media such as the comic strip, which gets by very well without it, or television, which serves here as the model of cinema (and perhaps is the key to its success). Like Inspector Kojak in the American television series, the heroes of *Star Wars* are not impassioned types; they act intuitively and are utterly disengaged. The passions that they come up against are fleeting and comprehensive, and without consequence. Rivals co-exist, calmly: an unthinkable state of affairs in the old adventure films where the rule was, in the Gresham's Law[5] of Hollywood fiction, that the hero chased the other man. In the fiction of *Star Wars* one finds the binary system which is the working practice of capitalism today: two heroes, virtually equivalent (and in the princess's heart, as strictly equivalent as the twin towers of the World Trade Center in the heart of New York), and incredibly, deliberately desexualized.[6]

The fictional system of *Star Wars* echoes the intense participation and great lethargy, deep involvement and great indifference that belong to the consumption of television. Where it all happens or in what historical period is immaterial; as is whether the young protagonists love one another or not (and whether the princess loves either of them); sex has no importance, nor does violence; nor even the dedicated totalitarianism of the 'Empire' (its nature, and what is implied by that); nor the death of Ben Kenobi (the old patriarch played by Alec Guinness). Everything is and is intended to be deliberately abstract, presenting itself as principle, postulate and conventional indicator and never the motor, dynamic force or launching pad of fiction.

Star Wars therefore breaks with the cinematic mania that in recent years has pushed films beyond any previously conceivable limits, towards extreme violence, hard pornography, disaster movies; the mania for bringing everything into the open in order to provoke a strong emotional response and a bellicose unanimism. In *Star Wars* all heterogeneity is admissible, all alterities and differences can be present, functioning in perfect narrative harmony, provided that all this takes place *in the absence of sex*. So the problem is resolved at its very root, if one can put it like that: no more sex, violence, passion, or even fiction, only cohabitation, intrigue, aloofness (such is the fate of these aloof heroes). Finish with sex and you finish with the risks of conflict, violent emotions, the force of fiction. No matter, the 'force' is elsewhere, as the film's poster ('May the Force be with you') puts it.

It is the quiet force of capital that has produced the film with remarkable economy; one precisely matched in the shooting and the special effects, in line with the film's ambition and budget.[7] It is a knowing film that renews the Hollywood spirit of wanting films to be in some way edifying; here, in what replaces fiction, is the film's whole concept.

This approach is one that has nothing in common with Kubrick's in *Barry Lyndon* where, for the battle scenes, he used long lenses to film thousands of extras as if he had only thirty, in story terms a pointless expense. Such is the twilight (noted by Oudart) of the Hollywood machine, clouded over by a crazy imagination which gives way to this calm and starry sky where technique triumphs over imagination; like all the rest, fed through the synthesizer. The story of the film's production would constitute a real science-fiction subject that would make one shudder.

Translated by Chris Darke

Notes

1 'Unanimism': a literary movement, concerned with an idealist notion of the collective, which flourished in France after the First World War. Its adherents included the writers Jules Romains and Georges Duhamel.

2 In fact it is wrong to pretend that the adventure film had disappeared from the screens (for some time it had worked mainly on the principle of the shock effect), and even Lucas's childhood had not been one surrounded completely by reassuring mythological spaces. There is a Golden Age ideology in *Star Wars*, a rewriting of cinema's history, just as the *auteurs* of the Western were rewriting American history. (Author's note.)

3 In the Terence Fisher films in question it is not so simple. Evil cannot just appear, it must be imagined as such on each occasion. In these films it is never a matter of a primitive accumulation, even if they are sometimes thought of as sequels to one another. *Star Wars* is happy to grind out the effects that cinema (American cinema) has taken years to build up, and it reduces the great cinematic myths (the adventure film in particular, but not exclusively) to narrative references, to the status of road signs. A sad fate, and a strange gift to give the children. (Author's note.)

4 Kubrick has shown that even a computer can fictionalize better than this, if you take the trouble. One recalls the awful chess game with the computer in *2001: A Space Odyssey*: the cosmonaut who plays poorly and who strips the computer's electronic brain, provoking in the victim an uncannily human moan. (Author's note.)

5 Gresham's law is the economic theory that bad money drives out good money.

6 This is all the more extraordinary if one recalls that in *THX* the two heroes were revolting against a world without either affective or sexual love, and that this was the motor of the fiction. (Author's note.)

7 In fact, the production costs of the film were remarkably reasonable ($9.5 million) compared to recent productions of the same type (*King Kong*, for example), and considering the technical inventiveness which had to be demonstrated: the 360 special effects (most of them never before seen), the John Dykstra workshop, the two thousand units of sound on the soundtrack, etc. (Author's note.)

31

FRANÇOIS TRUFFAUT'S *LA CHAMBRE VERTE*

(*Cahiers du Cinéma* 288, May 1978)

Pascal Bonitzer

Absence diminishes mediocre passions and increases the great,
as the wind extinguishes candles and lights fires.

La Rochefoucauld

Given that, for those who possess eyes to see and ears to hear (for cinema, of course, is also a matter of sound) *La Chambre verte* is the most beautiful, most profound of Truffaut's films – and without pushing the point, one of the most beautiful French films of recent years – I will first consider Truffaut the actor. And first of all, his voice. This voice is a symptom – a symptom of the laziness and stupidity of a good deal of film criticism in France. A laziness and stupidity that is signalled by the adjectives 'monotone' or 'Bressonian' that invariably crop up as soon as there is a sound or an emotion different from the usual expressive modulations. Truffaut's voice, right through the film, is at once disturbing, deep, arresting. The intelligence of the performance is striking: words like 'monotone' or 'Bressonian' suggest to those who may not have seen the film (and they are intended to be off-putting, of course) a voice made lifeless, deadened for the sake of the text. But whilst the dialogue is consistently admirable, Truffaut's voice carries it to the level of incandescence, giving it an accent at once violent, vigorous and appropriately passionate. What we hear throughout the film in Truffaut's voice, the voice of his character Julien Davenne, is the violence of passion – of obsession, of the heart on fire – and, like the vocal response to the silent cries of the dead, their mute demands, an insistent, untiring supplication to them in their utter weakness in the face of time and forgetting. So it is with both character and actor alike, overwhelming and admirable. But I should also like to talk about Truffaut's gaze, those truly strange eyes, which seem to reflect nothing, to suggest an ineradicable anguish.

Clearly it is not for nothing that Truffaut portrays his protagonist Julien

Davenne, in whom actor and *auteur* are so closely interwoven. Seldom will a film as a cinematic statement [énoncé], or group of statements, have been more prone to a 'shifting' of subject positions than here, riddled as this film is with the marks of the subject of the enunciation [*énonciation*]. To put it more simply, seldom has a film-maker committed himself to this extent – committing his very body – in his film. Committing his *body* (understanding the word in all its ambiguity, in view of the film's funereal atmosphere) and including 'his' dead; merging the dead of Julien Davenne with the dead of François Truffaut in the chapel of rest in which the meaning of the film culminates.

The film fascinates just as much for the ebbing and flowing of its meaning in a double direction: from the general to the particular (the highly singular meaning that the film has for Truffaut, his intensity), and from the particular to the general (the link, as much submerged as celebrated, between the cinema and death; our relationship to ourselves, the viewers, each of us interpellated into this present-day chapel of rest where love is one with death; the cinema as a necrophiliac art). The singularity of this story, so detached in appearance from the preoccupations of the day, so like its solitary hero – yes, point them out, those films that resemble their characters! – makes the film a manifesto on cinema, and Truffaut here is not only the *auteur*, actor and character, he is also a critic, all these roles being linked together, interwoven, inextricable.

The green room of the title, the chapel of the dead, with the photograph of Cocteau, and even that of Oskar Werner (a curious form of repentance[1] for the author of the 'diary' of *Fahrenheit 451*) – those darkened rooms where there burns a fire at times material, though it is the subtle fire of a desire for eternity, all this of course is cinema. Those corpses frozen at the moment of death in newsreels, in movement (during the title sequence, with the superimposed face of Davenne–Truffaut in First World War soldier's uniform), or fixed, not for ever but fragilely on glass plates (broken, in a brief scene, by the mute child) – here indeed is the truth of cinema. And here we must bring in André Bazin at his most metaphysical and most religious:

> Before cinema, we only heard about the profanation of corpses and the desecration of graves. Thanks to film we can today desecrate and expose at will the last of our temporally inalienable human goods. The dead without a requiem, the eternal living dead of cinema!
> ('Deaths every afternoon' in *Qu'est-ce que le cinéma?: 1*)[2]

In his manifesto Bazin denounced what he called an 'ontological obscenity', that pornography of death which certain documentaries stoop to by showing live – if that's the right word – people in the act of dying; the outrage of violent death converted into documentary sensationalism; the outrage of such death deprived, as never before, of peace and transformed, through its cynically permanent projection, into a histrionic version of its own suffering. On the surface, the story of Julien Davenne, inspired by *The House of the Dead* by

Henry James (himself also present in a photograph and a brief biography in Truffaut's chapel) and several other texts by the same author, seems exactly to contradict Bazin since it deals with the, as it were, vital importance of conserving images of the departed. In reality, however, the film precisely follows Bazin, shares the same preoccupation.

The preoccupation with preserving the image of the departed, certainly (and what film is not moved to show the departed as living?);[3] but not the image of their corpse or of their agony, for it is from this that begins what is justifiably called (and which Bazin in the same text called) their perversion. Julien Davenne is neither in the least perverted nor a necrophiliac; he has no 'vicious taste for dead bodies', as the narrator of [Georges Bataille's] *Bleu du ciel* says, his love of the dead is free of any erotic element, if that is possible. From this emerges the absolutely clear meaning of the scene – one of the best in the film – where Julien Davenne, having commissioned a wax effigy of his dead wife reacts in violent horror to the reality of his fantasy (a reality, however, that could not be better executed since, if I saw it right, this wax figure is in fact the actress portraying the dead woman, made up for the occasion with, as in the films of Cocteau, open eyes painted on her closed eyelids), and demands that the sculptor destroy her on the spot.

No explanation is given us concerning the character's horror, which verges on panic. However, it is clear that the wax effigy, this body made doubly inanimate, appears as a monstrous parody of death, and in some way makes her die a second time; hence the need to destroy, to kill this sacrilegious image. This scene is not, to my knowledge, from James; it owes too much to the cinema not to be from Truffaut alone. Impossible not to notice for example that in this scene Julien Davenne behaves in exactly the opposite way to characters in Buñuel (Archibaldo de la Cruz, for example). And the scene makes this appear superficial. For how not to discern, beneath its surface, disgust and horror, a protest in the face of a certain shamelessness in cinema, its degrading, suspect facility for producing bodies, the image of bodies, in place of what they cannot represent?[4]

Truffaut does not believe, any more than James does, in the existence of sexual relations (or, if you prefer, in the possibility of their being represented), as if, like James, he seems to be saying that the work of art alone, as a work of love, *might* compensate for this failing, this non-existence ... Might, but it falls short here, since it is unfailingly undermined by what haunts it, the famous 'figure in the carpet', or, in *The House of the Dead*, as in *La Chambre verte*, the candle that inevitably misses the flame, since it is that of the warden, the officiating priest and the witness – in short, of the artist who cannot find pleasure in his work.

Julien Davenne's passionate undertaking recalls another in cinema. I do not mean the one in *L'Homme qui aimait les femmes* which, in a slightly more trivial mode and with a less elevated tone, in fact describes an analogous trajectory, but rather that of James Stewart in *Vertigo*. Possibly Truffaut, in writing the scene of the wax effigy with Gruault and then in filming it, was thinking of Buñuel, but from an opposite perspective. He was almost certainly thinking of Hitchcock. The audience, in any case, will think of Hitchcock. And of this exchange between the two directors:

HITCHCOCK: There's another aspect to this which I'd call 'psychological sex'. Here it's this man wanting to recreate an impossible sexual image. To put it plainly, the man wants to go to bed with a woman who's dead; it's a kind of necrophilia.

TRUFFAUT: Yes, the scenes I like best are when James Stewart takes Judy to the dress shop to buy her a suit exactly like the one Madeleine wore, and the care he takes in choosing shoes for her — like a maniac.[5]

The difference is that, as I've said, in *La Chambre verte* it is a question not of 'going to bed with a dead woman' but of keeping love alive. The essential point, though, is that this is just as impossible, just as hopeless (in the scene that follows the one with the wax effigy, in the cemetery, it's this hopelessness that Davenne admits, as he confides to his wife's grave). A 'maniac' — a man possessed by the impossible — is exactly how you might define an artist.

Here is the essential resonance of *La Chambre verte*: no film, and no book, can actually keep alive a dead person or a love; or, as Proust wrote (and he is there himself, in effigy in the film's chapel), 'Our hearts change, and that is the greatest sadness.' Communication with what we have lost is impossible — that is just the point being made by the mute child in the film (brother to Antoine Doinel and 'the wild child',[6] as the scene of the theft reminds us); but this impossibility is also proof of a fidelity which is the only thing that counts.

We can love the dead more than the living, we can devote all our care to them, we can go on and on talking to them and only them: they are mute and will not reply. So we must die. This being the film's theme (which is also that of the original story), we can understand the sniggers with which it was greeted by some French audiences. But who can fail to see that 'the dead' here are only the extreme image of those whom our love pursues, and who are in any case unable to give the secret response we await from them? So those sniggers take on a different meaning. In the cinema as elsewhere it is risky to try to make the naked language of love heard. With *La Chambre verte*, Truffaut has taken this risk to its limit. And that is what makes this such a powerful and beautiful work of cinema.

Translated by Chris Darke

Notes

1 Truffaut's diary of the making of *Fahrenheit 451*, published in *Cahiers* 175–80 (February–July 1966), was less than complimentary about the attitude of his leading actor, Werner, during the filming.

2 For a fuller quotation from Bazin's essay, see Ch. 17 in this volume, p. 212.
3 Elie Faure: 'Do you see resurrected before you the woman you loved twenty years ago, alive again in front of you, whom you had stopped loving, whom twenty years ago, at the moment you were abruptly separated from her, you loved to death? Do you see the dead child resurrected?' (*Fonction du cinéma*, Gonthier, p. 66). The quotation pinpoints the theme of Truffaut's film fairly well, I think, but clearly Truffaut himself takes as his starting point a basic dissatisfaction with the slightly simplistic emotions suggested here by Elie Faure. (Author's note.)
4 The 'facility' here is, in film theory terms, the reality impression. (Author's note.)
5 From *Le Cinéma selon Hitchcock*, Paris, Seghers, 1983, p. 273. Translated as *Hitchcock*, 1984.
6 The reference is to Truffaut's *Les quatre cents coups* and his 1969 film *L'Enfant sauvage*.

32

AN ACTIVE FEAR (*THE PASSION OF JOAN OF ARC*)

('Une peur active', *Cahiers du Cinéma* 292, September 1978)

Jean-Pierre Oudart

What are film-makers like Dreyer, Eisenstein or Lang experimenting with during the era of silent cinema? With a violence of the signifier that overturns the cherished perspectival organization of the image and which organizes, in an urgent, graphic manner, a medley of simulacra where the editing – oblivious of the match-cut – plays a straightforward game with the imposed frontality of each scenographic decision. From the moment the material enters the scenographic apparatus, the filmic signifier is that which *fronts* what we call a *shot*, and which resounds with the scenographic decision as a scansion, a noise rebounding from the imagination, foreclosing the shot's depth.

The Passion of Joan of Arc is a film composed straight out of the shot. I mean by this that the film-maker not only ignores depth of field, but does his work in the single, infinitely modulated space of a contrapuntal callibration of body and shot. Resulting from this is a tension sometimes allied, as in Eisenstein, with a paradoxical exhilaration in the cinematic *écriture*.

Active within this violence is a kind of challenge to the impossible: how to shield the filmic body from its *defection* (the premise of which I borrow from Jean-Louis Schefer's text *Le Déluge, La Peste, Paolo Uccello*).[1] It is as if this cinema were haunted by the deathliness and imbecility of its matter (that of the filmic body, for there is no other matter), which it must dispel, hold at a distance, ward off through a metonymic pursuit of the effects of the real, *tangible* signs of suffering.[2] In certain films of this period there is only one thing at stake: to evade the death of the filmic body which is inscribed in the very matter of its ghostly reproduction (Victor Sjöström's *The Wind*).

In the repeated fragmenting of its materiality through the shot the filmic body here makes itself a martyr (and a witness) to the denial of its defection. As if another texture, acting as a shield against this matter, could manufacture, through an edge of light, the photographic fiction *of the invention of another body*. As if, in the strangely documentary aspect of the shots of Falconetti's face (as Bazin notes), it were perhaps less a case of clothing the original (pro-filmic) body with the signs of its suffering than of imposing on the filmic body the memory of this other matter, of doggedly capturing the body in this other texture, thus tearing away this matter's veneer of discretion from its primary indiscreetness. This body would be nowhere more tangible than in the fiction of its photographic invention. It is sometimes only to be seen in this fiction, as if by an unseeing telescope exploring an unknown planet. What is at stake in these shots is often not to focus on a figure but to take a bearing on the state of its matter.

Without solution of continuity the filmic body is here divided between two scenographic positions: pinned in a flat plane (on the inside edge of the frame, as though secured at an angle in the shot) or as a deposit floating in its amniotic bath (a balloon, a windbag – the judges' heads recall Eisenstein).[3] These positions are those of a *pre-diegetic* body (a body that the fiction has not yet set right about the regulations of cinematic language, which don't apply here), divided between the burlesque evidence of the theatrical body via cinema (burlesque being contemporary with *The Passion of Joan of Arc*) and its reappropriation into an apparatus that makes of it the decisive element in *an active fear* (in Lang's first films the punctuating intrusion of the signifier dislocates the body, opening a perspective of terror that, logically, precedes the diegetic procedure of match-cutting on the look). The body vacillates, secured to an apparatus that contracts the dramatic enactment in a strategy of limit-framings,[4] in a conflict of deframed positions that leaves in its wake the swollen heads, the balloons, the calculated idiocy of the Eisensteinian close-up.

In this scenographic violence, just as in Expressionist films, one can read the filmic body as stupefied by its signifier (its dislocation in Lang, its shock in Dreyer and Eisenstein). Caught in their aftermath, these films renew what fascinates us in the films of Lumière. The very particular fascination of shots in Lumière, the fluent geometry of the paths that cross within them, stems from the fictional possibilities that appear in the symbolic punctuation of figures entering the shot. In crowd shots, the diegetic impulses fade away from the periphery to the centre as if, on their being seen, the filmic bodies were moving *from one side of the strip recording them to the other*, effacing their symbolic obliteration in order to return to their amniotic state (that of shadows, ghosts).

In *The Passion of Joan of Arc* the body is thus subjected to two contadictory operations: the strategy of a limit-framing (which is very rarely transgressed, save in the shot of the entrance of the executioner, who advances like a sleepwalker into a scene of which his body has not yet taken the measure) manufactures it as a still latent pre-diegetic energy which overwhelms, recovers the visual field – the photographic instant, fixing on the body as matter, as texture, suspends it, confronts it with the assumption of its defection, without any possibility of absorption into the staged drama (but this photographic obscenity is also this drama's *sacred supplement*, and it is what produces the body as a sacrificial object).

The motif of the Passion thus represents the violence of the symbolic through the punctuation of the scenography by effects of the real – so that the symbolic stems from the reality of the suffering (the work) of a woman (of Falconetti, the actress) and through which the body simultaneously produces a dilation of the signs of her suffering and their tangible support (how else to affect the filmic body if not through producing its photographic obscenity?).

This violence that precipitates the torture (the fictional image of the contorted body is, as in Eisenstein, allied to a kind of metaphysical awakening), the fire, the uprising and repression of the crowd, recall the violence of Sjöström's *The Wind*. The two films, Dreyer's and Sjöström's, seem hewn from the same stone, carried along as they are by the violent nature of their signifier. The fiction of *The Wind* stems solely from the wild pursuit of a body by a fear that becomes consubstantial with it. The wind that sets Lillian Gish's hair ablaze produces a state of voluptuousness in the filmic body, as a paradigm of the ghostliness of its matter, the cause of its defection. This is the one thing at stake in the fiction: that the body, buttressing itself against the storm, resists being smothered by the sand, by the emulsion of the film stock, by the night without memory of celluloid.

I ought to say something about the way in which Dreyer's film is now offered to the public. Why has the ridiculous musical accompaniment (as a sweetener, the inevitable Albinoni adagio), which has nothing to do with the film's internal rhythms and which disturbs their proper appreciation, been preserved? Why the film's reprinting in sepia, with its redundant connotations of the hues of an older age? And why, when Antonin Artaud comes to announce the death sentence to Jeanne, the emphatic intertitles? These liberties taken with the film's material truth attest to a preconceived notion of archaism that affects all the films of this period. Because they are silent they require music, a surplus of drama and soulfulness and, since they are prehistoric, a surface that presents them as the filmic equivalents of ancient manuscripts.

Notes

1 A portion of Schefer's work on Uccello was published in *Cahiers* 236–7, February–April 1972, under the title 'Sur *Le Déluge universel* d'Uccello'. A passage from this article, in which Schefer comments on the interaction he sees at work in Uccello's *The Deluge* between the material state of the fresco (its decay) and the subject matter of its scenography (The Flood) may help to elucidate the idea of 'defection': 'the cracks, the flakes peeling off the body plastered against the arch induce a kind of dizziness in the viewer, as if, simply by picking at it with a fingernail, one could uncover another depth in the text. However, this can only be guesswork since the window in which the fresco is framed allows it to be seen only in its surface coloration. But this coloration might also allow the appearance of what is at work in this other textual depth. And what is 'proved' by these peeling fragments . . . might perhaps be only the *defectibility* of the painting'. Oudart's borrowing of Schefer's

notion of 'defectibility' is inflected by the material emphasis of *Cahiers*'s critical interests during this period, as well as by its interdisciplinary approach (cinema alongside painting and photography). Bazin's idea of the cinema as 'embalming' reality throws light on the concern here with the *body* (*on* film, *of* film) and its *material* (of flesh, of celluloid). The 'challenge to the impossible' that Oudart writes of appears, then, to be cinema's desire to disavow this element implicit in its signification process – 'impossible' because the body's 'defection' is inscribed in the material on which it is recorded. (Translator's note.)

2 For 'effects of the real', see Volume 3 in this anthology, Ch. 14, 'The Reality Effect'.

3 See Nick Browne's 'Introduction' to Volume 3 in this anthology, pp. 9–10: 'The impression of a continuous, homogeneous, "realistic" fictional world is extended by syntactical forms – what *Cahiers* calls the "scenography" of the classic film – to the effect of sequences or entire texts. A set of rules pertaining to screen direction, glances, off-screen space, scale, etc., which, when integrated with narrative requirements, institutes an (imaginary) spectator unity that sets up and guarantees a (codified) cinematic institution of the Real.' (Translator's note.)

4 Oudart uses the phrase 'stratégie de bord' to condense the similarities in the extreme foreclosure of the *mise en scène* and the use of close-ups on faces and figures he sees at work in Dreyer, Eisenstein and Lang. (Translator's note.)

APPENDIX

Cahiers du Cinéma in the 1950s, the 1960s and the early 1970s

This volume of material from *Cahiers du Cinéma* covers the period 1973–8. Volume 1, first published in 1985, covered the period 1951–9; Volume 2, published in 1986, covered the period 1960–8; Volume 3, published in 1990, covered the period 1969–72.

Volume 1: 1951–9

When *Cahiers* was founded in 1951 it inherited many of its critics (André Bazin, Eric Rohmer, Jacques Doniol-Valcroze, Pierre Kast, for example) and many of its critical concerns (and even its cover design) from the earlier journal *La Revue du Cinéma*. It was here in the 1940s that Bazin and Rohmer had developed much of their thinking about realism and the evolution of film language, and it was here that American cinema had been championed. These were both crucial components in *Cahiers* in the 1950s: attitudes to Italian cinema – neo-realism and Roberto Rossellini in particular – and to American cinema as a whole are strongly represented in Volume 1. To the *Cahiers* critics – both the older critics and the soon distinctive 'young Turks' François Truffaut, Jean-Luc Godard, Jacques Rivette and Claude Chabrol – Italian cinema and American cinema offered much that was found to be lacking in contemporary French cinema, particularly an engagement with social reality and an inventive freedom of form. Throughout the 1950s, as *Cahiers* increasingly established its own identity and importance as a journal, its critics engaged in fierce polemics over French cinema, as well as making short films themselves and criticizing cinema very much from the standpoint of future film-makers. Volume 1 thus traces the development, in reviews and discussions, of the *Cahiers* critics to their acclaim in 1958–9 as directors of the so-called *Nouvelle Vague* or 'New Wave'.

The international impact of the 'New Wave' films drew much attention to *Cahiers* and in particular to its controversial positions on popular American cinema. These positions – centred on the contentious concept of the *politique des auteurs* (the '*auteur* policy', which became known later in Britain and the

USA as the '*auteur* theory') and around associated ideas about *mise en scène* – were to initiate intense critical debate in Britain and the USA, ultimately producing radically changed critical assumptions. As well as general articles on the nature of American cinema, on authorship, on genre and on technological aspects such as CinemaScope, Volume 1 offers a range of *Cahiers* writing on *auteurs* such as Howard Hawks, Alfred Hitchcock, Fritz Lang, Samuel Fuller, with a short critical dossier on Nicholas Ray, one of the American film-makers most revered by *Cahiers*.

Volume 1 seeks to reflect the broad range of critical interests and polemics which characterized *Cahiers* in the 1950s, perhaps its best known and most influential period.

Volume 2: 1960–8

By 1959 *Cahiers* was well established as the major influence in French film criticism. Its polemical positions on American cinema, in particular, had begun to generate enormous controversy in critical circles both in France and elsewhere, notably in Britain. At the same time, there is little doubt that this controversy would not have received the attention it did had the films of the French 'New Wave' not dominated critical attention as extensively as they did in the period from 1958 to the early 1960s. Although by no means all the new French film-makers came from the ranks of *Cahiers* critics, enough important ones – Truffaut, Godard, Chabrol, later Rivette and Rohmer – did, and the prestige won by their films forced even critics hostile to *Cahiers* criticism to take their critical interests and judgments seriously. Thus, Richard Roud:

> I wonder how many English critics would have included (in their lists of ten best films of the year) Hitchcock's *Vertigo*, Samuel Fuller's *Run of the Arrow*, Douglas Sirk's *A Time to Love and a Time to Die*, or Nicholas Ray's *Wind Across the Everglades*. One's first reaction might be to conclude that these men must be very foolish. And indeed, until a year or two ago, one might have got away with it. But today it would be difficult, I think, to maintain that film-makers like Alain Resnais, François Truffaut, Claude Chabrol, Jean-Luc Godard, Pierre Kast and Jean-Pierre Melville are fools.[1]

The combination of prestige and controversy brought the circulation of *Cahiers* from around three thousand in the early and mid-1950s to around twelve thousand in the early 1960s and to a peak of over thirteen thousand in the mid- and late 1960s.

A great deal of the supposed critical 'excess' of *Cahiers* belongs to the early 1960s when Eric Rohmer was largely responsible for editorial policy. It was an excess marked by the growing influence of a group of critics, often identified as

'MacMahonists', after the MacMahon cinema in Paris which specialized in American movies, but pulling along with them others on the journal, including Rohmer himself, and shifting the central focus of criticism to an almost abstract conception of *mise en scène* and to a group of newly acclaimed *auteurs*, among whom figures like Joseph Losey, Raoul Walsh, Fritz Lang, Otto Preminger and Italian epic director Vittorio Cottafavi were pre-eminent. Perhaps out of modesty, but nevertheless surprisingly, relatively little was written about the French New Wave in the early 1960s. Certainly, the interest in European cinema, and particularly Italian cinema, which had been so important in the 1950s now seemed in decline. There is little doubt that these directions of *Cahiers* worried some of its earlier editorial leaders who continued to be associated with the journal. Jacques Doniol-Valcroze and Pierre Kast, for example, both left or liberal, were concerned about its increasing 'apoliticism', if not its drift to the right. Godard was arguing in 1962 that no new ideas were coming out of *Cahiers*: 'There is no longer any position to defend . . . Now that everyone is agreed, there isn't so much to say. The thing that made *Cahiers* was its position in the front line of battle.'[2] Jacques Rivette and Michel Delahaye wanted to see more discussion in *Cahiers* of 'new cinema', new cultural theories, politics – directions which Rohmer did not find very sympathetic. In 1963, as a result of these dissatisfactions, an editorial committee was imposed on Rohmer, who was soon after replaced as chief editor by Rivette, who remained there in the period 1963–5.

To be fair, the early 1960s were not in fact as narrow as this account implies. The contents of Volume 2 show that alongside the 'extremist' work on American cinema, there was a growing interest in quite different areas, such as the influence of Bertolt Brecht's work on film-making and film criticism and the developments in *cinéma-vérité* and Direct Cinema. Such new directions were given considerable impetus, however, in the mid-1960s, with the very conscious encouragement of an interest in current theoretical work in areas like anthropology and linguistics which were relevant to film – represented in Volume 2 by an interview with Roland Barthes. Probably most important was the development of a polemic for a 'new cinema' and for a conscious politicization of criticism. Inevitably, these new directions involved a reassessment of the stance *Cahiers* had taken on American cinema in the past, as well as a recognition that American cinema itself was undergoing significant changes. Certainly, overall, one needs to think of *Cahiers* in this period as beginning to question assumptions which had been fundamental to its earlier views on American cinema: questions about the concept of authorship, questions about the ideological function of American cinema. To be clear, this was not a *rejection* of American cinema, rather a *re-thinking* in the context of a more rigorously political and theoretical critical practice.

Volume 3: 1969–72

These more rigorously political and theoretical positions are, of course, those generally associated with *Cahiers* in the post-1968 period, but it would be wrong to see the events of 1968 as a sudden turning point: very clearly, the journal was already moving in these directions from the mid-1960s onwards. Paradoxically, *Cahiers* changed owner-publisher in the mid-1960s and was redesigned to look more 'popular', just at the time it was beginning to become less 'popular' in the areas of cinema it valued and hence less 'popular' in appeal. During the short but very intense period covered by Volume 3, *Cahiers* lost readers and went through ownership crises, ending the period with a very austere cover design and a new financial structure.

If the critical identity of *Cahiers* had been clear and influential in the late 1950s, then less distinct in the 1960s, it now became, in the post-1968 period, once again polemical and a source of enormous influence and controversy. This time, however, the polemics – more political, more theoretical – had less widespread appeal: whereas the critical controversies around authorship and American cinema and *mise en scène* in the late 1950s subsequently entered, in however crude or partial a form, writing about film generally – in newspaper reviewing, for example – the theoretical work of *Cahiers* in the 1969–72 period had its effects in the narrower field of serious film writing and film teaching.

Those effects were, however, very radical. They had to do, essentially, with the elaboration of a 'politics of cinema' in the wake of the events of May 1968[3] and the upheaval they caused within left-wing politics in France and, within those politics, radical thinking about the function of culture and cultural work. The crucial areas of debate became those embodied in the title of a celebrated 1969 *Cahiers* editorial: 'Cinema/Ideology/Criticism'.[4] Central to this debate was the concept of 'dominant ideology', formulated by philosopher Louis Althusser in his re-reading of Marx, and the manner in which such a dominant ideology was carried in cinema. As Volume 3 puts it, part of what was involved was a definitive break with the 'idealist' representational aesthetic of realism associated with André Bazin, so central to *Cahiers*'s past, and its replacement with an aesthetic based on 'montage' and its association with dialectical materialism, in particular its relationship to Eisenstein and the Soviet cinema of the 1920s, which became a major area for 'rediscovery' by *Cahiers* in this period.

The nature and function of criticism itself also became central: what was the status of the 'scientific' criticism *Cahiers* wished to practise, with its borrowings from the post-Freudian psychoanalytic work of Jacques Lacan, in relation to the spectator as 'subject', and from grammatologist Jacques Derrida, in relation to the process of 'reading'? As well as a rediscovery of Soviet cinema, this period also produced sustained work in the 're-reading' of French and American cinema of the past, in analysis of the new cinema of film-makers such as Miklos Jancsó and Jean-Marie Straub and Danièle Huillet, and in systematic ideological analysis of contemporary 'political' films, such as those by Costa-Gavras.

Notes

1 Richard Roud, 'The French Line', *Sight and Sound*, vol. 29, no. 4, autumn 1960, p. 167.
2 Interview with Jean-Luc Godard, *Cahiers* 138, December 1962; trans. in Tom Milne (ed.), *Godard on Godard*, London, Secker & Warburg; New York, Viking, 1972, p. 195.
3 For an account of the events of May 1968, see Sylvia Harvey, *May 68 and Film Culture*, London, British Film Institute, 1978.
4 Jean-Louis Comolli and Jean Narboni, 'Cinema/Ideology/Criticism', *Cahiers* 216, trans. in Volume 3 in this anthology, pp. 58–67.

INDEX OF NAMES AND
FILM TITLES